Finding Myself
Through Travel

Finding Myself Through Travel
The Backpacking Adventure Of A Lifetime

By T.D. Powell

Sunwater Press ~ Gulfport

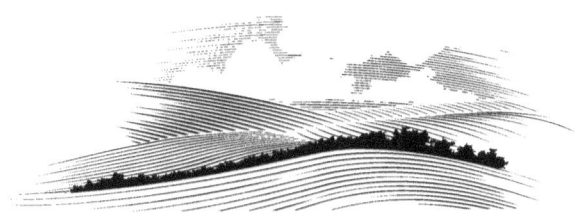

Dedications

This publication is dedicated to my many friends and family members who have supported me in this project. Secondly, this publication is dedicated to the incredible people I met while abroad – this story would be nothing if it weren't for you. A special thanks to Noe, Claire, Tanja, Zach, Jay, Nora, Josh, Paula, & Kelly for taking part in my journey and contributing immensely to the experience. May we remain friends forever. The "Mississippi Bohs" chapter is dedicated to the Dublin Bohemian FC, and particularly to "Freddy," "Osi," "Seanie," Deaglan, and the other unnamed lads who made my experience so memorable. I thank you. Further, I dedicate this publication to my 8th grade students, particularly the class of 2026, who enjoyed hearing many of the stories detailed in this publication while it was still in the editorial stages. Your honest feedback spurred me to continue the laborous work of bringing it to publication. Stories from this manuscript will continue to be told to my classes when deemed appropriate for and relevant to learning topics. Lastly, I can't thank my friend Jeff enough for graciously volunteering to typeset and format my manuscript for me as well as provide some invaluable tips, guidance and general encouragement. You and Shelly have been such a blessing and I know God will bless you 10-fold. Thanks again to everyone. God bless, enjoy the story,....and go have an adventure!

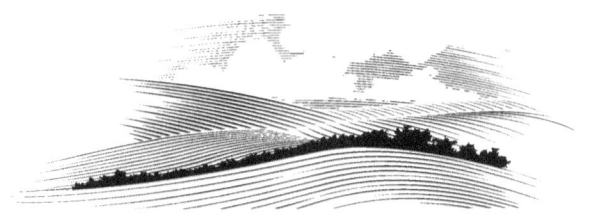

Contents

Part I: Taking The Leap

Part II: Ireland

Part III: England

Part IV: France

Part V: Italy

Part VI: Germany

Part VII: The Netherlands

Part VIII: Germany (Again)

Part IX: Belgium

Part X: The Journey Home

Part I: Taking The Leap

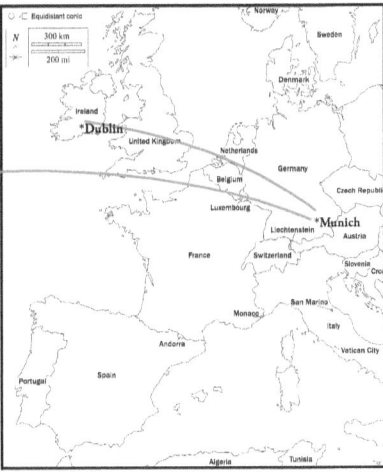

Map Left of The USA: https://d-maps.com/carte.php?num_car=24593&lang=en
- Lines, circles, and words with asterisks are author's annotations and not on original map
Map Right of Western Europe: https://d-maps.com/carte.php?num_car=13509&lang=en
- Lines, circles, and words with asterisks are author's annotations and not on original map

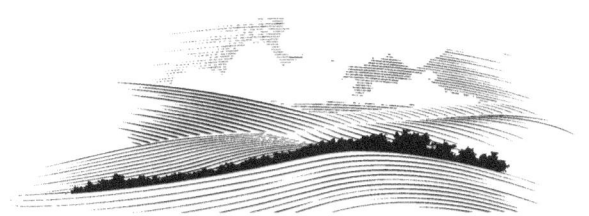

I Need An Adventure

University, 2011 - 2013

As I sat sleepily in my 8am World Geography class at my University on the Mississippi Gulf Coast in 2011, my mind begin to wander. My professor, whom I really liked, lectured away, but I could not stop my thoughts from drifting.

"How incredible would it be," I thought, "to go and see with my own eyes such things I had been learning in my medieval European history classes."

Things like castles, monuments, historical sites, architecture, and so much more danced through my mind. This fantasy was highly romanticized but was a nice break from my current reality.

"Tim!" My professor said suddenly, jarring me back from the momentary adventure in my mind.

"Oh! Uh, yes sir?" I replied, trying to appear as though I had been paying attention as much as my eyes had suggested.

"What do you think?" He asked thoughtfully. My mind raced through the overall theme and class discussion before my thoughts drifted away. I couldn't remember much but felt like I had enough for a vague answer.

"I agree," I said confidently. "We can't truly understand and appreciate other places and cultures unless we go and see/experience them for ourselves."

My professor looked at me thoughtfully for a moment then smiled.

"Very good." He replied satisfied before continuing his lecture.

Weeks later, the crazy fantasy was still strong in my mind. I found myself contemplating places I would like to visit during downtime or lying in bed at night. Some of the ideas were pretty ordinary, such as touring a medieval castle in England or visiting the Pantheon in Rome. Other times they could get as wild as casually running into and having a couple beers with a celebrity like Alan Rickman in a pub while asking fan-boy questions about the Harry Potter films. Over the next two years, my fantasy grew even stronger, which ultimately evolved into a genuine goal.

By the time I graduated from University in May of 2013, my crazy idea had become a serious intention. My parents were aware of it and allowed me to move in with them for a year to save money for my trip while I worked a $1,000/month job. Of this income, I put $600 away each month along with any holiday money (birthday, Christmas, etc.) I received specifically toward my trip costs.

My trip plan at the time was still extremely vague but it was a plan nonetheless. The route of my trip went through various changes including an idea to follow Apostle Paul's missionary journey across the Mediterranean. Such big ideas changed upon learning the cost and time required for such ventures, but to be honest, I also became a little overwhelmed. I then sought advice from a local travel agent my dad knew for guidance. She answered tons of questions for me and provided really valuable advice with no sales pitches or ulterior motives. She understood my desire to plan my own trip rather than purchase a cookie-cutter "5 countries in 3 days" type trip. After this council and with the help of a book, a more detailed, realistic plan started coming together.

It wasn't until the Spring of 2014 that it really hit me. Every morning before going in to work, I would spend time planning and doing research for my trip. During this time, I would occasionally find myself feeling extremely anxious. Despite having a blast putting it all together and imagining what I might experience, the thought of physically going through with it scared me to death! I had never left the country before. Hell, I had never even flown on a PLANE before, and my first ever flight was going to be across the ocean?!

"What if the plane crashes?" A voice in my head would ask. "With you're luck, you'll die before you get there, and all this planning would be for nothing."

"What if God doesn't want you to go?" Said another voice. "Will he still be with you?"

"Do you even have what it takes to do this?" A third one would ask jeeringly.

These questions petrified me some days. I would have to stop planning and put my computer away. I spent a lot of time praying, but felt I heard nothing back. I wondered what validity these voices had. If my fears of the plane crashing was silly and God had no problem with me going, the final question still remained. "DO I actually have what it takes to go through with this?"

I had always fancied myself as an adventurer. My school/university buddies and I loved to go on what we considered adventures. Whether it was adventuring to a party in an unfamiliar city, making videos of us getting into mischief (nothing too crazy or technically illegal), or going on a 1600-mile road trip to see Dave Matthews in concert, we enjoyed the thrill of the unknown together. Hopping on a plane for the first time, then traveling to another country alone, however, is an entirely different animal. I had always fancied myself an adventurer, but really, didn't fully feel it. I felt like I had been planning this trip for the adventurer I wished I was, not the one I was in reality.

As mere months turned into weeks, then weeks turned into only days, my anxiety skyrocketed. I made sure to see my close family and friends once more before I left, lest I never return. This thing was now real and happening, and the voices in my head had neither subsided nor been answered. Is God against me going? Do I have what it takes to go through with this adventure? Will I even make it back alive?

After returning home from seeing my closest guy friends the night before I was scheduled to leave, I sat in my car and wept. These tears contained my terror at the possibility of these still unanswered questions being answered undesirably. After calming myself back down, I opened up the notebook that would become my travel journal and wrote my first entry. My first words were, "I Am Afraid."

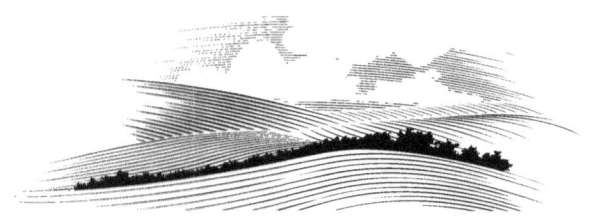

I Am Afraid - Journal Entry #1

Monday June 2nd, 2014 - 12:31am

I am afraid. I cannot recall a time in my life where I have been so afraid. For the past week or more, I have been fighting anxiety attacks. Tonight, I finally lost it...

I am uncertain why I am so frightened. Perhaps it is the whole deal -- 1st time on a plane, traveling through different countries all alone, and not having every detail planned out...

I'm told, "That is the way you want it! That freedom!"

Maybe it is all the unknown variables and risks involved. But isn't that what it's all about? Isn't that what an adventure IS? Dreaming about, imagining, and especially planning this trip has been extremely exciting and entertaining. However, I sense there is a twist.

I have always dreamed of being an adventurer,...however that guy has never been me. While dreaming about, imagining, and planning this trip, I believe I subconsciously planned my trip for **that** guy.

[After much contemplation]

I now realize...that my fears are what make an adventure an adventure. I must embrace it if I am to survive and enjoy the experience. I can only hope that God is indeed involved in my endeavors. What I can say for certain [i.e. what I believe and hope] is that He is with me always...even across the sea.

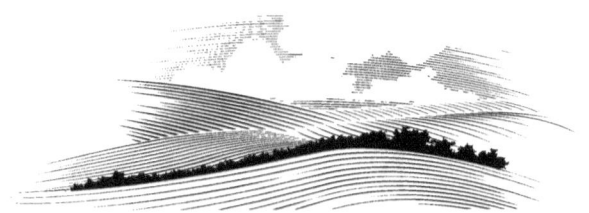

The Flightful Journey

Monday June 2ⁿᵈ, 2014 -1am

After a restless night, I woke up feeling a little better. It seemed that my tears had resulted in some sort of resolve. I somewhat reconciled with my possible fate, and although there was great temptation to abandon my path, I chose to move forward with it.

As my dad drove me to the airport, I expressed some of my fears and anxieties. I left out the part about voices in my head and the three scary questions they posed. He had flown hundreds of times for work and was able to provide some comforting words. Ultimately, I resolved to simply NOT be nervous. He gave me a hug, promised me I'd be alright, and wished me a great time. This made me feel a lot better. Once the first of three planes took off, there would be no turning back. The first plane will therefore be the hardest: Home to Charlotte, Charlotte to Chicago, Chicago to Dublin.

"I'm going to be fine." I reassured myself, trying to put full faith in my dad's confidence. I then continued through security and into the waiting room to await my flight. Yet the longer I sat, the stronger the temptation grew to call it off all while the three voices sang to me in unison.

"You don't have what it takes! You'll never return home! God is not with you and you're going all alone!"

Despite my fears and insecurities, I was determined to go through with it. Scripture said that God would never leave me, so I chose to trust it. If God chose to let me die, then die I suppose I would. Do I have what it takes? I don't know, but if I don't go through with it, I'll never know. All I could do was jump; to take an incredible, dangerous leap into an adventure, only hoping I make it back.

As soon as my flight was called, I hurried to board. I found my seat and strapped in as quickly as I could. Even seated on the plane, my eyes drifted towards the exit. The temptation to abort was strong. Even though I knew I would regret the decision to run for the rest of my life — not to mention losing all the money I'd already spent down the drain, the temptation to bail weighed heavily on me. Yet by some power that was not my own, I managed to stay seated until the plane begin to move onto the runway. I gripped the armrests.

Soon, the tiny jet began to rumble as the engines warmed up. I put in my iPod with music blasting. The next thing I knew, I felt a great force forward like a roller coaster, then a steep climb up with occasional teetering movements. I clenched both armrests hard for dear life as if it would make a difference and kept my eyes shut tight with full anticipation of feeling the aircraft begin to fall back to the ground,…Only it didn't. It instead climbed and climbed and climbed. After several agonizing minutes, I opened my eyes. I then removed my earbuds and asked the guy sitting next to me whom I had warned about this was my first ever flight,

"Is it going to feel like this the entire time?"

"Actually," he replied. "I think we're still going up."

The pilot eventually came over the radio to announce we had reached cruising altitude and provided our expected arrival time in Charlotte. I noticed that at cruising altitude, there were fewer ups and downs. Yet, the random bumps and slight movements of the plane made me weary. I just hoped we wouldn't suddenly drop out of an air pocket like my dad had warned me about. I was pretty certain I would freak out if it happened.

Looking out the window somehow calmed me slightly. When every so often I would feel sudden shakes - the plane dipping a little or hearing the engine on the wing turn off, I would look out the window. I guess seeing that we were not falling out of the sky made me feel better. The worst part was that it sometimes felt as if the plane had abruptly stopped moving forward — almost staying still. This is obviously impossible, but that's what it felt like, which was very disturbing.

Fortunately, the ride wasn't too terribly long, and soon I felt the plane gently descending through the clouds. I held on tight.

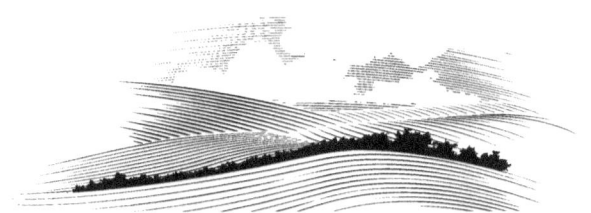

Not Dead Yet

Monday, June 2nd (Part II)

The plane landed smoothly, and all was well. I had made it over the first great hurdle. I also wasn't dead yet. I decided I liked the landing much better than the takeoff. I felt the motions of the plane, but I could say to myself, 'Obviously we must drop in speed and altitude to land.' I even felt comfortable enough to look out of the window as we landed. Although I was still quite nervous, I was much more at ease now than I was earlier.

I got off the plane and found my gate in Charlotte pretty easily. This, however, is where the trouble began. As I waited for my flight to Chicago, the intercom came on to announce that my plane was having maintenance issues. Great. That's exactly the kind of thing I wanted to hear (sarcasm). This will be the plane that goes down. So the flight was delayed an hour or so, then, there was a bigger maintenance issue discovered, then there were air traffic/weather issues in Chicago, then there were MORE maintenance issues! Naturally, my confidence and peace of mind grew with every announcement of another issue that this was going to be the plane that crashed. FIVE HOURS LATER to my relief, they announced that my plane was going back to the terminal, and my flight had been changed. Despite my annoyance with the layover time, I was extremely thankful to be changing planes.

The new plane had no issues -- I mean, that I was aware of. This plane was also much bigger and much nicer than the original. It was at this point that my experience met an unexpected, positive turn.

After finding my seat on the new plane, I met two older ladies sitting next to me. The one sitting closest to me was Sue, and next to her was Chris. Chris and Sue were sisters-in-law who had also become best friends and were traveling together to Chicago. These two gals were the coolest women I had ever met. Sue's husband had died ~11yrs ago, so she decided to start traveling, 'It's now or never,' she said. Her husband also hated flying, so she had been restricted in her travel abilities. Sue, on the other hand, LOVED to fly. She said she had, 'absolute confidence in the pilots,...they don't want the plane to go down either, you know.' Sentiments like this and others she made comforted me very much. Both of them were very kind and helped me to relax before and during the flight. I told them about my travel plans, and they were very interested. They were also kind enough to offer to buy me a beer, but it ended up being on the house for me as a consolation for having to change flights. This saved them from having to pay $7 for a 12oz can.

The flight into Chicago was magnificent. Sue & Chris pointed out notable things like the Cub's stadium, the big park, and Sears Tower. Seeing the big metropolis was really exciting. All in all, it was an incredibly pleasant flight thanks to my two new friends.

Just as we were about to get off, the intercom came on. The announcer called my name saying that I needed to check in with the clerk as soon as I exited the plane.

"I bet missed my flight," I said out loud to myself.

Now, it just so happened that there had been a cute flight attendant girl who I'd made eye contact with a couple times but had not spoken to. She apparently heard me react and looked over, realizing that they were talking about me. She jokingly called me a troublemaker (for having to be called up to the clerk).

"You know, I try not to," I said, "but it's inevitable." She jokingly gave me a disapproving head shake, and again called me a trouble maker. I responded, "I just like the attention."

"Yeah?" She asked.

"Hey, I got yours, didn't I?" I concluded with a smile. She returned the smile and added,

"[Well...] Yeah.." After this, I thought to myself,

"If they put me in a hotel instead of on a new flight, I know who I'll be hanging out with this evening."

As I got up to get my stuff, the guy in front of me turned around and said to me with the hint of an accent,

"You said you were going to Dublin?" He had apparently overheard me talking about my trip.

"I sure am!" I replied. With a smile, he handed me a $20 bill.

"Have a pint or two on me!" And that was my first contact with an Irishman [whose act of warm, welcoming, and friendly kindness would later prove to be a staple in my mind of the Irish people].

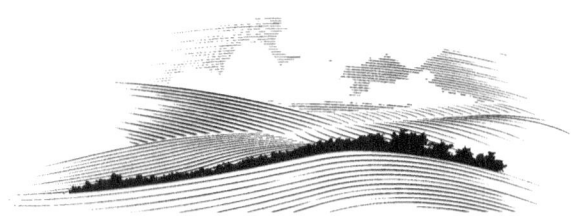

Flight Change

Monday, June 2nd (Part III)/Tuesday, June 3rd

I got off the plane in Chicago and went to the receptionist's desk as instructed. The receptionist confirmed my assumption. I had indeed missed my flight to Dublin due to the delay in Charlotte. My immediate thought was to see if I could catch up with the cute flight attendant, but the receptionist then informed me that I had been re-booked for the next available flight leaving in a couple hours. I honestly wasn't sure whether to count this as a fortune or misfortune. This flight would be an overnight trip on the German airline, Lufthansa, which would take me from Chicago to Munich (8hr flight) before catching a final plane on Aer Lingus from Munich to Dublin (3hr flight). A direct flight from Chicago to Dublin would have been a little over 7 hours If I had waited for a flight tomorrow, I might have been able to hang out with the cute flight attendant, then have a direct (not-overnight) flight from Chicago to Dublin. For better or worse, I thanked the receptionist and began looking for my next gate. Somehow I felt that God just might be in control so I trusted Him.

It didn't take me too long to find my gate. I entered when called and found a seat. This plane was enormous. I had never even seen a plane with two levels! It not only had stairs but a full kitchen too! There were three rows of seats from window to window. Two seats sat alongside the windows while another 3-seater row was in the middle. I was on the aisle seat in the middle row.

Looking around, I noticed Germans, French, Middle-easterners, Italians, and other people from different countries. My seat ended up being right next to a German woman whose name I cannot recall. She was very nice. We had simple discussions about food, beer, Germany, and America. The only problem was difficulty understanding her through her thick accent. Whenever she would say something I did not understand, I would simply agree and pretend I had. I just hope I didn't somehow sign up for something without realizing it.

It was nice talking to the German woman next to me, but it was nothing like having Sue and Chris along. My nervousness returned as the lights dimmed and the plane begin to move. The one thing I found comfort in was the screen attached to the seat in front of me. It was primarily for listening to music or watching pre-loaded movies, but also had a GPS feature that showed our global position on a map, our speed, our altitude, flight time/flight time remaining, and our ultimate ETA. As I did not have a window seat, knowing that all this information was being tracked gave me a better sense of ease.

The ride was surprisingly enjoyable once we got up in the air - for the most part anyway. It was the smoothest yet, and I barely felt the enormous plane move. The flight staff took orders and passed out food a couple hours after takeoff. I was surprised to find it pretty tasty. The meal was spicy chicken and rice, bread, a small salad, pudding, and a choice of drink (I got a beer). I then attempted to get some shut-eye after eating, but this proved to be nearly impossible. The pillow provided by the airline was not comfortable at all and the seat did not allow for much stretching out. I tried to pull the grade-school desk-sleeping position, but that didn't work. Attempting to sleep on this plane was like trying to sleep on a Grey Hound bus. In fact, the sound it made as well as its movements very much seemed like a bus. I attempted to convince myself I was on a bus as I attempted to fall asleep. Every so often I would actually manage to drift off, but would either start having a dream that the plane was going down and wake up or suddenly remember I was flying and jolt back up. Fortunately, I do believe I was able to get a little bit of sleep somehow because I remember waking up.

The plane landed early morning in Munich. It was now Tuesday, June 3rd. The air was a bit chilly as I stepped off the plane and walked across the ramp. The airport seemed huge, but not packed, and very quiet. Several of the passengers and I seemed to have the same idea in mind: find the restroom.

Here in this bathroom was my first experience attempting to communicate with people who did not speak any English whatsoever. Indeed, while trying to wash my hands, the sink was very different from what I was used to. I couldn't figure out how to turn it on! I know this sounds silly, but it was nothing like I had experienced before. Most everyone else who had previously washed had just left. I stared confused until a Middle-eastern looking man came out of a stall. I had no-ticed him on the plane as he was the first person I had ever seen (in real-life) wear a turban. He saw my confusion and spoke to me, but I didn't understand him. I looked at him and smiled awkwardly.

"Uh,…English? Ha…" I asked. He looked at me thoughtfully and chuckled. He did not know any English. Yet, this was not going to stop him. He then used hand motions and sounds from his mouth to express how to use it. It took me a second, but then I got it.

"AHHHhhhh!" I exclaimed with a big goofy smile. I wanted to say 'thank you,' but knew he wouldn't understand me. It's funny. Despite speaking completely different languages, our facial expressions and the looks in our eyes communicated perfectly. My eyes indicated that I was trying to think of how to say thank you until I finally put my hands together and gave a slight bow with a grateful smile. He returned the gesture and said something in a language I didn't understand. I will never forget this experience. It was just so unique and cool! Two guys from completely different cultures, who speak completely different languages were able to communicate confusion, explanation, understanding, thankfulness, and pleasure in assisting without uttering a single word — only facial expressions and small gestures. Seriously, how cool is that?!

Anyway, after about an hour or so of waiting, I boarded my next plane to Dublin. This plane was much smaller and rocked a good bit. Once, I'm pretty sure we hit a large bird according to the loud thump we heard from the bottom of the plane followed by a short but obvious drop in altitude. Everyone on the plane had the same concerned expression at this. Fortunately, the flight only lasted two hours and landed at the Dublin airport at 6pm Dublin time. I had crossed the ocean without a plane crash. I felt almost invincible now, and I had had some nice experiences so far. Could God have a supportive hand in this? I don't know. Technically, I still have to get back alive so there's still that, but by that point, I will have already had the adventure....that is, if I really have what it takes to spend the next 2 months traveling alone in a whole other world without running out of money or worse. But first thing's first: collect my luggage, find an ATM to get money, then find a way to my first hostel. Surely nothing can go wrong there, right?

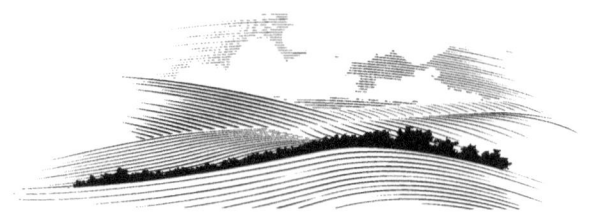

The Adventure Begins

Tuesday June 3rd

After hopping off the plane, thrilled to be done with flying for the next two months and ready to begin my adventure, I went to collect my luggage. I found the luggage carousel where I expected my bag to appear and waited. Bag after bag came by, but none were mine. I looked at the next carousel over to be sure I wasn't at the wrong one. From what I could tell, I thought I was at the correct place. However, this was all still very new to me. I still didn't feel certain. After what seemed like twenty minutes of waiting and two or three groups seemed to have gotten their luggage and made their way out, I finally saw a red Kelty Redwing backpack. Relieved, I moved in that direction, but before I could get there, another guy grabbed the bag and carried it off! It wasn't like my bag was generic. It was the only one of its kind I had seen since leaving Mississippi. I chased him down and yelled for him in hopes that he spoke English. I felt my chances were good since he was in Dublin, Ireland. After yelling for him a couple times, he heard me and turned around.

"Do you speak English?" I asked hopefully.

"Um,..yeah?" He replied in a confused and somewhat defensive American accent.

"I'm sorry. I haven't been able to find my bag and this one looks just like it. I've been looking for it for a half-hour. Would you mind checking the tag just to make sure?" I asked. He held his tag up and looked to confirm that his name was indeed on it. I exhaled in defeat. It appeared that I had made it across the ocean alive, but would now be required to figure out my next move without any other clothes than what was on my back and my small University string backpack I had taken as a carry-on containing my electronics and a few other items.

"Sorry, man. I really hope you're able to find it. I'm sure it will turn up. Maybe check with security? I gotta run though. Best of luck!" The guy then continued on his way.

I looked around to find security or some sort of attendant. I noticed one standing near the back wall so I approached him and explained how I wasn't able to find my luggage. Without any explanation, he pointed me to a desk. I approached this desk and explained my situation. This person pointed me to a different desk across the way. I followed the instruction to this other desk, and the same thing happened. After being sent to a third desk, I finally got somewhere. This individual was very nice and reassured me that my bag would be found within the next 24 hours and delivered to me. The attendant took my name, where I would be staying, and other relevant information. In the event that I did not receive my bag within the next 24 hours, he provided me with a number to call.

"This probably happened because your flight changed," he calmly explained. "It happens all the time, so don't worry. They'll get it here and we'll get it to you."

I left this attendant feeling much better about my situation. I was thankful that I had everything I needed to finish out this day and I could wear these same clothes the next if need be. I still had my phone, tablet, chargers, wallet, and identification. My next step was to get some money and then find my way to my hostel.

I left this area and got through customs relatively quickly. I couldn't get over how serious the customs agent was. He was so serious, that I was really tempted to mess with him. I only didn't because it would be my luck that they send me back.

"Why are you here?" He asked plainly in an Irish accent that was not welcoming or cheerful. I wanted to say something ridiculous like, 'to single-handedly overthrow the government and make Guinness the official currency of Ireland.' Who knows? He might have laughed,…but I decided not to chance the possibility of him not laughing or laughing as he helped me on the next plane home.

Once past customs, I found an ATM where I withdrew money. Thanks to my Bank of America credit card, I didn't have to pay anything extra to convert dollars to euros. With money in hand, I then continued toward the exit and grabbed a free map from a stand on the way out.

The weather was drizzly and quite cool. It wasn't quite cold enough for a coat, but I really hated I didn't have my light pullover with me (it was in my backpack). According to my hostel information, I was booked at a place called The Four Courts Hostel on Merchant's Quay. I looked at the map from the airport to the hostel provided by the hostel in an email I had saved. It didn't look too terribly far, but I didn't fancy walking down what appeared to be a busy highway system. I, therefore, decided my best option was to take a cab and let the driver take me to where I needed to go.

"It's sort of their job to know where everything is, right?" I thought to myself as I moved near a sign to my right with a "cab pickup" sign. Just about that time, a cab pulled up, a group of people put their luggage inside, they hopped in, and the car drove off leaving me and a small group of people waiting for the next car.

The group seemed to be together, and I happened to overhear them speaking. Once again I was surprised to hear them speaking English with an American accent. Not only that, but a familiar southern dialect as well! A woman happened to look over at me. Her eyes told me she wasn't sure if I spoke English, so she simply smiled.

"Hey, how's it going?" I asked.

"Oh! You're American!" She said. "Where are you from?"

"I'm from Mississippi," I replied.

"Oh my gosh! Small world!" She exclaimed. "Honey!" said turning to her husband. "He's from Mississippi!" An older man then turned to me with a smile. As it turned out, this family was from New Orleans of all places. We had a nice chat together until the next cab pulled up. We wished each other happy travels as they hopped inside the cab and took off. Something about meeting some fellow Americans made me feel a little at ease about being in this completely different country by myself. Stepping outside the airport into a foreign country is a unique sensation. I was a little nervous and feeling a slight sensation of culture shock, fear, and anticipation. Meeting the American family from New Orleans of all places made me feel better; like something was saying to me, "Everything's fine. You're not so alone."

Another cab pulled up only a couple minutes after the New Orleans family had left. The driver hopped out of the cab expecting there to be luggage. When he discovered it was only me, he cheerfully invited me to hop in. He sat down and turned his head to me.

"Good mornin'! Tha' name's Paul! What's yours?" He asked.

"Hi!" I replied. I was pleasantly surprised by how cheerful and positive he was. "I'm Tim."

"Very good! So where are we headed, Mr. Tim?" He asked.

"The Four Courts Hostel on Merchant's Quey,.....if you know where that is?" I answered.

"Hmm,…" He said looking into the air. "I know Merchant's Quay, though I'm not positive where that hostel is. But we'll find it! Not to worry. I think I know abouts where it's at!" And with that, we were off.

Paul ended up being a Dublin native. He was friendly, warm, and welcoming. He told me all about the city and some of its history. He explained how the queys (which are pronounced keys) are sections divided by the canal and were intentionally named. He told me I should never walk into a restaurant that doesn't have the menu with prices printed outside (if they don't, it's probably expensive). He also explained some cultural elements typical of Dublin and Ireland in general such as "what's your story" meaning "what's up" and how Irish people hate seeing others sitting alone/being left out and will often absorb them into their groups if said individual is alone.

I didn't take everything Paul said as absolute fact because he might be speaking purely from his experiences or personality, but I definitely made mental notes.

After what seemed a relatively short drive and a wonderful conversation with Paul, we pulled up to the Four Courts.

"See!?" He said cheerfully. "I told ye we'd find it!" Although he had made it an intention to inform me that, unlike in America, patrons of services don't need to worry about tipping, I chose to throw him a ten since he was so friendly and provided me with tons of valuable information to run with. He reassured me that it wasn't necessary to tip him, but after I insisted I wanted him to have it, he thanked me graciously.

I walked through the large green doors of the hostel and found myself in a small lobby with a desk. The young guy behind the desk welcomed me cheerfully and got me checked in. He then provided me with another map with iconic places enlarged. It was a map specifically for tourists, which I appreciated.

"So we do breakfast every morning through that door." He pointed to the door just to the right of where I was facing him. "The locker room to store your big luggage, if you need to, is down there," he again pointed just on the other side of the desk, "…and your room will be up those steps and down the hall." He pointed to the steps nearby. "Do you have any questions?" He asked finally.

"Yeah, man. I'm starving and could really use a drink. Got any recommendations?" I asked. Despite being tired, I was starving and could really use some food in my belly and a cold drink to unwind after my long journey.

He laughed. "Sure! Let me see your map." I handed it to him. With a pen, he pointed. "We are here. Over here is the famous Temple Bar district. It's where all the music bars are and where tourists usually go."

"Ahh, well I'm not looking to get wild. Just something good to eat and a nice beverage. Going for casual and chill." I confessed.

"In that case, I recommend Capel Street. Lots of good places with decent prices." He replied. "Just cross the canal here, and carry on until you find something you like."

I decided that Chapel street was likely my best bet. I thanked the attendant and continued past the desk to find my room. Inside my room, I found four sets of bunk beds. Two of the beds appeared to be taken already judging by the unmade bedding. I chose a lower bunk furthest from the door. There was a curtained window that overlooked the street below allowing natural light to enter with wood flooring. Under each bunk set were 2 cages. I looked at the bunks mentioned earlier to see that luggage was stored inside these cages. I didn't have any luggage to lock away. I hoped mine would arrive soon. I was glad that hostels provided pillows and sheets for the mattresses.

I sat down on a bed and relaxed for a minute to begin registering the fact that I was in fact still alive and had made it to an entirely different country. It was strange how there was so much that was familiar, yet as it were, unfamiliar. I spent only a few minutes wrapping my head around my new reality before getting back up and leaving the hostel in search of a pub with grub.

I managed to find Capel street with ease and had not walked too far before noticing a casual-looking pub called The Boar's Head. There was a short menu list written in chalk just outside the entrance, so I decided to walk in. The pub was very nice looking despite the reasonable prices noted on the chalkboard. I chose a seat at the bar and was almost immediately greeted by the bartender who showed the same warm and welcoming spirit as Paul. After a short conversation with him, I decided to order the lamb stew and a pint. Naturally, being in Ireland I ordered the only pint that made logical sense. A Guinness.

I had tried Guinness before in America. I was really never a fan. It just didn't taste that good to me. This Guinness however was a whole different world. My mind was blown by not only the presentation but the taste and consistency as well. I couldn't believe how thick the beverage was while also having such full flavor with a distinct hint of chocolate. In the words of Jonah Hill's character in Super-bad when describing what it was like to stare into a different character's eyes, "it was like the first time I heard the Beatles." Yes, that's how good this Guinness was. The lamb stew was great too, but the experience with this pint greatly overshadows it. I also learned from the bartender that the difference between this Guinness and what I had tried in the States is that Guinness in Ireland comes from the brewery here in Dublin. The Guinness available most everywhere else comes from a brewery in South Africa and is thus not as high of quality. This made perfect sense to me as I took a blissful and frothy swig of my second glass.

This whole time, there had been a group of three guys sitting two seats down from me. As I relaxed and enjoyed my tasty beverage and traditional Irish lamb stew, I slowly found myself getting pulled into this group's conversation. It's funny. Paul had told me this was likely to happen, and it did just as he said. The next thing I know, these three guys are introducing themselves to me and essentially absorbed me into their little group. Their names were Henry, who was 40 years old and catching jokes about being old from the other two. He was sitting furthest from me. The guy in the middle was Allen (pronounced "Aln"), who was about 30, and next to me was Steve, who was also 30. They were there betting on a horse race on tv via a kiosk around the corner and having a few pints in the process. They won a few and lost a few, but I think they lost more than they made.

Steve was tall, skinny, and red-headed. His buddy (or 'mate,' as they say in the UK) Allen was just as tall, but thicker than Steve and had short black hair. Henry ended up leaving not long after I joined the group because it was late for him (which gave the other two more reasons to give him a hard time about being old). Steve, Allen, and I continued chatting away as if old friends. It turned out that we had several things in common, especially when it came to sports. We all really like American football and they loved when I told them that Brett Farve was from Mississippi and I drove by his home on numerous occasions to get to a friend's house. Then Steve said something unexpected.

Steve looked at me for a moment, trying to decide if he knew me well enough to ask, then obviously decided to go for it. Out of nowhere, he asked,

"So how GAY is baseball?" He asked followed by a laugh. I nearly spit out my mouthful of Guinness at this having not expected it and simultaneously agreeing with the sentiment.

"I KNOW, right?" I replied laughing. This began a conversation about how we three all disliked baseball especially compared to American football and Soccer. This conversation was then followed by a question from Steve and Allen both that was more serious and sensitive.

The UK and Europe are very anti-gun for the most part. If it was legal to have a gun, it was extremely hard to obtain as far as my understanding. America on the other hand is very gun-friendly for the most part, especially in more rural areas like the better part of Mississippi. Hunting and outdoor living is a huge piece of American culture. With this in mind, Steve asked me what my feelings were about guns and if I agreed with them being illegal.

"Well, I don't personally own a gun. I do agree with them being legal, however. It's like this…" I presented two scenarios. Both scenarios involved a gas station and a 'bad guy' with a gun. In one scenario, guns were illegal while in the other, guns were legal. In both scenarios, however, the 'bad guy' had a gun. The point was that bad guys don't obey the law so if guns are illegal, it only prevents law-abiding citizens from getting guns while 'bad guys' are going to find a way. "One of my best buds, Ian, is a young war veteran," I explained. "He always carries a small pistol (concealed) wherever he goes. He's a good, law-abiding citizen. If some nut job 'bad guy' were to start firing inside a public place, Ian would have the ability to take action and likely save the lives of other law-abiding citizens (especially since he has military training which obviously helps). I feel safe when he's around. Both Steve and Allen naturally had mixed feelings about the issue, but completely understood where I was coming from.

Finally, we discussed the facts and fiction about "Pikes" (pronounced "pie-key"). These were sort of gypsies featured in one of my favorite Guy Richie films, Snatch (2001) starring Jason Statham, Brad Pitt, and others. Brad Pitt played a Pike and his gypsy clan became a vital role in the plot's outcome. However, I always wondered whether they were real people or a fictional group Richie made up. According to the guys, they were in fact real and quite disliked. Some were known to move into people's houses while they were out on holiday, change all the locks, and somehow prevent the homeowners from reclaiming their homes without a great deal of effort. The whole Pike idea was fascinating to me.

"Alright then, Tim!" Allen said after drinking down the last of his beverage. "Let's catch a cab and go have some pints!" I looked at him curiously.

"I thought we just had a few pints!?" I replied chuckling.

"Oh no, it's time to really drink some pints now!" Chimed Steve with an excited grin.

I told them I really appreciated the invite and explained that if it had been another day, I might join them, but I was very tired and jet-lagged from my journey which forced me to decline. They were disappointed but understood. We then bid one another a kind farewell and parted ways. They caught a cab to another bar in Dublin as I walked down Capel street back towards the Four Courts Hostel.

When I arrived back at the Four Courts, I discovered something very interesting happening. Sitting in the common room (where breakfast was served) were two guys quietly playing guitars. I decided to stop and enjoy the entertainment for a moment. The next thing I knew, a small crowd of hostel guests were gathered and the two guys were putting on a bit of a concert. After several tunes, they came to a point of not knowing what to play next. I decided to take the opportunity to ask if I might play one. They kindly agreed and I carefully slipped one of their guitars over my shoulders.

Representing the South, I chose to play, "Am I the Only One," by Dierks Bentley, which the crowd really liked. The guy whose guitar I had also enjoyed it and encouraged me to play another. With his blessing, I played my favorite country song, "Barefoot Blue Jean Night." The crowd really liked this one too. I then handed the guitar back to its owner like a good fellow musician. I didn't want to be that guy who basically tries to steal the show. I then stayed a little while longer and listened to the two guys play a few more tunes. When they took a break, I spoke to them for a minute. It turned out that they were both Americans. They were originally from Missouri, but were living in Chicago and decided to do some traveling.

After this chat, I looked at my watch to realize it was 10pm! I then promptly thanked them again for the chance to play and said goodnight.

Part II: Ireland

Map of Ireland: https://d-maps.com/carte.php?num_car=104831&lang=en
- Lines, circles, and words with asterisks are author's annotations and not on original map

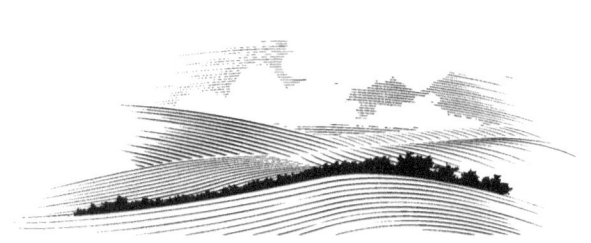

The Church and The Temple

Wednesday, June 4th

I woke up this morning around 2am and was wide awake. I couldn't figure out why this was the case considering I had gone to bed at 10pm after such a long day. I knew I had slept hard after getting to sleep (usually it takes me at least an hour to fall asleep whereas last night, I was out shortly after my head hit the pillow). I eventually gave up trying to return to sleep and got up. I later realized I had forgotten to change my watch last night. As I turned out, I had actually gone to sleep at 8pm local time, and it was just after 7am. Getting up at 7am meant I was just in time to get the breakfast provided by the hostel.

I walked into the common room after getting ready for the day and discovered a variety of food items prepared. There were loaves of bread with jams, unique-looking toasters, juices, coffee, cereals, and fruit. I prepared myself a bowl of cereal, toast, juice, and coffee, then found a seat.

I first bit into a piece of toast that I had spread apple jam over, only, it didn't taste like apple jam. It had the look of apple jam, but it rather almost tasted like honey but not nearly as sweet. In fact, perhaps because I was in Ireland, it had the unique hint of Guinness.

As I ate, a few others trickled in and requested to join me. I of course happily obliged. Their names were Rachel from Michigan, Jake and Riana from Australia, and Ryan from Canada. We talked casually albeit slowly as no one was completely awake yet, however, it was nice to talk to people from different parts of the world. Ryan in particular was fun chatting with because of his sense of humor. At one point, I told him about the jam that reminded me of Guinness somehow. His response completely caught me off guard.

"In Ireland, it is only natural that everything tastes like Guinness." He said so matter-of-factly. I cracked up. A few minutes later, Jake was eating a Neutela-looking spread on a cracker. He explained that it was a harsh, acquired tasking spread but that I was welcome to try it. I decided to take him up on it, so he put a tiny bit on a cracker for me. I plopped it in my mouth and chewed. It was not good at all! The whole table eagerly awaited my reaction in silence for a moment before Ryan asked in a sarcastic tone, "Does it taste like Guinness?" I nearly spit out the cracker as the whole table roared with laughter at Ryan's question. No, it did not taste like Guinness, but I doubt I'll ever try it again.

I stepped outside into the Irish morning air after breakfast and was again reminded that my luggage was lost. It wasn't quite cold, but a little too chilly for the t-shirt I was wearing. There was also a unique, 'misty' rain that seemed to drift down from the sky. I had a light jacket that would be good for this weather, but it was on some plane somewhere in my big backpack. There was therefore only one thing I could do: buy a new one. So, I found the familiar road from last night and followed it past the pub until I came to a small clothing shop. I found a blue pull-over jacket and tried it on. It fit perfectly and I was really surprised by how warm it was despite being a super-thin material. Even better, it was water-resistant! I really didn't want to spend my first 30 euros on a jacket before I even started my exploring Europe, but I had no alternative, so I bought it.

Next, I followed the map to the first big landmark which was Christ Church Cathedral. I'm not sure exactly why I chose this place first. Was it because I knew European cathedrals were supposed to be medieval and beautiful? Was it because it was simply the closest thing to me? Or did it have something to do with wanting to thank God for not letting the plane go down as I journeyed across the sea? It may have been a combination of the 3, but in any case, I walked along the canal until I came within view of my first ever European (British in this case) cathedral. After allowing a truck carrying at least 30 kegs of Guinness to pass by, I stepped across the street onto the church grounds.

Christ Church was beautiful on the outside; grey stone with castle-like fea-tures. I had never seen architecture like this (in person anyway)! The problem was that I didn't know where to go to see the inside. It was a functioning church, so I figured most doors would be locked on the inside. Fortunately, as I looked around, I saw a stone mason — a real-life stone mason! He appeared to be rebuilding a stone wall on the side of the church. He had a kind-looking face, so I decided to approach him.

"Um,..excuse me?" I said conservatively. He looked up from his work with high eyebrows.

"Oh! G'mornin'!" He replied. "Can I help ya?"

"Yes sir," I continued. "Is the church open? I'd really love to see the inside. It looks like a beautiful church."

He ended up being really nice and happily pointed me in the direction of the church's entrance. I then asked him what he was doing and he was delighted to explain that he was mending that part of the wall to protect it from further erosion. The church was apparently very old. The kind gentleman and I spoke for a few minutes before I continued on to find the entrance door to the church.

The enormous wooden door was already opened to expose a small foyer made entirely of stone. Facing the door was a carving carved seamlessly into the wall. A dim, yellow light shown on it to immediately catch the eye. It's hard to even describe the feeling I had already. It was almost like walking through a Disney World attraction, except everything was 100% real and completely solid…..and I hadn't even gotten inside the church yet. I was steaming with anticipation.

As I found my way to the main area, a young guy positioned behind a small podium like at a restaurant asked me if I was there for a tour or for the service.

"Oh! There's a service about to happen?" I asked.

"Yep! We have a short prayer service at 10am. You are welcome to stay for the service, or you can come back later for the tour."

Something just felt right about staying. It somehow made sense spiritually that I begin my adventures by attending a church service to honor God and offer thanksgiving for his delivering me here safely — or at least merely not allowing a plane to crash or doing something to stop me from arriving due to disapproval. I needed to feel like He and I were ok and that He wasn't angry with me. Therefore, I chose to stay.

I walked inside and chose a seat towards the back and took in the site. It was really beautiful. The ceiling was high and arched. There was dark-stained wood everywhere. Gold items twinkled in the light from the stain-glass windows. I was truly in another world, yet about to worship the same God.

Around 15 minutes after I had arrived, an older gentleman walked in from the side towards the front. He appeared to stand around 5 to 5 '6 by my best judgment. He had white hair on his head, wore glasses, and sported a black robe. He also seemed to have a nice pep to his step. As soon as he saw that everything was ready, he started speaking. He welcomed us all and announced that the prayer service was now beginning. The next thing I knew, however, he was speaking Latin! Having taken Latin in college, I recognized some of the words he used but was not fluent enough to translate quickly and without the aid of a dictionary. I did, however, manage to get the gist of what was going on. Using my limited Latin knowledge, inferences, and the pamphlet the young guy had provided me, I participated as best I could. During a couple prayers I didn't understand, I spent a little time praying my own prayer and simply agreeing with whatever was being prayed in Latin. Despite being unable to understand the bulk of it, the service overall was lovely.

After the service, I decided I would go over and say hello to the priest. He seemed to be a nice man, and I would expect someone of the cloth would be kind to strangers. I walked over to him and said hello as I offered my hand for a shake. Mr. Jimmy, as I learned his name was, could not have been more tickled and excited to meet me. He explained all that had taken place during the service, confessed that he was merely a lay person charged with leading the prayer service — not a priest, and told me that their priest was one of the first female priests ordained into the Anglican church!

After this merry conversation with Mr. Jimmy, he showed me around the church and explained the many items to look at and to get a photo of while giving me the history of the church. It turned out that this church existed as far back as Henry VIII!

I really appreciated how enthusiastic he was about showing me all these things and I'm not sure I'll ever get over how incredibly friendly he was! After showing me all around the historical areas of the church, he took me down to the crypt. He stayed for just a moment but then confessed that he had work to do and bid me a kind farewell.

The crypt was SO NEAT!! It was small, cool, and sort of dungeon-like. Displays inside were dedicated to the church's history and beyond. There were medieval-old carvings from stone and relics from the past. Further, costumes worn by actors and actresses playing characters on HBO's The Tudors series were displayed! Apparently, several scenes from the series were filmed at the church such as weddings, coronations, and baptisms. The crypt itself was used as the interior of the Tower of London. Finally, and most humorously, there were the mummies. Apparently, in 1850, a cat chased a mouse into an organ pipe and they both got stuck. The result was mummification. The mummified bodies of the cat and mouse are now displayed in the crypt.

After spending a bit too long in the crypt, I finally made my way back out to the street. From Christ Church, my next destination was Dublin Castle. Visiting castles was my number one priority for the trip, so I was of course extremely excited! Best of all, it ended up being Free Tour Day! The tour lasted about an hour and I got to see many rooms, artwork, and historical items and learned some history of Dublin. It wasn't exactly the castle experience I really wanted because the castle had been slightly modernized. It still felt really old and authentic, but I suppose I was looking forward to more exposed stone walls and such. Still, it was a wonderful experience and it didn't hurt that the tour guide was pretty cute too.

Next, I visited Dublin's National Archeology Museum which had been recommended to me by my university history professor, Dr. Jestice. The museum was quite huge and featured several sections broken up into subjects. I forget all the options I had but decided to go with Viking Ireland, Kingship & Sacrifice, and Medieval Ireland. It took me a couple hours to get through but was really cool! There were lots of ancient and medieval artifacts that gave me a better sense of what it was like to live during the time. There is something really meaningful about seeing something like a tool, a plate, or a weapon commonly used hundreds of years ago that reminds you that these people from so long ago were still merely people just like us. I left the main section of the museum feeling a great sense of satisfaction and appreciation.

Connected to the museum at the front was a small cafe. I decided to stop and try a cup of authentic Irish tea and a snack before going and finding lunch. I ordered a mint tea and was told to have a seat. I was expecting them to bring me a cup of hot water with a tea bag inside as I had experienced in the States. This experience turned out to be pleasantly different.

The waiter came over carrying a tray. On the tray was the snack that I ordered, a small teacup, a dish filled with sugar cubes, a small container of what I assumed to be liquid cream, and a full pot of steaming hot tea that filled the air with a delicious aroma. I was blown away. All of this (minus the snack) cost as much as a single cup typically costs back home. I carefully poured myself a cup of tea, added a couple sugar cubes, and took a sip.

The flavor was out of this world! Hot tea to me usually tastes like water with flavor. This, however, was flavorFULL. Had it not been so hot, I would have thrown it back because it tasted so good. Fortunately, the temperature forced me to savor each sip and simply enjoy. After 20 minutes or so, my tea and snack were gone so I left the cafe in search of real food for lunch.

My final planned destination of the day was Trinity College. It was an incredibly old place, but very well kept. The oldest buildings were neatly preserved while there were other modern buildings in view. I eventually found the small museum, the end of which featured the famous Book of Kells. It was a nice stroll through the exhibit and really cool to see the old book. I next found my way into the Trinity Library which was the inspiration for the Jedi Archives of the Jedi Temple in *Star Wars Episode II: Attack of the Clones*. All that to say it was big, beautiful, and impressive with its two-story shelves and high vaulted ceiling.

My tour day came to a close as I left Trinity College. I wandered back to my hostel hoping that my luggage had possibly arrived. I was overjoyed and relieved when I came in to discover it waiting on me behind the front desk! I grabbed it and immediately went to my hostel room to settle down and take a nice shower to refresh before going to find dinner.

When I opened the door to my room, I discovered a cute girl sitting on a bed across from mine. I sat down on my bed to rest a moment and began talking to her. She was French and had just arrived. It was around dinner time, so I assumed she might be hungry just as I was. With this in mind, I told her I planned to go find some dinner after I showered if she'd like to join me. She agreed and recommended a burger place she'd been to before even though she apparently wasn't hungry after all! The fact that she agreed to go with me to get a burger but not eat anything herself naturally suggested that she was really interested in hanging out. I then promptly got showered and into clean clothes in preparation for dinner (and maybe drinks afterward).

The burger place she led me to was about a 5-minute walk from the hostel in what is known as the Temple Bar District. The restaurant was called Gourmet Burger Kitchen. Frankly, I would have preferred somewhere else such as a traditional Irish kitchen or pub like last night, but since she seemed to think I'd really like it. We sat down and were soon greeted by a server. She ordered a Diet Coke. I meanwhile ordered a burger, fries, and a beer.

She and I talked about several things though it was slow going due to having to speak carefully. She spoke English, but wasn't superb at it and had a thick accent. I spoke little to no French, so I was no help in that area. Still, the conversation was nice despite being a bit weird. One major topic that she brought up was fast food. She asked me what my favorite fast food place was.

"Um,…I'm not sure," I said a little puzzled."I've never really thought about it. Chick-fil-a for sure, but I don't really consider that fast food. Do you have a favorite fast food?" To this question, she responded in a way that almost seemed like she was offended that I asked.

"No. I don't eat fast food. It's very bad. I will eat like a burger sometimes, but most of the time, no. I don't eat fast food. It also makes you fat and I don't want to get fat," she said.

As we talked about our two cultures, fast food, and her apparent fear of becoming fat, her perception of America, her judgment of me, and the reason we came to a burger place became clear. She assumed that because I was American and Americans are all fat (apparently), all I ate was fast food. She therefore had assumed that I likely had a favorite fast food place, and would want a hamburger for dinner.

"Ok, so she's pretty ignorant," I thought, "But that's fine. I'm probably not the most aware person either in many cases. She's still cute and we seem to be having a nice time." When the waiter came to collect a payment, however, things took a turn for the worse.

As mentioned before, she had simply ordered a Diet Coke (I now realized why she specified diet — fear of getting fat) while I had ordered a burger, fries, and a beer. The waiter explained that the whole thing would be cheaper if I put her Diet Coke on my tab which would make it a meal, then paid for the beer separately. Obviously, this made way more sense — it would save me like €1.50. I told the waiter to go ahead and do that. I had planned to pay for her Coke anyway. Besides, her drink was maybe 50¢ so in my world, it would be ungentlemanly of me not to pay for her. Unfortunately, however, even though the drink cost next to nothing and it made more sense financially for me to make it part of my meal, she wouldn't have it! Not one bit! She adamantly refused to let me pay for her 50¢ drink. It took me a minute before I realized that she didn't want me to pay because if I paid, it would make this occasion a date! Really?!

Finally after much convincing and reassuring her that I was offering to pay simply as a gentleman (because she didn't want to be on a date with a fast-food-loving American slob like me apparently), she let it go. Yet, even as I paid for the meal, she dug through her purse until she found a few coins and made me take them. I was absolutely blown away, not to mention low-key insulted, and pissed. I mean, I get it if you're not into me, that's fine, but absolutely refuse to let me buy you a damn Diet Coke even when it benefits me to do so by saving me money??

Sheez. I didn't want to be frank about how ridiculous she was since I was sleeping in the same hostel room, so I stayed as polite as I could until kindly bidding her a good night upon leaving the burger place. She headed back to the hostel while I turned toward the Temple Bar District strip. I needed to find a way to end on a high note after that mess.

I didn't wander too far down the road before coming to The Temple Bar by which the district was named. I walked in to find an enormous pub that was packed out. I made my way over to the bar and ordered a Guinness and found a spot to stand near a set stage. I was glad to find two guys there who started playing just about the time I found my spot. I was glad to have something more to watch than my drink. Had there not been live music to watch, I would have felt awkward standing there by myself.

The band was great, but there were only a couple songs I had not heard a billion times as it was all overplayed and mostly American music. I was really hoping to hear some authentic Irish music and/or iconic drinking songs. The whole place also seemed to be filled with nothing but tourists rather than interesting locals. Yet, I stuck around to enjoy my beverage and take my mind away from that strange French girl.

As the music played, I asked a guy sitting at a table nearby if I could set my drink on the end of his table. He readily obliged. When he spoke, I realized he was American. I then also realized I recognized him.

"Wait a minute! "Did I run you down yesterday and accuse you of stealing my bag?" I asked jokingly. Sure enough, it was him. We got to talking about his own backpacking trip which was actually coming to a close (he was headed home after Dublin). I shared with him my travel plans and he gave me encouragement as well as a few tips regarding places he'd been. A few minutes later, he and the guy he was with, left to get some sleep before flying out in the morning. They left the table, and before anyone else could grab a seat (there were lots of people standing), I sat down.

As I sat down, I noticed a couple had come up behind me quickly and an Italian-looking guy sat down in another seat. There were only two seats at this table. This left the girl this guy was with to stand next to him. As a southern gentleman, I was disappointed that this guy would let his girl stand while he took the seat. After a few minutes, I couldn't stand it any longer. I stood up and motioned for the girl to come over and sit down.

The Italian guy was very grateful to me for giving up my seat and asked what I was drinking. I told him I was having a Guinness, so he promptly bought me another. I was grateful since I was about to switch to a cheaper brew to conserve money. Ireland was my first stop so I didn't want to blow through cash too soon. The couple and I really started talking when the band went on break. I naturally told them about my backpacking plans. When I mentioned Italy, they got really excited and insisted that I visit a place called Cinque Terre, which translates to "the five villages." I thanked them for the suggestion but didn't put much stock into it. I figured I probably wouldn't make it there because I had my own agenda. Shortly after this conversation, I decided to find one more spot before heading back.

I left Temple Bar and wandered into another bar down the road. This one was even more packed than the last! I managed to squeeze my way to the back, past some stereotypical American girls going on about something, using 'like,' every other word. The music here was more overplayed than that from the previous bar. I stood there watching the band and contemplated whether I should grab a beer and stick around or just head back to the hostel. When the band started playing "Don't Stop Believing," by the band, Journey, which is probably the most overplayed song in the world, I took it as a sign to call it a night.

I got back to the hostel to find the two musicians at it again. This time I wasn't as tired as I had been the night before, so I asked if I could grab my own guitar and join them. They were happy to have me join, so I ran up to my room and grabbed it. Soon after I returned with my guitar, we were all three jamming and singing to whatever songs we knew. I entertained them with my skills on the slide guitar and had them play or make up a few blues songs to jam to. Finally, I dropped out and turned my guitar into a drum as we sang a 3-part harmony to "Man Of Constant Sorrow" as recorded in the film O Brother, Where Art Thou (2000). After this excellent ending to my day, I retired to bed, ready to see what the next day had in store.

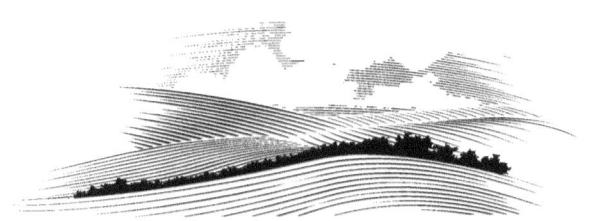

The Wax Irish and
"The Real" Irish

Thursday, June 5th

I woke up this morning in pain. My knees, particularly my right one for some reason, really hurt! I had no explanation for the pain, but there was nothing I could do. I eased out of the bed and hobbled down to the common room for breakfast. As I was eating, the two guys who had been in my room (I hadn't officially met them yet) joined me. Their names were Jakobi and Woi Fe. They were both from Germany. It was apparent that I was in pain, so they asked about it. Jakobi, who spoke better English than his friend said it was probably an irritated tendon from walking much more than usual. This assessment was based on his own experiences. He suggested, and even went and got me, a bag of ice to put on it. He said it would be sore for a few days but should feel alright soon. I hoped he was right since I didn't want to spend the euros on a doctor.

"So what are you guys doing today?" I asked.

"We're going to the wax museum," Jakobi replied

"Oh yeah! I passed that place on my way to Trinity College yesterday. It looked like it would be a fun time." I said.

"What about you?" asked Woi Fe.

"I was planning on going to the Jameson distillery and the Guinness brewery, but I heard from some people that it is cool but overpriced," I explained. Jakobi and Woi Fe had already gone and confirmed this.

"Well, the wax museum is supposed to be cheaper, so if you're feeling up to it, you're welcome to come with us!" Jakobi said enthusiastically.

"And don't worry," chimed Woi Fe, "if you aren't able to walk, we can carry you." We all had a laugh at this, even though I think he was actually half-serious. Both of them were extremely nice and encouraging. I obviously didn't want to waste a day sitting around due to my knees, so I agreed to join them. I said I might need a shoulder to lean on, and they were happy to provide it.

After grabbing my things, we three left the hostel and headed toward the museum. The pain was pretty excruciating for the first little bit. We would have to stop every couple of minutes and/or walk slowly for the first half of the journey. Fortunately, however, the pain eventually eased and the walk became easy. I was relieved. Soon enough, we arrived at the Dublin Wax Museum.

The museum ended up being a lot of fun! They had the history of Dublin in life-size wax scenes (which included the ancient and middle ages). After the historical aspect, there were featured wax figures of iconic fictional characters such as Gollum (Lord of the Rings), young Harry Potter, Star Wars characters, Batman, and others. The final room was dedicated to famous musical artists such as Elvis, Michael Jackson, Jim Morrison, and other recognizable celebrities (past and present).

After the museum tour, it was time for my new German friends and I to part ways. They had to go find a car to rent for the next part of their journey while I had an excursion planned. We said goodbye and exchanged contact information. While they headed one way down the road, I headed in the other back towards the hostel. My plans were to travel to a town called Waterford where I had pre-arranged to spend the night at a monastery! The photos looked absolutely beautiful and medieval, and I was super excited to meet the monks who lived there. The next morning, I planned to travel from Waterford to another town called Limerick to explore King John's castle.

While on my way back to the hostel, I ended up getting a little bit lost,…and hungry. Fortunately, I felt very safe in this city so I didn't worry too much. Dublin isn't huge, so I figured it wouldn't be long before I found my way again. Being hungry, I wandered into a small restaurant advertising kebabs. I had never had a kebab before but remembered my dad who had been overseas numerous times for work telling me about them before I left. I walked inside to find a huge piece of meat slowly cooking on a spit. The kebabs looked like tacos in the picture, so I ordered two assuming they'd be small. The woman instructed me to take a seat and she would bring them when they were ready. A few minutes later, she brought me a plate of two, quite large, taco-looking items. I took a big bite of the first one and was blown away. It was delicious! I then ate my fill without being able to finish the second kebab.

As I wandered further down the street feeling sure I'd find my way soon, I noticed a shop advertising crests and family history research. I had never seen one of these, so I walked in. I found the inside to be extremely small, not too much bigger than a large walk-in closet. The clerk behind a counter greeted me with a friendly tone and immediately complimented me on my beard, which I appreciated (it's a guy thing). I asked him about the shop and he explained that they had a database of surnames and their origins. They used this to find people's family crests, then craft them for customers. I thought this was pretty cool, so I gave him my last name. After typing it into his computer, he found that my last name was a Welsh house of lords (nobility) and showed me my family crest. Further, he provided me with a basic history of my last name, my family motto which is apparently, "always looking up," and some other interesting facts such as (supposedly) having "lovely singing voices." I must confess that I rather enjoyed the idea of having noble blood. This would mean that we potentially had our own castle, servants, perhaps a small army, and the audacity to fight the king on the occasion that he attempt to over-extend his power onto us. How cool?

Eventually, I did find my way back to the Four Courts. I quickly gathered my things and checked out. I found it odd the look the guy working the counter gave me when I told him I was checking out. His tone seemed surprised yet accommodating. In any case, I left the Four Courts and made for Heuston Train Station down the road a little ways. I was excited because this would be my first experience on a train EVER (not counting monorails at Disney World)! When I got there, I asked a few friendly Irish strangers for guidance on how to know what train I was to get on, who to ask for information once on a train, and how to activate my EU Rail Pass. Soon, I had boarded my first train, taken a seat, and was bound for Waterford.

No description will really do it justice. Nor will any photos I took. Yet, I express in vain how unbelievably beautiful this Irish countryside was as the train flew across rolling green hills for miles, flower-filled meadows, and stone bridges across small rivers. I had always heard that Ireland was green but never had I ever imagined it would be so green. We passed through several tiny villages, some I was tempted to stop in and visit. Girls would use the term "cute" and "adorable" to describe these little towns, but since I'm a guy, I'll just stick with "pretty" and/ or "quaint." The whole trip was very aesthetically pleasing to the eye and such a beautiful experience.

At one of the stops, a man boarded the train and sat in the seat across the aisle from me. He was nicely dressed in a sweater, tie, and khakis. After sitting, he began to sing casually to himself. I had trouble understanding the words through his thick accent, but he had a nice voice. Judging by his dress, I thought perhaps he was heading home from church or something. After he seemed to finish, I got his attention and complimented his singing ability. I asked if he had been singing a hymn and he told me that it was actually "Take These Chains," by Ray Charles. He then sang a little more before engaging me in casual conversation. I unfortunately only understood about half of what he said through his heavy accent, but there was something about visiting his daughter, government conspiracy, the "real" Irish, and something about caravans. It made me wonder if he might be some type of "Pike" like Brad Pitt's character in the movie, Snatch (2001).

At some point, the gentleman happened to notice the watch I was wearing. It was a basic digital watch that had a few basic functions. I bought it at a sports store for around $15. He asked me how much I paid for it and told me he liked it.

"Can I have it?" He asked me point-blank.

"Ha! No." I replied, thinking he was surely kidding around and essentially complimenting me on it more.

"I'll give you 20 euro for it." He replied plainly. There was no smirk on his face. His eyes were wide. He didn't laugh. This guy was completely serious and wasn't going to give up easily.

"No," I said a little more sternly but still kind of laughing. To be honest, I was a little bewildered by the situation.

"Do you play cards?" He asked, clearly trying to get me to gamble using my watch. I couldn't believe it. It wasn't that my watch was expensive. I just really needed a good watch and this one was perfect for my trip, and for such a great price!

"You're not getting my watch," I said very firmly. "I need this." I then turned away and ignored him. He made a couple more attempts before eventually giving up. Perhaps he realized he'd annoyed me and felt bad or perhaps he really was just joking with me because that was his sense of humor but I didn't realize it and didn't understand what he said when he tried to express that it was a joke (by which point I had already turned and was ignoring him anyway). In any case, he bought me a cup of tea from the trolley and left me alone.

When the train stopped in Waterford, I played it safe. I remained in my seat until after the gentleman got up and exited the train. I still waited as long as I could before covertly exiting myself. After getting inside what ended up being a tiny train station (about the size of the waiting room in a doctor's office), it donged on me that I had completely forgotten to look up where the monastery was or how to get there! The obvious thing to do was to seek out an official and ask for help. I found this person in the form of a security guard.

"Sorry, but it looks like you've missed the bus that would take you there." The security guard told me.

"Oh no! Is there any other way?" I asked frantically.

"Well," he replied, "you could catch a cab, but it'll be expensive. The monastery you're talking about is 30 miles away from here and there is only 1 bus that comes between here and there." I then explained my plans to him for clarity. During our conversation, I also learned that there were only 2 trains that went from here to Limerick. There was one that left at 7am and another that left at 4pm. I still pondered on dropping the cash for a cab ride, but then considered the 30-mile bus ride back from the monastery to catch a 7am train plus the time I would have to be back on a train to return. I ultimately decided that it wouldn't be worth all the trouble (and money for a cab) to make it happen.

I called the monastery to cancel my reservation only to find out that I was actually a day early! Even still, I decided to go ahead and cancel my reservation after learning how much trouble it would be to get there and back. I thought perhaps another time I might try again. Unfortunately, they did not do refunds, so I had to eat my reservation. In any case, I was glad to realize I had an extra day, and I didn't count it wasted. I got to see the beautiful Irish countryside and meet an interesting character. I would still visit Limerick, but instead of stopping in Waterford, I would simply take a direct train from Dublin to Limerick, which I knew ran constantly.

An hour or so later, I boarded the next train back to Dublin. This ride too featured a very interesting individual. A tall, skinny guy with shoulder-length black hair sat down next to me. He looked freakishly similar to my buddy Will back home. We got to talking after I heard a sound that my tablet made, which was his phone. I asked him if he had a Galaxy phone because my tablet was a Galaxy. From that point, we started a casual conversation that got very unusual very quickly. Although his accent was different and easier to follow than the singing gentleman, I still had trouble understanding some of the things he said because he spoke so quickly.

This guy was apparently set on getting everything for free from the city. He claimed that The Powers That Be brainwash us to think we have to pay for things that should be free for everyone. His primary examples were water in your house and electricity, but it didn't stop there. He and his friends also refused to pay tolls, even taking videos of themselves (which he showed me) driving straight through the stops for that very same reason. Unsurprisingly, he was also big into conspiracy theories regarding government control, the Illuminati, and other such things as well as stuff about "the real Irish." Again with the 'real' Irish...

I got off the train in Dublin and was immediately troubled.

"What if all the rooms got booked and I no longer have a place to stay?" My mind wondered. I made the journey from the train station to the four courts trying to think of what I would do if this was the case. I wondered if I could find help at Christ Church. I didn't know where any other hostels were even though I knew they were there. I felt very alone.

"Hey! You're back!" The guy behind the counter said as I went in. It was the same guy who checked me out and had given me the weird look.

"Yeah," I replied. "I got a day ahead of myself."

"I was wondering," he chuckled, "but figured you knew what you were doing. Anyway, I assume you want to get another room?" His mere asking of that question gave me a huge sense of relief. I hoped to goodness I would still be able to stay the night.

"Uh, yeah," I replied sheepishly. "Please tell me you have a bed available. Otherwise, I'm not sure what I'll do."

"Well," he started. My heart sunk and prepared for the worst. "The only thing is that the room you originally had is now booked so I can't put you in there." I said nothing, frozen, my mind already accepting the reality that I am about to have to figure something else out all alone — no safety nets. "But if you're ok being in one of our large rooms, there are several available beds." He concluded.

"Oh, thank GOD," I exclaimed. "Yes, yes, that's fine. I've never stayed in a large room full of strangers like that, but a bed is a bed." I'm not sure why that 'GOD' came out of my mouth. I still wasn't sure if God approved my trip even though I had at least made it across the ocean alive. Nevertheless, my joy prompted me to give him thanks. Maybe this would make him happy that I still thank him even if it was merely a coincidence. Regardless, I felt safe again knowing I had a place to stay. Even better, the price for the bigger room was cheaper than the smaller one I had originally! Therefore, I booked this night and one extra night since I had gotten a day ahead.

I walked into the large room which was indeed quite large. There were bunk beds everywhere like one might find at a summer camp, only about 4 times as many. Each bunk bed was evenly spaced apart so it was easy to walk in between them. I found one near a window and chose the top. Just like in my previous room, there were lockers under the beds. I locked my big backpack up and grabbed Indie (that's my guitar's name). I found a nice place to sit and play outside the hostel and did so until my belly told me it was time for dinner.

After finding and eating at another kebab shop for dinner, I decided to take a stroll down Capel Street in search of some local or merely authentic Irish music — unlike what I found in the Temple Bar District. The night air was very refreshing and relaxing so I really just wanted to chill, have a drink, and hear some casual music.

During my stroll, I came across what appeared to be a music shop. In the window, there were violins, banjos, and other instruments. I continued passed it supposing a music shop would be closed by now anyway but might check it out later. I continued wandering down Capel until the lights began to fade and the buildings appeared to become more residential. I turned a little disappointedly and headed back. I figured I might pop into the pub where I met the 3 guys betting on the horse race for a Guinness, then return to the hostel. However, as I walked passed the music shop again, I could swear I heard music. I stopped and listened. I took a closer observation of this music shop to discover a small sign that read, "McNeil's Pub"!

I pushed on the door to find it unlocked and as it opened a wonderful spectacle appeared. It was small but of high quality. There was a long, oak-looking bar. The establishment looked like it had been around for a century but remained very well maintained, and most everyone there seemed to be Irish (as to say not tourists). It was exactly what I had been looking for in an authentic, local Irish pub! Best of all, sitting around one table were several musicians very casually playing traditional Irish music!! I immediately entered the pub and bought a beer (Guinness of course), ignoring the odd looks I got from those who were probably curiously wondering, "who is this guy? I've never seen him before."

I found a chair at a table to sit at facing the musicians. They had just finished a song when I had entered so I sat with great anticipation for the next one. Their accents were also thick, but understandable. They seemed to discuss what they ought to play next. Then, the guitar player began to play a chord progression. A violinist joined in followed by a flute, then a guy with a hand-drum, then another flute player, and finally a banjo. 7 instruments by the time it was done, plus a guy playing an egg-shaker if you count that. It was absolutely incredible! I really felt like I was in Ireland, experiencing life as a local, listening to traditional music — a style played for centuries. It was at that moment I knew I had fallen in love with Ireland. What is more, it wasn't over. After a few wonderful rounds of instrumental music (that I could have listened to for hours on end), the music stopped and a girl decided to sing.

The girl had a very lovely voice as she sang an old Irish folktune called "The Balled Of Accounting" (as sung by Peggy Seeger & Ewan MacColl, 1973). She sang completely acapella, and it was beautiful and meaningful. Everyone in the bar stopped any conversation and respectfully listened. It was dead silent until she finished. When she finished, the entire place erupted in applause. My soul was overjoyed with gratitude at my incredible luck in discovering this place. Did God somehow lead me here? I wondered if perhaps he wasn't completely against my trip. In any case, I lifted up a silent prayer of thanksgiving.

I ended up having a great chat with a really sweet local girl after the band winded down. She recommended I go to a town called Gallway because I loved music. I told her I would try to stop by there. We chatted for a little while until I couldn't take it anymore. Between the scene, the music, and chatting with a cool local girl (nothing about conspiracies, the 'real' Irish, or attempts to buy my watch this time), my senses were now reaching their overload point and I needed to take my leave.

I laid my head down back at the Four Courts and slowly processed my day. SO much had happened, which had included some troublesome circumstances that I managed to handle, then I ended on such a high note! I couldn't believe how much fun I had had despite the troubles, and to think that my trip is really just getting started.

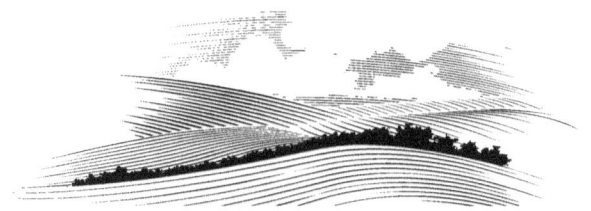

The LOTR Eucharist

Friday, June 6th

Saint Patrick's Cathedral was the only real thing I decided to place on my agenda. Otherwise, it was sort of a "wander around and explore" day; casually step off the beaten path and see where it takes me. I did, however, decide I would stop by Christ Church again to see Jimmy and attend another prayer service. So after breakfast, I crossed the canal and wandered down Capel Street.

The first time I ventured down Capel was specifically in search of food. If it wasn't food, I didn't notice it. The second time, I was in search of a pub with traditional Irish music. If it wasn't a pub, I didn't notice it. Therefore this time, since I wasn't on any sort of mission, I noticed many things I hadn't seen before. The first was a shop with an enormous marijuana leaf sign. Curious, I stepped inside.

This shop, called The Hemp Company, featured all sorts of hemp-related items. Everything from hippy clothes and merchandise, posters, coffee and teas, incense, and candles. The most interesting feature was a tiny museum in the basement entirely dedicated to the history and campaign to legalize marijuana. There were photos, newspaper clippings, journal articles, government documents, and other assorted materials in support of the legalization campaign. It was all very interesting and did a fair job of making its case.

After leaving The Hemp Company, I discovered a music shop — an actual music shop this time as opposed to a pub disguised as one. It was about the size of the guitar section inside a music store on the MS coast called Pinkston's Music (which has closed since the writing of this manuscript. The walls were lined with stringed instruments while drums sat along the floor. I noticed their most popular brand of guitars were called Sigmas, which were from Scotland. I pulled one down and played for a minute to find the tone was nice. I might purchase one someday.

I continued walking up Capel street simply looking at, and in, different shops until I was stopped in my tracks. There seemed to be a pleasing aroma drifting out of a small place called Brother Hubbard that compelled me to investigate. Judging by the name, I had no idea that this small shop was a cafe until I stepped inside. There before me was a counter with Baristas making coffee and teas for people in line. Along the walls were books, bags of coffee, and containers of teas available for purchase.

"G'mornin!" A young guy called, greeting me from behind the counter.

"' Mornin!" I returned. He must have instantly recognized my southern accent and, judging by my demeanor, correctly assumed I had not been there before.

"This yer first time here?" He asked politely.

"Yes sir!" I replied. "I was walking by just outside and it smelled so good in here, I absolutely had to stop in!"

"Ah! Well, welcome to Brother Hubbard!" He said merrily.

There were containers of tea on a shelf that one could smell, and from that, choose the desired tea. I smelled a few and found that the Moroccan meant tea smelled the best. I placed the order and within minutes was holding a small hot tea that actually tasted just as good as it smelled! Without even adding any sugar, the sweet, minty flavor was very pleasant and refreshing. It was so good in fact, that I seriously thought about purchasing a bag to take home, but ultimately decided it would likely get messed up before I returned home (if I made it back alive).

I decided to head back in the direction of Christ Church and Saint Patrick's at this point, so off I went in the direction I had come. Yet after crossing the canal into the Temple Bar District headed towards Christ Church, I noticed a shop down an alley which enticed my curiosity. It was exciting to walk down a narrow alley like this — something I wouldn't have done at night. To my amusement, it turned out to be a pet shop entirely dedicated to reptiles! It was called Reptile Haven.

Inside Reptile Haven were all kinds of snakes, turtles, and lizards – big and small. It had everything from tiny little corn snakes, to large iguanas, to 6ft long pythons! My favorites however were easily the two chameleons – I want one now.

The clerk was real nice, and about my age. He got them both out (one at a time) and allowed me to play with them. They crawled from my hand, across my arms, and attempted to climb on top of my head! It was so interesting to feel how strong their little toes were and how every movement was tested carefully, lest they fall. They didn't make any sounds, except once when the older one hissed. It was not an angry hiss, but more like the sound a human makes when he thinks he's about to fall. He made this noise while I was trying to pull him off my arm, so it may have scared him. Anyway, it was a really cool experience.

After spending perhaps a little too much time playing with the lizards, I continued on to Christ Church. It turned out that Jimmy was not there today, but the guy at the front desk told me that Eucharist would be held later and I was invited to the service. I excitedly made a note of what time the service would be held and told him I would be back.

St. Patrick's was more or less the same as Christ Church to be honest, albeit bigger. It also featured a large courtyard with greenery which was unfortunately closed to the public. The church also seemed to function more as a museum than a religious space. The museum was obviously dedicated to the history of St. Patrick, his affiliation with historical figures, his mission, and the legacy of the cathedral itself. There were also many statues, burial monuments, and pretty architecture. My favorite piece of architecture was a stone spiral staircase which begged me to climb it, but it was off-limits. Being a musician, I also couldn't help but notice how brilliant the acoustics were inside. Strike 1 chord, and everyone would hear.

Suddenly it occurred to me that I hadn't been watching the time. I looked down at my watch in terror to realize the Eucharist service would be starting in FIVE MINUTES! I really didn't care so much that they wouldn't let me take communion due to being protestant. I still really wanted to attend the service!

With my backpack jumbling all over my back and making constant calls over my shoulder of, "excuses me!" "Sorry!" from my panting mouth, I made like Forest Gump and RAN back down Patrick Street to get to Christ Church in time. Fortunately, I made it just as they were about to start. Still sweating and half panting, I found my way to the small area in which the service was being held.

Unlike my expectations, the service was not in the main area like the prayer service. Instead, it was located in a small area behind the choir loft. It was a circular space made entirely of stone. The seats were literally a part of the wall with tiny columns on either side of them to form the sides of the would-be chairs. Cushions were placed on the "seat," part. Entirely made of white stone they were, from the ceiling to the part that molded into a seat. Then down to the floor it went, which was laden with artistic tile. On each piece of tile, there was either some sort of fox or a typical medieval-designed lion.

A lay person I had met while with Jimmy the other day was there as well. I turned and asked him if I was allowed to take communion being that I was a protestant and all. To my surprise, he said I could!

"Oh no! You can!" He explained. "This is an Anglican church."

Up to this point, I had assumed for some reason that Cathedrals were all Catholic. I suppose I had subconsciously known otherwise, and that is why I asked in the first place. In any case, however, I was glad I would be allowed to partake.

A minute or two later, a woman came in and began the service in a similar way that Jimmy had done to start his (simply came in and started speaking). We jumped right into the service, which was in English this time for the most part. I read along in the pamphlet I was provided. There were prayers, responsive readings with scripture, and readings from the patron saint's writings. The woman gave a very short "mini-sermon" as we call them back home that lasted maybe two or three minutes.

I really loved every second of the woman's speaking. Her voice was so calming and relaxing, and her accent was beautiful. As she spoke, I kept waiting for her to recite the monologue at the beginning of The Lord of the Rings: The Fellowship of the Ring. (2001). Her voice, however, was more soothing than that of the one in LOTR. The sensation is hard to describe but very good, to say the least.

Eventually, we took Holy Communion. I was surprised that the bread wafers provided did not taste like cardboard as I'm used to getting at my home church. The wine was honey whine distilled with water and was delicious — we each drank from the same cup the way Catholics do. After taking the elements, I did as the others had done and said, "amen."

Following the service, I went over to speak to the woman to tell her how absolutely beautiful the service was. When I spoke, her face did similar to what Jimmy's did. She was extremely kind and very welcoming — obviously not expecting a random southern American to have been here for Eucharist.

As it turned out, this woman was a priest. She preferred to be called a female priest as opposed to a priestess or sister. We discussed things such as the Anglican Church, its ministry, and its similarities with the Methodist Church (the one I belonged to). When she explained that the Anglican church was formerly called The Church of England, everything suddenly made sense. The Church of England was King Henry VIII's church which was separate from the Catholic church. The Church of England became Anglican, which falls under the umbrella of Protestantism. Thus, I was allowed to take communion because Anglican is the Protestant Church of England.

By the time all this was over, it had gotten late, and was time to head back. I managed to find some cheap Chinese food for dinner before returning to the Four Courts. Even for a casual day, I went to bed exhausted.

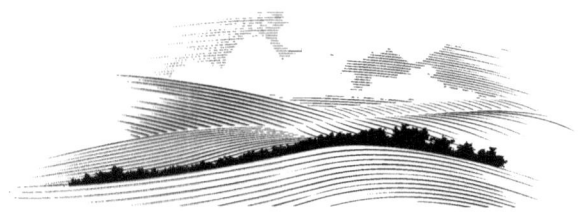

King John's Castle

Saturday, June 7th

When I woke up this morning at around 7:30am, my eyes shot open. It was Limerick Day, and that meant King John's Castle day! I was particularly excited about this one as opposed to Dublin Castle. Having done my research beforehand, I knew that this castle belonged to John, the brother of King Richard I aka "Lionhearted," both of whom played key roles in the legendary Robin Hood stories.

I found a bus stop this time and climbed aboard. To be honest, I had never ridden a bus before. I was thankful that Irish people are so friendly because all I had to do was ask someone to help me. An older local woman in this case was all too happy to explain how it worked. I managed to pull the rope alerting the driver and get off at the right stop thanks to her. Once off the bus, I walked into the train station and was headed to Limerick within a few minutes.

I left the train station in the lovely town of Limerick and in the direction of the castle according to my map. As I walked, I noticed it would rain lightly on me on and off for a few minutes at a time. I found this quite bizarre, but it didn't cause me any trouble. I passed by a gorgeous cathedral and asked a couple nearby if it were Catholic or Anglican. To my surprise, it was neither. Instead, it was Dominican. I wasn't familiar with the Dominican church and considered going in, but was too eager to explore King John's castle. Thus, so I carried on.

I finally arrived at the castle with the excitement of a '90s girl at an N'SYNC concert. Well, maybe not quite that excited, but comparable. I went immediately into the lobby where tickets were purchased. I bought my ticket and took a brochure with information about the castle. Before getting to the actual castle part, there was a museum to explain the history of the castle, significant facts about its current state, and why parts were missing (such as the entrance where the lobby building now sat), and a brief history of Limerick concerning the castle.

I went through the museum rather quickly, reading descriptions and listening to audio recordings regarding featured displays and models. As much as I would love to have taken my time to learn, my excitement at walking through the grounds of this medieval fortress prevented me from moving too slowly. I didn't want to be in the museum all day when there was a castle to explore!

"Besides," I thought, "If I want to learn all this about the castle, I can do deeper research myself! I am a trained historian after all!"

When I finally made it onto the castle grounds, I was in awe. I essentially fell in love with the place. It was all too surreal, I couldn't believe it. I felt the walls with my hands and looked down from the towers, attempting to imagine what it must have looked like in its time. It was so incredible that attempting to explain it seems impossible.

While exploring, I found an armory display of authentic (though likely merely replica) medieval armor and weaponry. Shields were hanging on the walls and weapons were secured in racks (which could not be removed). Further, there were a few shields and helmets available that weren't locked into place! Without hesitation, I picked up a large wooden shield that was quite heavy. Next, I chose a helmet and placed it on my head. There was a woman with her child also checking out the room who kindly agreed to snap a photo of me with my armor on. To make it better, I held a long spear in my hand that was attached to one of the racks. I was obviously nerding out super hard. Something else I found really cool were actual cannon balls in large barrels. These balls of rock were not much larger than my fist, yet weighed at least 20 pounds each if not more.

I probably spent an hour or more walking around the castle grounds, climbing the towers, and looking at the displays inside tents meant to recreate a setting that one might have found in its prime (chairs, maps, medieval military paraphernalia, etc). I stayed until I simply couldn't take any more in. Similar to my feelings at the pub, it was like a beautiful sensory overload. I could not have been more grateful for this incredible experience. I hated to leave, but I knew it was time.

The next thing on my agenda was to visit a place called The Hunt Museum, which I had noticed on my way to the castle. I'm still not quite sure what its purpose was, but it contained some really interesting historical artifacts and artwork. I went through this museum rather quickly as well, snapping photos, then headed back to the front towards the exit.

Before leaving, I decided to stop for a snack and some tea at the cafe attached to the lobby. I realized I really needed a little time to process and digest my day so far. The pot of tea and snack combined cost me only around €1.50, so I couldn't argue against it. I sat and enjoyed my treat for twenty or thirty minutes to "sober up" from my experiences.

From the Hunt museum, I headed back to the train station where I passed by some Scottish bagpipe players. I was thinking along the way that I'd return to Dublin, find some food, a beer, and then go to sleep. Nothing crazy.

While nearing the station, I was drawn to a sign claiming that the building was a casino. This casino did not look anything like the casinos we have in Mississippi or from what I have seen in pictures or movies of Los Vegas. This casino looked just like all the other buildings around it except for the sign indicating it was a casino, which simply read, "casino." Out of curiosity, I walked down the alley and into a stone courtyard where the entrance to this 'casino' was. I peeked through the glass windows to see the inside. It seemed very crowded with nothing particularly interesting to see (just slot machines), so I left. As I was walking out of the alley, however, an Irish guy my age stopped me. It was then that things took an unexpected turn….

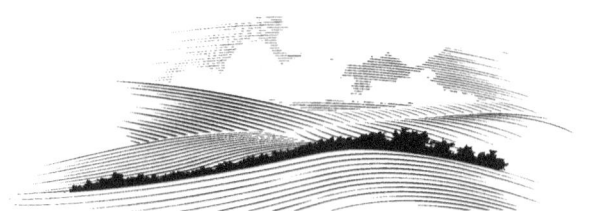

Mississippi Bohs

Saturday, June 7th (Continued)

The following story is dedicated to the Dublin Bohs Football Club, Freddy, Osi, Seanie, and the other lads who made my experience so memorable. Names of all individuals may or may not have been changed to protect their private identity (because I'm no 'journo'). The original version of this manuscrip was sent to "Seanie" for approval.
Also, it might benefit you to watch the original Green Street Hooligans (2005) film staring Elijah Wood~*

"What's the craic, mate?" He asked in a merry tone. "What's yer story?"

The guy caught me completely off guard, so I wasn't sure how to respond. Then, I remembered Paul the taxi driver telling me that this was a common greeting, equivalent to, "What's up man? How's it going?"

"Not too much," I replied, still a little surprised.

"Are ya goin to the match?" He asked.

"Match?" I replied confused. Even as I said this, I made a very exciting and enticing assumption.

"Yeh, the football match! Dublin Bohemians and Limerick City!" He explained. My eyes lit up.

"Oh, man! I didn't know about any match! I love football! ……could I join you?" I asked.

"Of course!" The guy exclaimed excitedly.

At that point, we introduced ourselves to each other. His name was Freddy, and I told him that mine was Tim. After talking for a few minutes, Freddy went around introducing me to everyone around.

"Hey! This is Tim from Mississippi!" He would say. Everyone he introduced me to was tickled and excited that a random Mississippian traveler was there and willing to come support their team. One of the guys, however, didn't seem too excited to have me along. He wasn't unfriendly, but he certainly seemed to be very stand-offish and didn't speak to me very much. I didn't let it bother me though, and soon we were all headed to the match.

As we walked along the road toward the stadium, I looked behind me to realize that there was a gigantic crowd of guys - just guys - of all ages walking with us. I had met a large number of people through Freddy, but I had no idea the mass that was associated with this group. I couldn't help but flash back to the movie Eurotrip where the main characters meet the Manchester United Football Club guys. I begin to wonder…then, about that time, Freddy turns to me. Out of the blue, he asks,

"So Tim. Do ya fight?" This random question along with my surroundings seemed to confirm what I had been curiously wondering. I had previously decided that while on this trip, I would adhere to the philosophy, "when in Rome, do as the Romans do." In this immediate predicament, I felt it was very important to be honest with this guy. Yet, I still needed to be true to the philosophy. I was on an adventure, and adventures require risks. Therefore I answered in the most honest, yet loyal to the philosophy.

"Uhh,…I wasn't planning on it." I said, suggesting that I could handle myself in a fight but hadn't had the intention of fighting this day in particular. In reality, I had never actually been in a fight before, but I wasn't about to let this stranger know that. Having a small amount of knowledge about European football, I could take an educated guess on why he was actually asking.

"Alright," he replied. "Well, I tell you what. If we get into a scrap, you throw the first punch, and I've got yer back." I agreed, and that was that. I reconciled to myself in that moment that as a new addition to this group of die-hard European football fans, there was a real possibility that we would end up fighting the die-hard European football fans of the Limerick City team. If we ended up fighting, I figured I would do a deep/old-south, fired-up redneck accent (and use southern words and made-up on-the-spot phrases they wouldn't understand) to scare them, then crow-hop the first guy out of nowhere like a crazy coonass, before doing my best to hold my own and not die. Solid plan.

"As the Romans do,……" I thought to myself as we continued toward the stadium visible in the distance.

As we walked along, some of the guys (or "lads" as they say over there) started referring to me as "the Yank." I assumed they simply meant American and didn't think much of it. If only I had seen a certain Elija Wood movie before this experience, it would have made more sense. Since I hadn't, I merely laughed along in fun having no idea of the events foreshadowed.

During the match, I spoke with several people about this and that. I even met the Dublin Bohemian Football Club manager who told me that the stadium we were in was the biggest in Ireland and was once used primarily for rugby. He also told me how rugby gave birth to American football (I can neither confirm nor deny the accuracy of this). I also witnessed, as expected, football supporters doing chants for their team. It was great to see it as well as be a part of it. It was often hard to understand what was being said through the Irish accents, but when I could understand, I tried to chant along. When a smaller group of younger guys who knew Freddy realized I was from Mississippi, I was honored that they made up a chant just for me that went,

"Missi-ssippi Bohs, na, na, na!," which was chanted repeatedly.

Sometime later, after constant chants and cheers (both positive and negative), the game ended with a Bohemian 2-1 victory over Limerick City. Freddy, a guy named Osi, and another guy I met walked down the street back to the train station. Freddy talked with me about cultural differences and pointed things out to me about Ireland that I had not noticed yet. After a good walk, a cab stopped. It was one of the lads from the group who made up my chant along with the Club Manager. They told us to hop in, and we rode back to the station with them. Before getting on the train, I learned that drinks for the ride back was a MUST. So, we stopped at a corner store nearby. As for me, I grabbed a sixer of Carlsberg. It was time to celebrate the win, and for me, the added bonus of not having to fight anyone! Yet, the night was far from over.

The whole train ride back was filled with chanting, singing, and drinking in merry celebration. I was thankful that the other passengers on the train didn't seem to mind us all carrying on. As we sang, I shared with Osi that despite having been in Ireland this whole time, I had yet to encounter Irish drinking songs.

"Is that even a real thing, or just some stereotypes we have in America?" I asked him.

"What?!" He exclaimed. "No, we 'ave plenty of drinking songs. Here, we'll make one for you!" He then gathered a few guys together and they explained one to me. It was really more of a silly game but I took it.

"Ok, so we're going to sing a song and at the end, you'll have to drink down your beer while we count. Ok? Here we go."

"We love Tim! He's our mate! We love Tim, he'll drink till eight!" They all chanted. "One…two…three," It was then up to me to drink down my beverage until they finished counting. The fun part about this game for them was that they controlled the speed with which they counted. Therefore, it could be a really short 8 seconds or a really long 8 seconds. Not wanting to get hammered in a foreign country without a trusted ally, I pretended to be drinking a little more than I really was to keep the count going. After they made it to 8, everyone cheered and I laughed in fun. After my "drinking song," the entire car erupted into the "Mississippi Bohs" song. Everyone pointed at me as I laughed and joined them. We chanted this several times until transitioning into another song, then another, then another.

The ride was so much fun, I decided I should stop and take a quick "mission Log" where I record myself explaining what is happening. However, while doing this, Freddy and Osi came over hurriedly.

"Try not to get anyone's faces," Osi warned me. "You could get them and or the club into trouble."

I didn't understand but certainly wanted to be respectful. I told them that I didn't have any intention of posting the video on youtube or anything — only documenting good times for myself. They both completely understood and didn't blame me, but explained to me what the issue was.

Elija Wood stars in a movie about an American who drops out of college and moves to England to live with his sister and her English husband. He has a journalism background and keeps a journal while there. During his stay, his brother-in-law introduces him to his friends who are all a part of a firm, or a football team fan club. Elija's character ends up receiving the nickname of "the Yank," from the guys and becomes a full member of the group. However, because of his journal of detailed accounts of the group's activities, he is ousted as a journalist — a traitor who sells these detailed stories and gets the individuals into trouble. In this film, journalists are called "journos." They are considered huge rats and are HATED.

Freddy and Osi confirmed once and for all that this group was in fact a group of hooligans (or "casuals" as they might prefer) as over-exaggerated in the Eurotrip (2004) film. Probably because I had turned up out of nowhere and joined them, because I was filming, and because they had jokingly been comparing me to "the yank," earlier on, they began to get genuinely suspicious that I WAS like that character i.e. an undercover journalist posing as a tourist to write a story on them. I of course had zero intentions of publishing a detailed story using their full names and descriptions. At the time, I was considering writing a blog that featured my daily journal entries which would feature every story from my trip, but nothing to get anyone into trouble! Freddy and Osi however assured me that they believed that I was not a journalist and told me not to worry about it. However, it was recommended I be careful about the filming, so I did. Despite this slight concern, the ride was still an incredibly good time.

Once back in Dublin, I found an atm and grabbed some cash before finding a kebab place. I was starving. Freddy and Osi joined me so they could take me to the hangout pub afterward where everyone was meeting. The hangout pub was called Davy's. After eating, we left and arrived at the pub just as another young guy I had met at the match came out followed by a large man wearing a fedora hat. The guy I knew greeted us and said he would be right back, but we were expected. As we walked in past the large man holding the door, the man closed the large wooden door directly behind us. I found this a bit odd in and of itself. I then noticed that there was also a large, old-school latch, which the man shoved to the left to lock the door with a notable sound. Further, in the middle and towards the top of the door, was another small rectangle latch that one might use to open to identify a visitor and perhaps request a password. I wondered what I was getting myself into now.

As we walked inside, I realized that there were only 2 older men sitting at the bar. Aside from the bartender and the two older gentlemen, there was only a small group of younger guys who I recognized from the match sitting in a group to the side on couches. I was forced then to assume that I was now getting to hang out with the inner circle of these Casuals at this particular pub. I felt pretty cool, I have to admit. Like being invited to the secret underground club of Mafia bosses (except not having to be worried that they might plan to kill you). I grabbed a drink, then went and sat down in the circle next to Freddy on my left, and across from Osi. To my right was Seanie, the guy that had been stand-offish to me all night, but by no means unfriendly. At some point, someone made a crack at me, which provoked Seanie to respond in a joking way, but with an undertone of seriousness,

"Personally, I'm still convinced yer wearing a wire." The guys laughed but knew he was really somewhat concerned. Their faces told me they anticipated my response. I laughed.

"You really DO think I'm a FRACKING JOURNO!" I replied, half-quoting the movie as some of the guys had said to me previously or heard them jokingly say to one another referencing the film. There with us was a red-headed guy everyone had been picking on at the match because he had an attractive mother. He was also one of the guys who knew I was harmless. In all fun, he demanded in a mocking-serious tone,

"ARE you a FRACKING JOURNO?!" He was half-quoting the movie back to me. Half-jokingly I replied.

"Do you want me to PROVE it?" The guys on the couch were jumping out of their seats at this exchange. All were laughing, some were equally amused with what was happening and very curious to see how this was going to play out. I then stood up right in front of Seanie, pulled my shirt and jacket up over my head to expose my entire upper body, and did a slow spin. The group of guys, Seanie included, howled with laughter. No one was expecting this, and Seanie's face was priceless. I then put my shirt back down knowing I had made my point. I then looked Seanie right in the face with a big grin and said, "Are you satisfied, or would you like me to take my pants off too?" As I said this, I reached down and grabbed my belt buckle. This was met with laughing shouts of "No, no, no!" I think they believed I was truly prepared to drop my pants to make the point.

After this humorous display of not being wired, I noticed that Seanie got up and pulled Freddy, Osi, and a couple other guys into a back room where they stayed for a while. I imagined it had something to do with me. When they came back in, I spoke Seanie, who I gathered to be the leader of this group,

"I want you to ask me questions." I said. "I've noticed you have been distant and suspicious of me all night, so I want you to resolve any concerns you have about me. I promise you, I'm not a journalist. I may put the experience I have during this trip on a blog, but I won't share anything that might get you or the club into trouble."

After this meeting with Freddy, Osi, and the others earlier along with my performance proving I wasn't a journalist, it seemed he now believed me for certain. He seemed to almost feel a little guilty for being suspicious of me. For the next twenty minutes or so, he and I talked. He even apologized many times for being so suspicious.

"I know you're a good lad," he said, "you're really just a tourist, and I'm glad you got to hang with us. But you can understand why me and some of the mates would be suspicious of you, having just popped up out of nowhere and started hanging out with us."

I assured him that I completely understood and I had no hard feelings. He let me ask questions about their group which he answered well, often referring to the Elija Wood movie to explain where some of the guys' suspicions came from. After this, I chatted with the rest of the guys a bit more before eventually deciding it was time to go. They all bid me a fond farewell and invited me to join them again the next time I found myself in Dublin.

The following morning was going to be a long day of travel to England for my next adventure. Being a little drunk at this point, Seanie, Freddy, and Osi helped me catch a cab back to the Four Courts where I found my last night's rest in Ireland.

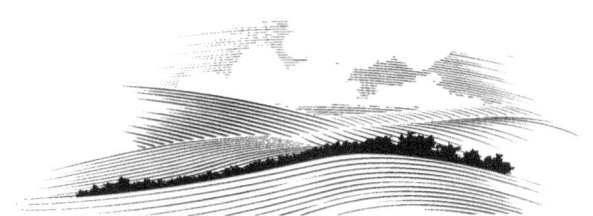

Rock-a-bye Ferry

Sunday, June 8th

Since departing from the United States, I had carried a small, string, carry-on bag with my University's logo on it. Somehow, it had ripped along the side which I had neglected to fix. The rip went from very small to large enough for things to start falling out (or easily stolen). Today was also a travel day where I would journey from Dublin to Liverpool, England to begin my England tour. I couldn't very well do this with a damaged bag. Therefore, my first goal of the day was to acquire a new bag to carry my most delicate items (phone charger, phone, tablet, journal, and some other things).

I chose to start my search at Penny's on O'Connell Street. In the States, this store is called JC Penny's. I wondered why but didn't care enough to start an investigation.

I walked around the store looking for bags, but most of them were bright yellow — not very masculine. I left empty-handed and continued my search. The next place I came across was a sports store that looked promising. I hoped I might find something like the bag I had already, but there were none. All they had were small, simple backpacks which I had noticed many locals using. Since these bags would likely prove to be more durable than my original string bag, I decided to go ahead and spend a little more money than I had planned for the quality. After buying the bag, I immediately transferred my things and left.

With my new bag in hand and my things secured, I returned to the Four Courts one last time to grab my luggage and check out before heading to Heuston Station. A train took me from there to the ferry port (quick trip) where I bought my €35 ferry ticket. I happily paid the amount because it was cheaper than flying and doesn't require flying — I'd had enough flying. The boat wasn't quite ready for boarding yet, so I took a seat and waited. The plan was to ride the ferry straight across the Irish Sea to Holyhead, Whales where I would then catch a bus that would take me to the local train station. A train would bring me to Liverpool, and from there, I would simply have to find my hostel called the Hoax Hostel near Matthew Street. It was kind of a lot, which honestly made me a little nervous. What if I get lost? What if I get on the wrong bus or train? What if something else happens? I pushed these things out of my mind as the intercom called for boarding.

The boat was pretty large with plenty of seats. I, however, chose to grab a spot out on the deck so I could see just how big the vessel was. Unfortunately, the deck was on the back side of the boat and my vision was limited. Yet, I was still able to enjoy the view of the open sea and coastline.

As the boat slowly pulled away from the harbor past the lighthouse, I watched the shore slowly fade away. About this time, the wind seemed to immediately begin picking up. Soon, it felt as if I were in the midst of a hurricane! Wind beat against me, requiring me to keep a hand on the railing lest it knocks me over! Droplets of icy-cold, salty water sprinkled my face as the largest swells I had ever seen (in person) crashed against the ship. I leaned into the wind, which was strong enough to hold me up, and gazed out towards the horizon. Meanwhile, Disney's The Pirates of the Caribbean films theme song played through my head.

"Adventure." I thought to myself. "Another adventure." There was no telling what lay ahead or if I was going to have what it took moving forward, but there was no turning back now. There was something inside me that was filled with excited anticipation simply about testing myself — to find out. No safety nets, and no one to call if things go south. I was on my own. I still hoped God would be with me, but didn't feel certain that he was. I wasn't dead yet, and to be honest, I felt REALLY alive! I hadn't been on this adventure across Europe long and had already been forced to overcome some unique challenges. I couldn't imagine what challenges would come my way next, but having overcome the ones I had so far gave me a little more confidence that I could somehow manage those that lay ahead. The only way to really find out, I realized, was to meet them.

My main deck experience was cut short when rain begin to fall. It wasn't so much about staying dry as it was to avoid the feeling of tiny needles stabbing my exposed skin. I ventured to imagine that even true buccaneers would doubtfully have endured this, given the choice. I, therefore, grabbed my things and eased back inside below deck just as the waves began to get noticeably rougher.

"If I were the kind of person who got seasick," I thought as the boat rocked up and down, back and forth, and side to side. "This would be the time for it to happen.

Sitting down seemed like the best option at this point. It appeared that everyone else had gotten the same idea. There were no longer plenty of seats available. I noticed an open seat at a table where a nice-looking family was and decided to approach them.

"Excuse me," I asked politely. "Do you mind if I join you?"

"Absolutely!" The woman holding a small child replied. "Have a seat!"

We began talking and I learned that she, her husband, and two children had recently moved to England from Australia for her husband's job and loved it. They were a super nice family and easy to talk to, although the woman felt as secure on a boat as I did on a plane. I tried to help her husband reassure her that the boat wasn't going to suddenly sink in the middle of the ocean and while the waves were indeed big, they weren't big enough to capsize us. To entertain them, pass the time, and distract the woman from the rocking boat, I told them about my travel plans. They were very interested and fully supported my intentions. When I expressed a concern I had about getting to my next hostel in Liverpool, the husband was so kind as to offer to drive me to my hostel if I wasn't able to figure it out — even though it was completely out of their way!

"Wow," I thought. "The kindness of strangers." Soon, we had arrived at port in Holyhead, Wales. The couple again reiterated that they would be happy to drive me if I needed the lift and they would stick around after they had gotten their car and look for me. I was overwhelmed by their kindness and thanked them.

I managed to find the bus without too much trouble, thanks especially to the occasional guidance of friendly strangers. Soon, I was on the train from Holyhead to Liverpool which was a magnificent experience. The landscape of Wales was absolutely breathtaking. There were steep, tall mountains that abruptly ended with a cliff overlooking a beach. Some of these small mountains were covered in grass rather than trees like they do in the States. Here the mountains seem to shoot up vertically out of the ground whereas the mountains I am familiar with are long rolls or gradual climbs. Watching these incredible landscapes go by, I could imagine an Aragorn-type character riding a horse to the top of one to get a view of the path ahead.

Coming into the English countryside was not quite as brilliant as Wales. It primarily featured sheep farms. Similar to Wales, however, the mountains in the distance and rolling hills were unreal. I felt like I had literally been transported back to 1300 riding by and making stops at all the small villages along the way. Most of them, I noticed, seemed to have Cathedrals in the center with houses all around with occasional remains of a wall on the outskirts.

I finally arrived in Liverpool and immediately noticed the architecture. It was incredible. Most of it was very classical European-looking with no space whatsoever between buildings most of the time. The other thing I immediately noticed was the police cars that came suddenly screaming by. I had only seen two police officers in Dublin, neither of whom were in cars. This was therefore my first time to see a police vehicle outside the United States (in person). The sirens echoed across the buildings as they came by, which was not a pleasant sound ("nehno-nehno-nehno"). I walked along the street following my map and with the help of a few friendly strangers, found my hostel.

After checking in, I found an Italian place down the road called The Filling Station. It served all kinds of food: Pizza pie, fish 'n chips, burgers, chicken, hot wings, and 3 types of kebabs. The kebab choices were Doner, chicken, and shish. I was unfamiliar with "doner," so I asked the guy behind the counter who explained that it was a mix of lamb and beef. It sounded good, so I ordered one. This is when the unexpected problem occurred.

I had intended to pay with my credit card since I had forgotten to exchange my euros for British pounds. It was also Sunday so banks were closed. There was no way for me to get cash. When the clerk called my name to get my food, I handed him my card.

"Sorry sir, we can't take cards." He told me. I couldn't believe my luck! I had no idea what to do. I wondered if it was a deal where they didn't take a card unless you spent a certain amount, but this was not the case. Fortunately, the clerk was really nice and told me that there was an ATM nearby that I could use to pull money out. I was very thankful as this would solve the problem at hand, while also letting me get cash out for the next few days. What surprised me was the fact that the clerk was willing to let me take my food with me to get money and then return to pay him. While I appreciated his vote of trust, I assured him that it was fine if I left it until I returned, which I did promptly before scarfing down my delicious doner kebab.

Before returning to the hostel, I decided to take a stroll down the famous Matthew Street where The Beatles used to hang out. I passed by several cool-looking pubs, but the people walking around, some of the venues themselves, and the atmosphere overall felt really sketchy. The strip was essentially an alleyway lined with pubs and clubs. There were very few (if any) cops and lots of homeless-looking people asking for money. I also noticed big mobster-looking guys in suits hanging out in places that were not well-lit. If I had not been alone, I might have checked out a few of the pubs, but I was very much alone. That being said, I chose not to spend much time there but noted that if I wrote a novel in the future and needed an underground crime location, I would definitely base it on Matthew Street.

Back at Hoax Hostel, I met two girls and a guy who were staying in my room. Jessie of South Korea, Susie of Ontario, Kathryn of Australia, and Jose of Portugal. We got to know each other a little bit, which made us feel a lot more comfortable sleeping in the same room. I then grabbed a quick shower and hopped into my top bunk bed. Once my electronics were plugged into the convenient outlet next to my bed, I went to sleep feeling satisfied with my handling of making it from Ireland to England.

Part III: England

Map of England: https://d-maps.com/carte.php?num_car=14753&lang=en
- Lines, circles, and words with asterisks are author's annotations and not on original map

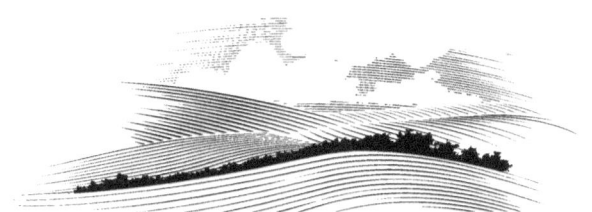

Beatles And Beers

Monday, June 9th

Before I ever considered this trip, back when I was still attending my university, I became friends with a few foreign exchange students. A few of them were Tanja of Germany, Claire and Noe of France, and Victoria of England. Before leaving for my trip, I made contact with all of these friends and they insisted I visit while I was traveling. Today, I planned to conclude my day by visiting Victoria in/near Manchester.

After waking up and having a €3 breakfast in the hostel lobby, I returned to my room to find my new friends from last night just waking up. We talked a little bit, then they invited me to go with them to breakfast. I had obviously already eaten, but chose to join them just to hang out. With that, we all went down to the lobby together. Even though I enjoyed my solo breakfast earlier, it was really great having this "second" breakfast with new friends. We enjoyed each others' company and shared in a few laughs. During the meal, we each shared our plans. It turned out that we all had intentions of visiting The Beatles museum and unanimously decided we ought to go together. Thus, after breakfast, we set out to find the museum using our maps.

We arrived at the museum without too much trouble. It was still very early and thus not very crowded. We showed our college IDs to get a nice discount at which point we were each given a pair of headphones and a small device for the audio-tour. This audio-tour was cool, but it meant it might take longer than necessary to get through the tour. I definitely didn't want to rush through it, but didn't want to take all day listening to detailed descriptions of everything. I'd prefer to simply snap a photo and move on. Since the tour used numbers to help guide your audio device, I stayed ahead a few numbers, and simply took in the sights. The others took their time a little more than me, but I think I managed to keep them moving. 'Slow but steady winds the race,' as they say. No dilly-dallying!

The museum was actually really something! I only wished I had still been big into The Beatles like I was in high school. The tour began with each band member's origin story, then the formation of the band, and how much influence Elvis Presley (king of rock and role from Tupelo, Mississippi) had on each of them musically. It continued from there to explain how they all found each other, their evolution as a group in sound, style, and look. Despite the "far out" evolutionary history, I was much more concerned with the physical history of the band. By this I mean guitars, clothes, early merchandise, etc. Again, I considered myself a trained historian who could do his own deeper research if desired later. This was my only chance to see physical items with my own eyes.

Towards the end of the tour, we realized we had somehow lost Jose! How you lose a grown young guy is beyond me. Regardless, Susie and I went back through looking for him, but couldn't find him! Seeing no other option, we resolved to exit without him. We felt forced to assume he had gone ahead without us since we hadn't found him in an earlier part of the tour. Besides, we were all hungry and didn't care to wait any longer. With food on our brains, we concluded our tour and went out in search of food.

The 3 of us found a strip of shops, a mall, and eating places. I was a little concerned about the price of things because England was more expensive than both the United States and the rest of Europe. We eventually came across a place selling unique-looking subs. These subs were really long and skinny, but ended up tasting great! After eating, my belly was satisfied, especially since it only cost £4! Now that I was sufficiently filled and my wallet still filled with money, I said my goodbyes to my new friends, exchanged contact information with them, and made my way back to the hostel to get my things.

After collecting my things from the hostel room, I went to the lobby to check out. I hopped in line behind a guy who had apparently just checked in and was inquiring about places to eat. While the girl behind the desk was giving him some options, I noticed that he didn't have a British or European accent. He also had a ring on his finger that looked like one from an American college. When he turned around, it all made sense. Big and loud, gold letters burst across the chest of his purple shirt that read "LSU." I must confess to how refreshing it felt to come across a fellow Southern American here in England. Since we both clearly had agendas (he to eat and me to leave), we merely said hello, shook hands, and wished one another safe travels. I left with a satisfied smile after checking out having had a brief encounter with an SEC alum (SEC = Southeastern Conference, an athletics league for sports in the US and arguably the best league in the country).

While sitting on the train, I took the opportunity to do a bit of journaling. My original intention was to keep a daily, detailed journal. However, I had gotten behind in my writing with so much going on and having so much to write about. This then seemed like the perfect opportunity — or so I thought.

"Hey, what are you writing?" A cute girl sitting in front of me turned and asked curiously. She had obviously seen me writing intently on her way to her seat.

"Oh, hi!" I replied. "Just journaling. I'm backpacking and have fallen behind."

"Oh, that's so cool!" She said.

"Yeah, it's been interesting so far." I answered, setting my journal down.

"I'm Carla." She told me.

"Oh, that's a pretty name!" I said. "I'm Tim. Very nice to meet you."

Despite my desire to keep a journal, I couldn't help putting it aside to have a chat with a friendly stranger, especially when it was a cute, friendly stranger. I had expected the interaction to fizzle out shortly after introductions so I planned to return to journaling. Surprisingly, however, this was not the case. Rather, we ended up diving straight into interesting conversation. I eventually asked if I could come sit next to her so she wouldn't have to sit turned around. She happily obliged.

Carla was a really interesting girl. Originally from a village in Romania, she moved to England a few years before to study, then chose to remain in the country. She was an artist by profession and showed me some of her work which was actually REALLY good! One was a huge mural of Mike Tyson she had painted inside a boxing gym. That was easily my favorite among those she showed me as well as the most memorable. Her and I ended up talking for the entire duration of the train ride up until it was her stop. She kindly ensured that I understood my own stop would be the next one (I had confessed my inexperience with the English train system) before leaving. I hated to say goodbye, but shook her hand again and wished her the best of luck.

Sometime later, I arrived in Manchester and immediately searched for a map. Surprisingly, there were none to be found. I was thankful to come across an older, very kind rail security guard who took one look at me and before I could open my mouth said,

"Let me guess,…YHA hostel?"

"What gave me away?" I asked laughing, pulling my large backpacking bag straps higher onto my shoulders. I obviously had the 'traveler' look going on. We had a quick exchange of humor before he helped me get my bearings. He provided me with not only directions to my hostel, but also a basic layout of the area and recommendations on where to eat. I was very grateful for his assistance for which I thanked him kindly before heading in his pointed direction. After setting out from here, I managed to make it to the hostel having only made THREE wrong turns! I was pretty proud of myself!

After checking in and getting into my room, I went outside and took a stroll. I wanted to get a better sense of the area. It turned out to be an excellent location. It was situated along a canal overlooking what appeared to be an old Roman half-ampitheater. There were flowers and swans everywhere (like seriously, SO MANY SWANS) with small, single-bed boat houses available for rent as a hotel for apartment. The one thing I didn't like, in fact it enraged me, was that they charged extra for wifi and in such a frustrating fashion. Let me explain.

The hostel itself was a bit pricey to begin with, but then they were charging a pound for every 20 minutes of wifi use! That breaks down to 5¢ per minute. Even worse, however, you couldn't buy an hour's worth. You could only purchase 20 minutes worth of time at a once. Thus, every 20 minutes, I would have to go buy another 20 minutes. Seriously?? I wanted to simply not use the wifi out of principal, but it was necessary that I contact Victoria so I reluctantly paid up.

I jumped onto Facebook and shot her a message to which she almost instantly responded back to. As it turned out, she didn't want to come to me and asked me to come to her.

"I'm really tired," she explained. "If you catch a 20 minute train here, I'll buy your dinner AND drinks." It was a tempting proposition, but I was pretty tired myself. I had only been at the hostel for a half hour and didn't want to get on another train so soon. However, after considering it, the offer of free dinner AND drinks ultimately led me to agree reluctantly.

It wasn't more than 35 minutes later that I again found myself back at the train station. The security guard was still there and made a joke about me leaving already. We chatted as I passed before hopping aboard the train that would take me to her small hometown/village of Macclesfield. Despite being tired, I was a actually excited about visiting. I would be visiting a small town that tourists likely never stopped at so I could really get a sense of local flare. Being with a local further ensured this, and best of all, my experience would be FREE. My tiredness would just have to wait. Like we used to say in college, "you can sleep when you're dead!"

Around 20 minutes after boarding the train, I arrived in Macclesfield. After exiting the train, I was able to get a better view of the lovely little town, which seemed to be placed on a series of steep hills. Narrow, cobblestone roads wound up the hills in between houses like a streams between banks of land and stone. These narrow roads seemed meant to connect the buildings to one another as if the homes were originally place on the side of the hills at random before roads were ever placed. The buildings along the roads — residences, shops, and pubs — all shared an old-English appeal. Again, I'll use the term "quaint," and very pretty to describe the scene. Ladies would likely use the word "cute."

As requested, I found Victoria waiting for me just outside the station. I had explained that I would prefer her to meet me at the station rather than have to find my way to the right place to meet her. I was tired and didn't want to have to think too hard or problem solve. I just wanted to eat, drink, and be merry. After meeting her, she led the way up a steep, winding road.

"What do you feel like eating?" She asked casually.

"Well," I laughed, "I have no idea what sort of options there are, so, why don't you pick? Just not a cheeseburger." I then told her the story about the French girl. I might have told her a story that was a little more dramatic than reality for the sake of humor.

"How about pizza?" She finally asked. Pizza in England would not have been my first choice, but since she suggested it and it was free, I just went with it. She said the pizza was really good, and it was the only place around that served proper lemonade. "Most other places will bring you a Sprite when you ask for lemonade." She explained. This blew my mind, and we both had a laugh at how crazy it was. After stopping for a quick photo of me in an iconic British phone booth that smelled horrendous inside, we soon made it to the restaurant.

I was surprised how how fancy the place was. Red tablecloth covered each table with wine glasses sitting face-down. Silverware was placed, wrapped up, waiting for a guest to take a seat. At the far end of the dinning area was a window wall that overlooked a small body of water and mountains in the distance. The view, needless to say, was exquisite! Well done, Victoria. Well done. When the waiter came to inquire about drinks, I requested a water while she ordered a lemonade. When he brought me my water, it came in a tall glass bottle and with a glass of ice.

"Is this free??" I asked. When you order a water in the States, you are brought a glass of tap or filtered water poured over ice. This water is also always complimentary.

"Probably not," Victoria answered chuckling at me. "But it's fine!" So much for being humbly economical since she was paying.

"Well dang!" I said. "I meant to get a free water. Sorry." She again assured me it was quite alright. Yet, I managed to make it last (no refills)

I next began looking over the menu. Everything seemed so expensive! I mean, I was happy to get a free meal, but I wasn't expecting something like this! I asked what she was getting to gauge a decent price range. Then again, I had also gotten used to my dinner budget being 8-10 (whether it be euros or British pounds/"quid") max. Anything beyond that was splurging.

"I'm not trying to 'break the bank,' I told her.

"Get whatever you want!" She insisted, meanwhile she planned on ordering a simple salad. I pressed her on it, but she seemed quite serious, so I found the most expensive thing on the menu.

"Ok, so if I get THAT [pointing to it], which is £15, it is totally ok?" I asked to test her.

"Yeah! That's really good actually." She replied with no hesitation. "You should definitely get it." Being as expensive as it was, I chose against her suggestion and asked what she typically got. She then pointed to 3 different things on the menu that ranged from 11-15 quid. The one that was £13 looked the best, so I chose that one. It also showed that I wasn't being cheap, but wasn't trying to be an expensive guest either. Besides, she was still taking care of my drinks afterwards too.

The pizza came surprisingly quickly, and although it looked funny (super thin crust), it tasted excellent. We discussed this and that as I smashed my pizza and she ate her salad. Topics of conversation included cultural differences between England and the States, as well as reminiscing about our time at university where we met. I felt really fortunate that we could discuss cultural differences more easily due to her having spent time in Mississippi. She could easily point things out to me that I perhaps would not have noticed, thought of, or possibly encountered yet. One phrase she taught me that I found absolutely hilarious (and SO British) was "tactical chunder." Brits really have a knack for making the worse things sound not-so-bad. A tactical chunder, as she explained to me, is when someone strategically lets themselves get sick ("chunder") so they can continue drinking.

Once we had finished dinner and paid, Victoria took me to a pub where she once worked. The whole pub was roughly the size of my parents' living room with a bar that stretch around 8ft (2.4 meters) across with no bar stools. Six beer taps stood on the other side of the bar near the 2 bar tenders. The bar tenders greeted us and asked what we'd have.

"What should I get?" I asked Victoria excitedly.

"Whatever you want," she said.

"Let me rephrase." I replied. "What do you *suggest* I get? I'm in a foreign country about to get a foreign beer, so I'm not sure which I should get — and don't want to waste your money if I don't like it." She told me she was getting one that was super hoppy. I knew I wasn't a fan of hoppy beer. Fortunately, the bar tender suggested one that I ended up really liking (the name of which I can't remember).

Victoria and I spend the rest of the evening enjoying quality British ale and talking with the two bar tenders. I found it interesting that on each tap, the alcohol content was clearly labeled. None of the beer we drank exceeded 4.6%, yet was better tasting than most of the beer with similar content I had tried in the States (which includes any domestic ending in *light*). According to the bar tenders, there was a tax levied in England on any beer with an alcohol content. The higher the content, the heavier the tax. Therefore, Brits had been forced to find a way to increase or maintain the quality of their beer without raising the alcohol content. Obviously, they succeeded brilliantly. Most higher quality/premium beers in the States come with higher alcohol content.

After a few delicious drinks and a new appreciation for the availability of trains (rather than necessity of a car), Victoria paid as promised before we both headed out. She walked me back to the train station to be sure I caught the right train and knew when to hop off. We said a fond farewell to one another, then I headed back to Manchester. It had been a fantastic day, but I was quite happy to finally be laying down.

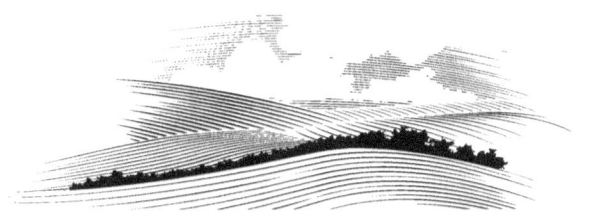

All Mixed Up

Tuesday, June 10th

This morning I woke up at 8am to enjoy my first, what was advertised as, a "Full English Breakfast." Unfortunately neither this nor any other breakfast was complimentary. This full English breakfast consisted of eggs, hash browns, sausage, mushrooms, cold baked beans, and fruit with your choice of juice (apple or orange), milk, and coffee. The fruit I chose was a pear, or at least what I believed to be a pear. When I bit into it, however, it was most definitely not a pear. I nearly spit it out it was so awful. Needless to say, I put it back down. Other than whatever fruit that was, the breakfast was pretty good. I didn't care all that much for the sausage, but even the cold baked beans were good.

After breakfast, I attempted to take a shower. I say *attempted* intentionally as I had so much trouble figuring out how to turn it on! I literally spent 15 minutes trying to get it to turn on until it finally worked. I naturally mission logged the whole thing because I could tell from the look of the would-be shower head that I was going to have some trouble. I just had no idea it would be this much. At long last, I managed to get it running the way I needed and freshened up.

I realized after going to the lobby that the hostel didn't have a place to keep people's luggage safe after they had checked out (like they did at the Four Courts). They did have have a locker room with large lockers, but they only locked with certain types of locks. Conveniently, there were locks for rent (of course) for €3. I was annoyed between this, the Internet, and no complimentary breakfast options on top of the pricey stay to begin with.

"Forget that!" I thought to myself. "No sir. Thank you." I put my bag and guitar inside one of the large lockers, then closed the door. "I'll just take my chances. Besides, I won't be gone that long, and if someone looks into my bag, they'll only find clothes — many of which are dirty." I then left the hostel and headed towards a museum of medieval history that I had read about before leaving the States. It looked really cool in the brochure I had downloaded so I was pretty excited. When I arrived, I discovered something very disappointing.

"Wow. Just my luck." I said out loud. "Closed." I had no other plans for the day, so I decided to simply walk around a while until it was time to head to Gloucester. To my shock and amazement, I discovered something that excited my soul. In what I had initially thought was a simple park was Roman road, a wall with a gate, and the ruins of two small ancient houses! Only the base of the walls were still standing which outlined the exterior and rooms within. I walked around the houses, stepped inside, and tried to imagine what it may have looked like in its time. I tried to imagine what each room could have functioned as based on their sizes. Based on the overall size and surroundings, I guessed it was likely the residence of a small farming family of ancient Rome. There was a good bit of land surrounding the area and no other structures of its time nearby (except for the gated wall).

I left this area and continued my walk where I discovered several Revolution sites, which I found very interesting. Unfortunately I was unable to recall too many specific details about the war, but key words helped jog my memory. What I remembered most was Charles the 1st being all caught up in his Divine Right, which made him incredibly stubborn and arrogant. He was pretty pathetic and lost the war miserably. On my way back to the hostel, I came across yet more Roman ruins. These ruins were obvious fortifications, ready to defend the village or city (and likely also used during England's Revolution).

I eventually made it back to the hostel locker room to find my things still where I left them. From there I made my way to the train station where I spoke to a rail worker to get my bearings. This was going to be my first time making several train changes in between destinations. I wanted to make sure I didn't somehow get on the wrong train! I thought if that happened, there's no telling where I might end up. That, and I wouldn't know where to stay. Therefore, I wrote down every stop, including the platform number and the time of the change. I felt extremely ready. There was no way anything could go wrong.

Oh, how wrong I was….

I found my fist train out of Manchester easily enough. I hopped off this train and onto my next one. So far so smooth. I expected to do the same thing at my 2nd stop, but when I got off and looked around, I didn't see my platform. I didn't see why this would be the case.

"Excuse me?" I asked a rail worker. "Where is platform," I forget the number I was looking for.

"Uh, we don't have that platform here." He replied.

"You don't have that platform?" I asked bewildered. He confirmed again that the platform I was looking for did not exist at this station. "What is this? Harry Potter?" I thought to my self. "What, did I just ask for Platform 9 and 3 quarters?!"

The man could see on my face that I was clearly confused and obviously lost. He then pointed me to a higher-up who could better help me. I immediately went and spoke to him. He was very kind, and able to figure out my issue. It seemed that despite my preparedness, I made a crucial error.

"It looks like you went the wrong way!" He explained. "You came North when you should have gone south! You were trying to get to Gloucester, right?"

"Yes.." I replied sheepishly.

"Right. So, you are right now in Lancaster." He said. Lancaster, as I found out was FIFTY-TWO MILES NORTH of Manchester! I was LITERALLY a little over an hour from SCOTLAND. The town I was SUPPOSED to be in was Leicester, which was 105 miles SOUTH of Manchester. Oh, I was so frustrated and mind-blown. While he was explaining all this, I half contemplated just going on to Scotland. It would be a cool adventure, but it would make my trip to Bath even longer. Therefore, I ultimately chose to go on with my original plans. After the nice rail man printed out a detailed train schedule for me (only 2 changes), I sat down and waited on my next train SOUTH. As I sat there, I realized what had happened.

The rail man who I spoke to in Manchester had a heavy accent and spoke quickly. The way he pronounced Gloucester (where I was trying to go) somehow sounded like "Gleicester" or "Glucaster," neither of which are cities. I, meanwhile was trying to get to Leicester. Because I didn't know that there was also a town called Lancaster, when he said Lancaster, I interpreted that to mean Leicester. Confused yet? Yeah, well, welcome to my world. To put it more simply, I interpreted his pronunciation of Gloucester/Glucaster as Gleicester, and thus Lancaster as Leicester, but Lancaster and Leicester were *both* actual cities while Gloucester *is* a city but *Gleicester* is not.

"What a story this was going to be for the guys back home." I thought, laughing at my circumstance. "They'll get a real kick out of this one."

After arriving in Gloucester 3 hours later, it donged on me that I actually had no idea how to get to my hostel and it wasn't even on my map! Out of the frying pan and into the fire, it seemed. I sought out a rail man hoping to God someone might be able to help me. I fortunately found one, and he knew the hostel I was trying to find. As it turned out, the hostel was just off the map. He even pointed to where it was probably sitting (just off the map) with his finger. I was grateful for his help. The place seemed like it was quite a far walk, so I resolved to find a cab pick-up. I found it quickly enough and happily paid the £8 required for the ride.

Once I had arrived at the hostel, I learned that renovations were being done, which would require me to have my room upgraded to a different building. This building was actually on the map, for which I was grateful. It was just outside the city center too! The manager took me in her personal vehicle and we had a nice chat on the way. She was very nice and excited to learn about my travel plans.

My upgraded room was actually really nice! It was a single-room with a tv and all the make-ups of a hotel room, but higher quality. There was a tv, private balcony, and my own shower to name a few luxuries I hadn't had since I left the states. It really seemed like someone's home that had been converted into a hostel — like an Air BnB.

Previously, I mentioned making contact with friends abroad before this trip. It just so happened that a guy named Zach, who I had become pals with at University, and who had been in the same Latin (language) classes as me, had fallen for and proposed to Tanja of Germany not long after graduating university. Zach was living with Tanja in Germany at the time and they both invited me to come stay with them for at time. Zach and I had also previously discussed the idea of meeting up in Rome for an adventure. Therefore, it was important that I keep in touch with him.

I got settled into my room and opened up my tablet to Facebook. It happened that I had a message from Zach! He was currently on and told me that we needed to Skype to talk about Italy. I told him that I had neither showered nor eaten dinner, but said I would call him ASAP.

I found a place called Cafe Rene that looked good and decently priced. They also advertised strong and free wifi. I entered and was seated quickly before putting in a drink order and turning on Skype. Zach and I were connected shortly after this and discussed our idea in detail. We decided we would spend a week in Rome, then he would return to Germany. Meanwhile, I would continue my travels and be up there with he and Tanja a week or so later. Since I was actively traveling, I got him to take care of booking the hostel, and I would pay my part upon arrival or pay him back when he arrived. The plan was then set. We both expressed our excitement, then I got off because my food had arrived (I had ordered during our conversation).

Dinner ended up being absolutely delicious. Spicy grilled chicken and mushrooms with onions and tomatoes with peas. It's crazy that I'm really not a tomato person, but these tomatoes were amazing! They were cooked, and almost tasted like grapes! I took my time eating, trying to savor every bite. I knew I'd probably never find tomatoes like this again.

After dinner, I had an interesting experience. I felt really safe on the quiet road, and even did a mission log as I walked through the night air. Then, I made a mistake. I passed by a guy wearing a backpack like mine and spoke to him.

"Hi!" I said. "You're a fellow traveler too, huh?" I expected a cheery confirmation. I was prepared to point him towards Cafe Rene and recommend the same thing I got. This, however, was not the response I got.

"Yeah, sort of.." He replied. I quickly realized that despite the map in his hand and his backpacker's backpack, he was homeless. Another guy suddenly came out of nowhere and asked me for a favor — money. I was immediately uncomfortable. If it hadn't been at night and there hadn't been two of them, and they hadn't both been slightly bigger than me, it would have been fine. I had been working out every day for a year before leaving, so I was in good shape. However, I wasn't sure I could take both of them at the same time if it came down to it. Besides, guys coming out of nowhere at night asking for money from a foreigner walking alone is probably not the most desirable situation for anyone. I stayed cool, though. I told them I was sorry, but had spent the money I had at the pub. This was *half*-true. I knew that if I even pulled my wallet out, they could be prompted to rob me. I followed up by telling them that I was meeting up with some buddies over the hill — I used *buddies* with a tone that implied dudes.

I continued walking with intention, but didn't want to appear as though I was leaving in a hurry. I kept casually looking off to the side pretending to look at something so I could covertly make sure they weren't running up on me. They didn't seem to be. As I came near the top of the hill I was climbing, I did a big wave into the distance down the other side,

"I'm coming!" I said loudly in a half-yell. My voice echoed down the otherwise quiet street. The two guys couldn't see over the other side of the hill from where they were. As far as they knew, I was waving at my buddies. I kept walking at a very intentional pace, then sped up quite a bit after I went over the hump out of eyesight.

I thought I was in the clear after getting over the hill, but then suddenly realized I had taken a wrong turn! I knew if I were to retrace my steps I could find my way again, but that meant going back past those guys. They would then realize I was in fact alone and there were no buddies expecting me. Worst of all, they'd know I was lost. Going back was not an option. So what did I do? I kept moving forward.

I walked through the night for 6 long minutes — maybe a little less. I didn't come across any other sketchy people, but I was ready to be back at the hostel. As I continued walking, I was relieved when I found a kebab shop. I went inside and told them my situation of being lost and asked if they would help me call a cab. They were of course happy to assist me. Before I knew it, I was in a cab, then back safely at the hostel and finally, in my bed.

Train confusion, setbacks, and sketchy homeless people. There never seems to be a dull moment on this adventure, and to think, it was still just the beginning. Yet, I was still alive and though I didn't quite feel like the adventurer I had planned the trip for, there was something excited in me, something more than myself. I never expected to encounter the issues and setbacks in this simple journey from one city to another, but I managed it. I figured it out, and even though I was alone, help was never too far away. Things seemed to work out and I made it unscathed.

"Perhaps," I thought as my eyes fell heavy, "maybe God *is* still watching over me. Maybe I do have what it takes......"

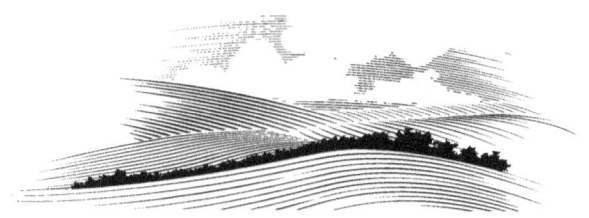

Of Witchcraft And Wizardry

Wednesday, June 11th

I realized after waking up this morning that there was no luggage storage place. Checking out was simply slipping my room key into a container before leaving. I also realized an unfortunate reality that could have been avoided. I had chosen to visit Gloucester for two reasons: 1, It was one of the two cities related to a medieval conflict between two noble families called The War of the Roses. There was museum that featured this conflict specifically. 2, there were castles and I wanted to visit them. I had, however, neglected to do deeper research before booking my stay. When I looked up the museum and castles online before checking out of my hostel, I realized that the museum was closed for maintenance (or something) and the castles were many miles outside of town. If I had booked another night or two, I might have been able to swing it.

Accepting my poor luck and mistake, I chose to merely go for a walk and explore the city a little bit. I further wished I had inquired from the manager about somewhere to store my backpack for a few hours, but there was really nothing that could be done at this point. I slipped my key into the container, tightened my backpack straps, slung my guitar over my shoulder, and secured my travel bag. It was going to be a long few hours of toting my things, which made me thankful for the training I had done in the form of rucksack hiking before I left for this trip.

It wasn't long after stepping out of the hostel door that I saw a large medieval-looking building in the distance. The closer I got, the more incredibly massive I realized it was — not to mention beautiful! When I drew nearer, I asked a little old woman in passing what the structure was.

"Oh! It's the Gloucester Cathedral." She said kindly.

"It's beautiful!" I replied. "Catholic?"

"No, no. Anglican, dear. You can go in if you'd like! They're very nice." She concluded. I thanked her and made my across the courtyard towards the entrance.

I stepped through the large arched entryway and into the main sanctuary area. Enormous columns holding arches separated the outer wall from the main seating area. Bright, natural light steamed in from a gigantic, beautiful stained-glass window that featured angels, Jesus, apostles, saints, nobles, abbots and bishops, and finally the shields of kings and nobles. Pieces of the window were constructed over time within the medieval period and told a rich, historical story. There were many lovely and artistic memorials like I had seen before. One notable and recognizable feature was an iconic casket made of stone and painted. This was the final resting place of Robert, Duke of Normandy, eldest son of William the Conquerer! Robert apparently died in 1134 as a prisoner under his youngest brother, King Henry I of England. How? Why? That's why I LOVE medieval history!!

After my initial look around, I saw that a small gift shop inside the church was starting to open up and stepped inside.

"Excuse me," I asked a clerk politely. "Is there any way you might let me set my things down for just a little while?"

"Sure," the woman said, "but don't tell anyone. We don't want everyone to think they can just pop in and drop off their things. Also, we won't be responsible for it." The stipulations were very reasonable.

"Thank you SO much! Yes, absolutely. No worries!" I replied gratefully. I placed my large backpack and guitar in a place she designated for me. I then returned to the main area and was stopped by a random older gentleman with thinning white hair.

"Hello!" He said merrily. "Are you looking for a tour?"

"Oh," I said a little surprised. He was dressed in regular clothes. "Do you work here?"

"My name's George. I'm a member of this church and I volunteer my service to give tours. Would you like one? It's free!" He replied.

"Free? Absolutely!" I said excitedly.

"Brilliant!" He replied. "Follow me. We'll start with the crypt."

George took me through the crypt which had many underground rooms which had been used for various purposes over the centuries. It was really fascinating. From the crypt, he took me all over different parts of the grounds while pointing out historically significant features. Such features included the area where monks would take baths, where children were taught, and the signature marks of stone masons who did construction on the grounds. The most fascinating were the burial places of King Edward and the Duke of Normandy. Also fascinating was the fact that during the Reformation period (bloody feud between Protestants and Catholics), this church was likely spared destruction due to being being the final resting place of a king (Edward) and the Duke.

"Destroying this church with the king and Duke would have probably sent a bad message to the public," George explained, "so for that reason, the church was spared."

"And a good thing!" I replied. "It's a beautiful church at that!"

I was particularly ecstatic during the tour when we walked down a certain hallway that seemed strangely familiar….as if I had seen it before. George's voice trailed off as I looked down the marble hall with stone wall and arched ceiling. What was so familiar about this hallway?

"And this hallway," George casually mentioned, "you might recognize,.." My eyes got extremely wide. I was actually thinking — slightly wishfully thinking, but didn't know for sure. "..from the Harry Potter films."

"OH MY GOSH!!!" I exclaimed literally jumping. "WHAT?! That's so COOL!" George laughed at my hysteria. "I KNEW I had seen this hallway somewhere, but didn't think that could be it!" I took a photo of the hallway, trying to get the same angle that was in the film. I went over and touched the corner column. It was the exact place where Professor Snape corners Professor Quirrell and asks, "Where does your loyalty lie?" Brilliant. I had chills of excitement.

"Yeah, there were many parts of the films shot here." George told me. "In fact, the boys' dormitory here that is in connection to the attached school was used for the Gryffindor Common Room. I would take you there, but they are doing renovations so I can't. BUT, there is one other place you might recognize we'll get to in a minute." First, I was floored that this was the home of the Gryffindor Common Room while equally upset that I wouldn't be able to see it, while simultaneously intrigued with what this other thing was that he would be showing me. It wasn't only the fact that I love Harry Potter, but also the fact that it's not every day you randomly stumble onto the film location of a major movie franchise purely by coincidence and as a result of some bad luck. Had the Gloucester museum been open, and/or the castles not been so far away, I would have never wandered into this beautiful church to discover the physical places where my favorite movie series was filmed! What were the odds?

We continued walking down the hallway until George stopped. I turned to him not understanding what was going on because he didn't give any explanation. He just smiled intriguingly and asked,

"Do you recognize this classroom here?" I beamed at him, then walked ahead in the direction he had indicated with a nodd. To my right was a large doorway blocked off by steal bars (like a jail sell). I peered inside to see an enormous room with a bright stained-glass window on the front wall facing me with stone paneling, and 7 rows of childrens' desks. In front of the desks was a short stage and a single desk in the middle. I couldn't believe my eyes! PROFESSOR MCGONAGALL'S TRANSFIGURATION CLASSROOM!!! I could see Rupert Gint and Dan Ratcliff as young boys running through the center as Harry and Ron, late for their very first class at Hogwarts where Maggie Smith playing McGonagall offers to transfigure both of them into pocket-watches so that one of them "might be on time." I was in *hog heaven* (as we say in the south)!

I left the cathedral and was headed down the street in the direction of the train station when I noticed an odd looking shop. Judging by the name of the store and the oddities displayed in the window, I gathered that this was some sort of witch store. I stared at it for a moment. This was something I had never seen or heard of. Part of me wanted to march straight on without giving it a second glance. Another part of me, however, was quite curious. The curious part of me succeeded and I chose to pop in if only for a moment. It's not ever day one comes across a witch store in England. I therefore approached the door and entered cautiously lest some sort of spell to be cast on me just by walking in. I didn't believe whole-heartedly in the reality of witchcraft, but even the Bible acknowledges its existence. I thus remained vigilant.

It was a tiny shop filled with weird things. Terrifying dolls, shrunken heads, demonic-looking displays, crystal balls, crystals, "potions," all sorts of herbs, and other curious items for purchase. An expectedly odd appearing fellow greeted me and asked what I was looking for specifically.

"Oh, I'm just looking around." I replied a little sheepishly. "This is my first time here."

"Oh ok, well let me know if you need help finding anything." He pointed out a few sales going on for a couple items around the store and mentioned a few new potions that had just recently been made. I thanked him for his help and continued looking. At the back of the store was a doorway. Beads fell from the top to the bottom so that the entrance was covered.

"What's back there?" I asked him. To be honest, I was a little scared to find out. He told me the head witch stayed back there and would tell me my fortune if I wished, but she was busy at the moment. I again thanked him, but said I was only curious and didn't need my fortune read. After another minute, I couldn't stand to be in there anymore. It was too creepy. I thanked the clerk and wished him a nice day as I exited hoping I didn't somehow offend him. If curses are real, I surely don't want one. Despite being a super creepy place, the clerk was really nice and friendly. As a Christian, it was just a little too much for me. Yet, I won't regret going in and poking around. I'll likely never have an opportunity like that again.

I next stopped at a pub called Westgate for a bite to eat. I ordered what I expected to be a simple, though overpriced sandwich. To my surprise, however, it was not simple. The sandwich was a double-decker with ham, melted cheese, lettuce, tomato, and bacon. It was excellent and around £5. I then used the free wifi to look up when my my train would be leaving for Bath as I ate. I found out when exactly the train would be leaving, how many stops, which stop to get off at to be nearest to my hostel, and around the time I should arrive. I was sure I would get it right this time.

Nope. I arrived at the station to find that I had somehow missed my train by EIGHT MINUTES! Apparently, I had gotten the time mixed up! I now had to wait a whole hour before the next train would arrive. I could have slapped myself. All that preparation for nothing. I couldn't do anything about it, so I reluctantly accepted my mistake and resolved to find somewhere to sit. I found a bench nearby, sat my things down, and pulled out my guitar.

An hour and a half after boarding the next train, I arrived in Bath, England. The station the train pulled into was called "Spa," which seemed very appropriate to me. I had a difficult time finding my hostel to say the least, and toting my heavy backpack, carry-on bag, and guitar didn't help. The only relief was how absolutely beautiful this city was. Aside from the lovely architecture of the city, there were tall trees and flowers everywhere with a large park in the center that featured a river flowing through it. The cool breeze and warm sun contributed to the overall blissfulness of the area. Regardless of how pretty everything was, I really wished to enjoy it without having to carry all my things.

After nearly 30 minutes of walking, I finally found my hostel. It was located in an alleyway that could be very easily overlooked. It occurred to me after discovering it that I had actually passed it and made the entire block (which was a long string of buildings) at least 3 times. I entered the narrow alley via a short flight of stone steps which opened up into a lovely, Romanesque courtyard with a nice fountain and green plants all around. There were small tables with chairs outside the doors with people casually eating and congregating. I wasted no time getting inside, checking in, dropping my things, and heading back out to explore with a map provided by the hostel in hand.

As I stepped out onto the street from the alley, I realized I couldn't read the map. It was not directionally clear. Which way was North? Which was south? I wanted to visit the Roman Baths and the ancient Roman circus area, but I couldn't tell where they were exactly relative to where I was. Oh, and I also couldn't figure out where I was! Fortunately, there just so happened to be a Bobby (aka British police officer) passing by. I stopped him and asked if he would mind helping me. He of course was happy to. He took a minute and affirmed that the map was a little hard to read, but pointed out where we were and where the other things were in relation to us. I then thanked him and made my way toward the great Roman Baths.

Walking down the stone street along the canal was incredible — especially without my heavy backpack on my back. The plants, the flowers, the water, and the mountains all around and the overall architecture of this city was absolutely beautiful. There was a real romantic flavor to the city I couldn't deny.

The walk down to the Baths took around 10 minutes. When I arrived, I was very disappointed to learn that they were closed for the day. There was a man playing music in the courtyard in front of the baths so I chose to stay and listen for a little so my trip would not be a complete waste. He ended up actually being really good. It was just him, his guitar, a looper petal, and a wireless amp. He played covers of familiar songs for a small crowd who had gathered to casually listen. I enjoyed for a few songs before dropping him a tip, then leaving to explore the city and find some dinner.

I headed in the direction of the hostel to get away from the main tourist attraction so prices would come down. I ended up passing a Spanish Cafe overlooking the canal advertising tapas for a reasonable price. I had never tried tapas before, but I remembered my buddy Will telling me about getting them while teaching English in Spain. He said they were good and cheap. The best part was that the advertisement said you got 3 tapas, plus a salad and a drink for the one price! It seemed like a good deal to me, so I went in.

It was a small and simple, but very nice restaurant. The waiter was friendly and sat me down by a window with a beautiful view. Through the window, I could clearly see the park with the river running through it and mountains in the distance. If ever a guy needed a romantic place for a date, this was it. I learned after being seated that they were having a special an sangrias — half off. I actually had never had a sangria before, so the waiter explained. It sounded pretty good, and since it was such a good price, I chose to go ahead and order one. Next, after looking over the menu, I chose my three tapas. The three I chose were fried fish, shrimp, and some sort of chicken dish that I never quite understood. As an appetizer, I chose to order some bread, which came immediately and was very good.

I leaned back in my chair and gazed out of the window as I waited for my food. I observed the lovely scenery and took it all in. I also happened to notice a castle-like structure at the top of a hill in the distance. A dangerous grin slipped across my face.

"If I have time, I've got to go check that out. I wonder how far of a trek it is." I wondered to myself. When my waiter brought my food, I asked about it. He said he wasn't sure how far is was or how I would even get there for that matter. I figured I could find out somehow and go check it out.

The chicken dish turned out to be similar to a "hush-puppyy," like we have in the south. The difference was that it was spiced differently and had soft chunks of chicken inside. Each tapas came on a small plate with three of the ordered item on each plate. All the food, along with the sangria was excellent. The sangria was just strong enough to give me a slight buzz — the sweet spot. I then paid the water and took my leave.

I walked back towards the Baths and beyond until I found a place called The Royal Crescent, The Royal Crescent Museum, and a magnificently beautiful park called Victoria Park. The crescent was merely a large string of buildings arranged in a crescent facing a green hill which tied into Victoria Park. The Crescent Museum was closed, so I 'd have to wait to find out what that meant, but the park seemed worthy of exploration. I naturally then decided to take a nice stroll.

The stroll was beautiful, peaceful, and very relaxing. There were tall trees, beautiful flowers, singing birds, and mountains all around in the distance. I ended up coming upon a woman who's fence and back gate bordered the park. I pondered as I walked, and decided that this beautiful place might make a great honeymoon spot someday — or at least a romantic get-away.

I finished my stroll and decided to head over to the Roman circus. To help me get there without consulting the map, I asked a girl on the street if she could point me in the right direction. She was really nice and happy to help me. I'm not sure if she was local or a visitor herself, or perhaps a recent transplant, but she ended up pointing me in the WRONG direction. It wasn't until I neared the city's edge past the baths that I realized this. I knew it was the city's edge because there was an old stone wall where there was once a gate. The road led through this entrance and there was nothing to see but trees and road ahead. Needless to say, I turned and walked back through the city until after consulting the map until I arrived at the circus.

I really didn't know what to expect at this "circus." I didn't know if there would be an old arena, if there would be pretend animals on display or what. I was excited regardless as I made my way up the hill beyond the alley that hid my hostel. As I followed my map to where the circus was, I felt a little disappointed.

There was no arena. There were not fake animals displayed. It was simply a huge, grassy, circular roundabout with flat (apartment) buildings all around it, and large trees inside. I was expecting at least some ancient arena seating or fake animals, but there was nothing. The one thing I did notice and appreciate were old, red stones on the ground buried under earth. There was also what appeared to be the remains of a small, red-stone platform where the ring master surely stood to direct the circus. That, however, was the end of it.

I stuck around for a few minutes to try to take in as much as I could. I appreciated what was left of the circus, but wished there had been more to see. I picked up a piece of the broken red stone and placed it in my pocket. Eventually, I headed back to my hostel as the sun started to set behind the mountains. Though there were disappointments, the day overall had really been great. I had stumbled onto a few film locations for Harry Potter, walked through a beautiful park, and had tried tapas for the first time. The next day, I would check out the baths. However, the following day carried with it some anxiety.

It occurred to me as I walked back to my hostel that this would be my last night of pre-booked hostels. I had a decision to make. I could either get on the horn and start pre-booking more hostels,..or I would wing it, and that idea scared me. What if I wasn't able to find a place to stay that I could afford? I was concerned that something would happen and I would find myself at a homeless shelter or something.

"You'll never make it!" Said a voice in my head. "You're going to die! You don't have what it takes." Although I had not yet died, and things had happened that suggested that perhaps God was in fact with me, this lingering voice was still strong. What if I couldn't do it? I've never traveled through Europe before. I've only been at this for what? Going on 2 weeks?

"But that's what you want!" Another voice in my head said. It was the voice of my buddy Will who had traveled overseas multiple times. "That freedom!" Will had encouraged me against pre-booking everything because it would limit my freedom.

I wasn't sure what I would do. My heart pounded at the thought of not being sure I had a place to stay every night. Yet, there was something deep inside me that adamantly agreed with Will. That freedom,…that adventure. Without some risk, without unknown/uncertain variables, it isn't as much of an adventure, is it?

"Am I a Baggins or am I a Took?" I thought to myself, thinking of The Hobbit written by J.R.R. Tolkien. I pondered this question as I laid in my bed. My anxiety was high, yet ironically, so was my excitement for adventure.

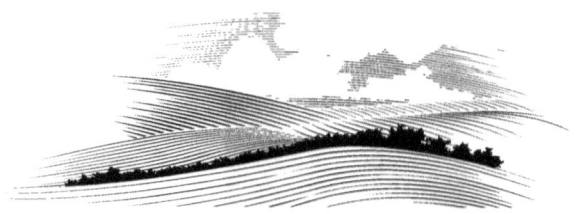

Roman Baths

Thursday, June 12th

I woke up this morning with resolve. The part of me, the "Baggins" if you will, had overcome the voices of fear and doubt. Was I still scared? Yes. Did I still have doubts? Absolutely. But something inside me said, "It's going to be alright." It takes the *most* courage, I think, to overcome one's own self. Today I would only have to remember to get online, find a hostel in London, and book it for tomorrow night.

After sitting up, I went ahead and checked the date of my Harry Potter Film Studio tour that I had booked before leaving the States. There was no WAY I was going to somehow slip up and miss that. I grew up reading the Harry Potter books and loved the films. The day I learned that the film studio was just outside of London and was available to tour, I signed up! I was actually more excited about this than seeing the Roman baths. I felt better seeing I was still on schedule to be there, then continued on with my morning. I showered, dressed, and went down stairs for breakfast.

Breakfast was nothing to write home about, but it was enough. I paid the small price of £2 for a cafeteria-style meal. I was provided with a trey and the freedom to fill it up with whatever I wanted. I found a friendly-looking guy sitting at a table and ended up joining him. It was clear that neither him nor I was awake yet as we had a very slow-moving, casual conversation while we ate. I consumed enough to feel adequately nourished for the day before wishing him a good day and heading out to see the baths.

I ended up becoming increasingly excited as I approached the now more familiar area. I really had no idea what to expect. I knew there was a hot spring, but didn't know what all it entailed. I also had seen pictures of what looked like a large swimming pool, but thought there must surely be a little more to it. There was also something magical about seeing authentically ancient structures with your own eyes, despite seeing the best professional photographs.

I followed the crowd gathered around the area through the large doors I had seen yesterday. I then learned that I could go around simply looking at things for free, but the price of a guided tour was only £10! I chose to pay for the tour, of course, so I wouldn't be left wondering what in the world I might be looking at. After purchasing a tour, I found the large swimming pool I had seen in photos and walked around it while waiting for my tour to start.

While walking around, I noticed particular groups of people would stop to take photos. The problem was that they apparently thought themselves models and had impromptu photo shoots with tons of photos and different poses in front of the fountain. They took up the entire pathway with their modeling which severely aggravated me. Each individual in these groups would have at least 30 photos each taken of them. I tried to be polite, but after the second person had taken 18 photos with 3 different poses, I pushed past walking straight between the girl and the camera. The group then looked at me like I had done something outrageously impolite. I considered attempting to explain to them how inconsiderate they were being to other visitors, but ultimately decided it wasn't worth it.

Next, I came across an older woman and a young girl sitting by the water at one end. They were dressed in ancient Roman-style clothing and were apparently playing the role of a master with her slave girl. I was impressed that they would not break character for anything! Everything we talked about remained in the context of ancient times, the wealthy woman's husband was off fighting the Gals, and the slave girl did her daily chores. In reality, I imagine it was a mother-daughter team. I ended up getting a photo with them before making my way to my tour's starting point.

The tour took me all through the baths, which ended up being quite large. I learned what ancient materials were used for cleaning, and the process people went through to get clean. The guide explained the culture and history of the baths, how the water from a natural hot spring was used, and allowed tour guests to sample a taste of the spring water (gently filtered). The water was very salty (full of iron, they explained). They said the water was good to drink and wash in, so they advertised the opportunity to take a dip in the pool for a steep price. I declined this offer, and was satisfied to merely dip my fingers in the pool as I passed by again.

I left the baths and wandered over to the Royal Crescent museum again. This time it was open! It was a short, cheap tour where I learned that the Crescent was built in the early modern era for wealthy people to come for vacations, banquets, holidays, and short-term events. It also happened that there was a school class from France touring the Crescent. I was amused as they ran past me, chatting in French and occasionally saying something in English. At the end of the tour,

I thought it was interesting and I was glad to know what it was, but I ultimately would have preferred to spend my time and money on something else.

Having toured the baths and found out what the Royal Crescent was, I now had the rest of the day to be spontaneous. I decided to see if I could visit the castle structure I saw in the distance, but after asking around, I learned that it was really far away (for a walk), and no one knew if there was public transportation that could take me out there. Therefore, I resolved to grab my guitar and lounge in the large grassy area in front of the Crescent.

I found a nice spot to sit simply relax for a while and watched people. As I had seen before, there were a lot of young people hanging out, relaxing, kicking soccer balls around, tanning, and pick-nicking. As I observed the natural culture, I strummed my guitar quietly. I was conscientious about playing too loud as to draw attention to myself and seem like I was looking for attention. At the same time, however, I did hope I would be noticed and engaged by some cool person or people. I hoped I might somehow make a new friend.

As I played, I started feeling more relaxed and became more comfortable. I cared less about appearing to be attention-seeking and just enjoyed myself. Soon, my playing got the attention of two guys who had chosen a spot not too far from me. They constantly turned around and nodded to me in approval. They eventually came over and said hello. They complimented my playing and asked to join me. I happily obliged. I attempted to come up with a song they might recognize, but was unable to do so. Instead, I played a few tunes I liked, which they applauded. The next thing I knew, I was making up a chord progression while one of the guys playfully freestyle-rapped. It was lots of fun.

Our commotion apparently then got the attention of a hippy-looking guy with long hair, long fingernails, and bare feet. He was nice and complimented my playing. He then asked me how long I planned to be there because he would like to go grab his own guitar and play with me. I was of course all too eager to agree. He fortunately lived nearby and took him less than 10 minutes to return. We took turns playing rhythm and lead, and he taught me some really cool jazz chords. We had a blast playing together and I really appreciated him sharing his jazz knowledge with me.

The hippy and I played together for a while, but I later started feeling antsy. I needed to get up and walk around. I therefore surveyed my surroundings and saw some girls and a few guys relaxing on a big blanket nearby. They looked like nice people, so I thanked the hippy for his company and wished him well before taking my leave. I admit that I did feel a little guilty about leaving him, but I just couldn't sit anymore. Relaxing time was over.

"Um, hi.." I said timidly to the group as I approached with my guitar in hand.

"Hey!" A few of them said together.

"You sounded really good on your guitar over there!" One of them said. "We were listening from here."

"Oh, you heard that? Well thanks!" I replied. "My name's Tim. I'm from Mississippi, United States and was wondering if I could join you."

"Yeah, sure!" Several of them answered, so I sat down. I asked if they were from Bath and they said they lived in Bath and were attending the University.

"It's a nice place, but we don't really like living here." One of the girls said.

"Oh, why not? I think it's beautiful." I replied.

"Yeah I supposed it is, but nothing happens here. It's boring." Another explained.

We talked collectively and some one-on-one conversations (with the girls in particular). They were all huge fans of the song Wonderwall for some reason, so I did my best to play it by ear for them to sing to. I did alright. They then asked me and were thrilled to hear me sing a little bit of Sweet Home Alabama. They really enjoyed hearing my southern accent, but commented upon the fact that I didn't sound like they expected (the stereotypical draw). I had to explain that I was a "coastie" and therefore had a different accent and that southern accents had variations depending on the region just like British accents.

After spending some time at the Crescent, one of the guys suggested we leave and go hang out at a pub called The Cork. I was invited to join them. It ended up being a relatively short time spent at the pub. After a drink or two, each started taking their leave. Although I was enjoying this time with these new friends, I was glad to call it an early day. Tomorrow was Harry Potter Film Studio day and I could hardly contain myself. After that, I would get to explore one of the most famous cities on earth: London, England! Despite being a pretty chill day, I was still exhausted. I eventually took leave from the group myself and found my pillow very welcoming back at the hostel.

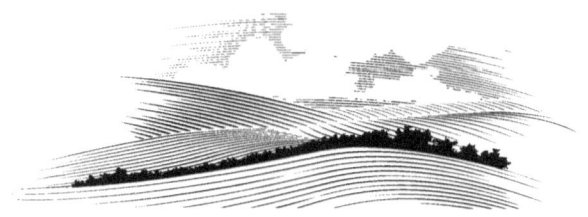

The Harry Potter Film Studio

Friday, June 13th

I sat up this morning in a panic. I had failed to book a hostel for the upcoming night! I went to the lobby and used their computer to find 2 hostel-booking sites. It seemed that every hostel with a price of £15 per night or less was completely booked! I scrambled through both hostel-booking websites as well as used general Google searches in hopes of finding a hostel with a good price and a good location. It was hard to find hostels with prices I liked that also appeared to be in (reasonably) safe areas and not too far from the city center or metro station. I considered simply booking another night in Bath. I could have survived another night in Bath, but it would make the next day to get to London and arriving for my Harry Potter Film Studio tour on time much more stressful. Yet, it was an option. I asked the hostel clerk about booking another night.

"Yeah, you can do that," he said, "but," he warned, "this hostel is filling up quick so you'll need to decide soon." The pressure was on. I spend what seemed like a half hour vigorously searching hostel options on the Internet until I finally found a place just outside the city center. I was relieved to say the least. I had to go over my budget, but at least I had a place to stay. I therefore booked my room at Palmer's Lodge in London before gathering my things and checking out of my hostel in Bath.

Despite the stress of the no-place-to-stay ordeal, I actually gained a sense of confidence. For a moment, I had experienced the complete unknown. Would I have a place to stay in London or would I be stranded? If so, would that prove that I didn't have what it takes? My phone and tablet would have died being unable to charge, I might have gotten robbed or something. Spending an unplanned night outside in a city is never ideal, but especially scary if it were in a foreign country!

Yet, somehow I had managed to handle it and it wasn't as difficult or scary as I had imagined. Now, I was safe. I had a place to go; a place expecting me. I'm not dead yet, and am still having a blast. I didn't enjoy the window of time where I didn't know if I would have a place to go, but I was thankful for the experience.

The train ride from Bath to London was around two hours. During this time, a nice older woman chose the available seat next to me. She ended up originally being from Manchester and was headed to London to visit family. She asked about my travel plans and was really exited for me. I then expressed my concern about using the London Tube (or Subway as we say in the States). I had never ridden on a Subway and the map I had seen didn't make a lot of sense. It turned out that she had a Tube map with her. She pulled it out and explained to me how it worked while answering questions I had along the way. After her explanation, she handed me the map and said I could have it because she had another one in her bag. I was very grateful and felt much better about using the Tube, though it would take doing it myself to get a complete grip on it. For now, I had a basic gist.

I got off the train and was suddenly struck with a thought. I met a kind British woman from Manchester headed to London. Isn't that a very similar scenario to when J.K. Rowling came up with Harry Potter? I chuckled at the thought of this woman actually having been Rowling as I was gearing up to see the movie film studio, and I didn't recognize her! I would have kicked myself every day for the rest of my life if it had somehow been her. However, considering the fact that she's a huge celebrity, I realized it was highly unlikely that this was the case as I'm sure she would have private transportation lest a media frenzy appear. Still though, it was fun to think about.

I didn't have to use the Tube to find Palmer's Lodge, and made it with relative ease on-foot. The place was apparently pretty popular as there were lots of people trying to check in around the same time I was. I figured it made sense for a cheaper hostel in London to be packed on a weekend in the summer.

After finally getting checked in, I found that it was HUGE. It was multi-leveled with a large parlor near the front desk on the first floor. The parlor had couches and chairs with coffee and tea available (bags & hot water). It had long corridors with high ceilings, wood paneling everywhere, and a wood stair case with large windows at one end overlooking the street and red carpet down the center of the steps. At the stair case's mid-level was a brilliant suit of armor that reflected the sunlight streaming in from the window. The hostel room itself was also enormous. Three levels of bunk beds were spread around everywhere. Each individual bed had its own curtain for privacy, a lamp, and an electrical outlet to charge devices. Despite being surrounded with 60 or so other men and woman (sometimes families) of all ages, it was pretty cozy and comfortable. People also seemed to be very respectful to one another. For instance, there were some people still sleeping. Those awake would let others know about the sleepers, and quiet the ones who were unaware (or were children).

I claimed a bunk for myself and locked my things away. I then ran down to a Chinese take-out place recommended by the host before returning to Palmer's Lodge until it was time to leave for my film studio tour. I relaxed in the parlor and sipped a cup of tea as I prepared myself to see in-person the real items and settings from the films of my favorite book series of all time growing up. I was going to Hogwarts!!

I left the Palmer's Lodge at 4pm and found that getting to the studio was really quite simple. I traveled to a bus stop that seemed to run non-stop from that place to the film studio. When I got off the bus, I saw a few large iconic set pieces from the films (namely chess pieces) outside the ticket booth. I next went to the ticket booth to claim the tickets I had pre-purchased. It turned out that my tour didn't start for 20 minutes, so I had time to walk around in the large front-room which contained a gift shop and a place to eat. I considered getting a bite, but feared I might miss my tour in the time it would take to stand in line so I decided to wait until after the tour. The prices for food items were also very overpriced I thought. Therefore, I simply grabbed a seat at a table and checked out some of the simple props hanging from the ceiling (miniature dragons and such) posters, and other iconic items.

Eventually, I heard my tour number come over the intercom. I immediately jumped up and made a B-line for the entrance. There was a zig-zag line at the entrance, but it wasn't obnoxious. Someone came out a couple minutes later announcing we would be let in shortly. Looking around, I noticed we were lined up in the entryway of Number 4 Private Drive! There was a door facing us. Next to it was a staircase with a framed photo of Dudley Dursley (Harry Melling) in a silly pose eating a large sandwich. There under the stairs was a cupboard with the door open and a lamp on next to a small bed.

The line finally moved, and I walked passed the Dursleys' front door and into a theater-looking room. I found a seat facing the front where a large drop-down screen dangled from the ceiling to the ground. The tour guide stood in front of the screen and after everyone was seated, provided us with some history of the props, fun facts about the actors, gave us a little trivia, then finally showed a video which was a message from the film actors talking about some experiences they had with things we were about to see. The actors shared a few memorable moments on set, some jokes, and finally a clip of them standing in front of the large door which was the entrance to the Great Hall at Hogwarts. After the video, the tour guide asked if we were ready.

"No, not quite yet. I think we need another video." One dad said jokingly. Most everyone else replied with an eager yet humble "yes!"

"Well then, it is my privilege to welcome you to Hogwarts, School of Witchcraft and Wizardry!" She proclaimed. As she said this, the large drop-down screen lifted up to reveal the same door we had seen the actors in the video standing in front of. The huge door slowly swung open. "Ejoy!" The tour guide said, then turned and led us into the Great Hall.

I have to be honest. I was a tiny bit disappointed in the Great Hall. In the films, it looks enormous. In reality, it really wasn't that big, but I can completely understand why. To make the Great Hall as large as Rowling's books describe, it would have cost a lot more money. It therefore makes sense to use a little "movie magic" to make it look bigger than it was. Regardless of the size, the Great Hall was really cool and the detail in every square inch was incredible.

Four long tables were lined against the Great Hall's walls so guests could walk through the center. Each of the tables had a different house theme that contained house robes and small props related to those particular houses. At the far wall opposite the entrance was a stage that featured full-scale manikins of Dumbledore and the other recurring professors (and Hagrid) dressed in full iconic costume.

Next, we passed through a (already opened) brick wall into Diagon Alley. Needless to say, it was exactly what I had seen in the films, only, once again, I realized how small it was. It was just large enough to be convincing with a little movie magic. There was Olivander's, the magical pet shop, the path down Knockturn Alley, Gringots Bank, and Weasley's Wizarding Weezies. What really surprised me about the whole thing was how the entire alley was indoors. The ceiling and lighting was done in such a way that it appeared to be outside in the films, but really was indoors the whole time. This blew my mind.

We turned the corner at the end of Diagon Alley, and the space we were in seamlessly turned into a giant warehouse. This warehouse featured all sorts of easily recognizable sets from the films. Everything from the inside of Hagrid's hut to Dumbledore's office, to even the mountain of furniture Harry and his friends had to climb to secure a horcrux. It was really amazing to see these sets in person and appreciate the brilliant details you'd never really directly notice while watching the film, but made a huge impact on the final product. It was perfect.

I won't go into all the things I saw through the tour (I could, and it was a lot of really cool stuff), so I'll just say it was incredible. I was thrilled to try a Butterbeer, which essentially tasted like a butterscotch soda. The finale was an enormous small-scale model of the entire Hogwarts grounds. It had to have been two stories high with mind-blowing detail. Rocks, trees, windows, doors, lights, water, you name it. This was obviously used for big shots over the grounds for the films. It was beautiful and unbelievably detailed. Hats off to the artists of this and the other sets and props.

The tour ended up taking a long time (completely worth it) so by the time I had finished, I was hungry. After leaving the gift shop at the end of the tour, I bought a simple meal from the food place of fish, chips, and a drink. I ate quickly, then went back to the bus stop. I hated to leave, but with this huge benchmark checked off, my next adventure could begin tomorrow: Exploring the city of London.

Back at Palmer's Lodge, I made a grave realization while unpacking some of my things. I had somehow gone off and left my toiletries in Bath! These items included my tooth brush, tooth paste, soap (body wash), shampoo, cologne, and even my towel! Not taking a shower was not an option, so I had to get creative. I grabbed a clean change of clothes with one extra clean shirt. I found the men's bathroom (men's as opposed to coed like many hostels are) and took the best shower I could using only water (no soap). To dry, I used my extra clean shirt as a towel, then put on my clean change of clothes. When I returned to my bunk, I laid the wet (still technically clean) shirt out to dry. I then laid down and hoped my drying shirt would be dry enough to re-pack by morning.

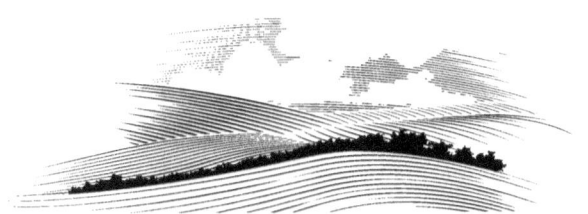

God Save The Queen

Saturday, June 14th

I loved taking the oak, red-carpeted stair case of Palmer Lodge past the full suit of armor heading down to breakfast this morning. I entered the parlor where breakfast was served and ate. I felt it was important for me to get good nourishment as I expected today to be a pretty big day. It was *London* after all. I had many things I wanted to see before leaving London, so I wanted to see as much as I could today.

I couldn't help feeling oddly nervous for some reason. I wasn't sure why exactly. Was it perhaps that I would be seeing so much of what I had only read about in history books and heard about in lectures? One of the courses I took at university specifically covered medieval England from the Tudors through the Stuarts. Many of the historical backdrops included the Tower of London, West Minister Abby, and The House of Parliament, among others. I couldn't get over the fact that I was about so see all these places as well as statues of historical figures. It was as if I were getting star-struck, preparing to see some big-name celebrity. This nervousness prevented me from eating much, but I ate what I could. After breakfast, I grabbed my map, charted my day's route, and headed out for an adventure.

My first point of interest was to find the Tube which would help me get around. I fortunately had no trouble locating it as it happened to be nearly a stone's throw from Palmer's Lodge! However, I rand into trouble after taking the steps down into the Underground. I was at a bit of a loss once I got down.

There were people all around standing at kiosks printing out cards of some kind before continuing on through a gate (the kind where you push past the spinny thing). I couldn't help flashing back to the Harry Potter film scene where Mr. Weasley is clueless as to how to get though the gate. Doing as the other people were doing, I found a kiosk myself and attempted to get a ticket. When I went to get a ticket, however, the kiosk didn't seem to respond. I decided then to get in line for a different kiosk behind two girls who were apparently having trouble as well. A rail attendant came over and assisted them so I listened to learn if I had done something incorrectly. Another kiosk nearby shortly thereafter came available, so I went over and tried this one armed with what I had overheard the rail attendant saying to the girls. I wish I had recorded myself trying and yet again, somehow failing.

"Need some help, there mate?" A young black man asked. He was the attendant who had been helping the girls.

"Yeah man, I'd really appreciate it! I can't believe I still haven't figured it out yet!" I replied laughing at myself.

"Don't worry," he assured me, "the system here is a bit confusing if you're not used to it — happens all the time." The gentleman showed me the simple error I had made and resolved my confusion before helping me purchase a 2-day Tube pass. Buying the 2-day pass was cheaper than buying the hours pass or single day pass since I planned to be here for a couple days.

"So where all are you planning to go?" He asked me after helping me get my 2-day pass. It was at this point that I suddenly realized I didn't actually know where some of these places were (or the Tube stops to get off at to get there). I told him my basic agenda, and he explained the best routes to get to each of them. He was impressed by my itinerary and mentioned that it was going to cost quite a bit of money to see everything — something I had not considered having assumed it would be free.

"Dang!" I replied after learning how much some of the things would cost (such as climbing to the top of Tower Bridge for £15). "I was really hoping to save as much money as possible." He laughed and suggested an alternative itinerary that would cost me a lot less yet still as enjoyable.

"Thank you SO much." I told him after he had made some great suggestions. "I really appreciate it."

"No problem! Glad to help. Have a great day!" He replied.

I continued past the gate thinking I might see if he'd like to go for a drink after work if he was still around when I returned. He was super friendly and had a great sense of humor. Being a local, I might learn some cultural things from him as well as where the locals go. I made my way beyond the gate and found the tube train. It was exactly as I had seen in films and tv shows that featured subways. Before I knew it, I was getting off at my first stop — West Minister Abbey.

The first thing I noticed after stepping off the train were how many people there were! SO MANY PEOPLE. I wondered if I had somehow been teleported to New York City! I flowed with the crowd of people away from the train and up the steps leading out of the underground. There was light streaming down into the stairwell as I ascended. My heart begin to pound in nervous excitement.

When I stepped out of the stairwell fully into the light, I was completely overwhelmed by the sights and sounds. My senses were so overloaded in fact, that

I almost turned and proceeded back down the steps to the subway. Cars, double-decker busses, motorcycles, and bicycles raced by on the street. The sidewalk was crowded with people — some tourists, some business people, some perhaps merely locals on holiday.

The architecture and iconic sites were enormous and vibrant as history seemed to hit me from every angle. There were historical buildings nearby and at a distance (some still big enough to seem nearby), statues of famous (or infamous) individuals from British history, and a beautiful green square in the middle with people enjoying the day. I looked up at one of the buildings towering above me and had to take pause. It was so impressively massive and stretched high into the sky. I had to lean my head all the way back to see the top. I had seen this iconic structure before in countless movies and tv shows, but could never understand what was so special about it. I now understand. If God Almighty were to erect a clock tower worthy of himself, I believe Big Ben would be that clock tower. It was almost actually intimidating the way it stood so majestically overlooking the city. I stood just outside the underground for a few minutes taking it all in, then attempting to regain myself before stepping forward to actually walk around and explore.

It was really convenient that all the major historical landmark buildings were around the same square. I walked around snapping photos of buildings such as Parliament and Big Ben and statues such as Winston Churchill. I attempted to visit the inside of a few buildings, but they were all charging more than I felt they ought to. Even West Minister Abbey was charging a high price to come in and look around (£15 if I recall correctly). I took photos of the outsides of these buildings, but chose not to go inside them. Maybe next time.

After spending a good amount of time walking around the London Parliament Square as I came to learn it was called, I wandered out towards the Thames River. I could see the London Eye ferris wheel across the water. This attraction too, from what I had read earlier, charged a pretty penny to ride. I appreciated it from a distance, but decided against riding. It wasn't just the price for the ride, but probably more about the idea of dangling in a bucket 443 feet in the air. I'm not about that life.

I next crossed the Westminister Bridge where an old Scotsman was randomly playing bagpipes hoping to earn some coin. Heading north towards the eye, I continued passed the London Aquarium. I paused and looked at it in consideration. I love fish and thus aquariums. Ultimately, however, I decided I would rather spend my time exploring the historical aspect of London. Perhaps next time. Besides, there were plenty of fish in the streets — and they were served with chips! I continued past the aquarium simply taking in all the sites of London before eventually crossing Waterloo Bridge and making my way toward Buckingham Palace.

As I neared the palace, an enormous, beautiful park that must have been either St. James Park or Green Park (I missed the sign indicating which one). As I walked down the pathway, I noticed people everywhere. Some were picnicking, some kicking a ball or throwing a frisbee, others were lounging in chairs enjoying the sun. The scene reminded me a lot of Victoria Park in Bath. What was curious to me was the number of people of all ages doing this. There were elders, children, young adults, and everything in between. Was there something special going on that I was unaware of or was this a common activity for Londoners?

Aside from the numerous people about, there was one other thing that really stood out to me: the TREES. The trees in this park were absolutely enormous! Hundreds of years old at the least! I tried to take some photos, but none will ever do them justice. I even attempted to take a selfie in front of a tree standing about 6 feet from it, but you still can't really see how large it is. If I had gotten much closer than 6 feet for the selfie, the trunk would have taken up the entire background. I should have asked a stranger to take one for me, but I didn't. As I admired the majesty of these beautiful, enormous trees, I couldn't help thinking about stubborn king Charles during the English Civil War (1642-1651). Charles, who was convinced that he was appointed by God to be king and therefore didn't have to consider the desires of the people, hid from his subjects in the branches of these great trees.

As I neared the palace, I noticed that many people who had been lounging were not collecting their things and making their way towards the palace. Meanwhile, I could see that a large crowed was gathered outside the palace gates.

"*What* is going on??" I wondered to myself. "Did every tourist in London decided that this day and time was the time to see the palace?" I was puzzled, but didn't think too much about it. As I approached, I noticed that the number of women and girls outnumbered what I could see of men and boys. This made sense to me since girls, American girls in particular in my experience, seem to be more often obsessed with modern royalty than guys. In the United States, the closest thing we have to a royal family is the Kardashians. Personally, despite my love for medieval history with its kings, queens, knights, and lordships, I have never had much concern for modern royalty. No disrespect to her majesty Elizabeth II of England, but royalty means very little in the modern era of democracy. There is more historical value than anything else. Therefore, with that being said, my plan was merely to pop in, check out the palace, snap a few photos, check my visit off the global bucket list, and be on my way. As it turns out, there was more to be seen here than I ever would have expected.

The crowd at the gates grew larger the closer I got so that when I finally arrived, it was as packed as a major music concert around the stage. My best guess was that I had been fortunate enough to arrive just in time to see the Changing of the Guard ceremony which I had heard was really cool to watch. However, I was under the impression that this had already taken place earlier in the day. My curiosity eventually forced me to finally turn and ask someone what in the world was going on.

"Excuse me, sir." I asked a guy standing nearby.

"Hey, what's up?" He said. He was an American. I instantly bet within myself that he was as lost as I was.

"What's going on here? Why are there so many people standing around the gate?" I asked. He laughed.

"Man, I have no idea. I'm trying to figure that out myself!" We both laughed at this.

"Well, if you find out and I'm nearby, let me know!" I concluded. He agreed, then we parted ways. He seemed to be less concerned than I was so I didn't put a lot of stock in him finding out. I, on the other hand, was now on a mission. I sought out an individual who somehow appeared to be British. A British person would surely know what was up. I found one and took a chance.

"Excuse me, miss, hi!" I asked a woman who looked like she might be British.

"Hello!" She replied in a British accent. I was relieved.

"Do you know what is going on? Why there are so many people hanging around?" I asked.

"We're waiting on the queen!" She replied excitedly. I was confused.

"The…queen?" I asked puzzled.

"Yeah!" She replied "It's her birthday! They've got the whole street blocked off for her parade. Her and her procession should be pulling up to the palace soon, then her and the royal family will retreat up to that place there!" She pointed up to a decorated balcony overlooking the courtyard. "Then they will allow us to go inside the gates and take pictures!"

I was beside myself. Of all the times I could have chosen to casually visit Buckingham Palace, I so happened to choose the birthday celebration of her majesty Queen Elizabeth II of England herself! Now again, with all due respect, I honestly could not care less about the queen or royal family outside of the history of British monarchism. I'm an American male (as opposed to an American female obsessed with the royals and flush with dreams of being a Disney princess) with no ties to royalty (aside from my apparent noble lineage of Wales as discovered in Ireland). The queen (as an entity) no longer plays any vital role in British government, the family has very little power overall, and are essential super-celebrities (but with a caliber of which the Kardashians could only dream of), yet maintain a historical tradition and significance that is absolutely undeniable. Her majesty Queen Elizabeth II represents one of the last remaining, authentic royal families in the world and has direct ancestral ties to what was once the most powerful empire on earth. Therefore, I had no choice but to stick around for this historic event (in my own life). It might be a once-in-a-lifetime opportunity for me, and I would never forgive myself if I walked away. My female friends would also have been PISSED if I told them I did so, so there's also that. Needless to say, I picked a good spot and planted my feet.

I patiently waited for what seemed like an hour. The entire time, more and more people slowly gathered, making the crowd grow thicker and thicker. The worst part was suddenly realizing that I needed to pee. At this point, however, leaving and returning was not an option. I therefore prayed to God that I could hold it at least until I got to see the queen. Suddenly I saw movement coming from the street beyond the gate.

Coming into the palace grounds atop great and magnificent horses were guards of some sort dressed in brilliant gold and red uniforms complete with gold feathers blooming from the top of their helmets, carrying swords that reflected the light of the sun. These guards trotted by, taking impressive formation along the outskirts of the palace grounds inside the gates. Once in place, the guards remained at attention. The next procession was similar. A brigade of mounted individuals entered the grounds decorated in gold and black, bearing brass instruments. I assumed this had to be The Royal Band of the Household Cavalry. They too settled into a formation of their own. Following this procession came a barrage of vehicles arriving from the front of the palace. One was a horse drawn carriage carrying the queen.

The caravan of vehicles pulled up and the entire royal family was quickly escorted inside the inner gate of the palace off the grounds through the great doors of Buckingham Palace. Once they were all safely inside and the courtyard became clear of horses and vehicles, the bobbies who had been keeping watch from the start, opened the gates to the public.

People streamed in like water from a bursting dam. Moments later, members of the royal family begin to appear at the decorated red and blue balcony overlooking the grounds followed then by the queen herself. The spectators all waved merrily to the queen and family and the family kindly waved back to the crowd. I felt it was kind of silly that people were waving. I thought perhaps an applause would have been more appropriate. However, as they say, "do as the Romans do," so I waved as well.

I stuck my hand up, half-heartedly to be honest, looking directly at the queen. Then, to my shock, as she looked across the crowd waving her hand, she panned across and looked directly in my direction, waved back, and smiled. I know it sounds ridiculous, believe me, but it is true. Yes, it is highly unlikely that she looked at me and only me and chose me to wave to. That would indeed be a very silly and presumptuous thought. However, she did look at me as an individual within group of other people to wave at, and she SAW me (or at least a blur of me). The point is, she didn't just wave at a crowd, she waved at people.

It was a really special feeling, and in that moment, I gained a significant amount of respect for this queen as a person. Despite her little power outside of wealth and tradition, her people love her, and she loves her people enough to spend time on the balcony of her palace looking down on them, waving with intention to ALL of them, being sure that she looks and waves TO every individual rather than blindly to a crowd.

The queen and royal family remained on the balcony waving for quite some time — long enough to have sufficiently waved to everyone. Then, several jets came roaring across the sky above the grounds, producing colored jet streams of red, white, and blue. The crowd cheered. Then, after one final wave to the crowd as a whole, the queen and royal family retreated back into the palace and the courtyard buzzed excitedly with people taking photos. I grabbed a few myself before leaving to finally use the rest room, grab lunch, and take a much needed rest before continuing to explore this amazing and beautiful city.

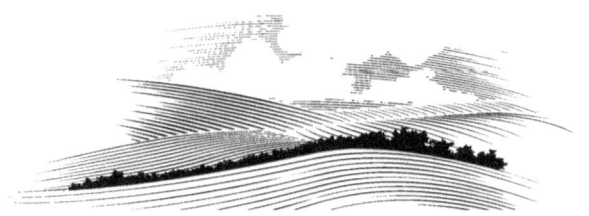

The London Players

Saturday, June 14th (Continued)

As I headed back into the inner city, away from all the (other) tourists, I came across the most curious sight. Coming down the road was a large group of people. Most of them were holding big signs while the others were yelling in heavy British accents and/or throwing beads and things. Was this some sort of Mardi Gras celebration? As far as I knew, Mardi Gras wasn't celebrated in England, but I supposed I could be wrong. If it was a Mardi Gras celebration, there were a lot of things missing, namely floats, a ton more beads, Mardi Gras colors, and of course the occasional drunk girl flashing for moon pies. I saw none of these things, which made me all the more curious. I then noticed that there were in fact thematic colors: rainbow.

"Oh, wow." I thought. "Is it a gay pride parade? Geez." I don't have anything against gay people. Most of the ones I have known (and still do) I have (and still) loved — they crack me up or are just chill about it (as opposed to in-your-face with it). A parade for being gay is a bit much in my opinion. Yet, I didn't notice anything overtly gay about any of the individuals. I scratched my head. Then I suddenly realized the music being played from a float (they had a couple but nothing like Mardi Gras) was a Christian song which I recognized. Then I noticed a few people were handing out crosses and Christian t-shirts. Next, a guy came walking past as a part of the group preaching about something. I distinctly heard the name Jesus followed by a familiar-sounding scripture.

"A Christian parade??" I thought. "That's something I've never heard of or encountered before." I found the whole thing to be as bizarre as it was humorous. There might have been more to it than a parade about being Christian, but I didn't look further into it. I supposed that it made sense in a way considering that

Mardi Gras started as a moving play of The Passion (Jesus' crucification story), but still. Weird. I thus merely laughed and continued my journey.

From here I chose to stop for a quick bite at a pub a my friend Cory recommended. He had studied abroad here and said it was really good. I found it to be a good place, but what was most interesting was the fact that each table had beer taps coming up. Had I desired to spend the day drinking, I could apparently pay for a cup, and refill it as many times as I wanted from the conveniently located tap. I thought this was super cool.

I walked around for a good while afterwards, simply taking in the city until I came across something that made my insides jump with excitement. There before me stood a HUGE white medieval fortress! It was made of solid stone with circular towers, a moat that went all the way around it, with green grass on the outside separating the castle from the cobblestone street. It was like coming up to a large Disney World attraction except it was 100% real (as opposed to wood and plaster designed to give the appearance of stone). It's authenticity reminded me of King John's castle in Limerick except still fully in tact! Obviously it was a requirement for me to explore this place no matter the cost. Even if it started pouring rain (which judging by the clouds was not unlikely), I would still ecstatically go exploring. Immediately, I looked around and found the ticket office which was located just across the street from the fortress' front gates.

"Hi!" A woman greeted me shortly after stepping inside the office. "Welcome to The Tower of London visitation office! What can we do for you?"

"Oh! This is the Tower of London?! Wow, I feel so dumb!" Having studied medieval history including medieval England, The Tower of London came up countless times, but I must have forgotten what it looked like. I didn't recognize it at all. I felt so silly but all the more excited to see it. I made a joking remark about this fact to explain why I felt dumb. She laughed and said something nice.

"So I guess you'd like to buy a ticket then, right?" She asked.

"Yes please!" I replied excitedly.

"Well," she said. "I have to tell you. I can sell you one now, but the Tower closes in a half hour." My heart dropped. I paused, still actually considering it for a moment.

"Are you open tomorrow?" I finally asked, feeling a little defeated.

"Yes, of course!" She replied assuringly.

"Ok,....I will just wait and come tomorrow." I replied.

"Alright! I think that's a good choice." She said." We'll see you tomorrow then. Bye!"

Despite my great desire to see it today, I knew I wouldn't be able to take it all in and really enjoy the experience with such little time. I left the office with a major buzz kill, but told myself that this would be my first stop tomorrow and I could take all day if I wanted to exploring the inner grounds and every guard tower of the Tower. I knew waiting was the right decision, but I still hated I couldn't see it this day.

As I crossed Tower Bridge to head back to the Tube, I began to find myself feeling increasingly melancholy and lonesome all of a sudden. I wasn't sure why. Was it the city?

London was really such a beautiful and romantic city — the water, the sites, the air, the breeze, the blue sky, it all felt so romantic in a classical kind of way. I further noticed couple after couple strolling together and sharing intimate moments by the water or in front of iconic structures. While I was glad to be free and able to do as I pleased without having to consider someone else's desires, I couldn't help almost wish I too had someone to walk through this city with. I recognized that what I really needed was a friend to hang out with — not necessarily a romance. With this in mind, I wondered if the nice Tube guy might still be there. I wondered if perhaps he might want to grab a pint and chill — just hang out and be guys.

I arrived back at the stop near Palmer's Lodge to find no one there. The Tube guy must have gotten off and gone home. I was a little disappointed, but it was what it was.

"Oh well," I though. "I suppose I can still go have a pint." It had been a long day of exploring and I could use a nice beverage and time to relax. "Besides, there's always the bar tender to talk to if nothing else, just to have a casual friendly conversation with someone." I therefore chose to check out a pub near the Tube called Ye Old Swiss Crescent Pub. As I approached, I happened to notice a table outside filled with guys and girls who looked around my age. I must have really been feeling quite depressed and lonely at this point because after I had grabbed a drink from inside, I went out and approached them.

"Hey, excuse me." I said to them. "My name is Tim. I'm from Mississippi and I don't have any friends around here. Could I join yall?"

"WHAT?!" They replied with surprise and smiles. They obviously never expected a random guy from Mississippi to walk up and ask to hang out with them. "Yeah!" The replied. "Come have a seat!" One of the guys in the group reached over and grabbed a chair from another table and set it down for me. They welcomed me into their group and immediately included me in their conversation. They asked what I was doing in London and what my plans were moving forward. They were all super friendly and a lot of fun to be with. One of the girls, Aine, was from Waterford, Ireland of all places (where I met the interesting guy on the train who wanted my watch). Her and I quickly hit it off. She had a really fun personality and great sense of humor. Her boyfriend, Tom, was also really cool. He was a London native and gave me the insider information on the city to help me over the next couple days.

As I got to know them all, I learned that they were from all over the UK. They were all players (aka actors) apparently about to graduate from the theater school and tonight would be their final theater performance as classmates before parting ways — possibly forever! Aine incidentally just so happened to have a spare ticked and invited me to come see the play. The others also insisted I come. I was of course very grateful and happily accepted the invitation. Then, after a few pints, we all went to the theater house a few blocks away. Fortunately, not everyone in the group was in this performance — Aine, for instance wasn't, so I wouldn't have to sit alone.

The play ended up being very interesting. Before going in, a few of them warned me that a lot of it might not make any sense because it was sort of an artistic play, but was still good. As it turned out, that was exactly correct. It had several funny parts, and others that I was completely lost on. I never quite understood what the overall plot was, but it was still fun. After the play, the group I had met at the pub originally returned to the pub where most of the other cast met us to celebrate the final performance and saying their last goodbyes. Since it was technically a cast party, Aine, Tom, and the others who had met me had to tell those in charge that I was their special guest so I could enjoy the night with them. It ended up being a really great time. The players were all very kind and made me feel a part of the celebration. One in particular who I hadn't met before was so moved that I randomly came from Mississippi and ended up coming to see their performance that he bought me a very high-priced drink out of appreciation. The night was wonderfully happy, yet also somewhat sad, and occasionally a little emotional due to their final night together, but overall very good.

By the end of the night, after I felt like I had gotten to know all the players there pretty well considering, I managed to experience a little taste of romance. It was nothing major; merely a brush, but it was just enough to appreciate and wonder 'what if.'

One of the actresses and I had ended up talking alone with one another quietly. She was a bit posh and one I would typically consider out of my league, but ended up really cool, down to earth, and laughed at all my jokes. There was something there, I just knew it. The way she held my gaze and smiled, the fact that even when we both seemed to run out of things to say for a moment, she didn't take the opportunity to politely excuse herself. As we stood very close, I couldn't help feeling that something was about to happen. I looked for her eyes to tell me, then someone called her name.

According to her calling girl friend, it was apparently time to go. Disappointment came across her face immediately as she apologized and reluctantly confirmed that she had to go. Her friend then came over as I took her hand and we said goodbyes. While her friend pulled her away, she held on to my hand as long as possible before out of arms reach. Even while her friend led her away, she continued looking back over her shoulder at me. For a moment, I considered going after her, but didn't.

"Come on." I told myself regretfully. "You live in the United States. She's starting an acting career here in England. There's no chance it would work out between you." I chuckled to myself about the whole thing. "Yeah," I agreed with myself. "It's probably for the best — for both of us. At least I had gotten to enjoy a little feeling of romance tonight."

Not long after this, the other players also began biding me a good evening and fond farewell. I stayed until the last one had left, wanting the experience to last as long as I could. Soon, however, they had all gone and I was strolling back down the street past the Tube entrance towards Palmer's Lodge.

"Wow," I thought. "What an incredible day." I had seen and experienced so many amazing things today despite being disappointed with the Tower of London being closed. I hated that I had somehow developed melancholy-lonesome feelings, but was blown away by how positively things had ended!

"It had to have been God." I thought. "Surely only He could have orchestrated the events of tonight so perfectly. ...maybe he isn't so angry with me about my trip after all?" I pondered this all the way back to Palmer's Lodge.

It then occurred to me that I had forgotten to seek out toiletries during my adventures, so my shower tonight was the same as my last. However, it just so happened that someone had left behind their bottle of body wash in the shower stall I was using. I'm not proud of it,...but desperate times call for desperate measures. I took a very small dab of this liquid soap to wash before rinsing extensively — lest some guy walk past me and notice I smelled like him. That would be an awkward conversation to say the least.

Once I was relatively clean, I dried with a clean shirt before getting dressed as before, then went and found my bunk. Before long, I had drifted off to sleep wondering what adventures await me next.

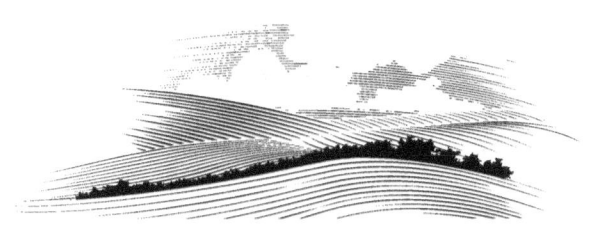

Mind The Crows

Sunday, June 15th

I woke up a little late this morning. I must have been more tired last night than I had realized. My agenda for the day, however, got me up and going quickly to lose as little more time as possible. Today's agenda was to go visit The Tower of London (priority #1, obviously) and Tower Bridge. I also really wanted to visit Baker Street, being a HUGE fan of BBC's Sherlock staring Benedict Cumberbatch and Martin Freeman. I also have a great general appreciation for the Sherlock Holmes legacy left by his creator, Sir Arthur Conan Doyle.

By the time I finished breakfast and head out, it was nearly 9am (which I considered late)! I hurriedly and excitedly raced down the street, hopped on the tube, got off at the correct stop, and made a B-line straight for the Tower. I found it funny how much more excited about this than I was at seeing King John's castle in Limerick. I supposed the Tower just looked a lot cooler — even having a moat for crying out loud! I couldn't wait.

"Hi! Back again I see!" The woman behind the counter said. She recognized me from the day before.

"Yes ma'am!" I replied. I then purchased a ticket and immediately made my way over to the Tower entrance. The gate was not yet opened and would not be opening for another hour. I chose to use this spare time to grab an early lunch. The obvious choice was authentic Fish 'n Chips, which I had not tried yet. There were several vendors nearby so finding a place to buy food was pretty easy. I chose one and ordered a plate of fish and chips with a can of Coke.

The plate-bowl on which the meal was placed was only a little larger than what one in America might expect to get an order of fries in at a baseball game. Inside were two very large fillets of fried cod on top a mound of French fries. The cod was thick, juicy, flaky, and delicious despite being also very greasy. Because there were so many people around as mentioned, I ended up having to stand for the majority of my meal until a small place to sit became available that was a few inches from someone else. I felt a bit awkward and looked around for something to stare at. I noticed carvings of large animals outside the walls. I inferred that maybe they once had animal shows here. I also of course gazed at the Tower's walls. I would be breaching them soon (via the opened gates). I imagined what I might find. As I did this, I sipped my can of Coke suddenly realizing how much I had always taken a wonderful iced fountain drink for granted.

After I finished my meal, I walked over to a peculiar site I had noticed. On the grounds outside the gates were a few oddly colored tents with people dressed in funny, medieval costumes walking about. One of them called out to those passing by inviting them to witness some great play at "the festival." It was obviously a professionally done thing (whatever it was) judging by the quality of the costumes so I wandered over to see what it was all about.

"Come! Join and see! A great festival this will be!" The lead actor announced. "For at half past the hour, we will be performing a play only just written by our director and my good friend, *William!*" This "half past the hour" was within the next five minutes, so I naturally stuck around to see. They weren't charging anything, so there was no reason not to stay. In any case, the play ended up being a goofy montage of some Shakespeare plays. The director, "William," of course ended up being a comical version of William Shakespeare. Following the comedy show, the actors took a slightly less silly tone (though not without still making plenty of jokes) to introduce a few medieval weapons and to demonstrate how they were used in their day. The players had a few audience members participate in comical demonstrations, but in a way that ensured no one got hurt. It was no Saturday Night Live, but it was fun. By the time they had finished, the gates had opened and people were rushing inside. It took me all of 11 seconds to get to the entrance.

I entered through the gate with high expectations. The Tower of London did not disappoint. I could never give it a just description, but it was probably the coolest place I had been to yet — not to mention extremely historical. It was very different from King John's castle in that it seemed still quite functional (and I learned later that people still live and work within these walls). Rather than following the crowd down the path, I chose to climb the steps up to the wall walk. This gave me a bit more of a bird's eye view of the lower grounds and I could also look over the wall towards the Thames.

Looking towards the inside I saw many doors and windows indicating residencies. There were streets, a large courtyard, and a very big square building towards the center that stood 4 stories tall, plus a high spire at each corner. However, what really grabbed my attention were the crows.

Crows are nothing new. I'm pretty sure they are a common bird most places in the world. Here, however, they were different. They were enormous! They seemed to merely hang around in groups near trash containers or benches and preferred to hop rather than fly. Looking down from the wall walk, they had to have been as big as wild turkeys! A friend back home who had visited London before told me about them, but I didn't think too much of it. When I saw them with my own eyes, however, I was blown away! I never would have imagined the biggest bird I would see would be a damn crow!

Pulling my eyes away from the mysteriously large crows, I tried to imagine what my surroundings (minus the crows) might have looked like in their prime: bowmen keeping constant guard along the inner and outer walls, great, beautiful ships with brilliant white masts and flags seen setting sail down the Thames or simply harboring along the bank, knights in their impressive armor training with sword and shield in the courtyard as the king attends an animal show outside the grounds with his family, perhaps hoping the beast might turn on its master to make things interesting for a change. How amazing it would be to travel through time to see it in its prime! Then, of course, I would return to modern day where we have good hygiene, medicines, and where people less often lose their heads.

I made my way along the wall walk to visit tower after tower. Some towers were larger than others and were used for different purposes. Each tower had a name and featured a historical aspect of that particular tower and/or information about the fortress' history as a whole. A few, based on the signs indicating so, were used as prisons. Markings could be seen carved in the walls, apparently put there by prisoners. One of the towers was dedicated to medieval weaponry and using the tower as a "war machine." Another told the story of The Peasants' Revolt with model depictions. The most interesting of them all was the Wakefield Tower built in 1220 for Henry III. It was decorated royally; complete with bed, a throne, fire place, and its own prayer room (when you're The Vicar of Christ and all, you obviously need a solid prayer room connected to your bed chamber that shows your piety).

After completing my journey around the exterior, I climbed the steps to the lower level and headed towards the large square building mentioned before. I was impressed by how big it was the closer I got. Somehow its shape gave the appearance of being a little smaller at a distance than looking up at it from its base. Located on one side was a modern set of wooden steps leading up to a door. I thought it odd there not being a ground-level door, but thought perhaps the door was on the side opposite me and the 1st floor was being used for something. That, or I needed to do some research into why there is no ground-level entry. In any case, I ventured up the wooden steps into the stone structure.

What I found inside made me completely 'nerd out.' This building was essentially being used as a museum featuring weapons and armor from the earliest of ages through the later middle ages! Everything from leather armor to metal armor, from swords to bows to spears, from small and large shields for men to fully armor clad horses! Indeed, manikins displayed all sorts of armor and weapons, while some riding atop manikin (or maybe hors-E-kin?) horses! Further still was different types of weapons and armor from different cultures! Some were honorable gifts of allies while others were taken as battle prizes. By the time I made it all the way through, I had decided that the Tower of London was officially one hundred times more awesome than King John's castle. The only thing King John's had on the Tower was that it was directly on the water and had a prettier view of the country.

I stopped at a few other exhibits on my way back towards the gate. One quick stop was an exhibit dedicated to the history of the first zoo of London (which explained the carved animals outside). Apparently, kings bought them and had them shipped in from all over the world. It apparently wasn't completely uncommon for an animal they didn't understand to escape and cause mayhem (lions will do that, you know). My second and final stop was see the Crown Jewels. They were cool and I appreciated it, but it really didn't do all that much for me.

As I left the Crown Jewels exhibit, I realized I was hungry. So hungry in fact, that I was starting to get the shakes! This wasn't good. I obviously needed to eat, but still had yet to see Baker Street!

"I can make it." I thought. "If I hurry and don't linger too long at any one thing, I can probably enjoy it before having to go into the next food place I see and smashing on whatever I can get the fastest." With that, I left the Tower, promptly crossed Tower Bridge, and headed straight for Baker Street which I had marked on my map.

Now, I must say that unlike the kings, queens, nobles, lords, and knights of medieval history that I had been enjoying so thoroughly, Sherlock Holmes was and remains to be a very fictional character. In fact, the current Baker Street wasn't even the original Baker Street Sir Doyle wrote about. Despite all of this Sherlock Holmes is to London as Spider-man is to Queens, New York...and then some. While Spider-man remains a super-hero in modern comics, Holmes has fallen into comparable legendary status as Britain's King Arthur and Robin Hood. That being said, along with the fact that I LOVE BBC's modern Sherlock series, missing Baker Street was not an option.

As I approached 221 Baker Street, the "residence" of the famous detective Sherlock Holmes, I realized I had become substantially more shaky and even a little dizzy due to hunger. I could see the door to 221 Baker open with a line coming out of the door and continuing half way down the street. My heart sank. There wasn't time. I needed to eat, but the Sherlock museum that was 221 Baker Street closed soon. If I got in line, I would be able to see Sherlock's place *eventually*, but would likely be miserable due to my shakes and dizziness at the very least!

"Ugh! Is it worth it though?" I thought staring at the long line. "Even if I passed out, is it still worth it?" I thought it over for a few moments, but ultimately decided (somewhat reluctantly) to simply snap a picture before turning around. I needed food, and at this point, the price was no object as long as it was at a close, sit-down/inside place and I could get it quickly.

After snapping the photo, I went quickly back in the direction of the Tube where I remembered passing what appeared to be a restaurant on the way. I found it again, and saw that it was indeed a restaurant. Without a second glance for menu pricing, I pushed the door open and went inside.

The class of the restaurant caught me off-guard as I walked in briskly. The exterior suggested it was a nice place, but I wasn't expecting what I found. Black table clothes covered each table, the lighting was low, a candle was placed in the center of most every table, waiters and waitresses were dressed in nice outfits, and the clientele blended right in. Here I was in a sweaty t-shirt, shorts, a cap (which I immediately took off), and a backpack. Unfortunately for any noses that might have turned up at the site of me (none of which I noticed), I really didn't care. I needed to eat pronto.

I was seated almost immediately after entering and ordered a water with the menu before I finished sitting down. When the waitress returned with my menu and water, I was blown away by what I found. I had every expectation to pay a steep price based on the ambiance. After looking over the menu for a split second, however, I found exactly what I needed for the perfect price: a burger and fries for only £8! It was my lucky day! I was relieved that not only was I about to eat a much-needed beefy (pun intended) meal in a very nice restaurant in London, but it also wasn't going to cost me an arm and a leg to do so! I still hated that I was going to miss seeing Sherlock's home, but I wouldn't have enjoyed it being shaky and dizzy anyway.

I left the restaurant and strolled back to the Tube station feeling full and happy. Despite not climbing Tower Bridge and not getting to venture inside Sherlock's home, I felt very satisfied with my day. After getting off at my stop, I chose to pop in to Ole Swiss pub hoping I might run into a couple players from last night — maybe even *her* by some odd chance. This turned out not to be the case. In fact, there were only two people there and both were much older than I. I still ended up grabbing a pint and sitting outside alone until a homeless guy wandered over. He ended up being really nice and was apparently just having a spot of bad luck. He didn't pester me or attempt to give me some sob story about how he got to where he was. Rather, he spoke more about being optimistic that he would be back on his feet soon. He did end up asking if I could spare a quid (£1) or two (£2), and I chose to help him out with what I had on me. We continued talking for a few minutes before he wished me a good night, thanked me for the quid, and went on his way. As I finished my pint and was about to leave, I suddenly realized there was one more thing I wanted to do.

Back home, there was a local band called Rosco Bandana. All the band members and I considered one another to be good friends, but the creator and leader of the band, Jason Sanford and I have always been close having known one another for a long time. A few years prior to my trip, Jason and his band had won the Battle of the Bands at the Hard Rock Casino in Biloxi (city on the MS Gulf Coast). Having won this competition, the Hard Rock sent them to London to perform for the London Calling Music Festival. Jason had told me that while he was in London, he would take his guitar down to the Tube and play because the acoustics were so good. Since it wasn't too late, I chose to run and grab my guitar from Palmer's Lodge and try it myself. Unfortunately when I tried it, I didn't notice much of a difference. Whatever Tube station he was playing in must have been better equipped for it.

After playing a few tunes in the Tube and speaking to a few random passerbys, I decided to call it a night. The following day I would be leaving for Paris. I couldn't wait, though honestly I wasn't too worried about Paris. If Noe hadn't been living there and with it a free place to stay, I would have skipped it altogether. Yet, a part of me was glad for the opportunity. As my head hit the pillow, it donged on me for the first time that I hadn't spoken a word of French since 10th grade.

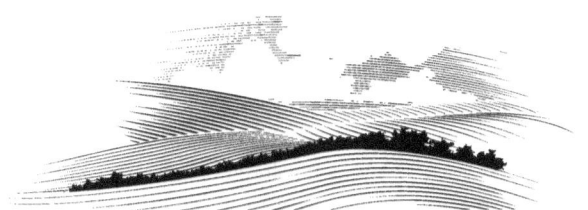

Pour Quoi

Monday, June 16th

I woke up this morning and immediately realized I had over slept! It was 8:45, which wasn't TOO bad but left no time for messing around and little time for error. Further putting me behind was having to check to see if Noe had sent me his Skype name and number so I could contact him upon reaching Paris. When I discovered that he had done so, I immediately wrote it down, threw my things together, and went swiftly down the red-carpet steps and past the suit of armor for the last time. I decided to go ahead and check out real quick before getting breakfast. After a quick bite, a raced out the door to the Tube where I ran into trouble that seemed to set the tone for my entire journey.

When I reached the Tube station, I realized that my pass had run out! I was forced to pay £8 for a single tube ride to London Station. Once at the station, I had a little trouble finding my train, and managed to make it before it left.

"Ok," I thought to myself once seated on the train. "This train will take me to Dover. From Dover, I will hop on the Ferry which will take me across the Strait of Dover into Calais, France. I won't have a whole lot of time before my train to Paris leaves Calais, so I'll have to be quick about it. Then, once I'm in Paris, I will find a wifi cafe to call Noe who will meet up with me and take me back to his place. Simple enough."

I arrived in Dover not long after leaving, though having narrowly avoided a mishap where the train split in half with the front going to Dover while the back half went on the Canterbury. I was relieved I had learned of this in time from the mention of a random stranger I somehow ended up talking to. I immediately found the first bus heading to the Ferry Port after arriving at the station. So far, so smooth. As I rode the bus, I looked out the window to notice how nice the city of Dover appeared to be. It seemed very quaint.

As the bus approached the port and the ship came into view I was blown away by the huge, beautiful, white rock cliffs that met the sea. As I watched the waves crash against the rocks, I was thankful that the waters seemed far calmer that the swells off the Irish coast. This ship also appeared to be much larger than the one, which I assumed would make for a smoother ride as well.

The voyage turned out to be even smoother than I expected. I could feel a very slight up-and-down motion but hardly noticed after a while. The best part was that the trip came with a food voucher (included in my ticket)! Passengers were called into the eating area by groups (like they do at air ports). I found a table and reclined until my group was called.

The "kitchen" we'll call it for lack of a better word seemed to me like a cross between a food-court and a cafeteria. The area was a quadrilateral-type shape with a few different meal options with a salad bar in the middle. I was provided a tray and the option to make my choices. I then loaded my tray with all the food that was allowed on the voucher, then found a table next to a window to sit at and eat. I ate merrily as I looked out over the horizon.

We made port not too long after I finished eating. I was excited to hop on my next train to Paris and see Noe. However, disembarking the boat ended up being a pain. To avoid too many people attempting to leave at once, the captain dismissed by groups and car-riders. I understood the reasoning behind all this, but I was very anxious about catching my train. It was already late afternoon/early evening and I knew I didn't have a lot of time to spare. I waited, sitting on pins and needles. More than once I considered trying to leave and sneak past security or whatever, but didn't. Then finally, after what felt like hours, they called my group and I exited quickly.

I stepped out into the cool air simultaneously preparing myself to be in a different country, where they spoke a different language, and had a completely different culture than anything I had yet experienced in my life. I just hoped I could remember enough French from high school to get me by and would find friendly strangers to help me along the way.

I found a bus which was leaving the port, but I felt hesitant about jumping on board. There was no markings indicating where it was heading. Fortunately, I bumped into a French-speaking American who let me know that it was headed into town and would be stopping at the train station. I then confidently boarded the bus and rode until it stopped across the street from the train station. I looked at my watch to see that I had a little time to spare, but no time to waste.

I walked into the noticeably small station to see that there was absolutely zero English anywhere. I stared at a tv screen showing train routes, but couldn't figure out how to read it — but was sure I didn't see anything suggesting a train to Paris. A little concerned, I went over to the desk in attempt to get help from the attendant.

"Pardon!" I said, remembering that for some reason simply saying, 'excuse me' like anywhere else was somehow considered rude in France. "Bonjour!" I was impressed that I remembered that from high school. Now for the real test. "Parlez vous Anglais?" I asked.

"No." She replied dryly. Great concern swept over my face.

"Non Anglais?" I asked clearly concerned.

"Ehhh," she replied. "A little." She seemed to be annoyed with me and was not excited to speak to me at all. I tried to explain to her in simplest terms that I needed to get to Paris. With every question I asked, she responded with a sharp, "No." She provided zero explanation or suggestion for an alternative solution. I couldn't help thinking that she would fit in PERFECTLY at my local DMV.

"No. No train." Was the most answer I got from her. She then abruptly informed me that her shift was over and she was going home. Without another word, she left the counter, locked up her area, and walked out. I was dumbfounded. I couldn't believe she didn't seem to care at ALL. I now had no idea where I was going to go or what I was going to do!

There was a bench there against the wall of the station. I stared at it and tried to wrap my brain around the reality of my predicament. I hadn't the first clue where a hostel was. No idea where to look for a cafe in this extremely tiny town where most of the buildings appeared to be residential, and the sun was getting closer to the horizon.

"I told you you wouldn't make it." A voice in my head sneered. "You never did have what it took, and now look at you. Alone, cut off, no plan, no escape." It was true. I was even having trouble thinking past the next second. I was freaking out.

"No!" I yelled inside my head responding to the negative voice. "I refuse!" I wasn't giving up and this was not the end despite the desperate feeling inside me that was overwhelming. I sat on the bench and thought. "Ok, worst case scenario, I sleep on this bench tonight, hope I don't get robbed or something, and catch the first train to Paris in the morning." Once I accepted this worst case scenario, I realized that it wasn't really all that bad. It would be extremely uncomfortable, and I likely would get little to no sleep, but I would be alright. As I accepted this, the fog in my brain began to lift allowing me to think critically and rationally.

"Ok, so I could stay here and accept the fate of sleeping on this bench or I could start walking down this street here and pray to God I find something useful (wifi) or someone who might be kind enough to help me." Still a bit flustered, a little confused, and definitely frustrated, I left the station and set out down the road. I said a prayer to God, begging him to please help me. I was desperate, and despite my resolve, scared.

Great relief came when I managed to find a small bar and grill. I went inside and did my best to order a beer if only to justify using the wifi to contact Noe. The waiter was a little kinder than the train attendant, but did not seem very pleased at all to speak English to me. Yet, he brought me my drink and provided me with the wifi password. Once connected, I attempted to call Noe for help via Skype, but it wouldn't go through. I used my only other alternative — Facebook to leave him a message.

"STUCK IN CALAIS! CALL ME ASAP!!"

I sat at the grill sipping my beer slowly in hopes that Noe would get my message and call me or at least respond, but he didn't. Eventually, I gave up and resolved to continue walking around in search of a kind and helpful stranger. I prayed to run into another friendly, French-speaking American, but none came. No one, in fact, was out. The city seemed dead, and the sun was starting to set. Not wanting to get lost in the dark, I made my way back to the train station where my bench — I mean bed for the night – was waiting on me. I felt trapped and wondered if God heard my prayer — or cared to hear it.

"He's not with you." A voice said in my head. You're alone. No one is coming to rescue you. Admit it." I couldn't do it. Despite my fears, doubts, and questions, a scripture, Deuteronomy 31:6, played through my head that promised this couldn't be the case. I put my hope in it, partly because it was the only hope I had left.

Just as I walked up to the station, I saw a young black kid (probably 16-18 years old by the looks of him) with what I assumed was his friend outside the station. They were dressed pretty normal and appeared to be nice. I approached them.

"Bonjour," I said politely. Their reaction suggested they thought I was homeless. "Parlez vous Anglais?"

"Uh, oui!" He replied in a friendly tone. "A little." In as simple terms as possible, I explained to him that I needed to get to Paris. This kind kid was happy to help me – the first one yet! We went inside the station and over to the kiosk. Through broken English and charades, he then explained that the last train to Paris for the day had left just moments before I had originally arrived (according to the kiosk)! However, he was able to help me find another train first thing in the morning. Then, like icing on the cake, he told me that there was a hostel down the road and around the corner so I wouldn't have to sleep on the bench! I was overcome with gratitude for this kid and for God having so clearly answered my prayer by sending this kind kid into my path. Just when I had given up and all seemed lost, this amazing kid shows up and takes the time (which was a considerable amount due to translation challenges) and helps me get a ticket, then points me in the direction of an actual bed for the night! I thanked the kid profusely for his help. I could have hugged him, but would have likely freaked him out. After I was taken care of, he and his friend continued on their way wishing me a *bon voyage*.

I found the hotel quickly and without any trouble. I was greeted by a friendly staff person who spoke a little English — enough to get by. I asked her for a room for which I paid €64. Obviously this was way more than I would have liked, but with the alternative being a free bench at the train station, I happily paid. Besides, it at least included breakfast!

I promptly went up to my room, set my things down, and took a long, hot shower using the provided toiletries. The shower helped me relax immensely before climbing into the big, soft bed. Leaning back, I then flipped on the tv while messaging Noe on Facebook and filling him in on what happened and when I expected to arrive (he was of course relieved I was alright). The first thing that came up, surprisingly, was an American show I immediately recognized — FRIENDS. I let the French-dubbed episode play in the background as I chatted with Noe until calling it a night. It was a relaxing end to a horrendous evening. Soon, however, I would be traveling to Paris where I hoped everything would go smoothly.

Part IV: France

Map of France: https://d-maps.com/carte.php?num_car=18005&lang=en
- Lines, circles, and words with asterisks are author's annotations and not on original map

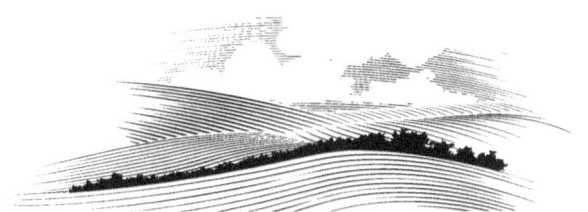

The Music House

Tuesday, June 17th

I woke up this morning feeling like a million bucks. I had slept really hard after the experience last night. However, after waking up, I realized it was 9am! I had only an hour left before breakfast ended! I jumped up and got ready as fast as I could and made it to the dining area with 10 minutes to spare. I then ate my *petit dejeuner* that consisted of cocoa crisps, Nutella, toast, coffee, and OJ. It was just enough energy to get me to Paris. After eating, I checked out and headed to the train station.

I caught my train easily and had no problems getting from Calais to Paris. I was thankful that it was a straight shot — no changes. My only issue was connecting to the train's wifi. I wasn't too concerned about it though. I was certain Paris would have plenty of cafes and such things where I could connect to wifi. I was thankful that so far, things were going really smooth. It wasn't too long before the train pulled into Paris Nord Station.

After getting off the train, I headed into the city where I chose to go into the first cafe I noticed. Finding a cafe in this area was no trouble at all. I found one and went inside. The cafe waiter was nice enough, but still didn't seem thrilled to speak English to me. He was not, however, rude at all. He handed me a menu and let me look for a moment (it was English friendly) before returning to take my drink order. I felt like the only appropriate drink to order right now, being my first time in Paris, was wine. I therefore ordered a glass of red along with an open-faced ham sandwich with pasta on top.

After eating, I asked my waiter if I could use their wifi.

"Why-fie?" The waiter asked puzzled. He had no idea what I was talking about. I was at a loss. What else do you call it?

"Weefee!" A voice came from over my shoulder. It was an American man there, apparently with his family. "They pronounce it 'weefee' over here."

"OH!" I exclaimed laughing. The waiter immediately understood.

"No, sorry. No weefee here." The waiter replied apologetically. He then backed away politely.

"Hey, thanks so much!" I said turning to the man who had helped me and his family."

"No problem man! Yeah, most cafes do have Internet and are called 'Internet Cafes.' This one just happens not to be one."

"Oh, wow," I laughed. "I picked the one cafe that doesn't. Classic." We had a laugh at that and chatted for a minute about where we were from and what we were doing in Paris. This family apparently vacationed to Paris every few years and were accustomed to how things worked.

"So do you need any help finding wifi or a ride or anything?" The man asked.

"Oh thank you so much. I really appreciate it, but I'll get it all figured out. I'm just trying to get connected to my buddy who I'm staying with." I then asked the waiter who was passing by where the nearest *Internet Cafe* was. He said the next one over should be, so I thanked the kind family again, exchanged well-wishes, and said farewell.

I left this cafe and headed to the next one over, but it wasn't as clear as the waiter made it sound. I couldn't find it. I searched up and down the street, but couldn't find another cafe. Either he was mistaken, or "the next one over," was a lot further than I understood. After walking around for a good 6 minutes or so, I finally found one and went inside. I confessed to the waiter that I only needed to use the wifi (calling it "weefee" this time) and he reluctantly allowed me to use it. I then connected as fast as I could and managed to connect with Noe. He sent me instructions on how to get to the place to meet him via the metro (aka subway). With these directions, I made my way back to the train station. His instructions were to ride the metro to Line 5 where he would be waiting for me.

I hopped off at Line Five and found him waiting as promised. I was so thrilled to see him.

"So," he said, "here's the thing. I'm actually not at my flat at the moment. My band is actually getting ready for a show coming up so we have been practicing. I hope that's ok."

"Are you kidding?! That sounds awesome! As long as I can sit down and chill out without having to carry all this stuff, I'm happy as a hound dog!" I replied cheerfully. Noe was actually a very talented clarinet player who loved playing the blues and jazz. At University, he and I would occasionally get together and play. I would play a jazzy or blues rhythm while he would lead over it. Before meeting him at Uni, I had no idea blues/jazz clarinet was a thing — even having played in my high school band! I was too excited.

Soon, Noe led me up the steps to a house and opened the door to an all too familiar setting. As a musician myself who has played in bands and has spent time with other bands, and been on tour as a roadie/merchandiser with Rosco Bandana, I was instantly comfortable in this space. There were cables running across the floor, amplifiers set up, computers out, and instruments on stands or being held by players. There was a guitar player, drummer, keyboardist, bass guitarist, a drummer — all guys, and a female singer.

Noe called to everyone and said some things to them in French. They all nodded their heads and smiled. He then turned to me and gave an explanatory smile before saying to the others (again) and to me (technically),

"Hey everyone. This is my friend, Tim from Mississippi. Tim, this is everyone."

"Hey! I mean, bonjour!" I said. There were a few who replied with "Hello!" while others responded with "bonjour!" Noe neglected to tell me if any of them spoke English, so it was a bit awkward but not bad. There was a lot of French spoken and it seemed that practice was going to continue as usual. Noe helped me put my things down and showed me to a place on the nearby couch. I was happy to be comfortable and no concerns. The next thing I knew, the band got ready to jump into the next song. I knew Noe could play well, but I was really curious and excited to hear how a blues/jazz band with a clarinet would sound. There was also no telling whether or not the band would be good — they might be awful, so I went ahead and resolved to put on a pleasing face just in case. When they hit it, however, I was blown away.

From the first note to the last, it was impressive. The full band set the tone, then Noe lit into it with the full power of his clarinet which was like adding salt to something sweet — delicious. Not only was the instrumental music good, but their singer was fantastic as well! She really brought it home! The combination of talent between each of the musicians as individuals combined with the unique sound Noe brought and the beautiful, soulful vocals of the singer was so beautifully refreshing. What is more was the absolute passion and spirit they all had in it. In my experience, there are two types of musicians. There are those who simply play music, and then there are those who release it from their souls. The passion and soul with which this band played enabled me to feel it despite not even knowing what was being said. This is actually what I love most about Rosco Bandana. Their music has so much soul and genuine passion. I knew then that this experience here in Paris was going to be one I would always remember.

Noe and I spent the entire rest of the day at "the music house" as we called it. The band would jam for a bit, then we'd all hang out, then they would jam some more, and we would hang out, and so on and so fourth until dinner. It turned out that everyone there spoke varying degrees of English and were very friendly. When having a conversation in French, they would pause occasionally and then explain to me in English the gist of what they were talking about so I could be included in the conversation. When I spoke to the group, everyone smiled politely, and then someone would repeat in French what I said to the couple who didn't speak as much English. It was so great getting to know everyone and they seemed to enjoy getting to know me.

For dinner, we all decided that we should cook spaghetti and all chipped in around €8. Noe and I then took the money down to the local market to get pasta ingredients and a couple bottles of wine (naturally). I was blown away by how cheap the wine was! I suppose that since France is a big wine producer, it would make sense for it to be cheap. I wondered what the prices for these brands were in the States. When we returned after picking up our groceries, we handed off the ingredients to one of the guys, Arnald, who owned the house and had volunteered to cook for us. He ended up doing a fantastic job, then after dinner, he insisted on doing all the dishes too! I tried to help, but he refused to let me.

"You are our guest! So no, please, go sit and relax. I have this!" It also turned out that Arnald, like Noe, spoke fluent English. He had apparently spent time in the States as well. He was really nice and had a fun sense of humor. After talking and joking around for a minute, I thanked him for his hospitality, then went and found a seat on the couch with the others. The remainder of the evening consisted of reclining while listening to music via the ipod(s) or Youtube, sipping good wine, and shooting the breeze. I also had the pleasure of introducing them to Rosco's music, which they really liked.

When it got late, they decided we should watch a funny movie. I looked around and didn't see a TV anywhere. I was curious as to how this was going to happen. Just about that time, I heard a noise and something moving out of the corner of my eye. It was a projector screen!

"WHAT?!" I laughed in excited amusement. "You guys have a projector?! That's so cool!" Everyone then piled up together on the furniture or on the floor with pillows to watch. The movie chosen was called "Les Clefs de Bagnole" or in English, "Car Keys." It was in French, but I strained my context clues and inference skills to follow what was happening. Unfortunately, I was pretty lost for the majority of the film. Some of the scene changes and character reactions were funny, and I would have occasional strikes of clarity before getting lost again. Yet, it was still fun. Eventually, I stopped trying to follow and just closed my eyes until the movie concluded around midnight.

After the movie, everyone found places to sleep — though space was limited. Along the side wall were some steep steps that led up to the attic. Me and a couple of the other band members made our way up these steps into the attic. Doing this would obviously not have been my first choice, but everywhere else seemed to be taken. I chuckled to myself as I climbed into the small space, crouching under the low roof.

"This will be a fun memory to have." I thought. "It will be yet another unique experience. Besides, a warm attic still beats a bench in a tiny train station any day of the week." I found a place to rest my head, and made my bed with the pillow and blankets Arnald provided me. Despite being pitch black, it was actually quite comfortable. After getting settled, I was soon fast asleep.

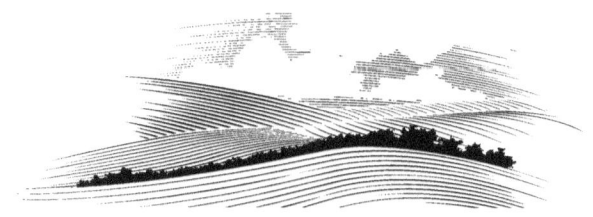

The Fleeing Eiffel

Wednesday, June 18th

I woke up this morning to pitch-black darkness. I was confused, and for a moment, didn't know where I was. As I woke up more fully and roused myself, I remembered that I was in the attic of the Music House in Paris, France with Noe. I sat up carefully, being sure not to bump my head on the declining ceiling and straining my eyes to see through the darkness. I turned my head in one direction and noticed a dim light vaguely emitting from what I assumed had to be the floor-door exit. I then gathered my pillow and blankets, moved to a crouch, and attempted to retrace my steps from last night. When I made it to the door, I pushed it open and was momentarily blinded by the sudden burst of light that streamed into the dark attic.

I climbed out of the attic and onto the steps. I set my bedding down, then surveyed the room. Semi-conscious bodies laid about inside blankets and sleeping bags all over the living room across furniture or on the floor. One of them was Noe.

"You ready to go?" He asked rousing, scratching his eye and yawning. I took a second to look for my things and I spotted them still over by the couch.

"Sure." I replied. "I am if you are."

"Ok. I need to wake up and get my things, then we can leave." He said sleepily.

"Sounds good. No rush!" I assured him. Indeed, I wasn't in a hurry, but I was really looking forward to getting a shower and starting my adventure in Paris.

After he woke up and gathered his things, we told those who were somewhat awake goodbye. Noe also noted that we would be back later apparently, which I was fine with. I liked these people and their music was great. After leaving the music house, we stopped by a pastry cart and bought a couple simple croissants for breakfast. I bought two chocolate chips croissants, which were very good. Next, we hopped onto the metro and were on Noe's street in no time.

"This is it!" Noe said, pointing up to a black gate as we strode down the road. We approached the gate and Noe punched in a code. He pulled the gate opened, then it closed with a "clang" behind us after entering. We proceeded from here down a short breezeway towards a case of stairs next to the smallest elevator I had ever seen in my life! It had a length of maybe four feet with a width of barely 2. There were no walls, but rather windows all the way around.

"So, we will need to take 3 flights of stairs to get to my flat,…or," he said, "you could take the elevator. I don't think it will fit us both with all your stuff."

I considered it, but wasn't sure I trusted the machinery to be honest. I expressed this to Noe in a comical way.

"Am I going to *die*?" I asked — mostly joking but at the same time suggesting my distrust of the elevator.

"I don't know." Noe replied chuckling. It was not the most comforting answer.

"Ugh, ok." I said. "I'll take the elevator rather than climb all the stairs, but if I die, it's *your* fault and you have to tell my family I said goodbye." He laughed and said "ok."

I squeezed into the elevator and rode it slowly up. Its elevation speed was so slow that Noe could climb the steps up (and around) nearly as fast as the elevator rose. If Noe had been in a hurry, he could have probably climbed up and down twice in the time it took me to get up once. That being said, we arrived on the 3rd floor at around the same time.

Noe then opened a nearby white door with black numbers and welcomed me to his flat. I was actually quite nice. It was simple, yet cozy and comfortable. Noe showed me to the couch where I would be sleeping and apologized for not having a spare bedroom.

"Hey man, I'm thrilled to be crashing with a buddy in Paris for free!" I said gratefully. "Besides, I almost slept on a bench the other night and slept in an attic last night. A comfortable couch is a considerable upgrade!"

I set my stuff down and inquired about the wifi. I told Noe about learning the correct way to pronounce it in France, and he got a kick out of it. I sat down on the couch and signed onto the wifi to check my Facebook just as Noe opened the fridge.

"Yeah, we're going to have to go to the store," he said. "I don't have much food left."

"Oh yeah, man. No worries. I'll throw you some money too." I replied.

"You don't have to do that. We'll just get a few things for now." He insisted.

After updating my Facebook so people (mostly my family) knew I was still alive and well, Noe and I left for the grocery store. It was a short walk to the nearby supermarket. It looked like any other ordinary grocery store in the States. It actually somewhat reminded me of the Win-Dixie back home. We grabbed a small shopping basket and walked around picking up a few necessary food items which included some cheese (I would say French cheese, but that seems redundant). It came in a round container like cream cheese does. I was a little confused, but trusted him — Noe was French, so he knew what he was doing.

Next, we found a section selling toiletry/hygenic items so I could buy some more. I was able to find soap, a tooth brush, and the other items pretty easily. The one thing we had trouble finding, however, was the deodorant. Where was it?? Slowly, Noe started chuckling to himself, then soon burst into somewhat of a giggle.

"What? What is it?" I asked starting to laugh as well.

"This is really not helping the stereotype." He replied. We both cackled a little bit. It was especially funny because he said it rather than me, and it hadn't actually even crossed my mind yet. We did eventually find some after what seemed like a lengthy search. The selection was also pretty slim, but I wasn't being picky. I chose some, and we moved on. Soon, we had checked out of the grocery store with bread, cheese, a few other food items, and an €8 bottle of good wine. If there's one thing I do love about France already, it's their wine prices!

Once back at Noe's I grabbed a shower, then prepared to start my adventure. Noe told me that he would be returning to the Music House later, so when I finished, I could either meet him back there or simply return to the flat and wait on him. He gave me very easy and specific instructions on how to get to both his flat and the Music House via the metro along with the key to his flat. I thanked him, and set off on my first adventure in Paris.

When I had prepared a basic itinerary prior to arriving in Paris, I loosely based it on the geography. Notre Dame was closest to the train station, so that was my first stop. As I emerged from the underground, I felt a sensation somewhat similar to what I had experienced in London. The only difference was that there wasn't quite as much to take in all at once. Still, it was like stepping into a whole other world. I did not, however, see the large cathedral. Only tall trees everywhere.

I continued forward into what appeared to be some sort of square. I saw a policeman keeping watch and thought perhaps he could point me in the right direction. I was sure it had to be close since the stop was named after it, but I just didn't see it.

"Pardon," I said to the officer, then asked if he spoke English to which he said he did. I told him I was looking for the Notre Dame.

"Yes, it's right over there." He said pointing. I looked and still didn't see it, but thanked him and moved in the direction he was pointing in good faith. Then suddenly, stepping out from beneath the trees, I realized the towering, legendary church had been almost right in front of me the whole time! It had basically been like looking at a zoomed-in photo of something huge where until you zoom out, you don't see what the huge thing is! The tall trees had prevented me from seeing the top of the church so all I noticed were buildings. However, as I moved further out from under the trees, I could see the enormous, structure in all its glory. None of the movies, pictures, nor documentaries I had ever seen did justice to how large this cathedral was. Just to get the whole structure in a photo, I had to stand at least 100 yards or more back! It really appeared to have been constructed by and for giants.

Being such an enormous and obviously legendary church, I assumed it they would be charging for entry. West Minister Abbey charged, so why wouldn't Notre Dame? To my surprise, however, I noticed a sign on the door as I came close that read, "free entry." I was blown away! Also at the door was what appeared to be a line, but was an awkward one. There were lots of gaps which suggested that perhaps the line ended before some groups who just happened to be standing there and other people assumed they were the line. I therefore saw an odd gap and stepped in. There were only a couple people ahead of me, so I didn't waste any time getting inside.

Walking inside the cathedral was astonishing. The ceiling alone must have been at least 4 stories high with absolutely massive pillars of pure stone! There were statues and pictures of recognizable medieval characters such as Thomas Aquinas (1225 - 1274). There were also medieval depictions of Christian scenes, stained glass windows, and beautifully decorated stone capsules containing the remains of notable (though not perhaps to me) people. I further couldn't get over the beauty of the architecture. It was so interesting how despite it being a holy place of God, it maintained a dark, Gothic tone. I even felt a sense of darkness in the place perhaps connecting to dark times in the church's history — like the church held memories. It was weird, but really cool, and very unique.

I noticed many people would come and sit in the pews facing the alter for a few minutes at a time. Some would simply look around in amazement, others would pray, and a few (older people especially) would simply take a rest. I felt moved to do the same. I therefore found a seat in a pew and sat. I took a moment to look up and around before saying a short prayer of thanksgiving and request for continued safeguard. I further confessed in that moment that if I was going to survive this grand experience and 'have what it takes,' I needed Him. Would he respond? I didn't know, but better to put it out there and move forward than to simply try to stubbornly go it alone.

I next visited a museum recommended to me by the same professor who had recommended the museum in Dublin. This museum was called Museum de Cluny, which was the national medieval history museum in Paris. With the recommendation of Dr. Jestice, I was excited to check the place out. When I arrived, I loved that the architecture of the museum looked very castle-like with high walls and round look-out towers. Inside was a testament to the medieval history of Paris complete with tapestries, sculptures, paintings, crafted/decorated stone, bath tubs, beautifully decorated stone coffins, weapons, armor, bowls, trinkets, and even books. The only drawback was that all the descriptions telling what I was looking at were in French.

After concluding my visit, I wandered back towards Notre Dame in search of a quick bite. I discovered a cafe called "Le Petite Cafe," which I felt was extremely cliché. When the waiter came out, I made a mistake. Instinctively, I ordered a water. When he returned, he brought a tall, chilled glass bottle along with a drinking glass. I felt so dumb.

"How much is this water?" I asked.

"Four euro fifty." He replied.

"How much would it have been for a glass of red wine?" I inquired.

"Red is three euro fifty." He said. "Will you be eating?" I then ordered a small €3.50 sandwich and a glass of red wine which was brought out promptly. It blew me away that both a glass of wine and a sandwich were (by themselves) cheaper than water!

My next stop was the Eiffel Tower. I had heard it was crazy expensive so I had no interest in going inside. However, since I was in Paris, I felt I must at least *see* it. It seemed that no matter where I was, the Tower was so tall that I could see the top of it above all the buildings and assumed it wouldn't take too long to get there. So, I started walking.

I passed by some really interesting buildings along with a park. Since the park looked nice, I chose to stroll through. I noticed as I walked some strange "artistic" sculptures. One was of a large, naked, muscular black woman titled "Standing Woman." I stopped and stared for a minute wondering why, then dismissed it as the type of weird "art" that normal people just don't understand. The other appeared to simply be a large pile of rocks melted together. The plaque read, "standing figure." Again, I dismissed it.

I pressed on through the park and beyond to journey alongside the Sine River. I walked for what seemed like a really long time, yet the top of the Tower really didn't seem to be getting any closer. Then, the Tower disappeared completely behind a series of tall buildings. I tried to find it again, but couldn't and managed to get a little lost in the process.

"Pardon!" I said to a stranger walking by before asking if she spoke English. "I am trying to get to the Eiffel Tower. Is this the right way?" The woman tried to explain it to me, but it was hard to understand through her broken English. I then thanked her and continued forward.

I managed to find the top of the Tower again after what seemed like another long amount of time, but again, the Tower did not seem to have gotten any closer at all. I decided to simply give up and return to Noe's. I was physically a bit tired, but the primary fatigue was my brain. It's interesting how being in a foreign country, especially one where you don't speak the language can cause your brain to work a lot harder than usual. At this point, my brain was so tired, I didn't want to even think anymore.

I let my brain shut off as I turned back. I used the map to tell me how to get back to the Metro and made it without any trouble. I decided then to go on to Noe's rather than the music house so I could simply sit alone and decompress for a while without using any brain power. My brain and mind needed that after being on overdrive all day navigating, problem solving (ie making inferences based on my surroundings), and straining to recall the small amount of French I had learned in high school whether for speaking or reading.

When I made it back to Noe's street having had my brain off for the duration of the journey, I decided to turn it back on for a quick trip. I needed to go grab some groceries for us since he had insisted on not worrying about it earlier. Since he was kind enough to let me stay with him for free, I wasn't going to let him supply all the food items. Therefore, I stopped in and found sliced cheese, turkey meat, sandwich bread, milk, a single beer (to enjoy for the evening), and another bottle of wine. After purchasing these items, I returned to Noe's. I put the groceries away and relaxed on the couch with my tablet.

Noe returned a few hours later with ingredients to cook dinner. He quickly whipped us up a simple yet delicious dinner and I told him about my day while we ate. He told me that he and the band had apparently done similar to what they had done while I was there, so I didn't miss anything. After dinner, we watched an episode of Game of Thrones on his laptop before calling it a night. I really could have stayed up longer, but my mind was still processing and needed rest. He then retired to his room as I climbed into my sleeping bag and was soon fast asleep.

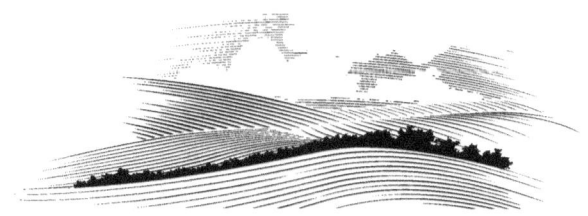

Gondor And Sex Shops

Thursday, June 19th

I woke up this morning and had a nice yawn just as Noe stepped out of his room.

"Did you sleep ok?" He asked.

"Like a baby." I replied lazily.

We chatted for a few minutes as we both took time to wake up.

"So what are your plans today?" He asked

"Well, the most important thing is to find somewhere to wash my clothes. All my clean clothes are now dirty. In fact, would you mind if I borrowed a clean shirt?"

"Sure, no problem." He laughed. "What else? Also, how long did you want to stay? I never did ask you, haha."

"Well, I haven't really put together an agenda aside from washing clothes, and I was planning on leaving Saturday morning." I explained.

"Ok." He said. "We can probably do your laundry at my father's. While we are doing your laundry, if you're down, there's a place I'd like to show you that I think you'd really like. There is a famous church there with a surrounding area that is really cool."

"Absolutely! That sounds great!" I exclaimed. "Also!" It had just donged on me. "I never did ask you when the show you are playing was. Next week some time?"

"Oh yeah, ha, I meant to tell you but wasn't sure how long you planned to stay. Saturday is Fête de la Musique, or "National Music Day" in Paris. We are going to play on the street outside a bar. It's a day when there is music everywhere and lots of bands or musicians play out in the streets." My eyes grew ten times larger.

"WHAT?!?!?!?!?!?!?" I exclaimed enthusiastically. "Why am I just now hearing about this?!?!" Noe laughed.

"I'm sorry! I didn't know how long you were going to stay and didn't want you to tell you about it if you weren't going to be here!" I understood where he was coming from, but still.

"Dude, I don't *have* to leave Saturday. I'm not on a strict time schedule. If you're willing to let me crash another day, I'd love to stick around to see your band and experience Music Day with you and the band! That would be incredible!!"

"Ok, ok!" Noe replied. "You are of course welcome to stay. I'm glad. Yeah, I wasn't sure what kind of schedule you were on. Great, so yeah, we'll go to my fathers to do your laundry, go pick up some things for lunch, I'll take you to Montmartre, and then I have to practice again at the Music House — you can come or not."

"Sounds like an excellent day! And I'll come to the music house tonight. I certainly don't want them to think I don't like them. Let's take it slow and easy today so we're not too tired for music practice." And that was that, the day was set. But first, we had to get breakfast.

After getting ready, Noe led me out of the flat, down the steps, through the gate, and down the street. There was a small local bakery nearby that displayed several kinds of croissants. There were cream stuffed croissants, jam stuffed croissants, chocolate stuffed croissants, chocolate chip croissants, chocolate drizzled croissants, and others. When it came to croissant types, you name it, they had it. The smell in-and-of itself was enough to make my mouth begin to water. With big eyes, I looked down and chose the chocolate chip (or really chocolate piece) croissant. After paying, I bit into it, and immediately understood why it was a French sensation. It was nothing like the croissants we have in the States (aside from its shape) and far better than the simple ones from yesterday. In the States, croissant bread is usually thick and sometimes hard on the outside. The best ones in my opinion are the Pillsbury crescent rolls, but they don't even compare to these. These croissants were hot, fluffy, flaky, buttery, hollow, and not to mention quite large and filled with tiny bits of melted chocolate. I probably could have eaten a hundred of them, but something told me that doing so might might make me sick. So perhaps another time.

We then returned to Noe's. We sat on the couch enjoying coffee and some of the buttered bread with blackberry jam Noe had insisted I also try. I was glad he did as they were most excellent. Since we weren't in any rush, we took out time and enjoyed the opportunity to talk. We hadn't really had the chance to simply catch one another up on life so it was nice to do so. During our chat, Noe introduced me to something I had never heard of before — Gypsy Jazz.

He explained that gypsies were true nomads. They wandered from country to country all together, but were eventually pushed out. For some reason, no one wants them. I wondered if they were like the "Pikes" in Snatch (2001). They didn't play music, so maybe not. In any case, this Gypsy Jazz was really impressive and very unique.

By midmorning, we were ready to go and Noe had called his father. We promptly left Noe's and arrived at his father's flat after a fair walk. As we walked in, Noe and his father conversed in French as I came in behind him. I heard my name mentioned, and his father greeted me with a smile, welcoming me. After what seemed to be a brief explanation, they switched to English. I was then introduced to Noe's father as well as his father's girlfriend who was also there. They were both very nice and had us all congregate on the couch. Similar to the Music House, they would speak to one another at length in French, then give me a quick explanation in English to keep me in the loop, then return to speaking French. I simply sat quietly and politely, and gave the person speaking my attention despite not knowing what they were saying. I tried to pick out words and use inferencing to gather the topics and mood of the conversation, but didn't have much luck. When speaking, I tried to use the tiny amount of French I could remember or had picked up since arriving in France, which was appreciated. The best part was when Noe's dad pulled out Noe's baby pictures to show his girlfriend and me so we could make fun of him. Noe *obviously* appreciated this (sarcasm). We then had some good laughs at Noe's expense, then Noe's father helped me get my clothes going. We stayed there, where we were provided a second (small) breakfast, until my clothes finished. Once my clothes were done, we returned to Noe's to drop them off. We left Noe's and stopped by the grocery store to purchase lunch items, then finally headed out for the day's adventure.

It ended up not being a long journey to get to the site Noe wanted to show me. After emerging from the metro, Noe led me to a street that shot up at an incline for a great distance. Once again, I was thankful for the training I did before leaving home.

The church was beautiful, even at a distance. It stood tall with three middle-eastern style domes, proudly facing the city it was serving. Its once white paint which was now turning grey beautifully contrasted the green trees and shrubbery growing around it. As we drew nearer, the masterpiece shone like a pearl among ocean weeds.

"Oh, and there is one very important thing." Noe said stopping when we appeared to be nearly halfway there.

"What's that?" I asked.

"Don't turn around." He said plainly.

"What?" I asked confused.

"The view from the top is really amazing, so it is best if you wait until you get to the very top before turning." He explained.

Now that he said this, it became really hard not to turn around. Once or twice, I had passed something that I wanted to get another look at. I almost blew it! Fortunately I caught myself just in time and had Noe watch behind me so I could walk backwards to get the second look. I wanted to look behind me so bad the higher we climbed, but somehow managed to resist the temptation.

Suddenly, the hill we were climbing turned into steps. These steps then gave way to three different levels of flat ground, and then up to a third level of steps which led to up to the church. There were so many steps, I couldn't help thinking of that famous scene from Rocky (1976) where he climbs the steps. I sang a little of the theme song out loud while doing a few punching motions, then did the Rocky dance at the top (and yes, people gave me funny looks). I was excited to have made it to the top! I couldn't wait to see this view that Noe insisted I wait for. I stayed with my back turned to catch my breath and so that Noe could catch up. Then, I turned slowly around.

"Oh. My. Gosh." I said aloud as Noe caught up with me.

"It's amazing, right?"

Looking out towards the horizon, I could see practically the entire city of Paris. From the village surrounding the church's hill to the Parisian suburbs, to the tall sky scrapers in the distance, and all the way to the foothills of the French Alps! It was a truly magnificent view. The wait was absolutely worth it.

Looking now at the church, I now saw in detail the beautifully crafted stone walls, tall pillars, and domed ceilings. Artistic carvings of Christian scenes garnished the over-arches with creative trims to create beautiful frames. Latin inscriptions in gold denoted the intricate carvings. I couldn't help but think of Gondor from Lord of the Rings, though this church was far too small.

After spending time enjoying this site, Noe and I returned down the steps and away from the village. We found a small park not too far where we decided to have our lunch. We pulled out the bread (French, obviously), deli meat, fresh sliced cheese, and bottle of wine. Unfortunately, we didn't think to bring cups, so we had to pass the bottle back and forth. While enjoying our sandwiches and wine, I noticed Noe start chuckling, then laughing to himself.

"What is it?" I said, now starting to chuckle myself at his behavior.

"This is so French." He said, then bursting into laughter. I joined his laughter when I too suddenly realized how stereotypical we were eating sandwiches and drinking wine in a park. I further pointed out that the usual stereotype was for a guy and a girl to be doing this yet here we were two (very hetero) dudes. We both then had a good laugh.

We took a different route back to the metro this time, which at first didn't seem out of the ordinary. Then, however, I realized there was something peculiar about this place.

"Wait," I said. "Are all of these....*sex shops*??" Noe laughed and explained that, yes, technically speaking, we were walking through the city's old Red Light District, which made sense. All around were "sexy massage" parlors, sex toy shops, and other sex-oriented places. While walking past one "sexy massage" place, I slowed to read an amusing advertisement. I hadn't stopped for more than 2 seconds when a woman stepped out and attempted to coax me inside. She offered me discounts, my pick of the girl to "massage" me, and promises of it being worth my while.

When I turned her down politely, she was displeased and responded with something along the lines of, "you probably wouldn't be able to handle it anyway."

"Considering it's still early afternoon, I probably wouldn't want to," I thought to myself while laughing at her as I continued walking.

"Ok, so we are about to be at the metro. I'm going to the Music House. Do you still want to come or go back to my flat?"

"I'll come!" I said happily. I was satisfied with the day and didn't have to think too hard having Noe with me. With that, we jumped onto the metro nearby and were back at the Music House in no time.

Back at the Music House, we kicked off the night by catching up on the latest two episodes of Game of Thrones via a laptop and the projector. After the episode, we all reacted to what had happened, then it was time for music practice. This lasted for a couple hours before eventually calling it a night. The night concluded with the decision to watch another movie. This time the group chose an English-speaking movie called Headshots, which I had never heard of. It turned out to be a parody movie of Top Gun staring Charlie Sheen as Tom Cruise's character. By the time the movie finished, despite being pretty hilarious, I could barely keep my eyes open.

"Do you want to stay here tonight or go back to the flat?" Noe asked. I considered it. I could go to bed immediately, but I would have to sleep in the attic, then worry about going back to Noe's first thing in the morning. On the other hand, if I could power through back to Noe's, I would be able to sleep on the couch and have a slow morning.

"Let's go back to your place if that's ok with you." I finally said.

"Ok, no yeah that's fine." He replied.

We told everyone goodbye and that I would see them again for Music Day if not again before.

It felt like a long journey back to Noe's due to being so tired, but it was well worth it. Not long after getting back, I was tucked into my sleeping back drifting off to sleep.

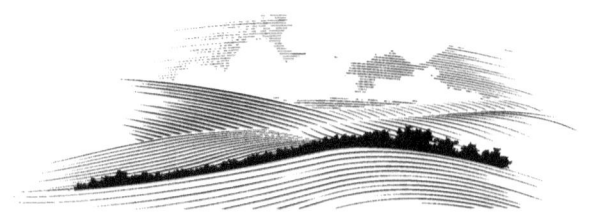

Bigger Things Appear Closer

Friday, June 20th

This morning I woke up slow. I had spoken to my friend Claire (a French-exchange student I had met at University) last night before and made plans for her, Noe and I to meet up for lunch so there was no rush. By mid-morning, Noe and I had both woken up. We ventured down the street for a couple croissants (I got chocolate chip again of course), then returned to Noe's for coffee and casual hang-out.

At around lunch time, Noe called Claire to confirm the meeting place and time before we headed out for the day. Noe had rehearsal with the band after lunch while I planned to visit the Louvre museum, walk the Champs Ulysses, and climb up to the top of the Arch of Triumph. That being said, we left Noe's flat with all that we would need for the rest of the day until we met again that evening.

Noe and I arrived soon to the meeting place and met Claire. It was a square near where she worked that had several food options. After getting food, we had a blast catching up and talking about the good times we had had while at university. Claire said she missed Mississippi every day and really hoped she could return one day soon. Unfortunately, our wonderful fellowship came to an end too early when Claire confessed she had to return to work. We hated to call it, but we of course didn't want our friend to get in trouble so we said our fond farewells and parted ways. I hoped it would not be the last time I saw her.

Noe and I then returned to the metro.

"So," he said. "I will probably be at the Music House all day and will be spending the night there. You can come meet me there or sleep at the flat. You know your way around there, so make yourself at home." He then gave me his flat key and explained the best way to get to my stop. There was apparently a line that stopped just near the Louvre museum, so he told me to get off there and follow my map to the Louvre. It seemed simple enough, so we fist bumped and headed towards different platforms.

I hopped off my stop and followed my map toward the museum. It occurred to me as I walked that I wasn't sure how it was pronounced, especially since French is weird. Was it pronounced the way the English say "Loo" (as in the bathroom) or if the "V" was pronounced to.

"Oh French," I thought. "The one language that often only pronounces a quarter of the word that is written." I tried it both ways when asking people, and no one corrected me, so perhaps it isn't that important.

Soon, I drew near to a gigantic, medieval-looking palace with a courtyard big enough to house a professional soccer and football field with enough space for spectators as well! Shooting up out of the ground appeared to be a gigantic, modern, glass pyramid that people kept taking pictures in front of. For several minutes while taking in my surroundings, this baffled me. The palace was very clearly dating back to the middle ages while this pyramid architecture was obviously very modern. The other puzzling thing was that despite many door and windows of the palace surrounding me, I saw no one entering or exiting them.

As I wandered closer to the oddity that was the pyramid, I noticed a line. I then noticed the line was moving into the pyramid. With no other alternative, I added myself to the line with the others. Eventually, and quite quickly really, I had reached the front of the line where I could see it going inside the glass pyramid then what appeared to be stairs going down.

After passing through and looking down over the rail before taking a staircase down, it all suddenly made sense. All the people came this way because it was the entrance (and exit too, technically) to the museum which (as I discovered later) fed into the palace that surrounded the courtyard, but it all started below ground. The giant glass pyramid being in the middle of the medieval courtyard which took visitors under ground before sending them up into the palace surrounding the courtyard rather than simply using the front door made (and still - as I write this - makes) absolutely no sense to me. Once again, I chalked it up to "art" that people like me just don't understand.

To make things even more interesting, I discovered after entering the pyramid that the stairs took me at least two stories under the ground which opened up into a giant atrium. All around were signs pointing to different museum exhibits separated by themes. This is of course an inference because all the signage was strictly in French. I was disappointed at this considering people from all over the world probably came to this massive museum and the most common language worldwide is English. Further, because the place was so massive, I was overwhelmed and didn't know where to begin. Being a huge Roman history lover, I definitely wanted to at least see this exhibit before I left but didn't know where it was.

I eventually found a museum map that was in English, but it didn't make sense to me in the slightest. The map was so busy in itself, I couldn't make heads or tales of anything. I ended up walking from one end of the large atrium to the other at least twice while asking museum workers a few different times where I was in relation to where I wanted to get to and how to get there. After far too long, I finally was able to get my bearings and found my way to the Ancient Greek & Roman exhibits.

The Ancient Greek and Roman exhibit led back up into the palace surrounding the courtyard which featured epic historical artifacts tastefully displayed through the halls, decorated in their original forms. My mind was absolutely blown. Statues and busts of recognizable historical characters, carvings, artifacts, paintings, tapestries,paintings, and did I mention beautiful paintings were everywhere (lots of paintings)!

The one incredibly frustrating aspect of the experience was the fact that there was absolutely zero English on anything. Unless I already had an idea of what/who I was looking at or could understand some of the French words based on my limited French recall leaning heavily on my recent Latin, I didn't have a clue. There were several things that looked really cool and I really wanted to know what it was, but was left to wonder.

The Ancient Greek and Roman exhibit was so long that despite not lingering too long on any one item, I finished just before the museum was to close! I didn't have time to see anything else such as the medieval exhibit like I would have wanted. I considered attempting to fly through it, but decided not to because I wouldn't be able to take it in and enjoy it. As I resolved to head for the exit, I noticed a large gathering of people attempting to see something. Curious, I walked by to catch a glimpse. Before the large crowd was a very small painting of a woman: The Mona Lisa. I was glad I happened upon it because of its fame for being the most photographed painting in the world, but I really didn't see its draw. Of all the historical artifacts and art in this enormous museum, the Mona Lisa was the least important of things I wanted to wait in line to see.

After stepping out of the pyramid, I took a moment to appreciate the beautiful medieval architecture around me. I tried to imagine it in its prime with medieval soldiers moving about in the courtyard as the king and his royal advisers stood and watched from palace windows. I concluded my visit with a few photos of the palace grounds before turning to look for the Champs Ulysses. I quickly realized it was just behind me and led straight to the Arch of Triumph. From where I stood looking toward the Arch, it appeared to be a good walk, but not too bad. I knew I could either return to the metro and ride to a stop near the Arch or step forward and march down the Champs. I chose to march.

I began my walk down the large street. There were many people out walking here and there with a few stopping at local shops, restaurants, and food stands. Suddenly, a very pleasant and familiar scent drifted into my nose. I instantly flashed back to the first time I had smelled this scent. Noe had invited me to a small gathering at his apartment while we were at University together. I walked in to find him wearing a cooking apron and running around making something in the kitchen.

"These are called crepes," he explained as he poured a small amount of pancake mix into the skillet. "It's a French desert. They are like a super thin pancakes that we add sweet toppings to. I have some on the table over there." I looked and saw honey, fruit, chocolate chips, Nutella, and powdered sugar. "The best part is," he continued, "they only cost around 50¢ each to make!" When he finished cooking, he put a fresh crepe onto a plate and handed it to me. I went and added an assortment of toppings. Then, when I took a bite, it was like the first time I heard the Beatles. Incredible.

I looked around and saw a small vendor (like a portable hot dog stand) selling crepes just off the Champs. I immediately approached and asked how much. My mouth was already salivating at the smell. I couldn't wait.

"Three euro." The man replied.

"WHAT?!" I exclaimed, looking at a crepe noticeably smaller than the ones I remembered Noe making. "THREE euro?"

The man confirmed the price, then pushed me to buy one as if he were selling them cheap and it was a great deal. I thought it over for a second. On one hand I really could use a crepe because they were amazing. On the other hand, I knew that the crepe he was urging me to buy for €3 likely cost him 25¢. I just couldn't do it. Besides, if I really wanted one, I'm sure Noe would be happy to make some. Therefore, I declined the man. I understood he was trying to make a living from tourism and would have paid €1 for a crepe, but €3 for a thin pancake with toppings is just highway robbery. I then carried on down the road stopping at a couple other vendors selling crepes in hopes of competitive pricing, but they were all the same.

After walking for quite some time, it seemed like I had gotten nowhere (little did I know at the time that the walk was a little over 2 miles/3.4km. Google Maps estimates a 43 minute walk). I looked behind me to see the Louvre palace, which still appeared pretty close. I then looked ahead down the wide, long Champs Ulysses to see the Arch, which didn't appear to have gotten any closer. I was reminded of trying to get to the Eiffel Tower which didn't appear to be too far away, but I never seemed to get any closer to it. I stopped walking and pondered for a few moments. I considered going back towards the Louvre and catching a metro, but wasn't sure if it would be worth it.

"What if by the time I walk all the way back to the metro, I could have continued walking and made it to the Arch by then?" I thought. I ultimately decided to press on down the Champs despite the objections I felt in my legs, and a faint voice saying I wouldn't make it. I ignored my legs and the negative voice as I continued putting one foot in front of the other and fixed my eyes on my prize. There was actually something inspiring about walking the Champs to the Arch, which helped propel me forward.

As I pressed on, I couldn't help notice a young girl dressed in Middle Eastern or perhaps Indian-looking robes with her head covered. She was barefoot, sitting on her legs in a bowing position. With outstretched hands she held a small cup. I noticed a few people would drop coins into the cup while passing by. I felt bad for her, but was puzzled because I had never seen anything quite like this before. Who was this child? Why was she alone? Why did she position herself in this way? Are there not institutions here to help children like this if they are homeless and without parents? I passed by her feeling a small sense of guilt for not dropping a coin and thought perhaps on my return trip I might. However, thirty to fifty yards later, there was another young girl about the same age, doing the same thing. I thought this interesting. Then the same distance ahead was another exactly like the last two.

"This must be some sort of organized thing!" I thought. "Someone is using these poor children to draw pity from tourists to make money!" There was no way such young children could be so organized and systematically distanced the way they were. "How sad." I thought. "Just sad."

When at last I reached the Arch of Triumph, I noticed there was some sort of event taking place. I couldn't tell what, unfortunately, but something that hadn't quite started yet. Individuals in military uniforms had gathered, holding flags all around the Arch. Yet, there were no signs that I could tell suggesting an official program (signs such as blocked off areas, security, someone directing foot-traffic, and other things one would expect to see at an official program/event). I walked around and investigated, but was unable to make heads or tales of what was going on. My best guess was some sort of veterans celebration outing.

"Maybe I should let it go." I thought to myself. "Just call it a bust." But I couldn't simply let it go! Another thought came to me. "I could do that, but then I would have walked all the way from the Louvre, down the Champs Ulysses, and up to the Arch of Triumph for nothing!" I couldn't let this be how it ended. I owed myself. So with that, I pushed past the assumed military veterans and made my way straight up to the Arch. In order to not seem rude if it was in fact some sort of organized thing, I tried to play "the oblivious American" looking around without any idea that something was going on. I hoped nothing was really going on, but just in case. Thus, with a hop, skip, and a jump, I made it to the ticket window at the bottom of the Arch.

After happily purchasing my €5 ticket (as opposed to the €50 or more to go inside the Eiffel Tower), I found my way to the steps going up one of the large legs of the Arch. Step after step I climbed taking me up and up and up and up! I don't recall how many stories I climbed, but it felt like quite a few. Eventually, I made it to what I thought was the top. There was a break in the stairs, but there ended up being a second level, then a third level. The third level was like a miniature gift shop and museum. The museum detailed the history of the Arch along with a few random historical artifacts. Unfortunately, like at the Louvre, all of it was in French so I hadn't a clue what I was looking at aside from the inferences I was able to make.

Finally, after climbing one final set of steps, I made it to the top of the Arch. The view I found here was absolutely incredible! There was a road that stretched out into the city at every direction and I could see for a hundred miles! It was really quite something and an excellent reward for my hike. I was even able to see the Eiffel Tower, which I now saw was a lot bigger than I had imagined. All the buildings around it appeared small in comparison. Even from where I was, the Tower didn't seem too far away. However, judging by the cars driving down the road, I could tell it was quite a hike and my legs at this point especially would not make it.

I stayed atop the tower for around ten minutes enjoying the breeze, taking in the view, snapping a few photos, and giving my poor lower-body a rest. Once I felt rested enough to keep moving, I headed back down the steps to the ground. This time, instead of attempting to walk all the way back, I chose to seek out a metro station. I could have stayed and explored some more, but I felt extremely satisfied with what I had accomplished for the day — not to mention the fatigue my brain was feeling again. Therefore, I chose to take the metro back to Noe's to rest both my body and my mind.

I hopped off the metro near Noe's street and stopped at a kebab place on my way. One of the workers was a young guy who ended up speaking pretty decent English. He and I got to talking and when I told him I was from Mississippi, he was blown away! He told me that he loved Mississippi because of the Blues and asked me questions about alligators. He was amazed to hear about people living on or near the bayou where alligators lived. I told them about how some people, whose back yards back up to the bayou, have had incidences where their dogs go missing due to alligators. However, I also told him that alligators are more frightened of humans than humans are of them. Crocodiles are the ones to really be careful of, but they primarily occupy the Mississippi River.

I got my kebab after sharing some laughs with this nice guy and bit into it. Of all the kebabs that I had enjoyed thus far, this kebab was by far the best. I told the guy I had been talking to, and he translated for the others. They were of course pleased. After finishing, I wished them a good day and promised to be back again soon.

The street seemed to be buzzing as I took the stroll back towards Noe's flat. The World Cup had begun, and France was playing! Bars and restaurants were packed out and guests' eyes were glued to the tvs mounted on the walls. I stopped and looked onto a patio bar to see that tonight, France was playing Switzerland. I considered going into a bar and watching, but really didn't want to spend the money and was of course exhausted. Instead, I resolved to continue on to Noe's and listen to the streets.

Soon, I was back at Noe's and sitting on his couch. As I relaxed, I listened to the reactions of the people. I could tell when something would happen because the entire city seemed to erupt in a positive or negative noise. At one point, there was a big negative eruption with positive noise mixed in. I wasn't sure what had happened, so I listened closely. The streets seemed to become filled with people which told me the match was now over. I looked out the window to see cars racing down the road, honking their horns, and waving Switzerland flags. Meanwhile Frenchmen could be heard speaking angrily. The drunker they seemed to be, the more angry their tone was. It was all pretty entertaining.

Suddenly, there was noise outside the door of the flat. The doorknob turned and the door opened. I wasn't expecting anyone, so I braced for whatever was coming.

"Hey, what's up!?" Noe said candidly.

"Hey! Uh, I thought you were staying at the music house tonight." I replied in surprise.

"Yeah,...that didn't end up happening," he explained, "but we have been invited to a party close by! You wanna go?"

"Ehh," I confessed, "I'm not really feeling up to going hard tonight. I'm pretty exhausted from the day. I walked the entire Champs from the Louvre to the Arch of Triumph."

"Wow, that's a long walk!" Noe chuckled. "It's going to be super chill though, if that makes a difference. Just hanging out and having some wine."

I thought about it for a moment. My body honestly said "You're tired! You need to go to bed." Yet, my heart whispered, "Dude, you're in Paris. YOLO. Get off your butt and go have another adventure!"

"Ok," I finally replied. "Let's go." So I returned the key to Noe and we headed out.

The party ended up being just as Noe described — super chill. It was in a small flat not far from Noe's with a few couches and chairs. There were only 7 guests including Noe and myself. Our host, Dagmar, was a lovely girl — cute, sweet, warm, and very welcoming. She insisted on speaking English to and around me at all times. Even if someone spoke to her in French, she would respond in English and immediately translate what had just been said to her in French into English. I don't think she knew and probably never will, but the fact that she did this really meant a lot to me. It was an incredibly kind and considerate gesture that was not necessary in the least. She will always be a warm memory.

Between my conversations with Dagmar, another girl named Ann, and others, it ended up being a wonderfully pleasant evening of good conversation and excellent French wine. It lasted for a few hours until Dagmar confessed it was time to call it a night — she had work the following morning. We then thanked her for having us and took our leave.

Noe and I returned to his flat. It was now very late and although I had zero regrets, I was now extremely tired. I climbed into my sleeping bag on the couch feeling warm, satisfied, and very grateful for my experiences that day.

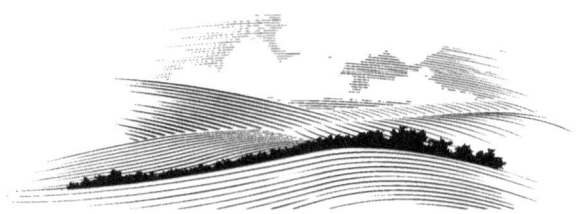

Music Day in Paris

Fête de la Musique
Saturday, June 21st

N oe left the flat early this morning to go rehearse with the band. I then had the flat to myself with no plans until Noe came to collect me for the day's festivities. It was a quiet, peaceful morning. I made myself coffee and enjoyed some toast with jam. Warm sunlight beamed in through the opened window as cool breeze gently accompanied it. The following day I would be heading to Avignon, the city of the famous Papal Palace. I was excited for this, but to be sure I had a place to stay, I went ahead and booked a hostel. After this, I turned on a bit of music.

I chose to turn on some country music via Spotify. I really wasn't a big country fan to be honest, but I needed to hear it. Being from the south, listening to country music seemed to give me a little taste of home. I heard the southern accent from someone other than myself, and the music talked about the things I love — being with friends, hanging out down by the water, back roads, "hunting, fishing, and loving every day." I wasn't home sick, but being away for over two weeks now was giving me a greater appreciation for where I was from — my home town, my state/region, and country too. If you ever want to realize how blessed you are, spend time in a foreign country. I think everyone should.

I had just gotten a shower and was rolling up my sleeping bag when the door suddenly opened. Noe came be-bopping in with excitement for the show. He asked me if I was ready, and since I was, we got ready to go. I gave him his key which he had let me hang on to while he was away (in case I needed to run out and get something) before we walked out not long after. I was really looking forward to the show. Meanwhile, I could tell Noe was a little nervous — and with fair reason. As we made our way down the stairs, I felt certain today was going to be an excellent, easy day with no troubles.

"Wait." Noe said suddenly just as we made it to the gate. He felt his pockets. "Did I give you the key?"

"No, I gave it back to you after you came in. Remember?" I replied. Time stood still.

"Are you sure?" Noe asked wearily with a look of concern creeping across his face.

"Yeah, I'm pretty sure but,—" I checked my pockets. "Yeah, no, I don't have them."

"Merde!" Noe grumbled. "I left the key in the flat." He paused. "My father's going to be SO pissed."

Noe continued feeling around in his pockets as I did my own. Both of us hoped that the other would magically produce the key, but to no avail. At this point, it seemed my brain went into overdrive working on possible solutions, worse case scenarios, and weighing potential options. While my mind continued to race, Noe and I returned up the stairs to see if the door by some chance had not locked. Noe turned the knob, pushed, and it started to give! For a split second, a rush of relief came flooding into my soul, but then was immediately dashed when it stopped. It wasn't over, however! Noe had another idea. He pulled out a credit card and slid it into the door. Hope returned to me. Noe slid the card, pushed the door, and yanked the handle, but it was of no use. My hope was again dashed. We were locked out. I recommended we call his father, but he refused, insisting that his father would be extremely upset with him and was intent on finding another way. Meanwhile, I had come up with several solutions and felt confident that one of them was likely to work out. No matter what, this day was obviously going to be an adventure. I just needed to be able to get my things in time to make my train the next morning.

"Well, there's nothing we can do right now," Noe said defeated. "Maybe if we find some x-ray paper we can get it open. For now, we just need to get to where we are playing."

After a quick metro ride and a long walk, Noe and I made it to where they would be playing. The bar, called The Null Bar Ailleurs, was on a narrow stone road called Rue de Cotte which was barely big enough to fit two cars on side-by-side. Just outside the Null Bar on the footpath was a white tent under which some of the other band members were getting set up. It could be dangerous at times because small cars would occasionally force their way down the road despite all the foot-traffic, but the police eventually blocked the road off.

While the band got set up, another group across the road at a place called The Troll Cafe started playing. They had a few guitars and a guy wearing a fedora played the harmonica. I was really impressed with their talent! All the songs they were playing from *Jonny B Goode* by Chuck Berry to *Crawlin' Black Spider* by John Lee Hooker were Blues songs! These guys clearly loved this style of music and really tore it up! My only disappointment was that the singer kept incorrectly singing "crawling *red* spider," and announced that as the name of the song after they had finished.

When the band's show concluded, I couldn't help but go over and compliment them on their job well done. I initially tried to tell the singer that the song was *black* spider, not *red* spider, but he wouldn't listen. I just laughed and let it go.

"Anyway," I also said, "ya'll sounded awesome! And you *killed it* on that harmonica! I would know, I'm from Mississippi!"

"Oh!" He exclaimed. "Thank you so much , my friend! That really means a lot!" I then heard him say something to his band mates in French that contained the word, "Mississippi." He pointed towards me then returned to me with a big smile. The band looked over with expressions of surprise and appreciation and several saying "merci beaucoup!" Once again, I'm sure it's not ever day a blues-loving Frenchman runs into a random guy from Mississippi where the Blues originated.

It wasn't long after the blues band finished that Noe's band started to play. They got in a quick sound check and jumped immediately into a great tune. Despite having heard them practice, I still couldn't get over how great it sounded. They had SUCH a great sound, and their female singer absolutely nailed it! It seemed that I wasn't the only one who felt this way either, for soon, a small crowd had formed in the street to listen. Some took a seat, some stayed standing, and some even begin to dance! It was a really excellent show and all who heard the music seemed to really enjoy the experience. Also, it's not every day one hears a clarinet player, which is typically associated with classical music, absolutely tear it up on a jazz song. It was definitely a show I will never forget.

After the show ended and I had helped the band load up their equipment, we all agreed that we should go find some food. We walked for several blocks where many bands of various types were playing on streets, in parks, outside of businesses, and anywhere else that was convenient. When we finally arrived at a pizza shop the group wanted to eat at, I noticed there was no seating. It was a single building with an order-window. Arnold volunteered to go order once we settled on what we wanted. We then agreed on a pepperoni and cheese, supplied him with money, then went to find a spot to hang out while Arnold went and got the pizza.

It didn't take us long before finding the perfect spot to relax. There was a small park not far from where we were that had gorgeous, tall trees and bushes all around with Victorian style buildings beyond. It was no surprise that there ended up being another group of young people in this area. They were really nice even though the dominate language spoken was French. I was asked a few simple questions and spoken to a little bit out of courtesy, but I mostly just enjoyed the scenery while trying to pick up bits of French I understood. Despite this, however, it helped distract me from how hungry I had become.

When Arnold arrived with the pizzas after what seemed like forever, I chowed down. The spice of hunger made the pizza so good that it was as if I had never had pizza before. My only concern was over the amount of pizza available and how much the others would eat. I was extremely hungry, but didn't want to eat more than my fair share. Thankfully, either because the pizza was quite large or the portions eaten by the others were a bit small, I inhaled several with there still being plenty to go around. By the time we had all eaten, there were a couple slices still left. Sufficiently filled, we gave our last couple slices to the group near us, then took our leave. I was full, had enjoyed a few cold drinks, and was ready to rock and roll for Music Day!

"Good news!" Noe announced to me as we were all getting ready to leave. I forget which one it was, but one of the band members, "...happened to have some x-ray paper. I told him about our situation, so he ran home and got some after we played before meeting up with us!"

I was thrilled! I had already mentally prepared for whatever fate befell us, but I much preferred to know where I would be resting me head in the end. Noe seemed pretty convinced that x-ray paper would do the trick, so without delay, we told the rest of the crew we would meet up with them later and then took our leave.

Through the gate and up the steps of Noe's flat we went. Noe pulled out the paper with all confidence and determination and slipped it between the door and frame. He jiggled, pushed, slid, and pulled, and to our frustration, none of it seemed to work. I also gave it a try myself, hoping by some chance I might just happen to accidentally do something right and the door come open. Despite my efforts, this did not happen. We were both able to get the paper down to the latch, but couldn't jimmy it the way we needed to. Then, the door to the flat next to us suddenly opened and a man's head appeared. He spoke in French, but I knew by the tone of his voice, exactly what he said.

"Excuse me,...can I *help* you?" He had obviously heard us and correctly assumed that we were attempting to break into the flat. At first, he was angry and suspicious, but after seeing the frustration on our faces, and the fact that we didn't run for it, he relaxed. In French, Noe explained to him who we were and our situation. The neighbor became friendly and stepped out. He agreed with Noe that x-ray paper was the best bet for getting the door open and gave it a try himself. Despite his effort, he was also unsuccessful. While this was happening, I took a moment to think.

"On one hand," I thought, "this sucks." We were locked out with no promise of a place to crash. We weren't sure if Arnold or anyone else was going to be at the music house tonight or we could stay there. Also, aside from being legitimately afraid to confess his mistake to his father, Noe said his father wouldn't be able to help at this point (for reasons I can't recall) and he now sort of regretted not saying *something* to him at the show (his father had been there along with his girlfriend in support of him). However, Noe was so confident that the x-ray paper would work that he didn't. Now, the future was completely unknown and there wasn't much

I could do about it. "Yet," my thoughts continued, "I can't help feel an odd sense of excitement."

I thought back to my very first journal entry the night before I flew out titled, *I Am Afraid*. I recalled how terrified I was about the unknown and the voices that were so loud and convincing, insisting that I was going to die, that I didn't have what it took, and that God was not with me; angry with me. I remembered quoting my friend when he told me, "that's the way you want it! That freedom" referring to all the unknown variables and risks involved. "Isn't that what an adventure IS?" I wrote.

At the end of the entry, I asserted that I had subconsciously planned this trip for "that guy," the adventurer I always dreamed of being but who I never really considered myself to be. Here in a moment when I should be more concerned, I had nothing but excitement about the unknown future. Would we have to sleep outside after a long night of festivity? We might. Yet, rather than thoughts of concern, a calm resolved thought came into my mind. "I will be mindful of where I go and what I do, I will get what rest I can wherever I can, and press through tomorrow the best I can." In this moment, I began to feel like the guy I had planned this trip for, and it was liberating!

Obviously, I would much prefer to find a good place to sleep tonight, but I wasn't too worried about it because I realized that literally, no matter what happened, it was going to be a great story! In fact, worst case scenario, I wake up outside, hung over, somewhere in Paris, have no idea where exactly in Paris I am, and no idea where Noe is! That voice I had been hearing, insisting that I was going to die and that I didn't have what it took called to me in a small voice, but I responded to it with laughter in my heart. I had absolute confidence that I was not going to die, and the worse it ultimately got, the better the story would be to tell later.

After around an hour of Noe and I trying, then with the kind neighbor attempting his hand, we gave up defeated. I remained positive, confident, and excited about the rest of the day and tried to encouraged Noe. I came up with positive "what if" scenarios that were plausible and that I had full faith that we would figure something out — even if it meant sleeping in a park somewhere.

The rest of the night was a bit of a blur. The sun quickly fell beyond the horizon, people filled the streets, and bands/musicians played around every turn. It was like a music festival that was very unorganized. We simply walked around and followed the sound of music that we liked until we found where they were playing. Then out of nowhere, a Brazilian marching drum-band rolled up and started playing. They played while people danced to the beat. No guitars, no horns, no music, just drum beats. It actually got old after around 30 minutes, so we moved on.

By around 1:30am, I was exhausted but knew I needed to stay up. I get cranky if I'm trying to sleep but am unable to, so since I might be sleeping outside, I felt it was probably in my best interest to simply stay up all night. As I went to tell Noe I was going to go grab a soda (for the caffeine), he motioned me to follow him away from all the noise. He seemed to have something to tell me. I followed him away to a place near the metro station entrance.

"Hey! Good news!" Noe said. "I found Arnold and he said he was going to be staying at the Music House tonight after all and gave me a key! So, whenever you feel like leaving, we can go."

"Dude that's awesome!" I exclaimed. "To be honest, I'm pretty wiped. If you're down to head out, then I am, but if you want to stay, I can hang."

"Actually, I'm really glad you said that because I'm about to pass out."

And with that, we climbed the steps down into the metro and hopped on a train. We arrived at the Music House a little before 2am and almost immediately crashed on opposite sofas. It had been a long, exciting day. The only question remaining was how I was going to get my things and be sure to catch my train to the next city, Avignon.

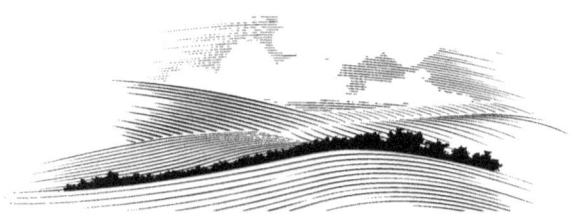

The Papal City

Sunday, June 22nd

Iwoke up this morning to see Arnold up and cooking breakfast in the kitchen. I was glad to see him. Since I figured I would never see him again, I took the opportunity to chat with him. He's a great guy, very nice and friendly. Since he had spent a lot of time in the United States, we talked about differences between our two countries and he provided some insight that I hadn't realized before.

"And yes, uh, if you hadn't noticed already," he concluded, "Parisians are jerks." I laughed. While I hadn't experienced a lot of direct jerk-ness, per se (though there were a few instances of it not described in this book), I confessed experiencing them seeming to get annoyed or frustrated with me because I didn't speak French along with the incident at the train station. "Yeah, that's pretty typical. It's gotten a little better over the past few years, but yeah. You would think that being a major tourist city, they would be more welcoming because tourists are a major source of income, but oh well."

After having a nice final conversation with Arnold, Noe finally woke up. Once he was awake, I said goodbye to Arnold and thanked him for his hospitality. Noe and I then took our leave heading back to his flat. We were still locked out of his flat and the only solution I could think of was for him to call his father, but I knew that would have to be a last resort for him. Fortunately, my train didn't leave until 2:27 so I had a decent amount of time before I needed to be concerned.

"I have a plan." Noe said as we walked. "I have the number for a locksmith. I'm going to call and have him get it open for us."

"Sounds good man." I replied, still thinking he should just call his father.

After getting off the metro train and stepping on to his street, he pulled out his phone and made a call. It was a short conversation —all in French. Noe seemed a little frustrated at the end of the call before concluding it. He crossed his arms, leaned back and exhaled deeply.

"The locksmith is too expensive." He confessed with a look of surrender and concern. "I'm going to have to call my father." Somehow I knew it would come to that.

"Ok." I said. He paused.

"There's a small cafe right over there if you want to wait inside." He said. "I am afraid this is going to be a long conversation."

"Alright man, I'll go order a cup of tea. Good luck. And hey, I'm sure he won't be *that* angry. It's not like you lost a million dollars or something." I said trying to encourage him. He still seemed convinced he was going to be in a ton of trouble, but there wasn't anything more I could do.

The cafe was a brick buildings with lovely plants and flowers around the outside and situated on the corner of two streets. The windows along the outside were cracked and the double-doors on the corner were opened and I could hear music coming from the inside. I strode inside to find a few tables and chairs, a waiter's table in the back, and 2 men talking to one another. I slowly approached them, not wanting to be in-courteous of their conversation. One of the men, an older gentleman, happened to look up at me and said something in French from across the bar.

"Sorry," I replied. *"parle vous Anglais?"* At this, it seemed both men became instantly irritated. The older of the two said something to the younger. Using body language and signals, I interpreted that the older instructed the younger to attend to me.

"Ehh,..a little." The younger responded, and appeared to reluctantly make his way toward me with an expression of anything but excitement or willingness. I asked if I could sit outside at one of the creatively designed metal tables. If I was going to be such an annoyance, I didn't want to annoy them with close proximity. He agreed and led me to an outside table near a window. He then asked what I wanted. I kept it simple by ordering a croissant and cup of tea. He wrote it down and promptly left. Within minutes, he returned with the tea and croissant. He set the items down before me, turned, and went immediately back inside without a word.

"Well, I'm sure glad I didn't need anything else," I said out loud to where he could have heard me.

Noe returned not long after I had finished my breakfast and paid. As it turned out, Noe's father wasn't angry with him at all (imagine my surprise)! Happy to hear the news, we went straight from there to Noe's father's flat to retrieve the spare key. Once there, I stayed outside in hopes of a speedy retrieval — I was ready to have a shower. Noe was in his father' flat for maybe 8 minutes before returning, then we set off for his flat.

By the time we returned to Noe's flat and I had gotten a much-needed shower, it was about time for lunch. I had a few hours before needing to catch my train to Avignon, so Noe volunteered to make us some pasta. Without allowing him to protest, I asserted that I was going to run down to the market for supplies. I figured I could at least contribute some bread for the pasta and something for dessert!

While at the market, I had trouble finding the (French) bread. I looked all over, but it evaded me somehow. Further, I could not recall the French word for bread to save my life! Finally, I decided to approach an elderly woman. She spoke zero English, but after managing to somehow communicate what I was looking for was absolutely thrilled to help me! It turned out that the bread had been right under my nose, only I hadn't noticed it. This experience with the woman was a welcomed 180 from the guys at the cafe. After obtaining the bread, I found a rum-cake that sounded good and checked out.

I returned to Noe finishing up the pasta and we enjoyed the meal together. We both realized that this could be the last time we ever saw each other so we tried to make the most of it. From this point until I left at 2:17, he and I chilled, talked about as much as possible, and listened to great music. When it came time to leave, Noe walked me down to the train station where we passed a black piano that Noe explained was for public use and occasionally a famous celebrity would stop and play. Just as we were moving beyond the area, someone sat down and begin to play. I only wished there was time to listen — it might have been a celebrity! I had never met a national celebrity and didn't expect I ever would. Still, anything is possible I suppose.

After arriving at the train, I gave Noe a big bro-hug and said goodbye. I was ready for my next adventure but was sad to leave my friend for what could be forever. Still, I next hopped onto my train. I couldn't find a seat next to a window as I prefer, so I ended up having to take one next to a random girl listening to music.

As the train pulled off with a slight jerk, we were soon flying through the French countryside — which is why I wished I would have been able to find a window seat. The girl next to me seemed to be very into her music and I didn't want to be trying to look out the window past her and her think I was being weird and staring at her or something.

At one point, we passed through what I later learned was known as "The Little Alps." The site of this mountain countryside was absolutely spectacular. A light blue, cloudless sky overlooked the fields of grass and grain moving swiftly by as the train hurled down the tracks. Farms, small villages, lovely patches of various tree types, and rolling hills braking against enclosing mountains far off in the distance.

Suddenly, I noticed we were headed straight for the side of a cliff! If I hadn't known better, I would have thought we were going to crash, but it obviously simply entered a tunnel through the mountain. When we came out the other side, I looked up and out of the window. Were were now completely surrounded by mountains! It was amazing! Like the scene from Indiana Jones and the Kingdom of the Crystal Skull where they find that secret place with the pyramid and the whole place is surrounded by mountain cliffs! From this side of the mountains, I was now able to see the peaking tops of rock and tree with clouds of mist hovering over them. In a few places, their heights varied so much that their design looked as if the mountain line were a sleeping dragon! Occasionally, I noticed a few small houses within what appeared to be walking distance from the base of the enormous mountain line. I couldn't help imagine what it might be like to live there, walking out the front door and spending the day climbing to the peaks of the valley walls. This was, without question, my favorite ride so far.

When the train stopped at Avignon Station, I half expected the girl next to me to leap up out of her seat and run off. She had never once acknowledged my existence and ignored me when I attempted to speak to her — at which point I would have asked if she would mind trading places with me. I was then forced to snap photos of the countryside from where I was. I tried to be as polite as I could and make sure she didn't think I was creepily taking photos of her or something. Yet, she never said anything — just listened to her music. As I got up, I left her just as I had found her: listening to music and ignoring (or rather taking a break from) the world.

I exited the train station in search of a bus stop that would supposedly take me to my hostel. However, despite my effort, I could not locate any evidence of a bus stop. I went back inside the station and asked a station worker for some assistance. They gave me some instructions to follow, which I did, and still couldn't find it. I could have gone back in and asked for clarification, but resolved to simply walk. It looked like a good hike on the map I had, but didn't look too bad. I figured worst case scenario, I take a break along the way as long as I made it before they closed for check-in. Recently walking the whole Champs Ulysses gave me some confidence in my ability even though that walk didn't include carrying my big bag, small backpack, and my guitar strung across my chest. One thing was for certain, though. Before I started, I needed to get food. I was very hungry at this point and knew that if I even had a chance of making it, I would need to eat.

I crossed the street and followed the road toward what I presumed would be restaurants. I came to what appeared to be a really nice, yet simple restaurant where I immediately felt under-dressed. In fact, I probably looked like a homeless person with what I was wearing and all the stuff I carried, but my hunger didn't care. I walked right up to the host desk and asked if they spoke English. To my surprise the waiter standing there not only confirmed that he did, but didn't seem annoyed to do so! I asked if I could sit outside — partly because the inside was so nice and I certainly was not dressed appropriately for it.

The waiter then happily showed me to a small table outside and handed me a menu. To my astonishment, this menu actually had English subtitles! I couldn't believe it! How is it that this restaurant in Avignon, which might have a quarter of Paris' tourism industry at best, have English subtitles on their menu while Paris, the tourism capital of the country, does not? In any case, I saw a burger with fries that sounded like just what I needed. Long story short, it was, and probably the best burger I'd ever had. Further, it came with a whole-cooked and seasoned tomato which was basically life-changing because I loved it and I have never liked tomatoes (outside of salsa or pasta sauce).

After paying and tipping the waiter (I insisted on doing so because he was so pleasant), I set out in the direction of my hostel. The journey took me back down the road toward the train station, then along the outside of the old, medieval city walls and toward the Rhone River Bridge. As I made it half-way across the bridge, I stopped to catch my breath. I leaned against the railing to look out over the water. I noticed a medieval-looking bridge that extended out into the water but stopped about mid-way. Following the bridge with my eyes back to its base, I finally saw it. The reason for making Avignon an intentional stop in my route through France: the Papal Palace.

To put it simply, a certain pope rather offended a few kings during the crusade period so the pope built himself a fortified palace where he hid for long periods of time. It later became a vacation spot for future popes. Because it has been so well preserved and has such an interesting history, it was one place I definitely wanted to see. It appeared to be surrounded by a medieval city of stone walls — which explained the walls mentioned previously. What was most interesting was the contrast between the medieval-ness within the walls (as far as I could see) compared to the modern-ness on the outside. I gazed at the old, stone city with its high guard towers, thick walls, and medieval architecture on the inside. Excitement rose within me such as I hadn't felt since touring the castle of King John back in Limerick. The excitement gave me a burst of energy, so I grabbed my things and pressed on.

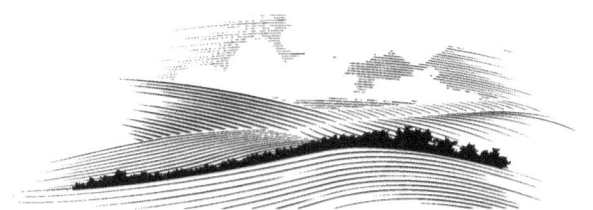

Midnight Scaling

Sunday, June 22nd (continued..)

As I came across the other side of the bridge, I saw what appeared to be some sort of summer camp facility in terms of cabins. There was a main, central building with a few cabins around it. If it hadn't been for the sign, I never would have guessed that this was my hostel. Therefore, I went into the central building that I presumed was where I would check in. Inside was apparently a mess hall of sorts with long tables complete with napkins, salt shakers, and pepper shakers. The aroma of food cooking could be smelled coming from an area with a sign that indicated a grill with a menu of burgers, sandwiches, and other simple items. There was a line in front of a cash register near the door, so I added myself to it.

In line in front of me were two black girls with backpacks like mine. One was short and wore glasses while the other was tall with an eye-catching hair style. They spoke quietly to one another, but I couldn't make out what they said. I did think, however, I detected an accent and wondered if they were perhaps from Africa. At University, I had taken a class on the history of Africa, which covered many areas and people groups. I have met a few Africans, and they are always so interesting to talk to. However, these hopes were dashed as soon as the two girls made it to the register and spoke up. When they did, it was clear that they were not African, and their accents sounded American but a little funny.

"Hi!" I said as they finished checking in. "So ya'll are from the US too, huh?"

"What? No!" They said.

"We're from Canada." The short one said.

"Ooh! Canada? Wow, you know, I've only met one guy from Canada since I started traveling." Referring to Ryan whom I had met in Dublin — "In Ireland, it is only natural that everything taste like Guinness."

"Really?!" The tall one replied surprised. "I heard Canadians were all over the place. We've run into several already!"

"I guess I must be looking in all the wrong places, haha." I joked. "What are your names?"

"I'm Nora," said the short one. Nor had a really friendly smile, and wore glasses. She then reached out and shook my hand. "And this is Jersh-" is all I understood. It was a name I had never heard before, and she said it so quickly that I wasn't sure what exactly I had heard. I smiled and shook Jersh's hand too, hoping I would hear her name again later and get it.

"You can just call me Jay," she said. "Most people do."

"Ah, Jay," I thought to myself shaking her hand. "That's much easier to understand and remember!"

"Well, ya'll seem real friendly," I remarked. "I plan on finding some food somewhere after a while and then doing a bit of exploring if you'd like to join me."

"Actually, Nora and I are craving pasta and had similar plans, so if your up for pasta, that sounds great!" Jay said happily. "We're gunna grab a nap first and probably shower, but if we catch you on our way out, we'll all go!"

"Sounds good to me!" I replied. "I'll probably be sitting outside playing my guitar."

After this quick conversation, I got checked in myself. I was provided a room key and walked over to my cabin. I found the inside to be very similar to the cabins at the summer camps I went to growing up called Camp Wesley Pines near Jackson. Here there were five bunk beds, a shared bathroom, and a wall unit air conditioning. There was an Australian guy named Jax who was also staying. He and I talked for a little while as I got settled in, then grabbed a quick power nap before grabbing my guitar and heading outside.

Just outside the central building was a large deck. Tables and chairs were set up with a few people eating or otherwise hanging out. I went into the central building to grab a soda, then found myself a place to sit on the deck. It was a beautiful early evening with the sun starting to head toward the horizon and a cool breeze drifted through the trees as I started to pick. I warmed up by playing things off the top of my head, then went into a few actual tunes I knew. To my surprise, those sitting around began applauding after I would finish a tune. I was humbled and thanked them. An hour or so after sitting down to play, Jay and Nora came out with another girl.

"Hey Tim!" They said "This is our new friend, Denise!" Denise stuck out her hand for a shake.

"Hello, I'm Denise." She said. Denise had olive skin, dirty blond hair, and spoke perfect English with a lovely Spanish accent.

"Hi Denise! Very nice to meet you. Where are you from?" I asked.

"Chile." She said.

"Oh, cool!" I replied. "You're the first person from Chile I have ever met." I then made a cheesy joke about letting me know if she gets cold. This was reacted to with chuckles and (expected) eye-rolls. What can I say? I can't help myself sometimes. After we were all properly introduced, we set off towards the city.

We crossed the bridge across the Rhone River and entered the old, walled city through the gates. I did my best to contain my nerdy excitement at being inside such a medieval place built in the pre-teens of history. What I found most interesting were the subtle modern additions to the medieval structure that didn't take away from the old aesthetics. Things such as electric lanterns hanging outside residential doors brought in modern-day technology, but were styled in such a way that didn't seem too out-of-place. Meanwhile great columns stood tall on either side of doorways that added a majestic quality to the scene. Narrow, cobblestone and brick pathways snaked their way through the city, separating rows of buildings lined up and connected. Two and three story tall architecture made of brick and mortar shot high into the sky with medieval-style with artistic depictions carved into the sides.

Occasionally, there would be more modern technologies such as dim, neon lights coming from shops and restaurants or random vending machines around a corner. One of them in particular, which I found both odd and humorous, was attached to a wall like an ATM and featured 8 different kinds of condoms. In the States, one might can find a vending machine of sorts inside the men's bathroom with a few condom selections, but I had never seen one such like this.

White-cloth covered tables with chairs were set up that featured candles as center pieces under a large white tent. Lanterns hung from the top of the covering illuminating the area. If one were looking for a romantic, but not over-the-top date spot, this would be it. The girls and I walked over to a small table and took a seat. A waiter then promptly came over and seemed to immediately recognize that we were not French.

"Bonjour!" He said happily. "What can I get you?"

"What? Twice in the same day?" I thought, referring to the friendliness of this waiter and willingness to speak English.

"What do you have in the area of wines?" I inquired after the girls had ordered their food. Strangely enough, I really wasn't hungry. The burger must have still be somewhat fresh on my stomach.

"What type are you looking for?" He asked.

"I like sour and/or bitter, so red?" I answered. "I'm not exactly a connoisseur of wine, haha, but I know the taste I like. I just don't like sweet wines."

"Alright! No problem. I think I know just the thing." He replied.

Several minutes later, the waiter returned with the girls' pasta and a glass vase for me that was filled 3 quarters of the way to the top along with a small wine glass. I poured it, took a sip, and found it to be perfect. The night was already off to a great start.

The girls and I sat, laughed, they ate, I drank, and after an hour or two, we reached our respective fills of wine and food. We paid the waiter, then set off again for more exploration.

While strolling through the night air, we came to a part of the walls that had a wall walk at the top like the Tower of London, only it was not meant to be accessed *per se*. Excited at the possibility to stand where medieval archers would have stood watching for any would-be attackers, I decided I must try to breach the wall. It seemed plausible because from the wall walk, there was a steep, stone slope that went from the ground on the inside of the walls to the wall walk. This would obviously have been handy for soldiers needing to get off the wall walk quickly without hurting themselves. Getting down would be easy, but getting up that same way would likely be difficult. However, I accepted the challenge.

"I'm going to climb it." I said with a 'challenge accepted' expression on my face. The girls stepped back and laughed.

"You're gunna WHAT?" They cried. "How are you gunna get up there? You're going to *die!*"

"Na!" I said. "I got this."

I surveyed the wall and its 12/12 slope from the wall walk. The height from the ground to the wall walk appeared to be around 15 feet. I looked for a space on the slope that looked to be slightly less steep than the rest. I found this space, and it was all I needed. I felt that if I could just get enough momentum, I could propel myself up to the top (and man, if I could have had some roller blades..). Unfortunately, the area between the start of the slop and the line of buildings was not enough for the ideal running start. It was only around 6 feet. Yet, I stood back as far as I could, did some comical stretches and jumping jacks to "get ready," and lunged forward.

"WAIT!" Nor cried halfway through my initial lunge forward. I stopped. "Let me get my camera ready. This is gunna be great!" I stepped back again and waited with an excited, confident smile. Truthfully, I had no idea whether or not I would be successful but the challenge in and of itself would prove worthwhile. I only hoped I could at least manage to touch the wall walk with my hand before sliding back down.

"Ok…." Nor said with her camera now ready. "Go!"

In the few steps that I had, I created as much velocity as I could manage. I rushed up the slope with all my force, half jumping, half running. Three big steps I got up the slope before I felt my momentum ending. In a desperate attempt to continue my motion forward, I lunged my body towards the top, stretching out my hand. Two feet was all I lacked when my momentum came to a complete halt and gravity overtook me, forcing me to slip and slide back down. Naturally, the girls got a huge laugh out of witnessing my valiant attempt. As I stumbled backwards off the slope with my momentum now working against me, they had assumed I would be done. They were, however, quite mistaken.

"I almost got it!" I shouted with excitement and new determination.

"Yeah, you were actually sort of close!" Nora admitted laughing.

"I'm going to try again." I said, and the girls got their cameras ready for a second try. In fact, twice more I attempted the feat. On these tries, I managed to touch the wall walk path the my hand but discovered it was completely flat with nothing to grab hold of. After the third try, however, I resoled to accept defeat and be satisfied with successfully *touching* the top at least. THEN, something unexpected happened.

While continuing to walk along the street following the wall walk, Denise pointed out something even more intriguing. Just ahead was a large, square tower that tied into the wall walk. The side of the tower stuck out from the wall walk, forming 3 sides. On the left side that met the wall, there were a number of stone pieces that had apparently cracked and fallen away to make brick-sized holes. Before I could even say anything, DENISE was already on the wall with her feet and hands in the spaces and beginning to climb! I immediately ran over and stood under her. If a stone brick came lose causing her to fall, I would want to be there to catch her lest she get hurt (I know, I'm practically a hero). After she had safely scaled the wall and climbed onto the wall walk, I hurriedly climbed up myself to join her.

While scaling up at around the 8 or 9 foot height mark, I narrowly evaded a fall. A hole I had placed my foot in suddenly gave way and my foot fell. Had I not been careful in making one movement at a time, I wouldn't have caught myself so easily. Scaling then to my left, I stepped off the wall onto the dirty wall walk of dust and clay. With both feet firmly planted, I looked out over the wall. I noticed immediately that we were a lot higher up on the outside compared to the inside. I looked around, taking in the moment. I then looked toward the tower I had climbed to see the wall walk leading inside.

I followed the path to find nothing worth getting excited about. Rubble, dirt, trash, and evidence of where a homeless person may be sleeping considering the empty bottles, blankets, and food remains. Still, I called Denise over to explore with me and she did. We walked around and found an arch under the outer edge facing the inner city. It made a nice place to sit and look out. We couldn't see everything, but was still a nice view.

"You know," Jay said. "You actually look pretty awesome up there." She looked at Nora. "You wanna go up?"

"WHAT?!" Nora replied enthusiastically. "NO, I'm not climbing a wall. I'm not about that life. You go ahead though, and I'll take a picture."

"Aw, come on Nora! It's awesome! You'll be alright!" Denise called down to her, but to no avail. Nora wasn't having it. Jay on the other hand wasted no time.

Jay set her purse down, walked over, carefully scaled the wall just as Denise and I had done, and was sitting with us in no time. We sat together for only a few minutes after Nora got her picture, then decided it was time to move on. We stood up, carefully climbed back to the wall walk, and half stood, half slid down the slope back to the ground. It was so much fun and I was thrilled to have had some great people to share the memory with.

After getting down, we continued exploring by the light of the stars and the lanterns along the walls of the streets. We had loads of laughs and took many photos along the way.

"Oh my gosh!" Jay said suddenly. "It's literally 3:27 right now."

"Holy crap! We should probably head back." The others agreed, and we started back towards the hostel. We had been having such a great time together, we hadn't realized how late it had gotten. By the time we made it back to the hostel, it was a little after 4am, but so worth it. We bid each other a good night and planned to meet up tomorrow to explore the city again,…at the crack of noon. I returned to my cabin-style hostel room, found my bunk, and crashed. It was a great first night in Avignon and I looked forward to the adventures to come.

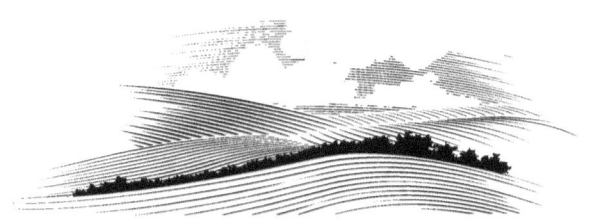

Zorro, Eroticism, and...
The Papacy?

Monday, June 23rd

I climbed out of bed at around 10:45am and went into the center building filled with anticipation for the day. I grabbed a €4.90 trey that contained a bowl of cereal, 2 pieces of toast, a glass of orange juice, and a cup of coffee. It wasn't exactly the Breakfast of Champions, but it would do. I grabbed a place at the long table and ate. After finishing, I went out to the deck where there were a few people hanging out. It was getting close to noon and I didn't want to miss Jay and Nora, so I decided I'd try meeting a few random people and talking with them to kill time.

There was a couple nearby who appeared to be nice, so I approached them and said hello. They were indeed very nice and introduced themselves. The guy was named James while the girl was Alycia. Both were from different parts of Australia! I was thrilled to meet Australians. I love hearing the accent — especially on women, which I think sounds very sexy. James was tall and well built. Alycia was a head shorter than me with shoulder-length blond hair, deep blue eyes, and a smile that could knock a boy over. The three of us were engaged in a nice conversation when Nora, Jay, and Denise appeared.

"Hey yall!" I greeted them. "Come meet my new friends, James and Alycia." Once everyone had been acquainted, I suggested we all go into town and explore together.

"Ah man!" Alycia said in her lovely Aussie accent. "I wish we could, but James and I have plans to do something else today. How about we catch up later for dinner or something?"

"Yeah, that sounds great!" Nora said, speaking for us all. So with that, we said goodbye for now and headed towards the city.

It was really great to see the stone architecture in the light of day. The guard towers stood impressively along the outskirts of the city with pointy spires reaching up towards the sky while statues of famous people and saints stood atop many buildings and flowing fountains. It was also nice to see people walking about, making it seem more alive than it was the night before. Passing by the restaurant where we had eaten pasta, we saw our waiter working hard again. He looked up just as we were passing by.

"Bonjour!" He shouted merrily. "Have a good morning and a great day!"

"Merci!" We yelled back. "You too!" He was such a nice guy.

After a short walk, we found our way to the palace. The entrance was much less grand than I had expected and hoped for so I was a little disappointed. Had it not been indicated on the map, I never would have guessed it was the entrance at all. What is more, I further realized that we had passed by it once or twice last night and I never noticed it.

"I wonder if this was not the original front entrance, but rather a side entrance now used as the only entryway." I thought. "Or maybe, considering how I now see that the city, the palace, and the walls all seem to be connected, the paranoid pope intentionally designed it this way for security purposes."

We entered the palace and paid the clerk for a self-guided tour. Self-guided in this instance really just meant to walk around and read signs describing what things were. No tour guide, no pamphlet, nothing, which was fine. The ticket was very cheap and I was very excited simply to be walking where the paranoid pope strode. To my surprise and gratitude, all the signs fortunately ended up including *English* text as well as French so I knew what I was looking at — unlike at the Louvre or anywhere else in Paris for that matter.

Inside the palace were many rooms filled with painted walls and ceilings, artwork, and (most interesting to me) artifacts. Medieval tools were displayed behind glass casings, sculptures were carved into the stone walls or stood in decorated corners. A few carvings had been detached from the wall somehow, but were still displayed. A gargoyle head, for instance was displayed on the ground (perhaps fallen?). Also featured were important stone tablets such as the dedication of the Church of St. Stephen in Avignon in the 12th century and hand-written documents including, "The Expansion of the Episcopal Palace at Avignon, December 13th 1316." Coolest of all, I think, was a section of crossbow bolt frames, crossbow nails, and the skull of a person who had been killed by a crossbow bolt.

Something I got a kick out of was what appeared to be a secret hiding place of some sort. It was a small room that would otherwise be unknowable, but the floor we were standing on had an area replaced by plexiglass and therefore visible beneath us. The pope who built this palace was clearly concerned about his capture. If the city walls had been breached by a king's army, he would have had a nice place to hide. Fortunately for him, this never happened.

From room to room we explored, climbing narrow, spiral stair cases, looking over old stone walls, sitting in small window-seats that overlooked the courtyard below, and taking pictures (unless it was a specified area that restricted photo-taking). Near the end, we stumbled upon an area that none of us understood. The contents of the area were extremely out of place both contextually and histori-cally.

"What IS this?" I asked out loud equally offended and tickled at the absurdity of it at same time. "Art??"

Apparently, someone thought this area of the papal palace (you know, the 'Vicar of St. Peter' on whom Jesus Christ said, "I will build my church,") would be the perfect spot for extremely weird, erotic-but-not-erotic art! There was a piano, for instance, made of black male genitals! Displayed nearby was an enormous pink, female vulva with a smaller, purple vulva inside it, and a smaller pink one inside that, and so on until it was tiny! The worst part is, the two I just described were some of the lest bizarre and 'erotic' pieces! Why on earth anyone would cre-ate such things is one thing, but then to put it in a place that is technically supposed to have religious connotations is another question altogether. Therefore obviously, I was ruthless in my making fun of it all until we had exited the area.

We exited the palace and re-entered the courtyard where many people were walking around or gathered together. Some were taking photos while others were reviewing their maps. Suddenly, I noticed something that was almost as out of place as the disgusting "art" I had just seen, but not grotesque. Standing nearby was a man dressed in all black. He wore black boots, black pants, a black tunic, black belt with a sheathed sword hanging from it, a black wide-brimmed hat, a black mask, and a black mustache to top it off. Yes, here in Avignon France was a man dressed like the Mexican crime-fighting vigilante, Zorro.

"DUDE! What the heck!?" I exclaimed in both surprise and humor. "It's freaking ZORRO!" I told the girls I would be right back and to wait for me. Speaking to Zorro was now the highest priority. They said they would, so I im-mediately approached Zorro with the old theme song from Walt Disney's Zorro (1957-1959) television series playing in my head.

I went over to where Zorro was and waited for a small group of other people to finish getting their picture with him. After they had finished, I went over.

"Zorro!!" I said excitedly. I wasn't sure what language to speak, but went with French. "Parle vous Anglais?" I asked.

"Yes!" Zorro said with a *Spanish* accent. This caught me off guard but at the same time made a lot more sense.

"So you're not French?" I asked trying to get some answers. He laughed.

"No, no. Colombia!" He replied.

The guy apparently was a simple traveler who made the money to travel by dressing as Zorro and getting people to pay him for pictures. I was impressed that he was able to make enough to do this, charging only €5 for a photo. I failed to catch his real name, probably because I couldn't believe I was in France talking to

ZORRO! It was also really cool that he had a thick, Spanish accent. Colombia is not Mexico, but it's the most authentic opportunity I will probably ever have — it almost felt real. I therefore obviously paid him and got a photo. After a minute or two of talking, I wished him the best and said goodbye. At this point, I wouldn't be shocked if I turned the corner to see RDJ in full Iron Man costume somehow flying up over the wall.

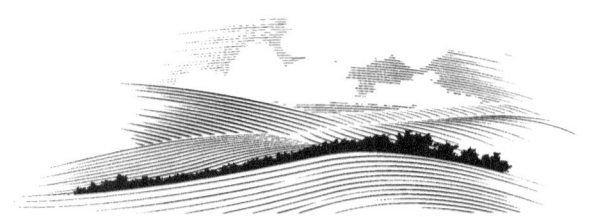

Water Under the Bridge

Monday June 23rd (continued...)

I turned to rejoin the girls, but they were nowhere to be seen! I looked around, walked here and there, but they were gone. I knew I had told them I'd be right back, and I wasn't gone for more than a couple minutes so why had they disappeared? I thought perhaps they went on ahead of me and we would meet at the Avignon Bridge (the one that sticks out half way across the water from the old city). So, I headed in that direction. Admittedly, I was a little frustrated at the though of them simply leaving me behind.

I climbed a set of stairs to get on the wall walk and followed the path around. I really enjoyed the view and the fact that I was walking where medieval soldiers once patrolled. I came to the bridge, but still no sign of the girls. I gave up looking at this point, and resolved to continue my day alone. Just as I was making my way along a certain section of the wall away from the bridge, I heard something that made me stop.

"TIM!" I heard a voice yell. "TIMMM!" Another called. Confused, I looked behind me, to my left, to my right, and over the wall. "TIM! Down HERE!" A voice rang out. I finally managed to look in the right direction where at last I found where the voices were coming from. It was Nora, Jay, and Denise!

"Oh, hey!" I called from the wall walk to the ground. I was still a little sour about being left.

"Where did you go??!" They asked.

"Well," I said, "I told yall to wait a second while I grabbed a photo with Zorro, but after doing so, I turned around to find you all gone. I looked around, but never found you, so I assumed yall got tired of waiting and chose to carry on without me.

"What?! No!" Jay exclaimed. "We've literally been waiting just around the corner in the shade this whole time! I guess we didn't hear and assumed you went to the rest room or something so we were waiting for you to catch up!"

"Yeah!" Chimed Nora. "I would step out every 11 seconds to see if you were coming. You must have snuck past us! Stay RIGHT THERE. We're coming up now!"

"Don't get lost this time, TIM!" Denise added with a gin.

I chuckled to myself in relief that I had not been abandoned. I don't want to sound like a wimp, but my feelings were hurt a little bit — the feeling of abandonment is not pleasant. My hurt over being carelessly abandoned was replaced by immense gratitude for having found such kind and loyal friends. I even felt a little guilty for thinking they had abandoned me so carelessly, but chose not to let it own me.

Once reunited, we continued along the wall walk to the bridge. The wall walk opened up past the primary parapet and became the bridge that stretched out over the water. The bridge was obviously very old and had chunks of stone brick missing in a few places, though not enough to make it structurally unsound. We strolled across the bridge all the way to the end where we looked out over the water. Then, we noticed small, natural steps leading from the pathway down to the water on one side. At the bottom was a space below the bridge created by an arch.

"Hey," I said to the girls. "...Do yall dare me to go down there?" To be honest, I really wasn't actually asking them to dare me. I was already panning on it, but wanted to gauge their thoughts on the idea. I didn't know them that well, and we were technically not really supposed to venture down considering the small gate blocking it off, so when I did, I wouldn't want one of them to run off and tell on me.

"YEAH!" replied Denise. "Let's do it!"

I laughed. Considering her enthusiasm about scaling the wall to get to the wall walk, I shouldn't have been surprised that she would be up for this adventure. Jay wasn't too keen on going herself, but didn't oppose us going. Nora made it clear that she was not coming, but didn't mind if we went. She only urged us to be careful. I really couldn't blame them for not wanting to go. It was definitely a bit dangerous, but I was too excited for the adventure not to risk it. With a smile like I had before climbing the city wall, I moved to the side of the bridge where the steps began.

Looking over the side, I could see the stairs leading down. I now realized the steps were much shorter than I had originally estimated. In fact, the first three steps were a whole quarter sized longer in width than all the others and I could see the sides of many had been chipped away. I could see algae growing on some of the steps which could make it slick and being old, a step could possibly crack and break off under me. The potential for a slip and/or fall was real, so it was imperative that I be careful. I looked down into the water trying to gauge how deep the water looked and how high up I was in case I were to fall. After calculating the risk, I determined it was worth it. I put my valuables in my backpack and set it down in case I ended up in the water. Then, I carefully hopped over the small gate and began my descent.

Each step I made carefully, not putting my full wait onto the next step until I had tested to make sure it wouldn't give way. When it felt solid, I could slowly put my whole weight on it while being ready to move if I felt it start to crack. I further stayed close to the wall figuring the weakest part of the step would be at the edge. The total length of each step was around a foot and a half (so not very big). With the girls looking on, it took me around 3 minutes to climb the 8 narrow, stone steps. Once I was down, I found myself on a stone-concrete island that gave way to the space under the arch. Here, I found another very short set of steps that suggested the existence of a small dock long ago. Under the arch was a place of old rock, dirt, and a few modern beer cans. A minute or two later, I turned to see Denise coming down the steps!

"This is so COOL!" She exclaimed in delight, looking out over the water. "Hey Nora! Jay! You need to come down here! It's really cool!"

"Where are you?!" Nora replied. "Please be careful!!"

"Don't worry!" I yelled up to her. "Nothings gunna happ-wo-wo-ah!" I then tossed a rather large rock into the water. I heard Nora and Jay gasp and come running over to the side of the bridge where I threw the rock. They looked down wide-eyed, expecting to see me in the water. When they discovered it was only a rock, we all had a good laugh. I was a little surprised at how easily they believed I had fallen in. To tell the truth, I was actually a little bit tempted to jump in. The water was pretty, and it was a pretty warm day, but I decided I didn't fancy being soaking wet for the rest of the day. Being this close to water also reminded me of home. All I needed was a cold drink to sip on and a nice chair to sit in, and I'd be happy as could be.

We didn't stay at the bridge too long, and soon were back at the hostel after walking around the city a little longer. Once back, I needed to decide where I was heading. My original plan was to go from here to Venice, Italy, but I had yet to find a direct connecting train ride.

"Maybe this is some sort of sign from God?" I thought. Despite being frustrated at not seeing a way to visit Venice, I sought other options. As mentioned, I had pre-booked my hostel stays up until Bath because I was afraid of not being able to find a place to stay. If I wanted, I could sit down and pre-book a bunch of hostels for my upcoming travels, but now that I had gotten my feet wet in travel, I rather liked the idea of taking it day-by-day and meandering from my planned route as needed. I knew that the next day, we would all be leaving Avignon. I didn't know where Nora and Jay were planning to go next, but Denise had mentioned her plan to visit another city in France called Nice. It had been really great meeting these girls and already felt like we had been friends for a long time. Perhaps if nothing else, I might join Denise in Nice before continuing towards Rome to meet up with Zach. "Choices, choices," I thought.

Unable to make a decision, I chose to put off making that decision for a while in exchange for relaxing in the nice weather. Inside my backpack, I carried a hammock (originally expecting to occasionally sleep in parks, but realized it probably wasn't safe — and I liked showers). I found two trees not far from the center building and got set up. Looking up from my hammock, was a beautiful green canopy of tree branches overshadowing me. Their trunks twisted slightly as they rose so that they were not straight in the way most pine trees in Mississippi are. Their branches became small and thick towards the top, which allowed them to block out most of the sun's rays. Yet, small windows of blue sky broke through providing just enough light to not be fully shaded. Meanwhile, birds chirped passively all around me, and occasionally a busy bee would come buzzing by. All of this, along with the gentle breeze that caused the trees to slowly sway made for a wonderful and relaxing afternoon. For the next couple hours, I listened to Rosco Bandana's album at low volume and journaled. It was a beautiful day to be in beautiful place at such a beautiful time.

Later, after later getting my things packed in preparation to leave in the morning, I grabbed a burger and fries from the grill in the main building. Alycia and James ended up coming in too and invited me to join them for dinner, but I declined. I didn't want to impose on their date and really didn't feel up to going into town just yet. As it turned out, the couple was not a couple after all, but rather happened to meet one another while traveling and decided to come here together. I wasn't certain James was sold on the idea of just being friends — and I couldn't blame him in the least if that was the case. Like I said, her smile alone was enough to knock a boy over. In any case, I confessed that I was still a bit tired from the day and wasn't ready to go out again yet, but we should definitely do something later.

After dinner, I reconnected with Nora and Jay, but Denise was feeling very tired from the day. We three agreed to go for a nice stroll around the city and enjoy our second and final night in Avignon. I also said I wanted to bring my guitar and casually pick while we walked.

"Oh yeah! Do it! I'm actually a jazz singer and could make up some songs." Jay said.

"Ohhh! This is going to be so fun!" Nora exclaimed in agreement. So, I ran into my hostel room and grabbed my guitar.

The three of us left the hostel and strolled into the city. I casually picked my guitar as we walked and the girls enjoyed it. We all agreed that the courtyard in front of the Papal Palace would be a great spot to hang out, play, and sing due to the acoustics. After walking through the streets as we had done the night before, we eventually arrived at the courtyard.

We found a nice place to sit and I began picking. The girls asked me to actually play a few tunes, so I did. Then I requested that Jay sing. She agreed, and I played a simple chord progression. When Jay started singing, I was blown away. Her natural speaking voice is very soft and sweet, but when she started to sing, her voice became powerful! I was also impressed with her ability to come up with words in the moment. After one of these made-up tunes, Jay remarked that she had written a couple. I immediately stopped playing.

"WHAT!? Jay! Sing them! We need to hear them NOW." I said sternly, but in an obviously un-serious sternness. She laughed and agreed. She then closed her eyes, swayed to the rhythm of the song and sang a beautiful tune. It was like being at a concert. What a night! Then, to make things even better, who came walking by but James and Alycia!

James and Alycia were taking a stroll after having just finished dinner. They were heading back in the direction of the hostel when they heard a guitar and singing, and decided to investigate. Together we talked, sang, and joked into the night with me taking every opportunity to make Alycia smile (without seeming like I was trying to). After a while, however, we all decided it was late and time to retire. This was probably a good thing because I still hadn't a clue where I was going to head in the morning.

After getting back, Jay, Nora, and I found Denise up and hanging out. We all sat and talked and got Denise caught up on our evening's adventure, then started discussing what our plans were for the next morning. As it turned out, Nora and Jay had a plan, but it wasn't rock solid. When Denise described Nice and encouraged us to come with her, we all decided that we should. And thus, my plans were made and Denise was thrilled. I now had a plan for the next couple days, and my new friends were going to be with me for longer! I was almost as happy about this as Denise was.

Finally, it got very late and time for bed. We said goodbye to our Aussie friends and bid one another goodnight. I still didn't have a place to stay booked, but at least I would have others in the same boat. I felt excited and couldn't wait to see what the future would bring.

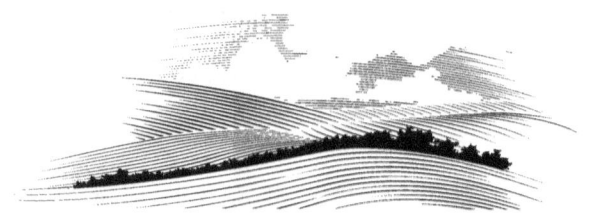

A Cheeseburger Economy

Tuesday, June 24th

This morning I went over to the central building after packing and enjoyed a €2 chocolate chip croissant. However, that was the entirety of my breakfast. Not wanting to lug our luggage across the city to the train station, we chose to grab a cab. Taking a cab allowed us extra time before our train left which we used to find a hot spot. The train station didn't offer it, so we left in search of perhaps a nearby cafe. What we stumbled upon was a park with a sign that said, "wifi park." It was a typical walking park, but with wifi available to connect to. It was perfect! We all sat down on a bench and began searching for possible hostels within a decent price range. Within a few minutes, we had found a place and booked it.

"Dang," I said now satisfied that we had a place to stay for the night. "I'm starving. Are yall?"

"Na, I'm ok." Jay replied. The girls echoed the sentiment.

"I think there were a couple places in the station though, if you want to run over and see." Nora suggested.

It was going to be somewhat long journey to Nice and I knew I needed to eat before leaving or I'd be miserable — not to mention cranky. We then made our way back to the station and I went in search for food. I hoped to find something both filling yet not too expensive. I tried a few places, but none of them allowed carry-out. Then, I saw a take-out sandwich shop liken to Subway. A sandwich seemed perfect.

"Pardon," I said politely to the man behind the counter. He didn't respond. I thought perhaps he was so hard at work, he just hadn't noticed me. "Pardon! Misure?" I said more loudly. This time he looked up.

"Wi?" He asked.

"Bonjour!" I replied. "Parles-tu Anglais?"

"A little." He answered.

"Merci! I would like the Sandwich Americano please?" I requested.

"No. We don't have that." He replied, then brushed me off and returned to his work.

I was very confused. There was a sign in front of the store with a list of items, all of which were in French. The only thing I could read was the sandwich in large, bold, colorful letters that read, "Sandwich Americano." I reviewed the sign to make sure I hadn't read it wrong. I wondered if maybe he had misunderstood me.

"Sorry,…you don't have the Sandwich Americano?" I asked, this time pointing to the sign. The man responded by mumbling something in French that didn't sound very happy before replying in English.

"NO. We don't have that." This time, he didn't even look up. He simply continued working and mumbled angrily in French again. At this point, I was really confused and frustrated. I had done nothing to deserve this type of treatment. It was fine if they didn't have the ingredients to make the sandwich, but if that was the case, he could have at least erased it from the sign and been more friendly about it. A good food service worker would have recommended an alternate choice.

I returned to the girls who had found a place to gather nearby while they waited for me. They had apparently met an engaged couple from Switzerland who were traveling together. I told the group about my poor experience with the sandwich guy, and the girl asked if I needed some help.

"I speak fluent French!" She said cheerfully. "I'd be happy to try ordering for you. What were you trying to get?"

"Oh thank you! I would certainly appreciate that!" I replied. "I was trying to get the Sandwich Americano. They might just be out of ingredients for it or something, but the guy would barely speak to me."

"Oh, that's terrible. Wait here, I'll go over and see if I can get it figured out." She said.

The girl left our table and went over to the sandwich place. I have no idea what the exchange was, but she returned fairly quickly. Her facial expression told me it didn't go well for her either.

"Don't even bother with that place, man." She said. "He's just being a jerk." I thanked her for her attempt, then said goodbye before parting ways.

As it turned out, our route to Nice included 1 hour-long layover in Marseille. Since Marseille was a pretty busy city, I immediately went in search of food after arriving. This station was in fact much bigger and busier than that of Avignon and had many more options. Included in the options was a McDonald's. This gave me an idea.

I went over to the McDonald's and found out what the price for a cheeseburger was. I compared that price to the typical expense of one in back home.

Considering these variables, I felt I could then estimate what the economy was like. An economical estimation based on the price of a McDonald's cheeseburger. For example, the price for a cheeseburger back home is around $1, which is ~€1.33. I had heard that a cheeseburger in Switzerland was around €10, which suggested that I would not be able to afford anything there. I called this strategy, "The Cheeseburger Economy."(*Disclaimer: This strategy for estimating an economy has not been approved the NEA - National Economic Association*).

I quickly found a sandwich shop after employing my Cheeseburger Economy strategy. I was able to order with ease and the server was happy to help me. After getting my sandwich, I rejoined the other girls who had also decided to get some food. I told them about my experience with *this* sandwich shop guy and expressed my gratitude for his willingness to serve me.

We boarded our train after the hour layover and found it to be somewhat of a challenge. There were many people riding this particular train for some reason, which made it impossible for us to all sit together. We attempted to save seats, but others would move our things or sat around it — rude. In the end, the best we could do was sit two rows down and on opposite sides of one another. Denise and I sat together while Nora and Jay sat two rows back and to the right. We preferred to all be together, but there wasn't much more we could do.

"Geez, it's kind of warm in here." Denise remarked as we waited for the train to pull out.

"It is, isn't it?" I agreed. Denise put her hand up the the vent.

"I don't think the A/C is working." She said troubled.

"Yikes. I hope it kicks on by the time the train moves or else it might get stinky in here." I replied.

Unfortunately, the A/C never did kick on. The only relief was the stops along the way where a blast of fresh air would rush inside whenever the doors opened. However, the view of the countryside almost made up for it. Looking out across a body of water stood a cluster of tall mountains. The water met the mountains directly upon their rocky feet. Meanwhile, a boat rode smoothly across the top, creating small waves for a few locals enjoying the cool, rocky beach. I had never been to Nice before, but I sure hoped it might be something like this.

As we pulled into the greater Nice area, the crisp, blue Mediterranean Sea met the sides of mountains as palm trees lined the rocky beaches reminding me of a cross between Florida and Rio De Janeiro (I've not been to Rio, but have seen photos). It's as if the two places had a baby, and Nice was its name.

After getting checked into our hostel, the girls and I parted ways for food. They wanted a cheap chain (like Subway) whereas I wanted something better. I had seen a restaurant on the main strip leading from the beach to where out hostel was that was advertising bison burgers! Since I had never had bison yet always wanted to try it, I couldn't pass up the opportunity. I just never imagined I would try it outside of North America. It ended up being delicious.

After dinner, the girls and I regrouped at the hotel and decided to take a beach walk and go for a dip in the water. As we made our way back down the main strip, we really took in the sights. In the main square, for instance, there was a statue of Apollo standing in the middle of a fountain surrounded by copper mermaids, seahorses, fish, and dolphins. Near Apollo was a large concrete grid-space with water seeming to leap up out of the center of 1 square, then disappearing into small holes in the next. A few children played in the area and could be heard laughing in amusement as water shot over their heads.

After making it to the beach, I noticed that rather than sand like back home, the beach was made up of stones. There were, however, patches of sandy beach featuring volley ball nets for public use and other patches for private enjoyment (i.e. owned by condos and such not available to everyone). Across the beach were people playing volley ball, lounging in the sun, or taking an end-of-day dip in the sea. Ahead of us to the east was a high hill (or mountain?) in the distance that looked like it would provide a great view of the city. We continued along the beach towards the hill until coming to a rocky peninsula that stretched out over the water. Near the end of the peninsula was a break in the rocks forming a rock "island" if you will.

I decided to jump from the peninsula to the "island" rock and take a seat. With the girls watching curiously. I then slowly began to sing Ariel's iconic song from Disney's The Little Mermaid (1989) at the top of my lungs as the water crashed against the rock I sat on. I managed to make Nora cry with laughter at how (intentionally) horrible my singing was — and imagining me as a mermaid.

After my comical display, I returned to the main peninsula where the girls and I found a great spot on the rocks with a nice view of the city across the water. We sat here for a while before returning to the beach walk and finding a place near the shore.

"So," Jay said. "Are going to for a dip or what?"

"Ehh," I replied. "I was planning on it but it's gotten a good bit cooler."

"Speak for yourself!" Denise exclaimed. Jay was right behind her and I followed.

"WHOOO!" I shouted as the water splashed against my belly-button. The water was *quite* cool. It reminded me of experiences as a kid at my buddy Will's river house in southern Alabama. We would jump in the water, scream at how cold it was, then hop out immediately to warm up in the sun before jumping in again. After a few cycles of this, our bodies would adjust. Here, however, the sun was down and the breeze was constant, and I didn't have a towel. Nora, meanwhile, had grabbed my camera and filmed my failed attempt to get in the water along with my retreat. She naturally made fun of me the entire time for being a wimp — and it was very warranted. It didn't help that each time a wave would hit my waste, I would emit a high-pitched, falsetto yelp in response to the water's temperature.

We eventually made it back to the hostel around midnight and briefly discussed what we should do the following day — that is, Jay, Nora, and I. This was sadly Denise's last night with us. For this reason, we all tried to stay up as long as we could to continue being together. We had all gotten so close in such a short amount of time, and were naturally very sad to be breaking up. However, exhaustion eventually won out. I bid the girls a good night and Denise a fond farewell before retiring for the evening.

After getting settled into bed, it suddenly donged on me that we had neglected to find a hostel for the next night because we only booked this 1 night! Those were my last thoughts before exhaustion overtook me and I slipped into a dream.

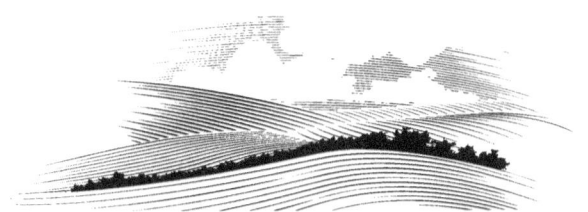

The Mountain Fall

Wednesday June 25th

My first thought upon waking up was, "We need book another night or find another hostel asap." I went down to the hostel lobby to wait for the girls to get up to make it a community effort. Meanwhile, I grabbed a cup of coffee and took a seat at a small table with wicker chairs. As I got to the bottom of my coffee, I became increasingly concerned. The girls had still not appeared and it was nearly 10am. Hostels go quickly in places like Nice, so I didn't want to end up having to pony up for an expensive hotel. I therefore chose to go ahead and book myself a room. I felt pretty confident the girls would book the same hostel. I also considered going ahead and booking them a room too, but was afraid they might book the room themselves and the hostels don't do refunds on reservations. I decided that the best thing to do would be to simply remain in the lobby until they came down and let them know what the deal was. An hour later, however, I got a message on Facebook.

"Good morning Tim!" Nora wrote. "Just so you know, this hostel is out of rooms for tonight, so we booked ourselves and you another hostel!"

I believe "palm-to-face" is the common expression for this type of circumstance. While I was touched that they were concerned enough to get me a room also, I had already paid for the night at a different hostel than the one they booked us for! I froze for a moment, then laughed out loud at the predicament. How could I not? Fortunately the hostel I had just booked wasn't too far away, so I immediately went over to see if I could get a refund.

The girl working the front desk at the hostel was nice, but said they didn't do cancellations. This was expected. However, I wasn't going to give up that easily. I explained to her my situation and tried to sweet talk her. I offered to go buy her flowers, lunch, and/or coffee. She laughed at my gestures and confessed that she wasn't a coffee girl.

"BUT,…" she added. "Maybe if you go to the bakery and buy me a croissant, I will speak with my manager when she arrives — if she comes in, to see if she will? I can send her an email and call her too."

"Done! Wait,…where is the bakery?" I asked. She giggled at my enthusiasm and cluelessness, then told me where the bakery was and how to order what she wanted in French. I could tell by her body language that she really didn't expect me to do this, but was getting a kick out of our interaction. "Ok!" I said determined, "I shall go and return with your croissant!"

I dashed out of the lobby and power-walked to the bakery. To her great surprise, I returned around ten minutes later with exactly what she wanted. With a big grin, she took the croissant from me and took a bite. She then immediately picked up the phone and spoke to someone who she instructed to deliver a message to someone else regarding my case. She then also sent an email to this person who could remove my reservation with no charge. I was very grateful for her help and thanked her. I stuck around and talked with her for a little bit before returning to my previous hostel to move to the new one.

While in line to drop our stuff off at our new hostel before check-in time, there were two girls ahead of us in line who ended up being from Canada and were checking in. Jay and Nora naturally hit it off immediately with them, and they seemed pretty cool. One was named Rene and the other was Ashlyn. Rene was a tall, lovely black girl with long bradded hair worn in a bun. She was really friendly, easy to talk to, and had a great sense of humor. Ashlyn was a little shorter with golden toned skin and long, dark hair. She was more quiet than her friend Rene. However, when her big brown eyes caught mine, I was taken aback by how pretty she was. I felt like Odysseus upon meeting the sirens! I started to speak to her a few times, but had trouble recalling words so I resolved to merely sit back and try to seem cool while Jay and Nora did most of the talking. Somehow we all realized that we all loved watching the sun set and thought it might be nice to watch it together.

"So, we'll meet at Apollo at 6, then head up to the hill for sunset?" Nora asked in conclusion. She was referring to the big hill we saw the night before.

"Yeah! Sounds good!" Ashlyn and Rene replied together. "We'll see yall there!"

I was very pleased with my luck. Not only would I be watching a sunset, but also get the chance to remember words and talk to Ashlyn! Today was already off to a great start. After getting our things secured, we planned to climb the hill (or maybe a better word would be *small mountain* because it was quite high), then go to the beach. We were eager to catch the high view during the day time for a great view of the city and also find a superb spot to catch the sunset later.

The journey from the new hostel to the hill was a considerable walk. From the hostel, we went down the main strip, past Apollo and his fountain, down along the beach walk, and beyond the peninsula from the previous night. The redeeming factor of the long walk was the scenery. Waves crashed onto the rocky beach as multitudes of people bathed in the sun or played volley ball in the sand patches.

Eventually, we came to the foot of the hill where we were met by stone steps. We climbed the steps up and up and up and up. Then the steps turned into a flat incline. We continued up until we finally made it to what we assumed was the top.

There was a nice space with a great view overlooking the ocean which stretched out for miles before the city and the bordering mountains to the north. We rounded a corner casually to discover that we could yet continue up, so we carried on up the path until we hit another level. This time there was an even better view of the east side of the mountain. Here, we could see a sea port with a very large ship coming in. The girls and I got a few pictures, and I scared them by sitting on the ledge with a leg hanging over the side (*sorry, mom*).

"If I slip," I thought to myself while peering down, "unless I am able to catch myself on a few limbs on the way down, that'll be it for me."

I felt really courageous doing this and having this thought. I wasn't particularly fond of heights, and I knew very well that if I wasn't careful, I really could fall to my death. Yet, rather than thoughts of fear, my thoughts were logical options for what I might do *were* I to slip. I think part of this was the fact that my greatest fear involving a plane had (for the time) been conquered. At least in the situation of falling, I would still have the ability to do something about it rather than merely hold onto my seat helplessly in a plane hoping only to God that I would make it.

Suddenly, my ears pricked up. I distinctly heard the sound of water coming from somewhere nearby, but couldn't figure out where. The girls were a bit tired from the climb, so I offered to go scouting to see if I could locate it, then come back and get them. They accepted.

I set off excitedly at a bit of a jog. I was once again thankful for my training as I still had plenty of energy. On my way further along the path, I discovered an excavation site! A real life excavation of an old cathedral tower was in progress! I wished so badly to go in and have a look, but there were signs making it clear that entry was strictly forbidden. I looked from the path for a minute to take it in, then continued along the path.

As I turned the next corner, I immediately found what I had been looking for. From the very top of the mountain came a huge waterfall and yet another lookout point with the greatest view yet! It was all very beautiful, but also extremely loud. The water crashed into the rock-pool below with a constant rushing sound and the mist pounded against my face. It was refreshing in the hot sun, but I knew that if I stayed too long, I would end up getting soaked. Before allowing the mist to drench me, I returned to collect the girls and show them to the view.

It wasn't long after I brought the girls to the fall that we realized it was getting near our check-in time and still wanted to hit the beach for a little while before checking in. After a couple more photos, we hurried back down the mountain and along the pathway that followed the beach. We chose a spot on the rocks directly in front of the main strip so that our route would be a straight shot from the beach to our hostel. Here we reclined in the sun, enjoying the beautiful weather and the view…which was amazing!

The waters of the Sea had the most beautiful coloring I had ever seen. In the shallows near the beach, the water had a crisp, teal color. Looking out beyond the shore, the water transitioned into a light blue, reflecting off the sun. Beyond this, to the horizon, the ocean became a deep, blue color, deeper than the deepest blue I had ever seen. The transition between these shades of blue were extraordinary, reflecting the creative design of its maker. However, there was one major con to this beach.

Although it was aesthetically pleasing to the eye, I absolutely hated the rocky beach of small stones. The rocks were loose and hurt to walk on, and not real comfortable to sit on either. I struggled with which I hated more. Sticky sand that gets everywhere, or rock that hurts to walk on. Both may be equally terrible. However, the rocky beach did not deter us from enjoying ourselves. We basked in the sun, enjoying the cool breeze off the water, and watched as crazy people attempted to body-surf the absolutely massive waves crashing against the beach. The waves actually ended up being so ferocious that the Beach Patrol eventually told everyone that the ocean was off limits. They walked by and called people out of the water. A few were even forced to leave for not complying. I told the girls that if this had not been the case, I probably would have gotten in. They just laughed.

After spending sufficient time enjoying the beach, we headed inland. It was time to grab our things from our last hostel, check into our new one, and get ready to go catch the sunset.

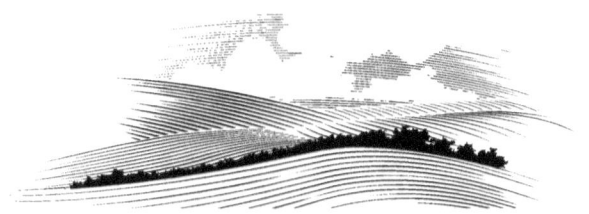

Waitin' On A Woman

Wednesday June 25th (continued)

W e still had plenty of time before we needed to meet up with Ashlyn and Rene after getting checked into our new hostel— or so I thought. I freshened up and was out shortly while the girls took more time. This didn't surprise me because girls always take more time to get ready while guys are in and out in no time (most anyway). I waited patiently as I thought about that song Brad Paisley did with Andy Griffith called "Waitin' On A Woman." However, I soon happened to look down at my watch to realize it was 5:45!

"Girls!" I hollered outside their door. These hostel rooms were two-bed rooms and the doors opened up to the lobby. "It's 5:45!"

"Oh! Uh, sorry!" They called back. "We're not ready yet."

I was afraid that Ashlyn and Rene might arrive on time and think we are no-shows. This would not only be very rude, but my second chance to talk to Ashlyn would be lost!

"Should I go ahead and meet the girls and let them know yall will be along in a bit?" I asked.

"Yeah, go ahead! We're coming!"Nora replied. And with that, I took off.

"So much for being cleaned up." I thought to myself as I grabbed my bag and hurried out the door.

I looked down at my watch to see that it was now 5:49! I had 10 minutes to get from the hostel to the fountain or else risk losing my second chance. The distance between the hostel and fountain was not exactly short, so there was only thing I could do: run. And ran I did.

With my hat backwards and the contents of my bag jingling around, people could hear me coming up behind them at ten yards away. As I ran past, I was given several weird/confused looks. Beads of sweat dripped down my forehead which made me thankful I had applied deodorant before leaving. I kept my breathing steady as I had done playing soccer and focused on maintaining a constant pace. Occasionally, I would slow my speed in hopes of not sweating TOO much, but never stopped completely. Eleven minutes after leaving the hostel, I arrived at the fountain.

I had half expected to see Ashlyn and Rene standing around waiting, but they were nowhere to be found! I was actually relieved that they seemed to be running a little late themselves. I took the opportunity to catch my breath, cool off, and wipe the sweat from my face and hoping I wouldn't stink. However, after waiting patiently for several minutes, there was still no sign of them. After ten minutes of waiting, I gave up and started making my way back disappointed.

I took an easy pace on the way back and kept my eyes peeled for Jay and Nora. At this point, I felt like it would be my luck that they would pass me headed to the fountain and I would end up at the hostel alone. To my surprise, I actually ran into Ashlyn and Rene.

"Hey!" I said.

"Hey…" The replied nonchalantly.

"What's up?" I asked, not sure if they were just late or if something had changed.

"We're headed to find some dinner." Ashlyn said.

"Oh," I answered a little confused. "So yall aren't going to watch the sunset with us then?"

"No yeah, we are! We'll catch up with you all on the hill after we get dinner!"

"Oh, ok! Cool. Sounds good." I replied.

I couldn't help feel a little annoyed. They were extremely late and didn't seem to be concerned about it at all. There were no apologies or mention of that fact. At this point however, being hot and tired from my jog in order to ensure that we weren't late, I cared little. I assumed that one of them had spoken to Jay or Nora, but wasn't worried about it if they hadn't.

"If it's meant to happen, then we'll catch up and it will happen," I thought after saying goodbye to Ashlyn and Rene. "But if not, then we won't, and I'm good with that." A casual walk later, I had made it back to the hostel.

Once inside the air conditioning of the hostel, I sat back and relaxed in a chair to cool off. The girls weren't in a big hurry, and were kind enough to wait while I changed out of my sweaty shirt and into a dry one. Next, I grabbed my guitar, we stopped for a quick bite to eat on the way down to the water, and soon arrived at the hill (or mountain).

Again, the girls and I climbed and climbed all the way up to the fall. Only this time, we saw that the path actually continued beyond the waterfall. We followed it a little ways and found yet another lookout point which was very nice, but the path did not stop. The girls chose to stay there, but I was eager to find the very top. I therefore continued and discovered what was clearly the very top! The view from this point was absolutely brilliant! The sun was now barely over the mountains and just about to set! I knew the girls would want to enjoy this view as it was far better than any of the others, but I also feared that in the time it would take me to retrieve them, we might miss some of the setting. Yet, because I am a gentleman, I chose to risk it and raced back to find them and bring them up.

I managed to find the girls and get them up quickly before the sun hit the tops of the mountain range so we didn't miss anything. I was disappointed that there had been no sign of Ashlyn and Rene, but accepted it for what it was. Instead, I focused on my excitement for the spectacle, and deep gratitude for the amazing friends I had with me to enjoy it with.

My bliss was suddenly interrupted when security guards started making people leave! The mountain closed at 7:30 and it was about that time. It was a complete buzz kill. We had managed to see the beginnings of the sunset, but there was plenty more yet to go. Part of me wanted to hide, then finish watching before quietly heading back down. Had the girls not been there, I may have. However, as it were, we reluctantly made our way to the bottom, hoping we might still yet be able to catch the last of the sunset down on the rocky peninsula.

As we walked along the beach toward the peninsula, who did we meet but Ashlyn and Rene! Apparently, they had gotten to the base of the mountain not long after we did, and were afraid they wouldn't make it before the sun set. They then found a spot nearby to watch and hoped they might catch us on our way up or down. Fortunately, the sun had no finished setting so there was still time! I suggested that Ashlyn and Rene join us on the peninsula to which they agreed, so I led the way.

Despite being kicked off the mountain, the evening turned out to be beautiful. We all sat together on the rocks near the water and watched the sun set over the mountains behind the city. Somehow, I managed to end up sitting next to Ashlyn AND was able to remember words to have a nice conversation. Better yet, since I had my guitar with me, I picked a few tunes and sang a few songs. She was impressed. I also picked some jazz chords so Jay could serenade us with her off-the-cuff jazz songs. I joked with Rene and talked to Ashlyn between songs and we all swapped stories from our travels so far. Jay, Nora, and I loved telling how we had randomly met in Avignon along with Denise, almost instantly became good friends, and how none of us had planned to visit Nice but had come with Denise because she was awesome.

After enjoying the cool, night air, we eventually decided to head in. On the way, we stopped at a local venue for a few drinks. We met a random guy from the UK there who ended up taking an interest in Ashlyn, and an American girl named Jen who was apparently also staying in our hostel. I stayed as long as I could, but was tired from the day and soon was forced to call it a night. I reluctantly said goodnight knowing that I leaving the UK guy with no competition, but I wasn't worth anything as tired as I was. I left with a sinking feeling, but hoped for the best.

"Maybe he'll mess up and make me look more appealing." I thought as my head hit the pillow. All I could do was hope for the best.

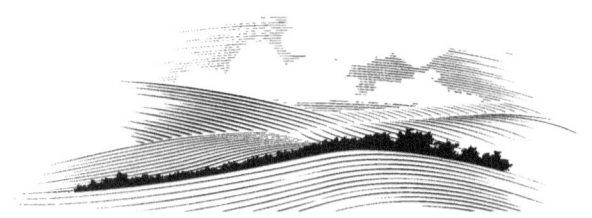

The Buzzing Opportunity

Thursday, June 27th

I woke up this morning from an excellent sleep. After yawning big and properly dressing, I went out into the lobby. Here I saw Jen from last night. She and I didn't talk much last night due partly because I was busy talking to Ashlyn, and partly because I didn't stay out very long. Seeing her sitting there, I decided to be friendly and join her.

Jen turned out to be an American from Texas! I was thrilled to meet an American and one who knows what grits (a southern breakfast item) are at that! While we talked, I noticed the door to Ashlyn's room open. My eyes lit up expecting to see her come out. Then a rock formed in my gut when the guy from the UK came out looking haggard and headed for the hostel exit with a bit of a swagger.

I then looked back at Jen who continued telling me something, but I didn't really hear her. For a few moments, I merely looked and nodded at Jen as if I were paying attention, but really wondered if things might have been different had I stayed out last night.

"Maybe he just got super drunk and crashed on the floor." I thought to myself."

"Oh, that's awesome!" I simultaneously replied to Jen who had mentioned something about skiing while on vacation somewhere recently with her family.

"Yeah, maybe," I followed up to my last thought," "but that swagger he had really said something."

Suddenly another door opened up. From behind it came Jay and Nora who joined Jen and I. We all sat and discussed what we thought we might want to do today as we sat.

"Jay and I REALLY want to go on a walking tour." Nora said.

"Yeah, and maybe we can also find a local guy to take us fishing!" Added Jay excitedly.

"WHAT?!" I exclaimed, then laughed. "No! That's dangerous!" Yet despite my concern and attempts to steer them away from such an idea, they wouldn't budge. They were very confident they could find a nice person to make this a reality for them and insisted on trying. I did not support their decision, but knew I could not stop them.

Jen, on the other hand, was very interested in finding coffee. As it happened, I also was very interested in finding coffee. Jen also hadn't been up to the hill yet and really wanted to do so, but would prefer not to go alone. In the end, I suggested that Jay and Nora go ahead and do their own thing while Jen and I went to find coffee. I also offered Jen my company up the hill since I really didn't have any big plans. At the end of the day, we agreed we would all meet back at the hostel for dinner. Now with a plan, we all parted ways for the day.

Having no idea where to specifically search for coffee, Jen and I simply picked a direction and started walking. Making like the Toucan from Fruit Loop cereal commercials, we followed our noses through the streets and down allies near the beach until we came to a small, local shop. We were seated at an outside table where we ordered coffees and a little something to eat.

The weather was incredible as we sat, talked casually, and took our time fully waking up. Unfortunately, the coffee didn't actually do anything to help wake me up, but it still tasted good. Jen and I discussed this and that under the shade of the large umbrella above us for around an hour until Jen voiced that she was ready to go. I could have sat there all day in the beautiful weather, but I understood her excitement.

On the way to the hill, we passed a wine shop and both wandered in. While browsing, she decided to grab a bottle. She offered to share, so I thanked her and offered to keep it in my small backpack for safe keeping. From here, we went directly to the hill and were there within several minutes.

We kept a steady pace up the steps and along the inclined path. I led her past the first lookout point the girls and I had discovered and instead took her to the second where the port was. I went over to the rock wall, placed my bag down carefully, and hopped up onto the ledge. I let both legs dangle down over the side and leaned back onto my hands. Jen stood behind the wall looking out and taking in the view. Then, to my surprise, she hopped up onto the ledge and sat next to me in the same manor. She was clearly and adventurer. Next, she reached down behind her and pulled the bottle of wine out of my backpack.

"Shall we?" She asked. It was really just a hair early, but considering the view, I couldn't argue.

"Sure." I agreed.

Jen then popped the cork, took a big swig, and handed it to me. I did the same. As we talked and laughed, enjoying the incredible view in the perfect weather, a large ship pulled into the harbor below. We watched as it came in and readjusted itself until it was flush with the dock before mooring.

"You know," I suggested after taking another swig. "We really ought to be careful. It's a long way down from here."

"Yeah, you're right." Jen agreed. "Is there another spot?"

"Oh yeah, for sure! There's a water fall ahead, then there's the very top. The top view is pretty incredible." I explained.

I handed the bottle back to Jen who took one more swig before popping the cork back in. We then carefully climbed down off the ledge. I then led her towards the waterfall that I had discovered, only something wasn't right. Last time, I had distinctly heard the sound of water. This time, I did not. As we rounded the corner to enter the waterfall area, we found that the waterfall was gone — off. The rocks were still there, along with the pool, but there was no water falling! It was all fake!

"Wow." I said. "Sorry. I guess this is a bit of a let down." All we could do was laugh. We explored the area for a bit and enjoyed the view of the city. Both being adventurous, we attempted to scale the inside of where water would have been falling. Unfortunately, this didn't last long as the rocks we were stepping on and clinging to were very slick. We decided we didn't feel like risking the fall into the water and thus getting very wet (the pool still had about a foot of water in it).

Next, I took her to the top of the hill where we could see the entire city, the ocean, and bordering mountains at the same time. It was beautiful. As I leaned against the railing into the wind and gazed across the city, Jen joined me. At one point, she confessed with a laugh that she was a bit of a light weight and despite the relatively small amount of wine we had consumed, she was a little drunk. Then, she seemed to move in closer to me. Out of the corner of my eye, I noticed her tilt her head and looked up at me with a smile.

She was about a head shorter than me, blond hair, green eyes, tan skin, and a bright smile. She wasn't hard to look at either — easy on the eyes as some might say. Perhaps due to the wine in conjunction with the scenery and atmosphere, there almost seemed to be a romantic vibe in the air. I turned slowly over my shoulder in her direction. She met my eyes and did not turn away. I immediately got the curious yet certain sensation that she both desired and was expecting something to happen.

"Should I?" I wondered in that moment. I considered the pros. "It would make good use of the romantic vibe, she is nice-looking, and it might make a nice story for my journal." I thought. "But then again, what would be next? I barely know her. What if I get to know her and she turns out to be bad company, then hangs around and prevents me from talking to another girl I could meet later?" All of this took place in my head in a matter of around 4 seconds. I then nodded my head, then turned back towards the view as if to silently (and obliviously) say, "yeah, this is awesome!"

Ultimately, my reason for not going for it was simple. It is not wise to make moves in such situations without being of sober mind and judgment. I myself was by no means drunk, but did have a calm, warm buzz.

"Let's wait." I thought to myself as I continued looking forward. "I'll take time to get to know her without the influence of wine, and if I decide I like her and she's cool, I will be confident from this experience that she's into me. Then, I can make a move."

As we were nearing the hostel on our way back, I noticed a market. Seeing it reminded me that there was a small kitchen at our hostel that we were allowed to use. Plus, the United States was scheduled to play Germany in a World Cup match this evening, so cooking a great meal before watching the match would make it all the better! I had no way of hearing anything from Jay and Nora, so I basically made the executive decision for them. I figured the worst case scenario was that there would be a little extra leftover.

"Hey!" I said to Jen. "Let's cook pasta for dinner tonight before the match!"

She supported the idea, so we both went in to find ingredients. I decided I also wanted to try my hand at from-scratch pasta sauce. I grabbed several fresh tomatoes, garlic, herbs, and other spices while Jen got the other items. I had never made from-scratch pasta sauce before, but was somehow extremely confident I could pull it off.

When we made it back to the hostel, Jay and Nora were already there. When they saw the ingredients in my hands, they were too excited. Without wasting any time, we immediately went to the kitchen and started getting everything ready.

Since I was not skilled in slicing tomatoes or crushing garlic, Jen offered to help. However, while I really appreciated her assistance, her attitude became very unpleasant towards me. She constantly made jokes at my expense regarding my inexperience and spoke to me in a way that was extremely condescending. I really knew what I was doing for the most part, but of course desired some help with a few things. Rather than simply giving me a hand, Jen would instead speak to me as if I had absolutely no idea what I was doing. If I said anything back to her, she would get pissed and snap back. At one point I asked her point-blank if something was wrong or if I had done something to upset her. She just gave ma a look and didn't really answer my question. She then kept attempting to takeover the cooking, but I wasn't having that. So, she resolved to constantly tell me to do things that I was either obviously already doing or was about to do, again speaking to me condescendingly and acting as if I had no idea what I was doing.

It ended up getting so bad that even Jay and Nora took notice. At first they assumed we were just playing back and forth, but then slowly realized it wasn't banter. In response, they both came over to say encouraging things about my work. Nora took it a step further even as to make a video of me cooking and commenting on my "awesome cooking skills" in the video. I was thankful for this, and it made me feel better.

"Seriously, you're doing fine." They both said while Jen had momentarily left the kitchen to get something.

"It smells great and I'm stoked to eat it!." Jay said reassuringly

"Yeah, you just keep doing you. Don't worry about what she says. There's no telling what her deal is." Nora added.

I knew what her deal was, or I at least had a good guess. The only reasoning I could come up with was for not making a move at the top of the mountain. She must have really been expecting something that she didn't get, so now she was punishing me. If this was how she acted when she didn't get her way, I was relieved that I made the decision to not make a move — or at least wait until I got to know her. Because of the way she treated me, any attraction to her I had developed previously died.

In the end, everything came out perfectly! The sauce, if I do say so myself, and which Jay and Nora insisted was the truth, was incredible! My only mistake, which you can bet that Jen had a ball with, was that I poured the sauce onto the noodles. I underestimated how many noodles were in the bowl, so when I poured the sauce, it drastically thinned out. I felt like such an idiot. I apologized to Jay and Nora many times, but they assured me that it was fine.

After finishing dinner, I tried to find the match on the tv, but couldn't. I asked the hostel clerk for help. Come to find out, France was not televising the match.

"SERIOUSLY?" I exclaimed both pissed and annoyed. "Are you KIDDING ME?" Yet then again, I was in France after all, so I couldn't be that shocked.

Instead, we chilled together at the hostel trying to decide what to do next. This was the end of our planned time together unless we chose to make another unanimous move. I still had plans to meet Zach in Rome, but had a few days to spare. I checked hostels in Venice, but all the hostels required the booking of multiple beds at once for the room rather than per-bed.

"I'm actually headed to a place called Cinque Terre in Italy," Jen chimed. "Yall should come!"

Jay, Nora, and I all sort of looked at each other. We were all thinking the same thing. We looked up pictures on our devices and saw how beautiful it looked. Since I was using my phone, I slipped over to Facebook and sent Jay a message.

"Look, I'll go if yall go, but otherwise I'm going to find somewhere else to go." I wrote.

"We were sort of actually just thinking something similar. So, I guess let's go for it! It looks amazing!" She replied.

Therefore, we planned to all go to this place together and were stoked not to be parting ways just yet. Next, we looked for available hostels. We found that nearly all of them were over priced. Eventually we found one in an area called Riomaggiore that was decently priced, but to make it so, we had to say we only had 3 people — not 4. The girls figured they could double-up so I could sleep in a small bed or something. We joked about us all basically sleeping together in the same bed (not in a sexual way). The funny thing is, despite having not known Jay and Nora for all that long, if I were forced to share a bed with them, it wouldn't be that weird. It would be like sharing a bed with my [then] friend Krista back home — my closest female friend. Anyway, we would have to be a little sneaky, but the money we would save on "three" people would be worth it. The only thing that could have made our plans better was to have had Denise with us again.

We relaxed for the rest of the evening before eventually calling it a night. With a plan to meet again in the morning, we all headed off to bed.

As I laid in bed, the name Cinque Terre resonated in my mind for some reason.

"Cinque Terre. Where have I heard that before?" I wondered. "History class?" Then suddenly, it hit me and my mind was blown. It was back in Dublin! Inside the Temple Bar where I met that Italian guy and his girlfriend! He had highly recommended that I stopped by a certain place in Italy while I traveled. Cinque Terre, or "the five villages," was the place. I had never heard of Cinque Terre before this and had forgotten about it completely until just this moment! How coincidental that despite me assuming I wouldn't be stopping there, here I was about to visit it the next day.

"This must be God revealing his sense of humor." I thought with a sense of assurance. I now felt like I was not alone, that God was in fact not only still with me, but close, and even planned to show me that I did have what it took to see this great adventure through.

I closed my eyes refreshed in my spirit, and looked forward to the next chapter of this adventure: Italy.

Part V: Italy

Map of Italy: https://d-maps.com/carte.php?num_car=14527&lang=en
- Lines, circles, and words with asterisks are author's annotations and not on original map

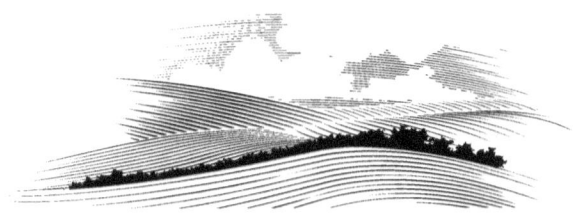

Riomaggiore Del Cinque Terre

Friday, June 27th

As we found seats on the Italian train the next morning, we all immediately noticed a change in the air. From the very beginning, our minds were blown by the hospitality offered by the Italian train attendants and the welcoming, happy atmosphere. They were very friendly, accommodating, and didn't seem irritated in the slightest that we didn't speak Italian! In fact, there was apparently an incident involving Nora having accidentally purchased the wrong train ticket.

When it had come time to show our tickets, an attendant had started down the isle. When he got to Nora, he paused. He spoke something quietly in broken English to Nora that was gentle, then spoke loudly and angrily in Italian to the passengers and made gestures towards Nora before speaking to her again in English. This happened a few times before returning the ticket to her and moving on.

"What was that all about?" I asked Nora puzzled.

"I somehow bought a ticket to a different train by mistake." She explained. "The attendant was really nice when he was talking to me and said it was alright. He understood that I had made an honest mistake. He told me he just had to make an example of me to the Italian passengers because the trains had been having problems with other people doing it on purpose — basically catching a cheap ride. But like I said, he was really nice when he was talking to me and welcomed me to Italy. He then told me to look upset when he handed my ticket back to me."

We all had a laugh at this. It sounded like the attendant had just cause to be ugly to Nora and technically could have kicked her off the train. Yet instead, he recognized an honest mistake and let it slide. We were definitely headed into a different, English-friendly country.

Around 30 minutes after pulling out of Nice, we arrived in Italy and quickly pulled into the tiny, single-attendant building train station of Riomaggiore in Cinque Terre. To our right was the Mediterranean Sea; to our left were bushes, trees, flowers, and and earth running almost straight up towards classical Italian buildings. As we exited the train and started down the street, we came to an enormous wall at least 3 stories high that featured a very large and beautiful mural that appeared to depict the old village — people working in a field, carrying baskets filled with what appeared to be wheat, and other classic labors, all with the backdrop of the sun shining down over the sea behind them.

We continued down the road past the mural and up two long sets of stairs. After climbing the second set of steps, we came to what appeared to be the main strip — a long, narrow pathway leading upward at an incline. It was fortunate that there weren't too many people out and about or else it would have been quite crowded.

As we walked, we passed all types of shops, cafés, and outside restaurants. A few places I noticed was a small coffee shop, a pizza hut (not the franchise, but literally a small hut selling brick-oven pizzas), carts with fresh fish sitting on ice, a butcher shop, bakery, a small grocery market, and lots of small souvenir shops. These souvenir shops were selling everything from beads, bracelets, little trinkets, miniature statues, and colorful jewelry. It was such a cultural experience, not to mention all sorts of greenery and beautiful flowers everywhere. I was blown away.

During our journey up the path, I couldn't help be reminded of Aladdin, my favorite animated Disney film growing up. I could almost hear the fisherman from the movie yelling at Jasmine as she passed by, "FISH, fish! We catch'em, you buy'em!" or perhaps the man selling jewelry, "Would the lady like a necklace? Pretty necklace for a pretty lady!" I wasn't sure what the name of the area or strip we were walking down was, so I chose to call it "the market place" after the film.

After several minutes walking up hill, we eventually came to what was apparently the hostel's headquarters.

"You three go ahead inside." Nora said.

"Are you sure?" We asked.

"Yeah, I'm going to go chill on that bench over there. Besides, we told them there would only be three of us." She was right, so Jay, Jen, and I went inside to see about our room while Nora sat down on the bench.

As it turned out, something had happened and the room we had been expecting was no longer available. Fortunately, the owner of the hostels had a few other places nearby. These places nearby were more expensive than what we had planned for and were obviously not going to pay these rates because they mistakenly overbooked. Therefore, we began negotiating what we would pay. During the negotiation, I noticed the owner of the hostel seemed to be rather taken by Jay. It appeared that she noticed this too and started being more flirty with him. Being a guy, I knew that if I left, he would feel more comfortable flirting with Jay, which would give her an even greater advantage (he flirts more obviously, she flirts more, he gives us a better rate). I therefore slipped out, along with Jen to let Jay work her magic.

I chose to go join Nora on the bench which was still in direct eye-sight and ear-shot of the hostel HQ's opened door. From here, I could still keep an eye on Jay and hear her negotiating. If I were to hear anything concerning (Jay in danger/made uncomfortable), I could be back inside in an instant to handle business as necessary.

Using her flirty magic, Jay managed to get the price of our room down below what we were expecting to pay for the one we came for! Better yet, the man said it had one of — if not the best — views! We ended up paying only €50 for 3 nights/4 days. The only kicker was that the man insisted someone show us to our hostel so Nora (again taking one for the team) followed behind us at a distance pretending not to be a part of our group. All the rest of us had to do was distract our guide from taking notice of Nora.

A couple minutes after this, a girl from the hostel came out, grabbed the three of us, and led us up the path and beyond the marketplace. After what seemed like a twenty minute climb up the inclined paths and a few sets of steep steps, our guide finally announced that our hostel was just up ahead. I almost didn't see the building. I saw a stone wall, the branches of a tree covered thickly with green leaves, and shrubbery coming over the side and along the top of the wall.

"Holy….." I said when I realized this was not a mere wall.

Trees grew up and created a large, natural canopy over the top of what turned out to be an elevated porch. Shrubbery grew along the sides and overflowed down towards the street. Bright pink, red, purple, and white flowers were everywhere. To the west, we could see where the road we were traveling down curved sharply to the right and followed along the mountain face. Across the mountain tops, we could see lush greenery and what appeared to be irrigation and farming. To the south, which is the direction the hostel faced, we could see homes that were built into the side of the mountain all the way down. Beyond this was the train station sitting near the Mediterranean coast.

Nearly hidden by hanging greenery and flowers, was an iron gate that opened up to a small stair case hiding against the side of the rocky mountain face. Walking under the canopy of green, pink, and white, the guide led us in single-file up the narrow stairway where the aroma of sweet honeysuckle flowers filled the air.

After climbing what ended up being the first of three short flights of brick and mortar steps, we came to a small space covered by a canopy of trees and flowers. To the left was a metal railing to prevent falling forward. Approaching the railing, we could look South to a stunning view of the entire city and Mediterranean Sea below. To the right, the mountain range continued and we could better see the tops of the mountains. If we looked closely, we could see the the occasional farm house atop the mountains.

Continuing up four more short steps was yet another space just like before. This one, however, was much larger. In the middle was a tree coming up from under the stone with a concrete base creating yet another natural canopy. Under this tree and directly in front of another metal railing were three small tables with chairs around them. This view was even better than the one before. Looking west, I noticed the semi-natural front porch continued along the outside of the hotel. It too featured a narrow canopy of trees and tables with chairs along the railing, and of course, flowers were everywhere. I kept half-expecting Diana of the Amazon to step out at any moment. Neither the greatest description, video, nor professional pictures would do what I've attempted to describe justice. It was easily the most naturally beautiful place I had I ever been.

After climbing through this unreal outside area, we made it to the actual door of the hostel — which was uniquely blue. Opening the big, blue door, we walked inside, passed through a tiny living and dining room, and into our bedroom. Our room was quite large with a small table and chairs, a chest of drawers, and two large windows facing south. A cool breeze lazily flowed through the windows brushing the red curtains to one side. Further, there was a single twin bed, a full sized bed, and a set of bunk beds. To top it all off was a painting of a sunset clearly depicting the scene from the porch. This made me excited to watch it in real life. The only thing missing was an A/C unit, but the weather was so pleasant, I doubted we would need one.

Thinking of Nora, who had continued past us down the road and was likely waiting around the corner, we thanked our guide and sent her back down the road toward the hostel HQ. As soon as the guide had turned the corner, I ran out and found her. I helped her with her things and showed her to the room. We were all super excited about staying here, but now it was time to get lunch. We were all very hungry. We decided we should go back to the marketplace in search of some lunch, then go for a swim.

The four of us hiked back down the mountain which was much easier going down. On the way, we chose to find that pizza hut we had passed and get a pizza. It seemed like the only logical first-meal to have upon entering Italy! Therefore, we found it shortly after arriving back at the market and considered the menu. The price for a pizza was a little higher than what we had expected, but considering the fresh ingredients and the fact that it would be made by local Italians in Italy, it seemed worth it. We agreed to go simple — pepperoni and cheese. Fifteen minutes after ordering, we had a freshly baked pizza before us.

As we opened the box, the aroma of fresh tomato sauce, basil, other herbs, and melted cheese filled our nostrils. We wanted to dig in immediately, but decided it would be best if we found a great spot to lounge while we ate — rather than a nearby bench — to really enjoy it. I then suggested we go sit on the rocks down by the water. The girls agreed, so we took the box and followed the street down toward sea.

As we followed the path southward, the street turned slightly, and abruptly became a steep decline. Then, the scene opened up into a small bay, surrounded by rocky cliffs from the mainland. There was no beach to speak of, only flat rock that met the waves. Crystal-clear blue water drifted into the bay from the sea and broke upon the rocks which either stuck up out of the water within the bay or where the water met the rocky surface of the land. All along the mouth of the bay, people were lounging on the natural rock formations over the water, soaking in the sun, and taking the occasional dip. A few small vessels were also docked in this area, such as motor boats, kayaks, and canoes.

We found a nice, semi-comfortable place right next to the water which was almost level with the waves casually braking against the mass of rock. Once settled, we threw open the pizza box and dug in. Still very hot, however, it was impossible to eat it too fast. I took a bite despite the heat, and chewed quickly to let the heat out before throwing back a soda I had picked up at one of the shops on the way down to cool it off. After a few bites like this, the pie cooled enough to really notice the flavor. I chewed the following bites slowly to enjoy the flavor, but was surprisingly disappointed.

"It's really not as good as I was expecting it to be." I finally said, turning to get the girls' reactions.

"Yeah, I agree." Nora replied. "It smelled like it was going to be incredible but is,….pretty ok."

The other two girls echoed these sentiments. It wasn't bad, but I had definitely had better and expected an authentic Italian pizza to be more impressive. The one decisive factor that did not disappoint was the freshness of the ingredients. However, I still felt like they should definitely bring the price down because honestly, a local place on the MS Gulf Coast called Brooklyn's Pizzeria is better.

After finishing the pizza, we decided to check out a part of the city we hadn't noticed before. We headed back up the slope then turned sharply to the right where there were wide steps leading up the side of a mountain. The steps were divided into 2 large levels. On the first level, there happened to be a gelato cart. I looked over while passing by and made a note to get some on the way back. It was my understanding that gelato was like ice cream, but different, and REALLY good. I had also been urged to get pistachio flavor.

On the top level we found a nice looking restaurant that had large, open, natural-rock patio seating area. The view from this area was very pretty, looking out over the bay with the city's colorful buildings on the rocks high above. I naturally had to stop for a photo.

Next, we noticed a path leading on around the mountain to the east. We followed it curiously and were led down closer to the water where there was a small dock. There was also a sign indicating this location as the local ferry port that people could take to hop from one of the five villages to the next. This was a good discovery as now we knew how we could go visit the other villages. A few men fished off both sides from the dock.

Continuing along the path, we were led further down towards the water and around to the other side of the mountain. As we turned the corner, I was filled with excitement and wonder. What came into view was yet another bay. This one, however, was small and featured a rocky beach similar to that of Nice.

As we climbed down onto the rocky beach, I surveyed they area. Small waves broke against the rocky beach as white clouds hovered over the horizon. To the right (west) was a jagged wall of dark rock with the narrow path from where we had entered leading away from the bay and around the side of the mountain. To our left (east) was a steep, rocky incline where the mountain's foot met the sea. This wall was more steep than jagged, with light vegetation growing from within the crevices. Behind us to the North was another wall made of stone brick, red arches, and a walking path above. Because of the ancient look and the red brick arches, a staple of Rome, I couldn't help thinking it might have been built by the ancient Romans! Sure, it could have been medieval or colonial, but I really enjoyed imagining it to be Roman.

With the magnificent scenery all around and the incredible view before me towards the sea, I couldn't help seeing pirate ships in my mind. I could see clearly in my imagination a pirate ship taking refuge in this small cove.

"Pirate's Cove," I named the place to myself. I then pulled out my camera and shot a short panorama video of the area while quietly humming Disney's The Pirates of the Caribbean theme song. Meanwhile, Jen went over and put her feet in the water.

"Woo! Nope!" She yelped. "Way too cold today!"

"Yeah, with the sun not out, and the water as chilly as you just suggested, we probably ought to wait till tomorrow to go for a dip. You know, when the sun's out." I said chuckling. This time, compared to last time in Nice, Nora and Jay agreed.

"Tomorrow then!" Recommended Jay.

"Tomorrow!" Nora echoed.

Instead of getting in, the girls and I simply relaxed and enjoyed the cool air, beautiful scenery, and fun conversation. After being here for a couple hours, I casually mentioned the gelato stand and wanting to stop by on our way out. This comment got the girls thinking about gelato too. Soon, we were making our way back up the side of the mountain, past the ferry dock, through the outside seating of the restaurant, and back down to the first level where the gelato stand was.

I instinctively ordered pistachio flavored gelato from the man at the cart, and put a spoon full in my mouth. Like a cross between ice cream and frozen yogurt, my taste buds lit up! Despite having cost more than I expected for the small container, it was worth every cent. Not even the high-end ice cream parlor back home called Marble Slab could compare to this man's simple gelato cart. There was no marble table for mixing flavors, no toppings to put inside, no chocolate syrup, or anything else to that nature was available. Yet, the texture and flavor of the gelato alone was better than all of those things combined.

As we moved away from the cart with mine already nearly gone, we wandered down the main strip through the market. This time we actually browsed a little.

There were small trinkets, miniature statues, jewelry, and some simple clothing items for sale in all the shops. We momentarily also wandered off the beaten path, but only found small residential flats. One feature I really appreciated despite the simplicity of the flats was the greenery and flowers everywhere which stood out beautifully against the sand-colored architecture.

After a while of walking, I pointed out that the sun was moving nearer to the horizon and suggested we head back towards the water to watch it set. The girls agreed. Soon we were back down and found a great spot on the rocks overlooking the bay to the southwest with the mountains to the north and distant west.

The setting sun reflected off the water towards us, creating what appeared to be a path of light leading out to sea. Between the water and the sun, a warm, orange hue formed, meeting the water below. Fluffy clouds lazily hovered over the mountain tops as a haze of cloud formed around the giant ball of fire, enabling bright reflections and gentle light to stream from within the great spectacle. Soon, the sun fell away to disappear behind the mountains, as the earth transitioned from day to night with the moon and stars beginning to arouse from their celestial slumber.

After the sun had set behind the mountains, we headed back up to our hostel. On the way, we picked up a bottle of wine to share for the night. We thought we might be able to catch a little more of the sun's setting from our high perch, but it ended up being at a different angle so not so much. Yet, we still popped open the wine and shared among ourselves while enjoying the weather, the incredible view over the city, and one another's company.

After a little while, I decided I needed a brief time alone with my thoughts and prayers. I therefore grabbed my guitar and went down to the street level to be somewhat alone. I picked tunes as I reflected on the day and talked with God. When I was finished, I rejoined the girls on the hostel porch. Here, I had a wonderful, deep conversation with Jay about her hopes and dreams for her future life — singing jazz.

"Speaking of" I said, "give us a song, would you?" I then began picking a jazzy-sounding chord progression. She smiled a big smile and began to sing whatever thoughts happened to be in her heart, and they were beautiful. She has such a perfect singing voice for jazz — strong, yet captivating. In this moment, I couldn't help think of Noe.

"He would have loved this." I thought to myself as Jay sang.

Nearly two hours later, we all decided it was time for bed. We discussed it, and agreed that the next day we would go village hopping via the ferry boat. We then all went inside the hostel to our room where I took the single twin bed while they shared the large mattress next to it.

What an amazing day. I couldn't wait for the adventures ahead.

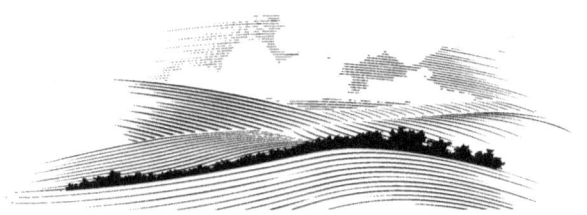

Village Hopping

Saturday, June 28th

After waking up this morning and getting ready, we made our way down towards the water. While walking through the market, we came by a small cafe selling breakfast and coffees. Here we stopped for a bit where ordered a croissant and a cappuccino. The croissant which wasn't as light and fluffy as those in France, but still very good. I ordered the cappuccino because it only made sense to order a drink that originated in this country.

According to history, the cappuccino was named for the coloration when the frothy milk mixes with the espresso. Apparently the color was similar to that of the robes warn by Capuchin friars within the Franciscan order of monks. It was a cool sensation to be enjoying a piece of history. As I sipped my drink and enjoyed my croissant, a girl appeared. Somehow, she and our group started talking. It turned out that this girl was traveling alone, so we invited her to join us.

"I'm Lilly," she said in a familiar accent. "I'm from Australia." Lilly was tall, fair skinned, and had long, dark hair. The girls and I formally introduced ourselves, and after the light breakfast, Lilly accompanied us back to where we had discovered the dock.

This time, a boat was tied off and passengers were climbing aboard. There was a woman selling tickets with a sign indicating that the boat was headed to the village of Manarola. After getting in line and paying the woman, we were soon taking our seats on the ferry. It wasn't nearly the size of the ferries I took from Ireland to England or England to France, but it was still quite big.

Looking down over the side, I was amazed by how crystal clear the water was. It was probably ten feet or so to the bottom, but it looked as if I could reach down with my hand from the surface and grab the sandy bottom. I don't believe I have ever seen water so clear. Not even the coastal waters of the Florida coast or the waves beyond the barrier islands of Mississippi (Ship Island in particular) was the water so clear.

After the boat reached maximum capacity, the line of people boarding was cut off. The boarding plank was removed, and the boat pulled away from the dock. The boat reversed for a minute or two away from the rocky coast, adjusted to face west, then blasted off. The cool ocean breeze instantly beat against my face as we roared across the horizon. Water would occasionally splash up as the front of the vessel broke swells beneath us. Yelps could often be heard from passengers as they were met with sudden cold showers.

At this distance from land, I could get a broader view of the mountainous coast. It was like nothing I had ever seen before! Massive, natural land forms rose magnificently from the water. At some points, the surf was met with jagged rock walls towering a hundred feet or more up. Greenery hung over the tops as if reaching for the waves below. In other instances, the sea rose up to meet the green tops as the mountain bowed down as if inviting us to make port at its foot. I couldn't help but feel a gratifying sense of adventure. For a moment I even closed my eyes, imagining that I was on a great wooden brigantine vessel (colonial era sailing ship) with huge, white masts catching the wind, whisking us off to places unknown.

We rode past many small residential properties along the coast before the vessal slowed and pulled into a village port. The colors of this village exploded against the gray, rocky shore where it met the water. Each building visible was painted yellow, red, blue, orange, pink, and white. Along one of the tall cliffs appeared to be an ancient Roman aqueduct (like a large power line, but for transporting fresh water all across the empire) followed along the side of the western cliffs. We had arrived in Manarola.

Once it was safe to exit the boat, the five of us hopped off and made for the market place ahead. Upon reaching the market street, the road opened up to expose a multitude of restaurants and shopping opportunities. I found a souvenir shop and purchased a tourist map of Cinque Terre which included maps of each village along with the top attractions to visit. Unfortunately, it didn't take us long to realize that while Manarola was very pretty, it didn't have much to offer us aside from shopping and eating (and the restaurants were all very touristy). Therefore, we returned to the dock and caught the next ride further west to the next village: Monterosso.

The boat pulled into the small port at Monterosso not long after leaving. This village was nestled between three great mountain forms, all sloping down toward the water around the village like arms cradling a small child. Unlike the previous village, Monterosso did not explode with color, but instead maintained a warm earth-tone. To the east, the mountain face was rock and grew as it drew away from the village, holding trees and shrubs above. To the west, the mountain turned into a corner created by rocky cliffs at different heights.

After stepping off the boat, we headed inland. Down the strip went, through the market, and past the touristy, area until we came to a small cathedral. It was white, and quite a bit smaller than what I had become accustomed to. Curious, I approached.

Through the double-doors I pushed expecting to see a typical cathedral. However this one was a little different. Aside from being almost miniature, this cathedral featured yellow walls with white trimming. Some of the stone pillars were stone-colored from the ground until about midway where it shifted into a stripe pattern of alternating black and white up to the ceiling. Other pillars featured this stripped black and white pattern from bottom to top. I didn't understand it, but still somehow looked cool.

The four of us spent a few minutes looking around the church before leaving and heading further inland. The further inland we got, the less touristy things seemed to become. While there were still shops, things appeared to gradually get more residential — flats lined the foot of the mountain, small gardens on the grounds, and children's bikes parked along the street. Eventually we came to a small grocery store and went in to grab some cold drinks. It tickled me with surprise when I heard The Gorillaz (an English hip-hop group from the 90's/early 2000's) playing from the speakers of the store. After leaving the grocery store with drinks in hand, we headed back towards the coast as we realized there was nothing of interest further inland.

Next, we found a road that lead up the west side of the mountain nearer the coast. We followed it on around where we suddenly came to a lookout place featuring a statue I instantly recognized! It was Francis of Assisi! Even better, it was the same statue featured in my university professor's slides when we discussed him! I reacted a little bit as if I were seeing a celebrity. The girls looked at each other confused.

"It's Francis of Assisi!" I exclaimed as if this would make any difference to them. They of course had no idea who Francis was.

Francis was a historical figure I learned about who lived during the 13th century. He committed himself to poverty and became a monk much to the disappointment of his father who desired him to become a wealthy knight. He, however, felt called (by God) to leave his home and spread the faith far and wide. He took his conviction so far even as to go on a Crusade where (as the story goes) he ventured into the Muslim camp, gained audience with the Sultan, and preached the Gospel of Jesus to him without losing his head! Apparently, the Sultan was so touched by Francis' "divine foolishness," as it was called, that he decided to simply send him away rather than kill him. Sometime after this, Pope Innocent III claimed to have had a dream where the Church was falling, but then Francis came and held it up. Later, Francis became known for his love of animals, and was ultimately named their patron saint. Finally, in 1209, Francis founded The Franciscan Order which is still a missionary operation all over the world today.

After getting a few photos, the girls and I continued along the path, leaving Francis and his dog peacefully looking over the city.

When we completed our path around the side of the mountain, we saw another large bay ahead and below. We excitedly made our way down along the path that led towards the beach. Then, we noticed this odd-looking structure to our left facing the sea. Thankfully there was a sign to explain what we were looking at. Thankfully even further, there were 2 paragraphs of writing. The first paragraph was in Italian, while the other was in English! If this had been France, English-speakers would have simply been out of luck. I looked down and read the English text:

From this panoramic 'window' you can admire Punta Mesco, the promontory of the mountain that closes the gulf of Monterosso. Its beautiful cliffs are home now to unused ancient sandstone mines. The same stone was used to pave the streets of Monterosso and of other cities. At its summit is 'il Semaforo' (the stoplight), an old abandoned lighthouse and the ruins of the Monastery named Saint Anthony of the Mesco built between the eleventh and fifteenth centuries that also served as a watchtower against enemy invasions. Further towards the tip of the point is a military bunker that dates back to WWII.

We looked out and could indeed see the large, black, circular shape of an old WWII military bunker with slits near the top, just large enough to stick a rifle out of with clear vision. It was a really interesting find, even thought I'm not super into WWII history. Still, it's not something one gets to see every day so I was grateful to have stumbled upon it.

As we continued past the WWII bunker, the view of the bay opened up more clearly. We became excited after realizing that this beach was actually sandy, unlike the one's we had seen up to this point! We could see people swimming in the crystal-clear, blue surf or lounging on the beach. Rows of chairs with orange umbrellas were set up (I assumed for rent) and a large section of what appeared to be kayaks, canoes, and tiny sail boats. Along the coastline we could make out "beachy" restaurants with a tropical themes.

Once we got down to the beach, the girls and I realized we were hungry and decided to find something to eat before hitting the beach. With the aroma of fresh tomato sauce drifting through the air, we agreed that spaghetti would be the best choice. However, upon investigation, we learned that every restaurant offering spaghetti offered it the same way and at the same price. There was no individual ordering. Instead, the order was per table and thus everyone had to get spaghetti. When they brought it out, it came in buckets and was shared. At €18 per person, we quickly decided to push inland away from the touristy areas in hopes of finding a cheaper deal. However, after walking ten to fifteen minutes, we realized the prices weren't getting better and we were getting very hungry. Every restaurant we then attempted to enter was full, making matters worse! Finally, we came to a small, local place with spare seating and immediately sate down.

I don't recall the name of the place, but we were provided menus and ordered quickly. I decided to go with ravioli, which was still more expensive than I would have liked, but I figured it would be filling enough. I fully expected a big plate of fresh, delicious ravioli with lots of sweet tomato sauce on top. After ordering, I sat with eager anticipation with the spice of hunger to make it even better. When the food was brought, however, my disappointment was unquestionable. Four pieces of ravioli sat on a small plate with a little bit of sauce splashed over the top. I was borderline pissed, as I had spent over €15 already on this meal along with a drink. The quality of the meal was superb, but having cleaned my plate in 5 bites, my hunger was far from satisfied. I would have happily sacrificed some of the quality for double or triple the quantity.

After we got down to the beach, we begin to realize how blazing hot the sun seemed to have gotten all of a sudden. The heat beat down with zero cloud coverage above. I was therefore very excited to go hop into the water.

"Oh! Wait!" Nora suddenly exclaimed. "My water bottle is empty! I need to fill it up!"

Jay and Jen also needed to use the rest room, so as to be sure we didn't get separated, Lilly and I said we would stay in one spot and wait for them. Then, once they returned, we could all go find a place on the sand. I hadn't really gotten the chance to talk to Lilly much, so I was ok with this opportunity. There was only one problem. I couldn't remember her name to save my life! Sure, I could just ask her, but we'd been together for hours now and I felt like I'd seem like an idiot. We talked casually, and I avoided needing to use her name as I desperately tried to think of a smooth way to find out.

"Should I try the middle school strategy of asking for her 'full name' with her first name included?" I wondered. "No, that's stupid and obvious." I continued thinking. Then suddenly, I was struck with brilliance. "TIM! You ding-dong! You've got a camera! Do a freaking video!" I then looked at Lilly. "Hey, I'm going to do a quick video since we're not doing anything. A video-log, basically of where I'm at, what I'm doing, and what I plan to do."

I pulled out my camera and started recording myself. There wasn't a whole lot to talk about aside from large statue of Neptune that I kept mistakenly referring to as Apollo. I mindlessly talked about the statue for a moment as my heart raced while trying to come up with a non-weird way to film her and thus introduce her, and ultimately learn her name without her ever knowing that I had forgotten! Then, yet another stoke of brilliance.

"So as you can see," I said to the camera, "there is a statue of Apollo over there and, —" I paused, then looked over at Lilly off-camera. "Did I say it wrong again?" I asked.

"Yeah," she laughed. It's Neptune." She corrected me.

"Ah! Thank you!" I replied, motioning toward somewhere off camera and pretending to laugh at my planned mistake. "Yeah, that's my 'home girl," I said to the camera.

"Hey, good'ay!" She said with a casual wave, leaning into the camera's view. She seemed pretty comfortable being on camera. I was in. At this I turned the camera to her.

"Why don't you tell the camera a little about yourself. I could have introduced you, but it's better that you do it!"

Just like that, she introduced herself as Lilly from Australia and explained why she was traveling. After this, I turned the camera back to myself, mentioned a couple more things, and concluded the video. Mission accomplished! Now all I had to do was make sure I didn't forget again. That strategy probably wouldn't work a second time.

When the girls returned a little while later, they did so with bad news. Jay was burning quite bad from the sun. She was trying to cover her exposed skin with clothing articles, but it wasn't doing the job. She was trying hard not to be the reason we left before even making it to the beach, but I could tell she was pretty miserable. Therefore, while I was really looking forward to swimming and exploring the Neptune statue, I agreed that we should head back for Jay's sake. It was the right thing to do.

We swiftly made our way back up the mountain, past Francis, and found the boat dock again. After a quick ride, we were back at Riomaggiore. Since we didn't get to hit the water earlier, Jay said we could still go to what I called "Pirate's Cove," since there was shade from the mountain side there. Sure, the rocky beach wasn't ideal compared to the one with sand, but it was a great compromise. I had no complaints.

Pirate's Cove ended up being more popping this time compared to last time.. It wasn't crowded, but noticeably more visitors. Once we had chosen a spot, I volunteered to take the first watch over our stuff. As the only man in the group, I felt it was my duty and obligation as a gentleman to do so. Therefore, I sat back and watched as the girls ventured down to the water, then looked out into the sea. I couldn't help think about the fact that I would soon be swimming in the Mediterranean Sea where, in this very place, ancient Romans once swam. I looked out onto the water and imagined triremes and quadriremes (Roman ships with 3 & 4 rows of oars) gently moving across the horizon, perhaps headed to and from Rome, delivering goods or military units.

After ten minutes or so, Jen returned and offered to take my place. Without hesitation, I hopped up and made my way across the rocks towards the shoreline. As I made my way towards the water, I half-wished I had brought a pair of water shoes. I cannot over-emphasize the discomfort I found walking across the large, loose rocks. Some of the rocks moved as I stepped over them, causing me to momentarily lose my balance and have to quickly take another step. Others were firm, but had points that would poke into my soft feet. I expected the rocks would turn into pebbles once I reached the water, which would be more comfortable. To my great disappointment, this was not the case at all. Despite this, my excitement and determination to swim where ancient Romans likely swam overpowered the pain in my feet, the aggravation at the unstable rocks, and the cold temperature of the salty sea.

I waded into the cold water around thigh-deep and cringed. I let out a soft, high-pitched, girlie yelp each time a wave broke against me. I pressed on, stumbling backward each time a bigger wave hit me, forcing me off balance. Stumbling backwards forced me to step back onto rocks that varied in shape, size, and stability. One of them ended up slicing my foot. If I continued in this way, it would only get worse. There was only one thing I could do.

With a deep breath, I plunged myself beneath the next wave. A rush of refreshing but very cold water crashed against my whole body. I then swam a few feet forward before coming back up to break the surface. As I came up, I let out a spew of water and air from my mouth like a whale taking a breath followed by a cry of "Whooo!"

I took a few good breaths while treading water, then set my feet down to judge my depth. At the bottom of my toes, I could feel the rocks — I must have been out around six feet. Looking around, I saw a large rock sitting just below the surface. A few people were climbing on it, but not having much luck staying on. I watched for a minute. When they gave up, I had a familiar thought:

"Challenge Accepted."

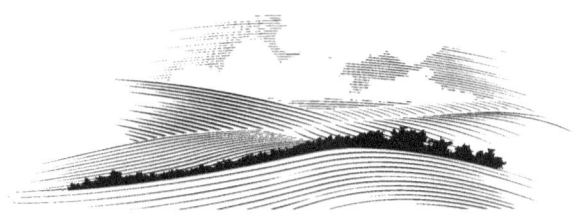

Massimos And The Tuna Surprise

Sunday, June 29th (continued)

I swam over to the large rock. After reaching it, I could clearly understand why the others were having such difficulty staying on. The rock was slick and when standing, the water was ankle deep. Waves rushed over it, making it very hard to stand still. Further, I now realized the waves rushing over the top were a little larger than they had appeared before. Nevertheless, I proceeded as planned.

I soon realized that it was a challenge to even stay near the rock long enough to hoist myself over top it without being knocked off and around by the constant waves. I finally decided to swim out to the south side of the rock, catch the back of a wave, and ride it to my desired destination. Once I was on, I had seconds to grab hold of tiny crevices in the rock with my fingers and toes before the next wave crashed onto my back shoving me forward. I clutched the crevices to withstand the next two waves, preparing myself to stand and dig in with my toes. The hardest part was not being able to see the waves coming, which came at different intervals so perfect timing was impossible. Yet, as soon as that second wave crashed against me, I stood in a squatting position facing south, grabbing the edge of the rock with my right foot's toes like a monkey does a tree while my left foot's toes clutched a divot in the rock's surface. Then, the next wave came in crashing against my ankles. I rocked my body with it hanging on with everything I had. I managed to hang on, then stood up all the way just in time to look up and see another, bigger wave coming right for me. I had a bad feeling about it, but remained steady.

"SWOOSH!" It said as it plowed into the rock and against the top of my shins! In a tenth of a second, I was forced to make a decision. I realized that as this wave hit me, my toes were being forced off the edge. My weight was shifting beyond my control. If I stayed fast, I would most likely slip and fall backwards onto the rock, but feel awesome because I managed not to fall off completely. On the other hand, however, I might hit my head and really hurt myself.

In that instant, I made my decision. I used my planted foot push off the rock towards the water just to the left. Then, half leaping-half slipping, I fell into the sea. As it hit the water, I felt a sharp pain in my foot. I then swam away from the rock into shallower water and away from the larger waves where I could examine the area of the pain. I lifted my foot and peered down below the surface to see that there was a little blood issuing from a small slit in my toe.

I wouldn't say I was paranoid so much as quite aware of the sea creatures that are drawn to blood in the water. It was in the middle of the day as opposed to sun rise or sun set and the water was crystal clear as opposed to murk. Yet, I didn't want to take my chances of a shark, who can smell blood from 3 miles away, just by chance be nearby. When we enter the ocean, we enter a kingdom that is not our own and must be ever mindful of what lies beneath the waves,…and respect them. Suddenly, it also occurred to me that I was some distance away from others, bleeding, and not great at swimming over constant swells. I was concerned that if I attempted to swim quickly across the surface, I would make a lot of noise, creating vibrations suggesting a distressed fish. Therefore, out of precaution, I made my way beneath the surf as quickly yet smoothly as I could back to the shore.

Once back to shore, I hobbled over to our spot and sat on a large(r) rock to investigate my injury. Indeed, I had scrapes and scratches on both feet from walking on the rocks that made up the sea floor and of course the one from falling off the large rock in the water. Despite the cost of these scrapes and scratches, it was completely worth it. I swam in the Mediterranean Sea where ancient Romans swam!!!

When we eventually left Pirate's Cove, it was getting close to dinner time. We discussed gathering some fresh ingredients and cooking dinner together. Our hostel didn't have a kitchen, but the hostel's HQ had one we were allowed to use. Thus, unanimously, we agreed that this was a good idea. Jay, Nora, Jen, and I would therefore part ways with Lilly where we would go freshen up/take showers before meeting up again at 6:30 at the pizza hut for dinner. Lilly was to meet us near the pizza hut. With this plan, we parted ways.

On our way to the hostel, we stopped by HQ so that Jay could make a phone call over the wifi and inspect the kitchen. Here, we learned that the Hostel HQ's stove was not working! Fortunately, the manager said there was another building with flat-style rooms we could use which was near the market. This worked out much better for us. However, by the time we spoke with the manager and found this out, then Jay made her call, we realized we were running very late! It was already 6:15! There wasn't time for us to trek back up to the hostel, shower, and be back down before Lilly arrived at the pizza hut thinking we had stood her up or something! Being the good gentleman, I therefore offered to stay behind while the girls went ahead to start freshening up. The girls then headed up towards the hostel while I made my way down to the pizza hut.

I arrived at the pizza hut at around five till. There was no sign of Lilly, but it was fine. Six-thirty came and went. Still no sign of her. After a couple minutes passed, I hoped it wouldn't end up being an echo of the time I waited for Rene and Ashlyn in Nice. Fortunately, around 10 after, just as I was about to give up and head towards the hostel, I see Lilly hurrying down the street towards me.

"I am SO sorry!" She said when she was just close enough to be heard. "There were several other people all in line for showers, so it took forever!"

"Hey, it's alright! I'm just glad you came!" I was further very relieved that unlike the last time, Lilly actually cared that she was ten minutes late even though I had some slightly bad news for her.

"Actually, I have a little bit of bad news so we have to apologize to you." I explained our situation and she took it well. "So, we can either wait until they get back at which point I will head up to shower, we can set up another time to meet and try again, or you can come with me to our hostel. It's got a beautiful view from the front porch where you can see all the way down to the sea and mountains all around."

"Oh wow, that sounds awesome! Yeah, we can do that." She replied.

"Cool!" I said. "But I do have to warn you,….it's a good hike up." She said she was fine with it, so we started making our way up.

I was actually pretty happy about this. The hike gave her and I a chance to talk 1-on-1, which went really well. It was really nice getting to know her. The fact that she was pretty also didn't hurt.

As we came up to the hostel, Jen came out. She immediately insisted her and Lilly go down and start looking for ingredients in the market. I was a little shocked since we had literally just walked all the way up and I hadn't even gotten to show her the front porch!

"Oh,..ok.." Lilly replied uncertainly.

"Jen," I interjected politely, "We literally just climbed up here. Why not hang out for a little bit then go down?"

"Because," she replied with the same condescending tone as the other night in Nice, "we need to get the ingredients so we can start cooking."

Lilly responded with a subtle facial expression suggesting to me that she noted the tone and wasn't going to fight it. Based on the last experience, I knew arguing wasn't worth it. Yet, I made one last ditch effort.

"You sure you're good with that?" I asked Lilly, ignoring Jen.

"Yeah, that's cool. I don't mind." She replied, seemingly without much choice. And with that, Jen and Lilly made their way away from the hostel back down toward the market.

"At least she won't have to come all the way back up again with the ingredients." I thought.

Jay and Nora were taking turns showering, so I waited patiently for my turn. During this time, I sat on the beautiful patio and took in the view. Eventually, both girls finished and I was able to hop in while they headed down to meet up with Lilly and Jen.

When I met the girls after getting cleaned up, I saw that there was an Italian man with them. I wasn't sure what to think of this. I gave the girls a look.

"This is Massimos!" Jay said. "We met him while we were walking around and invited him to dinner."

"Oh,..ok," I replied a little uncertain. Massimos smiled, shook my hand, and said hello in an Italian accent. I was a little confused, but went with the flow. He had a humble, kindly demeanor and thus didn't seem threatening. However, I kept an eye on him as we walked over to the hostel where we would be using the kitchen.

We went in and climbed the stairs to the correct flat and entered. The girls set everything down and we got to work on preparations. When I reached down and turned on the stove, however, we discovered that it didn't work! I tried several things, as well as Massimos, but nothing happened. At that same time, one of the girls suddenly realized we had forgotten to get the ground beef! Two things now gone wrong.

"What are we going to do now?" I asked in frustration.

"How about we go upstairs and ask someone if we can use their stove?" Nora suggested. I laughed.

"That would be a very unusual request, but, if anyone had the personality to ask and make that happen, it would be you, so....go for it!" Indeed, as described before, Nora had the type of personality that made everyone love her — cute, sweet, genuine, and kind. Basically, if you know Nora and don't absolutely love her, you're a freaking monster.

"What about the meat?" Jay asked. "The market will probably be closing soon, and we're not sure where the butcher is!"

"Actually, I don't eat red meat." Jen replied bluntly. This explained why she didn't eat the spaghetti I made in Nice. I had assumed she was just annoyed with my cooking and refused to eat it.

"Well, you picked the right time to make this known." I retorted. It appeared that we would be eating spaghetti sauce and noodles.

"I could go get some mushrooms." Jen offered, but the rest of us agreed that we needed something more filling than just mushrooms.

"You can use tuna!" Massimos chimed in with a thick accent. We all looked at him bewildered.

"Tuna??" We all said together.

"Trust me! It is delicious! I will make it for you!" Massimos seemed extremely confident. "You use some different ingredients than with beef, but it is still so good! Trust me."

Although tuna spaghetti sounded ridiculous, when you have a native Italian man offering to cook for you who insists that he can make tuna spaghetti and it be delicious, you let him. Make a note of this and keep it forever.

"OK." We all agreed. It seemed we didn't have much of a choice anyway unless we wanted pure veggie spaghetti.

"I will be back." He said. "I will go get tuna and other ingredients." And with that, he left us.

"This is going to be interesting." I said, half laughing. But hey, it isn't an adventure without risks. I went ahead and decided that even if it was terrible, I would force it down. Terrible, cooked food, is better than no food. "By the way,.... who IS that? What is he doing with us?"

"Ohh,.." Jay replied laughing. "When we were walking around before you got here, he came over and met me."

"He basically fell in love with Jay." Nora added.

"Yeah, he's a little unusual, but he didn't seem creepy." Jay assured me.

"Though he DID suggest yall get married." Nora laughed.

"That he did, haha! I thanked him, but said it wouldn't work out." Jay replied.

Jay was obviously also very flattered by the guy, and as I mentioned before, he didn't seem threatening. Now, as it would seem, he was going to cook for us! That is,...if we could find an oven that worked!

Nora and Jay then went upstairs to the other flats and knocked on a few doors. Jen, Lilly, and I were delighted when Jay returned to announce that the couple above us were kind enough to let us come cook in their hostel-flat! It's funny how kind travelers are to one another — there is a unique, unexplainable sense of community.

Lilly, Jen, and I followed Jay up the steps and into this couple's hostel-flat. The couple, Greyson and Rianna were both from Canada and had recently gotten engaged. They were both very friendly and welcoming to us. As the girls and I continued prepping, kept the door open to listen out for Massimos coming up the stairs and talked happily with our kind hosts.

Not long later, we heard Massimos coming up the stairs and called to him. He then appeared at the door with tuna, sardines, and a few other ingredients. After saying hello to our hosts, he took total control of the kitchen and went to work.

"You sit. Relax! I will take care of everything!" He said insistingly, so we stepped out of the way.

While he went about chopping, stirring, and heating, we watched and occasionally asked for cooking tips as he very clearly knew exactly what he was doing. Soon, the warm smell of tuna combined with the tomato smell to produce a unique, but freshly delicious smell that mixed with all the natural spices Massimos masterfully employed.

As the food simmered with Massimos carefully crafting the pasta, Jay fulfilled a small dream of hers which was on her bucket list. As a jazz singer, one thing she dreamed of doing was serenading a young couple. Greyson and Rianna were happy to help her fulfill this dream. Once the couple had granted Jay's request, Jay then sat up tall on the stool she was sitting on, took a deep breath, closed her eyes, tilted her head, and begin to sing an old tune made famous by Frank Sinatra.

"My funny,…Valentine…" she sang with the grace and elegance she so fiercely commanded. From the open window, it seemed as if the entire village of Riomaggiore fell silent to listen. After she had finished, we all applauded in appreciation.

Just as Jay had finished singing, Massimos announced that dinner was ready. We all found a place at the table to sit while Massimos insisted, yet again, on fixing our plates for us. I'll admit, I was still a little weary of eating fish-spaghetti as he set it before me. Fortunately, it was at least fresh tuna, not canned, so it wouldn't have that distinct canned taste. It also surprisingly smelled really good, so I hoped this indicated it would taste good. I picked up a bit and brought it to my lips.

Flavor exploded in my mouth. Never in my wildest dreams would I have ever imagined spaghetti made with tuna would taste good — much less incredible! We each looked up at one another with wide eyes confirming how delicious it was. Massimos beamed at our reactions.

"Is good?" He asked with a grin.

"Oh my gosh! This is ah-MAZING!" Nora exclaimed, speaking for all of us."

"YES," we all agreed between chews.

I couldn't help but chuckle to myself considering that we'd been in Italy for two days now and had not eaten spaghetti because it was so expensive. Then, in comes this Italian man who makes us spaghetti from SCRATCH using not beef but TUNA of all things, and it cost us next to nothing because Massimos went out and bought half the ingredients himself! "Hashtag blessed" doesn't begin to describe the blessing that bestowed us. I said a silent prayer to myself thanking the Lord for such a splendid, random, undeserved blessing.

After dinner, we stayed and carried on in conversation until the girls and I eventually decided it was time to go. We thanked the kind couple for their hospitality and wished them a happy engagement. We thanked Massimos as well for his hospitality and cooking service. I knew I would never forget him. At this point, I would have been happy to have him come along with us, but I later learned that Jay didn't want to lead him on — which I understood.

After we left the hostel-flat, we said goodbye to Massimos and went back to the hostel HQ to return the key to the hostel-flat we initially attempted to use. We further informed them of the problem with the oven. I assumed we would be heading back to the hostel, but Jay, Nora, and Jen suggested we grab a bottle of wine and go sit on the beach under the stars. I naturally approved of this idea. However, Lilly then confessed that she was ready to call it a night.

Since Lilly's hostel was on the way to the beach, we walked her there. Once we got there, she and I got to talking and remained there while the other girls carried on down the road. For five or ten minutes we stayed talking without any unnatural pauses. Then suddenly, I somehow said something that indicated the conclusion of the conversation (I don't recall what it was that I said). I didn't know how to recover without forcing the conversation's continuance, which would have made things awkward. I felt like an idiot, but there wasn't much I felt I could do. So, we just hugged, said goodnight, and she went inside.

I left her hostel disappointed at how it had so abruptly ended. I also failed to get any contact information from her so I would never see, much less talk to her ever again (most likely). It seemed to be a trend that I meet really cool people shortly before moving on. Freddy and the lads in Dublin, the actors in London, Ashlyn and Rene (sort of) in Nice, and now Lilly here in Cinque Terre.

"Oh well," I thought as I headed toward the beach. "Such is life."

I soon made it to the beach with a bottle of wine in hand and sat down with the girls. I popped open the bottle, took a few sips, then laid back to gaze up at the stars strewn across the clear sky. I closed my eyes as Jay sang another pretty jazz tune while the waves gently crashed against the rocky shore in the background.

Tomorrow, the girls and I would be parting ways. I was headed to Rome to meet up with Zach, while Jay and Nora had plans of their own. They actually planned on being in Rome a couple weeks later and wished I could prolong my visit, but I couldn't. Despite this sad thought, I felt good knowing that Jay, Nora, and I would likely be friends forever. We felt like family at this point even though we had only known each other for a short time. However, despite this bitter end, the sweetness of a new adventure was on the next horizon with new and interesting people still to meet. I looked forward to seeing my old pal Zach with whom I had spent 2 years studying Latin with at University and exploring the ancient city we had learned so much about during our time as undergrads.

After an hour or more lounging together on the rocky shore, we finally decided (somewhat reluctantly) to conclude the night. It was a beautiful ending to a wonderful chapter of such an incredible adventure. There was no telling what challenges lay ahead or what trouble Zach and I would find ourselves in as college buddies in Rome. My only hope was that whatever happened, it would make a great story.

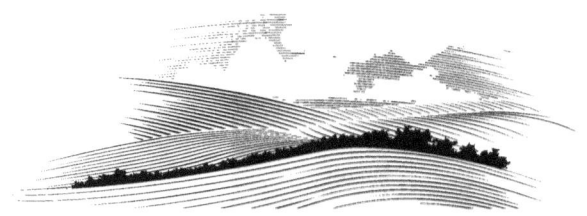

If Beggars Had Beaks

Monday, June 30th

I woke up this morning at around 9am. I grabbed my blue backpack and went down to the train station to inquire about getting to Rome. The woman manning the station was very kind despite not speaking very good English. She explained that I would need to catch the train to La Spezia first. From there, I would be able to hop on another train headed to Rome. She even provided me a time sheet so I could see what train(s) I would need to catch. Once I was certain I knew what needed to be done, I thanked her and made my way back up toward the hostel.

Just thinking about going to Rome was exciting for me. Not only had I studied its ancient history and language at University, but I had also played and beaten Ubisoft's *Assassin's Creed: Brotherhood* game. This game featured the character Ezio Auditore da Firenze, through whom I had spent many hours racing across the rooftops and exploring the city of Rome, Italy in the 16th century. The game took me through such places as the Forum, Colosseum, and the Pantheon. I was truly as excited about visiting this ancient city as a 13-year old girl in line for a Taylor Swift concert.

On the way back up, I stopped at the cafe where the girls and I had stopped previously for breakfast. For €4.40, I purchased an orange juice, a cappuccino, and a croissant. As I enjoyed my peaceful breakfast, I opened my tablet and connected to the wifi. Next, I used an app to look up train routes to chart my expected journey. The woman at the station said the trains to Rome ran constantly, so I only needed to decide when I wanted to go and make sure I caught the correct train from La Spazia to Rome. Once I had chosen my times and made note of the train numbers and platforms, I sat back to soak in the culture for the last time. I allowed the sights, the smells, the colors, and the sounds to invade my senses as the cool breeze coming up from the water, into the market and through the cafe brushed across my face. This place was so beautiful and romantic, I hated to leave. Yet, I was still very eager for my next adventure.

When I arrived back at the hostel, I found a note from the girls letting me know they were at the HQ doing laundry. I chose then to take advantage of this time alone at the hostel to relax in my favorite spot — on the porch, under the tree, overlooking the city and water — for a bit of journaling. It was hard to stay focused on what I was writing with the view and weather being so perfect before me. I couldn't help again trying to soak up as much as I could. I knew I might never have the opportunity to return, so I wanted to be sure I could remember. With my eyes closed, I wanted to be able to remember the climbing up the mountain to get here, the view of the ocean, the cool breeze brushing against my face with the warm sun beaming down, the sweet smell of honeysuckle, and the color of countless flowers dancing in the wind. After spending ample time journaling and soaking in my surroundings, I got up to go pack.

After getting my things together, I made my way down the mountain. I found the girls at the hostel's HQ washing clothes and using the Internet as the note had expressed. I was glad to be able to have a nice goodbye and wish one another well for the future. I hugged Jay followed by Nora and we wished one another safe future travels and a fond farewell. Jen was inside washing clothes, so I simply waved to her and said goodbye. I then somewhat reluctantly turned and took my leave, hoping that one day, I might see Jay and Nora again.

As I neared the end of the market before taking the road toward the train station, I suddenly realized that I was hungry. I wasn't starving, but considering the long ride ahead, I knew I had better eat something or else risk being hungry on the ride. I looked around and noticed a local pizza shop. This was not the same one from the other day, so I decided to give it a try. I then purchased a small pizza for €8 and was shortly thereafter presented with a fresh pie.

Despite being very similar to the one the girls and I had the other day, this one was much better. Perhaps they added salt? Who knew? Whatever the missing ingredient(s) was that the other shop had failed to add was evidently included in this one. As I finished the pizza and thereby satisfying my current and future hunger, I looked at my watch.

"2:41!" I exclaimed in my head. My train was scheduled to leave in the next 10 minutes! I had to leave right then and book it to be sure I made my train. Therefore, I took off with all haste towards the station.

"Me scusi! Me scusi!" I called out to a train main leaning out of the train. "Est 2:52?!"

"Si, si!" He called back.

"Gratsia!" I replied quickly hopping aboard. He nodded as I passed by him seconds after the train was scheduled to leave. I was grateful in this instance that Italian trains weren't quite as punctual as those in the UK where if you aren't on board at the exact time they are set to leave, the doors shut, and you are simply out of luck.

The ride from Riomaggiore to La Spezia lasted a mere 10 minutes. I smoothly exited this train and was quickly on the next headed for Rome. While on this train, something very curious happened that I had not yet experienced. In fact, it made me wonder about the security they had on the train.

Out of nowhere a man came onto the train. He walked down the isle begging anyone for a penny. His appearance was unkempt with long hair and beard stubble. With one hand he presented an open palm. With the other, he rubbed his fingers together as if to symbolize change. All the way down the isle he walked doing this, looking at each individual sorrowfully. When he came to me, his face showed particular hopefulness. Considering my luggage and "Mississippi, USA" hat, he likely and correctly assumed I was an American, and further assumed that I was therefore rich with money to give. Unfortunately for him, I didn't have anything to provide him. After hesitating next to me for a moment with an empty palm, he continued past disappointed.

Shortly after this, a woman also came on board. She looked about like the man did. She came along just as the man had done, only this time, passing out slips of paper with words typed in both Italian and English. The message read exactly as follows:

"I am very poor with four child. We don't have a house and no job. Please help us as you can. God protect you. Thanks."

After passing by, she continued to the next car beyond ours. A few minutes later, she returned holding a container. She jingled it around as she passed by each person along the isle. When she passed by me and I didn't respond, she seemed noticeably surprised.

"You're not going to give me anything?" Her face seemed to imply. Honestly and truly, I had no cash to give, even if I had felt so inclined to drop some in her bucket. However, oddly enough, I didn't. I couldn't help feel weird about the whole thing. The way she and the man had come in, and especially with her pre-printed text to hand out, it felt really dodgy. Besides, how many people in desperate situations go to the trouble of printing out enough text to hand out to a multitude of people on a train? There further seemed to be a very distinct difference between the type of mere homeless people I have encountered in the United States and these who actively begged. Perhaps it was all real and genuine, and I'm a terrible person, or maybe it was an organized, money-making system. Who knows? All I can say is that I had no money to give and the whole thing felt weird.

The train pulled out shortly after this incident and I arrived in Rome some time after. I exited the train to find an enormous station. I followed the crowd leaving the train toward the street. There was a large breezway where a multitude of people were all clustered together. I managed to find a station attendant who spoke English so I was able to get my bearings (i.e. the direction I needed to head in order to find my hostel).

While moving through the crowd of people, I noticed many individuals that, based on their appearance, were homeless. They all looked very rugged and dirty, sitting around full of sadness. Perhaps because I felt some guilt for not having any money to help the man or woman on the train and perhaps because I felt sympathy for them, I decided to do a good thing.

I went over to an older man who was sitting down, leaning against a pillar and asked him with my words and hands if he needed some food. I pointed to the kiosk that was selling hot dogs or something. His eyes lit up, and he started doing a similar gesture as the man with his fingers and palms. However, in this gesture, the man kept putting his fingers in his palm then his mouth and saying, "num, num, num."

I told him yes, and he followed me over towards the kiosk. Then, as if this action had somehow alerted every other beggar within 50 yards, they turned started coming towards me from every direction. Some, who were lying on the ground, suddenly jumped up and came my way. If they had anything to sell, they brought it. They came limping, struggling to wheel a wheel-chair, looking sad and pitiful, showing their old age, showing great sorrow, whatever they could while swiftly converging on me. By the time I had pulled out my wallet and started to pay for the food I was ordering from the kiosk, hands were literally everywhere; poking me, pushing me, surrounding me! It was like being a kid at the park with bread and trying to feed a duck (which you shouldn't do as I recently found out that this is actually bad for ducks)! Other ducks will see the one duck getting fed and will literally come flying across the pond or swimming over. Soon, there are 30 ducks all quacking for a damn piece of bread until one finally snaps at the bag and they all jump on it while the feeder is sent stumbling back as the devour they entire loaf. This was the experience with these beggars.

"No!" I tried telling them. "Get back!" They hardly responded. Thankfully, a few larger men from outside the large circle of beggars surrounding me noticed what was happening and came to my aid. They had to physically force them away from me as if they were animals and began calling for the *Polizia* (police) to help.

"You can't try to help them because this happens." One of them explained in English with an Italian accent. "You should probably go somewhere else if you can [otherwise they'll just keep coming]."

I knew from having looked at the map on my tablet (provided by the hostel) that the hostel wasn't far. I thus decided to take the man's advice and leave. I went outside and saw the cab line, but it was very long. Instead, I simply walked away from the station, passed by a group of beggars whom I ignored, crossed the street with purpose, and did not stop until I had put a good distance between myself and the station (along with its beggars). At this point, I consulted a map of Rome I had picked up shortly after exiting the train.

Of all the maps I had seen so for, or had ever seen in my life for that matter, this map of Rome was by far the most confusing. I knew where I was relatively based on the simple map the hostel had provided me, but was not entirely certain of where I was specifically in relation to the more detailed map of Rome. Still, I tried to maintain an expression and air of confidence lest an undesirable person attempt to take advantage of a lost tourist. Fortunately, a friendly-looking passerby came along and I asked him for a bit of assistance. He then pointed me in a direction with some instruction. I followed these instructions, but didn't completely trust him — I recalled the incident with the girl in Bath who pointed me in the exact opposite direction. I then happened upon two young, friendly Asian guys. I stopped and asked them for directions as well, and they were happy to help me find my hostel as they were headed in a similar direction. To my relief, it turned out that I was very close!

When I found my hostel, I thanked the two guys as they continued on. The next issue was how to enter. The door was very big and there was no knob. In the center of the door was a large sphere. I pushed and pulled, but nothing happened. I then noticed a small button. I couldn't be sure what it was for exactly, but since I didn't have much other choice, I pressed it.

"Hostel Beautiful!" An Indian voice announced from an unseen speaker. I didn't see a microphone, so I spoke in the direction the voice came from.

"Um, hi! I'm Tim and have a reservation here I believe." I explained. The voice welcomed me and told me to come in. However, I confessed that I couldn't figure out how to open the door.

"There is a latch to the side." The voice said. I looked around for a moment still confused, then noticed what the voice was referring to. As I opened the door, I hoped Zach would have issues too so I wouldn't feel so dumb.

Up to the third floor I went and checked in with the kind Indian man working the front desk. I asked if my friend had arrived yet, and he said no. After verifying my reservation, I was checked in and shown to mine and Zach's room. The room featured two twin beds and a window. Our view out of the window was the brick wall of building across the narrow ally. The ally was so narrow in fact, that I could reach my hand out and miss touching the other building's brick wall by mere inches. As for the shower and toilet, the hostel featured a community-style bathroom down the hall from our room.

Shortly after getting settled in, I heard a deep, southern, Mississippi accent coming down the hall. There was only one person that could be! I immediately went out and excitedly greeted my old pal Zach and helped him get inside. Although he tried to act all stoic about being in Rome, I could tell he was just as excited as I was.

"Man, I don't know about you, but I'm starving." He said after getting settled in himself.

"I passed a nice looking cafe in the little square on my way here." I said.

"Sounds good. Let's go." He replied. And with that, we were off.

Around the corner from our hostel was a square of cobble stone. The square featured several shops and a grocery store. On the corner across from the grocery store stood a small cafe with outside seating. Metal chairs were set around small, circular tables under umbrellas in the inviting scene. Zach and I claimed a table and within a minute or so, an Italian man appeared. It didn't take Zach and I long to decide upon splitting a pizza since I really wasn't all that hungry and Zach wanted to have pizza being his first time in Italy. Along with our pizza, we ordered large beers to celebrate.

We sat there and relaxed for the next hour and a half or so, catching up on our recent ventures, talking about Professor Doleac's Latin class at University and how he looked like Tom Cruise when he wore his sun glasses with his long hair. It was so refreshing to see my old pal again, and especially to hang out with someone from Mississippi for the first time since I left. After being full of pizza and beer, we walked back to the hostel and turned in, excited about the adventures ahead.

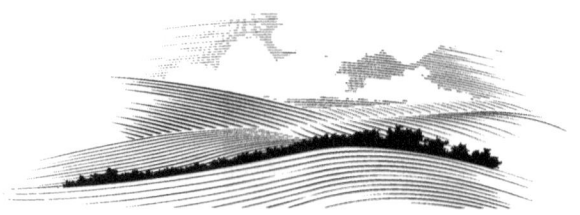

It Never Hurts To Ask

Tuesday, July 1st

Zach and I kicked off our first day in Rome a little slow. We had simply been so excited about being in Rome and reconnecting that we lost track of time and ended up staying up later than we had intended. Rather than seeking out breakfast, we simply finished off the leftover pizza and I found a coffee machine.

"So,..what would you like to do first, Tim?" Zach asked with his strong, yet articulate southern draw between sips of coffee and pointing his finger at the map. "We could hit the forum and Colosseum, go to the Vatican, take a tour of the Pantheon, or something else." A burst of excitement shot through me as he said each of these things as we had discussed all of them in our class together.

"Well," I replied taking a look at the map. "Since the Forum, Palatine Hill, and Colosseum are all right there together, why don't we go check all that out today? We're off to a bit of a late start, and since the Colosseum looks like it's the closest to us on the map, we wouldn't have to rush."

"Alright," Zach replied. "Sounds like a plan to me!" Shortly thereafter, we were walking down the steps of our hostel and out into the streets of Rome.

As we walked down the street in what we believed to be the right direction, we both realized how absolutely impossible it was to read the map! It made no sense, and it was nearly impossible to figure out where we were in relation to the things we were trying to find. I told him that I had to ask for help from strangers when trying to find the hostel the day before. We were both vaguely aware of how to get back to the train station, so we chose to find that first to better get our bearings. Yet, even with the map in hand along with our memories from the previous day, we had to ask a stranger for a bit of help.

After a few minutes of walking, we again saw the station. As we walked down a narrow Roman street, I suddenly realized something. The street smelled like Bourbon Street in New Orleans, LA. If you have ever been down Bourbon Street, you will likely recall at some point the smell of stale urine drifting into your nostrils. This street in particular reeked of the smell! Needless to say, Zach and I picked up the pace a little bit to swiftly move beyond this less-than-enjoyable smell.

Once we made it to the train station, we again consulted the map, which Zach jokingly referred to as "the consortium"(which is not a word, but sounds Latin and was funny at the time). We compared it to the compass on my watch and asked a stranger for a little assistance. The stranger was kind enough to point us in the right direction and validated that the map was really quite confusing. The way the streets wound, twisted, and stopped abruptly was enough to throw the most experienced navigator off. Of course, it's important to keep in mind that the city has existed for over 2,000 years and "city planning" wasn't really a thing as it was developing. Still,…a better designed, modern map would have been helpful. After a fifteen minute walk and only a couple wrong turns, we looked ahead to see the glorious Colosseum coming into view.

As we approached, we both shared a sense of celebratory victory in finally finding it. While Zach kept his composure, I reacted like a Justin Timberlake fangirl. The Colosseum even from a distance was enormous! Walking down the old, dusty road, I couldn't help but imagine the Colosseum and the surrounding area in its original glory.

Spartan warriors kept the roads safe as people from all over the ancient world traveled to Rome. The came either to watch or to participate in the legendary Roman games that embodied the virtues of the empire. Whether it was watching a chariot race with great, beautiful steeds or cheering on their favorite gladiator in a fight to the death against man or beast, all came to witness the spectacle. For while a strict social class separated the haves from the have-nots, all were equally enthused by the thrill of the games.

All around the outside of the Colosseum, people were taking photos, on tours, waiting in line to enter, or sitting in a shady spot. I also noticed guys with backpacks filled with water bottles selling them for €1. This was obviously unlawful for some reason because whenever a policeman came into sight, they would all start yelling, "plicia, policia!" and scatter.

While Zach and I were heading towards the line, a girl stopped us. In an American accent, she asked if we had been inside yet. When we told her no, she asked what all we had seen. After telling her that we'd only just arrived, she made us an offer.

"We are a private tour agency," she explained, "and right now, we are offering a special deal. You pay us the same price you'd pay to get into the Colosseum, but a) you can go right in and not have to wait in line, b) you get a private tour guide who will give you some historical background before you are free to walk around, then c) one of our tour guides will walk you over to Palatine Hill, Caesar Augustus' house, a few other sites, and the Roman Forum. Tips for the guides are encouraged, but not required. What do you say?"

Zach looked at me and I gave him the same uncertain look. We both asked if we could think it over and get back to her. She gave us a card and told us where she would be, but we only had a few minutes to decide before the group was booked up. Once she was gone, we considered our options.

We both felt like it was a little bit sketchy. We were supposed to pay in cash, then wait to be called up for the tour. It would be so easy to trick a gullible tourist into handing over the €30 cash and taking off. Yet, we figured there were a lot of tour groups around such a site. After mulling it over, we chose to take a chance on the tour. We went over to the girl, paid, received a wrist band, and found a spot near a large arch closely resembling the Arc of Triumph in Paris (though much smaller) to sit as we waited (and hoped) that the tour guide would in fact show up. I, of course, kept a close eye on the whereabouts of ole girl, least I see her appear to make off with our money.

After around 20 minutes of waiting, we saw a short man stand up on a rock and begin calling. We realized with much relief that this was in fact our tour guide. Zach, myself, and a small group all gathered around. Once we were all counted, he asked if we were ready. A very nice looking older woman asked us all to wait while she went to get her husband and kids, so we waited a couple more minutes. As soon as they joined us, we headed toward the Colosseum. To be honest, I didn't even notice the woman return with her husband and kids. I was too busy gazing up in anticipation at the ROMAN COLOSSEUM!

Just as promised, our tour guide lead us straight inside, skipping everyone else in line, and took us around to the right just inside the gates. He then gathered us all around him so that he could give some historical context to the structure. Having just recently been through an in-depth class on ancient Rome, written multiple papers on the Roman Games, and had taken 2 years of Latin as a second language, I was already familiar with most everything he said. However, when the tour guide told everyone that the Jews built the Colosseum, Zach and I both couldn't help but chuckle because that wasn't true. There is not nearly enough historical evidence to support such a claim.

As the tour guide talked, I pulled out my camera to record a short Mission Log of where I was. I held it as high as I could to get above the heads of those standing around me, and canvased the area all the way around, then back. During this video, the husband of the woman mentioned whom I had not noticed before just happened to remove the hat he was wearing to adjust his hair. He further casually turned around to see my camera facing him, then immediately put his cap back on and turned to again face the front. I was so busy looking at the structure itself, I didn't even notice this. Zach, however, did. As soon as the tour guide finished talking and gave us instruction on where/when to meet for the rest of the tour, he grabbed my arm.

"Tim!" He said quietly but with shock and excitement. "Do you see that guy over there?" He motioned toward the man I mentioned previously. He was wearing a blue plaid, button down shirt, khaki pants, a blue hat, and dark sunglasses. He also happened to be two to three heads taller than anyone else around. All that to say, yeah, I saw him. He was hard to miss.

"Yeah?" I asked. "What about him?"

"…I think that's Conan O'Brien." He said with a big grin. Conan is a successful late night talk show host and comedian in New York. I thought Zach was crazy.

"No it's not…" I replied rolling my eyes and laughing at him. "Come on. There's no way." I had never before run into or met any major celebrity, so there was no way I was about to assume something like that. To me, clearly, he was just a very tall, fair-skinned American guy.

"No, I'm serious!" Zach insisted quietly. "I'm about 99% positive it is." I still didn't believe him. If THE Conan O'Brien were to tour Rome, wouldn't he get himself a fancy, super-private, exclusive tour as opposed to a random, touristy tour group for "normal people?"

"Well," I said, "if you're so certain, why don't you go ask him?"

"Oh no, I can't. I'm too nervous." Zach said.

"Ugh, ok fine then. *I'll* go as him just to prove you wrong." I declared. At first Zach didn't want me to because he didn't want to bug him, but then his desire to know for certain overcame him and he allowed me to go. So, I waited until there weren't a lot of people around (you know, in the 1% chance that it somehow actually *was* him). Then, I went straight over.

"Excuse me sir," I said very politely. He looked at me and bent slightly. His wife and kids turned and watched. "I'm sorry to bother you, but me and my friend back there," I pointed to Zach, "were arguing. You see, he thinks you're someone and I told him you weren't but I decided to just come ask." I paused, then asked, "Are you Conan O'Brien?"

Without skipping a beat, the man pulled off his hat and sunglasses. He leaned down a little because he was so tall. He stuck out his hand and said,

"Yes I am! How ya doin?" My jaw dropped. I had never understood why people got nervous around celebrities. They're just people like anyone else. Well, this day I understood because I became immediately starstruck. I shook his hand but was unable to speak for a moment. Meanwhile Zach came from behind me grinning like a 13 year old boy who just got his first Red Rider BB Gun.

Conan engaged us for a moment asking where we were from and what we were doing in Rome. I couldn't believe how nice he was. Zach and I then asked if we could each get a quick photo with him, but tried to be discrete as to not draw attention. He was there with his family after all, and not doing the celebrity thing. He was kind enough to allow us a quick photo. After this, we initiated an exit, wanting to be respectful of his time with family. I think he probably appreciated it.

Zach and I left and begin touring the great Colosseum, but to be honest, neither one of us could stop thinking about the fact that we had just met CONAN O'FREAKING-BRIEN in ROME! The craziest part was......HE WAS A PART OF OUR TOUR GROUP. When we had finished touring around the Colosseum, we exited but stayed around the area where our next tour guide was said to meet us. We tried to keep our distance and not draw attention to the fact that Conan was a stone's throw from us ALSO waiting on the next tour guide. I really appreciated how anyone who recognized him would receive a positive, friendly response. I had heard stories about some celebrities who could be very rude and unappreciative of "normal people," excitedly recognizing them. One story I heard was of Brad Pitt and Angelina Jolie [this was while they were still married] showing up at a small bar in or near New Orleans. According to the story, Pitt was very friendly and politely spoke to fans, that recognized him, allowed photos to be taken with him - even joked around with them. Meanwhile, Jolie allegedly ignored them for the most part and didn't want any photos taken. Conan, on the other hand, was very much like Pitt in this story. I observed this one scene where one of the guys selling water walked past, recognized him, and excitedly said, "Hey! Conan!" And went for a high five. Conan responded in a like manor with an enthusiastic high five. It was really great to see a celebrity in person and see him act so kindly and appreciatively to fans, or at least merely recognized him and knew who he was.

The second tour guide eventually showed up, gathered us around again, and took us to Palatine Hill. The guide was really nice, informative, and gave the audience a chance to answer history questions. I got really tickled when he would ask a question and Conan's daughter (probably around 10 or so years old) answered the questions correctly. She was adorable and impressed me with her apparent love for and knowledge of Rome. We then continued on, hitting a few other historical sites, but most of it had been reduced to less than ruins. Finally, we came to the Forum where we received a final history lesson and left to enjoy the rest of the site.

After the group had departed, I did a video. The theme was, "holy cow, we just toured Rome with Conan O'Brien and his family." Zach and I both confessed in the video that it was hard to keep our heads "in the game" of taking in the sites because the whole time, all we could think about was "OMG, Conan O'Brien is walking alongside me right now." At one point, I had asked Conan if I could ask him a question for my buddy Cory He obliged me kindly as we walked from one site to the next. I told him Cory was a huge fan of his, and that he was an idol of my friend. Cory was a journalist at the time, but really wanted to write comedy (he is hilarious, so I'm sure it will happen one day). I asked Conan if there was any advice I could bring back with me to give my friend.

"Tell him to start writing spec comedy." He said, then went on to explain how doing this is what he did and it really helped him. I was again blown away by Conan's kindness and generosity, which further goes to show how nice he was. It sounded like great advice.

"Tell your friend good luck." He concluded after a couple minutes of talking. I thanked him, then left him alone for the remainder of the tour, again wanting to be respectful of his time with his family.

Zach and I spent the next half hour walking through the Forum until we realized we were both completely fulfilled at this point, not to mention a little exasperated after being on tour with CONAN for the past 2 hours. Considering all this, we decided it was time to head back to the hostel. We further decided to visit the grocery store on the way back to get some breakfast items and some pasta ingredients to cook for dinner. Thus, we did as planned and were soon back at the hostel with groceries, which included a few beers that looked interesting.

Once back at the hostel, we sat back, relaxed, and listened to Spotify while enjoying a couple beers. Having no plans for the evening, I pulled out my tablet and begin searching for nearby bars we could check out after dinner. I found a few interesting options, and discovered that Irish Pubs were all over the place. I found one nearby, and Zach approved. This night also just so happened to be a World Cup match, and Germany had been doing very well. My plan suggestion was to grab a shower while Zach begin cooking our pasta, then we'd head down to the pub for a few pints and to watch the match. Unfortunately, while I was in the shower, Zach hollered at me that while we had assumed the small kitchen would have some oil, there was none, so we would have to dine out.

At the Irish pub, I ordered a burger and we watched the game as planned. Germany did really well, and I was excited to see them come so far. Their defense has been really on point this series. After the match, Zach and I caught a cab back to the hostel and were shortly thereafter fast asleep.

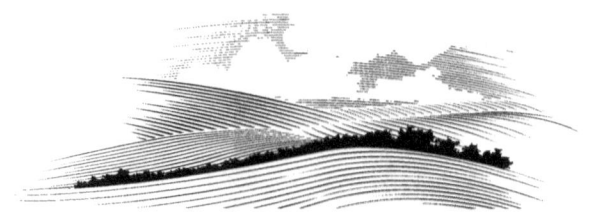

The Eye Near The Ghetto

Wednesday, July 2nd

Zach and I chose to sleep in a little bit this morning, but still woke up by 8am. Once up and ready, we agreed that the famous Pantheon should be our destination for the day. I was of course very excited to see this building. It had great historical significance as a religious icon from the ancient Roman days. It was erected as a temple where one could worship all the gods (hints the prefix pan) in one place. Later, it was converted into a Christian icon during the 7th century AD and remains to this day. At the top of the structure is an inscription that our Latin professor once assigned us to translate for extra credit. The inscription is thus:

M•AGRIPPA•LUCIUS•L•F•CONS•TERTIVM•FECIT

The inscription reads (literally), "Marcus Agrippa Lucious-Son-of Consular third term built." Better translated, it reads, "Consular Marcus Agrippa in his 3rd term built this temple." Agrippa was Emperor Augustus' right hand man who became a consular in c. 63BC and initially constructed the temple. It was later damaged, but then restored by Hadrian in c.126 AD before Severus (ruled c. 193-211) and Caracalla (ruled c. 198-217) made some final modifications.

I was obviously very excited to see this building I had learned about not only in Latin class, but also Dr. Doleac's Roman History class. Further, just like as mentioned previously, Ezio's story took me to Rome in the video game. Through Ezio, I had explored the area around the Pantheon, walked (and climbed) through the inside, and made one crucial assassination. Now, I would have the pleasure of visiting in-person and seeing it with my own eyes. I couldn't wait!

Zach and I set out down the street with our nearly useless map in hand. We fortunately noticed during this journey that the street signs were actually marked on the sides of buildings rather than street signs like we were used to! This made the map slightly more readable, but still not very helpful. We made a few wrongs turns and had to ask for directions a few times. It was so frustrating, we considered calling and paying for an expensive cab ride. Then, we stumbled onto something interesting.

"Hey," Zach said suddenly looking up. "What's that?"

"It appears to be a religious structure." I replied. We both looked a little closer form across the street, then he pointed.

"There, see? There's a small sign above the arches that says 'Basilica.'" Zach then tried his hand at reading the Italian sub-text but was unsuccessful. "Well," He continued. "We know that a basilica is some kind of church. Would you like to stop and check it out?" Partly due to wanting a free break from the heat and partly due to genuine curiosity, I agreed.

Zach and I then approached the ancient-looking basilica made of red stone brick. As we entered, there was a shocking contrast. While the outside looked very old and crumbly, the inside was bright with marble, extravagant color, beautiful artwork and statues, and not to mention a very noticeable change in temperature. The ceilings were extremely high with great columns and arches, and as we walked around, slow, calming chanting could be heard gently echoing through the halls from a place unseen. I was blown away. This place that looked pretty rugged on the outside turned into a beautiful, fully functioning church on the inside complete with a choir loft, pulpit, and pews.

There was such a peace in this place that Zach and I spent at least 15 minutes inside either walking around or having a rest in a pew. Aside from the gentle chanting, all was quiet. Other visitors were also respectful of this ambiance of peace and kept communication to a soft whisper while some took time for prayer. I probably could have spent an hour here, but Zach and I were on a mission so we couldn't deter for too long. Once we had cooled off and relaxed, we again set off.

Further down the street, we came across a brilliant, ancient-looking building which was now the capital building of Rome. Although built in the first half of the 1st century AD, it looked prestigious as ever. It's hard to describe how enormous and interestingly it was designed, but it really embodied Rome's ability to express the empire's power and authority without uttering a single word. White columns rose high above the ground with impressive arches before, around, and above it, all with perfect symmetry. A crescent formed like open arms as if to say, "ROMA HIC ES," *THIS is ROME.*

After a few more wrong turns and a constant questioning of the map, Zach said he believed we ought to be nearly there.

"After consulting the consortium, the Pantheon should be just through there." He said, motioning toward a street that went between buildings just up ahead. I was uncertain. I didn't see any tall structures come up from behind the long buildings as I would have expected. I thought we would at least see the top of the Pantheon from where we were. Thinking back to Assassin's Creed, I always took Ezio over-top buildings to get here rather than walk down the road.

"There's no way." I thought. "Surely we're lost."

We continued walking and entered the narrow way between tall buildings on a road that was probably just wide enough to fit a compact car though. Next we stepped out of the passage into a large square with a beautiful fountain in the center and people gathered everywhere. Beyond the fountain, standing impressively before me with huge ancient columns and the famous inscription at the top, with all the epicness of a tale worth telling, was the Pantheon.

Despite the fact that the structure was shorter than the apartment buildings surrounding it that made up the square, it was absolutely massive. It was far bigger than I had even imagined it to be. The people all around looked like mere ants in comparison. Sure, I had been there as Ezio, but being there in person, standing before it, taking it all in at once, was breath-taking. The Colosseum was obviously much bigger, but that meant you could only take in pieces at a time. With the Pantheon, you could take it all in at once — and what it had to say was quite a lot what with its shier mass and intricate detail.

Zach and I stopped at the fountain to get a few photos where we were approached by young blond girl. She had a German accent, but spoke perfect English.

"Hello! Are you planning on entering the Pantheon?" We said we were. "Well, it is free to go inside, but if you are willing to pay €10, you can have a private, guided tour."

Like the other girl from the Colosseum, she was running a small tour company. Since it was only €10, Zach and I agreed. She was wearing a badge of some type like the last girl, so we felt pretty good about it. She thanked us and said our guide would be with us shortly so we should stay where we were.

After a few minutes, another girl approached us. She introduced herself as Amanda and said she would be our guide. Amanda reminded me of Victora in many ways. She was about the same height and build, and had a heavy British accent. While at the fountain, Amanda first asked what we already knew about the Pantheon and was happy to know we knew a little already. She then told us about what we would be seeing upon entering.

"It's extremely loud inside because there are so many people in there right now." She explained. "So rather than trying to yell over the noise, I thought it would be better to explain outside, then take you in. Once we are out, you can ask me to explain anything you have questions about." After she had provided a detailed explanation and answered any initial questions we had, we went inside.

We then walked away from the fountain, past the enormous columns, and through the giant-sized entry that gave way to a vision one could only describe as immaculate. The faded color of the stone, the carved statues, the inner columns with flourishes on the tops and bottoms, the unbelievable inner architecture, the high dome ceiling, and the famous *oculus* (Latin for *eye*) at the top was almost too much to handle. It blew my mind looking up at the oculus that, as I knew, was an absolute feat of Roman engineering. It was not held in place by anything, which makes it a marvel that the ceiling never fell in, much less last over 2,000 years! Scholars and architects to this day are still baffled by how such a structure was created with the known resources available to the ancient world. The Romans were known to be incredibly innovative, but this really takes the cake.

"So what do you guys have planned for the rest of the day?" Amanda asked after we had gotten back and answered a couple questions.

"This is really about it for today." I replied. "We visited the Colosseum, Palatine Hill, and the Forum yesterday which we toured with Conan O'Brien and his family — no big." She of course knew who this was and we told her the story. She added that she had actually heard he was around but thought it was cool that we met him. "Tomorrow, we are thinking of hitting the Vatican, but that's about it as far as planned adventures." At some point during the conversation, I mentioned the fact that I was pretty hungry.

"Are there any good places to eat that aren't super touristy?" I asked.

"There's actually a great pizza/pasta place not too far from here in the Jewish Ghetto." She answered casually.

"The WHAT?" I exclaimed both surprised and curious.

"Yeah," Amanda replied. "It's an old part of Rome that is still primarily inhabited by Jewish people." Neither I nor Zach had ever heard of this place.

"Oh wow! That's really interesting!" I said. "So would you like to join us for lunch......and show us where this place is since we don't know?" She admitted that she was tired and not very hungry.

"We promise we don't expect you to provide any type of tour or further details about the site." Zach said

"I'll even buy you a beer for your trouble." I added.

"Ok,.." She finally said. "I guess I could go for a beer."

It was tough to resist asking some questions here and there about things we saw, but we did our best. Fortunately, Amanda ended up giving us a little explanation without being prompted which was nice. Not long after setting off, we arrived at the restaurant and took a seat.

Zach, Amanda, and I discussed cultural differences between our two countries and Rome (and Italy in general) while we waited for a server. One thing that Amanda expressed frustration with was the educational system surrounding the ancient architecture in the city.

"It's really hard to become a tour guide as a non-native because native Roman citizens have first priority." She explained, which made perfect sense. However, there was more to it. "It seems like most of the natives don't know and don't actually care that much. They aren't educated well on the history and therefore the public isn't well educated on it. That being said, in order to become a tour guide, you have to take a test. The test results of non-natives are judged harshly while the locals hardly have to pass."

"Wow, that's crazy!" I replied. "But it makes sense. While at the Colosseum yesterday, our local tour guide tried to tell us that the Colosseum was built specifically by the Jews!"

"SEE?!" She exclaimed. "That's what I'm talking about! Yes, there are some rumors about that, but little to no actual evidence to support it! They most likely participated in building it, sure, but using the Jews specifically to build it? NO!"

A very interesting cultural phenomenon I was unaware of that Amanda explained to us was the mob's control over the city. This control apparently abounds throughout the city and particularly in its politics.

"As an example," Amanda explained. "All the local shops and restaurants are heavily taxed a high percentage. They don't seem to realize that it is not in fact a tax, but a sort of bribe being enforced on them. They don't legally have to pay it, but are scared not to.

When the waiter came out, I ordered a white pasta with a glass of wine and a beer for Amanda. Zach ordered a red pasta and a beer. My pasta ended up being good, but nothing to write home about. After eating, we stayed there and enjoyed a good conversation during which Amanda told us about her manager named Christine. Christine had apparently just sent Amanda a text informing her that she was finishing up and wanted to go shoot the breeze down by the Tiber River.

"Do you guys want to come?" Amanda asked. Since Zach and I had nothing better planned and Amanda was pretty cool, we happily agreed to join them.

We followed Amanda out of the Jewish Ghetto and away from the tourist attractions. After a ten minute walk, we arrived at a particular spot along the Tiber and waited for Christine who arrived not long after.

"Guys, this is my manager, Christine." Amanda said, as a tall, blond haired, slender girl came over.

"Hello!" Christine said with a pretty smile and German accent.

"Christine, this is Tim and Zach from the tour." Amanda said to Christine. Zach and I said hello. After introductions, we engaged in conversation. For the next while, the four of us carried on shooting the breeze and skipping rocks across the water while watching the sun set over the Tiber and ancient city of Rome.

"Well,.." Christine chimed once the sun had fully set. "I think I might like to find a drink. Would you all care to walk around a bit?" She then looked at Amanda then to Zach and I. "Amanda and I could show you some more of the city."

"Oh! We should take them to the fountain!" Amanda exclaimed.

"The fountain?" I asked.

"It's where young people gather and there are often street performers." Christine explained. I looked over at Zach.

"You down?"

"Sounds like a plan to me!" He replied enthusiastically before skipping another rock across the water. And with that, the plan was set.

Covert Op And The Night Bus

Wednesday, July 2nd continued...

The four of us left our cozy little spot by the water and returned to the street. Zach and I then followed the girls back towards the city. As we crossed a bridge, we stopped for a moment to observe the view and appreciate the talent of a man playing the guitar. He was playing an electric guitar through a battery powered amp on wheels that resembled a baby stroller. I smiled and politely dropped a euro into his open bag to which he acknowledged with a "grazie!"

Next we stopped at a corner store that reminded me of a gas station without gas pumps. Inside I grabbed a 40 of Peroni, my favorite Italian brew. This ended up being a poor decision on my part because by the time I was 1/3 finished, I made a grave realization. I needed to pee.

I asked the girls where the next opportunity to visit the rest room would be. To my dismay, they said it would probably be another *mile and a half or so* before there was a free public rest room. This was not good at all because I was definitely not going to make it that far. I looked all around as we walked for cover. It was now dark, so if I could find a large tree or a bunch of shrubs, I felt confident I could make it happen. Unfortunately, there was nothing but stone and concrete, hardly any green at all. I looked down allies thinking perhaps I could sneak around behind a dumpster but there were none and open windows lined ally faces. There was nowhere to hide in order to secretly relieve myself without risk of being seen. I had only one other option. Zach and the girls didn't completely believe I was serious when I told them.

I started looking inside restaurants as we passed them. I knew that if I was honest and simply asked politely to use their rest room, they would require me to pay — which I utterly refused to do on principal. All I needed to do was slip past the servers without being noticed, swiftly locate and gain entry to the rest room, and do my business. If I were to get caught after that, what could they do? I felt confident that as long as the servers were occupied, I could slip past them inconspicuously. I just needed to have an educated guess as to where the rest room might be judging from my view outside the door and could therefore make a b-line in that direction. Suddenly, I saw my target. There was a single woman inside a certain restaurant cleaning a table.

"Wait, wait!" I called to Zach and the girls. "I think I found my target." They all stopped and looked. Then I looked at Zach and said the three magic words that began so many a great story in the south: "Hold my beer."

Handing my beer to Zach, I immediately moved closer to the restaurant's entry so that I could get a better view of the inside without being noticed by the worker inside. Here I patiently waited for the right opportunity to make my daring move. From this vantage point, I could see a small hallway towards the back. I was so confident that this was most likely where the rest room was that I could have bet money on it. Fortunately, in Europe, male and female rest rooms aren't usually separate. At this point, however, I really didn't care if they were. As soon as the woman cleaning turned her back and started walking in the opposite direction and I could see that no one was tending the bar further into the establishment, I make a break for it.

As briskly as my feet could carry me without making any noise or drawing attention to myself, I dashed straight for my established destination. Taking long strides while attempting to appear oblivious to anything else, I flew across the dining area. As I cross the half-way point thinking I was in the clear, there suddenly appeared behind the bar another woman. While my focus was completely on my destination, I saw her come around the bar at the corner of my eye! She saw me dead on. She reacted to seeing me, prompting the other woman to turn around as well!

"Me scusi?" The older woman said politely. I meanwhile maintained my fain obliviousness, pretending not to hear her.

"Um, me scusi?" The woman repeated a little more forcefully this time as she started moving toward me.

For a split second, my good natured character nearly forced me to stop and give her my attention, apologize, and request to use the facilities. This would have obviously resulted in required payment or being kicked out. Thankfully, I controlled this urge and pressed on still pretending not to hear while subtly yet intentionally increasing my pace.

"EXCUSE ME!" The woman shouted in an ordering tone, now clearly realizing what my intention was. "YOU HAVE TO PAY!"

At this point, both women were now racing forward with every intention of preventing me from reaching the rest room! I was almost there! Just a few... more...

I jumped my last two steps without my eyes ever leaving the door. I reached what I now clearly saw was rest room. As fast as I possibly could, I yanked open the door, closed it behind me, and locked it just as one of the woman reached the knob and attempted to pull it back open. She jerked on the knob and beat on the door angrily.

"NO! YOU HAVE TO PAY! I CALL THE POLICE!!" She cried angrily, but it was too late. I had succeeded. If she did call the police, I would be out and gone by the time they arrived. I couldn't help chuckle to myself as I concluded my business. There was something so satisfying about reaching my desired destination and the thrill of breaking a stupid rule. Yet, despite my victory, it wasn't over yet. I now needed to escape.

I had been listening to the women outside as soon as I knew I was safe (for the moment). After first making it inside, the woman continued to stand outside the door banging. Then, seconds before my business was concluded, she stepped away and begin expressing her aggravation to the other woman in Italian who apparently was in the back again (probably phoning the police). After finishing, I quickly and quietly washed my hands, carefully and silently opened the door, then bolted for the exit.

Again, the women caught me making my escape and yelled at me saying that I had to pay and that she had called the police. I laughed out loud (I couldn't help it) as I jogged out the door and motioned to Zach, Amanda, and Christine that we needed to leave immediately. I told them how it went as we made our way in the opposite direction and they got a kick out of it.

"I'm sure the workers will always remember this occasion as fondly as I do,…" I joked

After a fair walk, we arrived at a large square called Piazza In Di Santa Maria Trastevere which was just outside the Santa Maria Basilica. Near the basilica was a large fountain with steps all around it for easy sitting. There were many people around either socializing near the fountain or sitting outside at bars that lined the square. Not long after finding a place to sit on the fountain steps together, a street performer suddenly lit double-sided torches and begin juggling them. We remained here talking to one another and watching the performer for around an hour until Zach and I remembered that the United States was playing a World Cup match against Belgium this night and we wanted to find a place to watch. We invited the girls to join us, but they decided it had actually gotten quite late and they should head back home. Zach and I thanked them for the pleasant evening, exchanged contact information, and said we would try to see them again before leaving Rome.

It didn't take long for Zach and I to find a place nearby that was showing the game. Before I knew it, I was sitting in a booth with a Corona while cheering on Team USA. Despite their efforts, our boys weren't able to pull it out, giving up a 2-1 victory to Belgium. I couldn't be too upset as both teams played very well and made it a great match to watch. However, at the conclusion of the match, Zach and I were both exhausted from our day. After consulting the map and asking help from a few kind strangers, we learned that there was a night bus that could take us to a stop not too far from the hostel! From here we found the bus stop described and waited for our ride. I expected a regular city-bus type vehicle to pull up. To my surprise, this was not the case.

Suddenly, like the Night Bus straight out of the Harry Potter story, a blue double-decker London style bus comes screeching up to the stop like Dale Earnhardt racing the Indy 500! It halted in front of us hard before swinging open the doors. Several people got off as even more hopped on. Climbing on board proved to be a challenge, and Zach and I ended up being a few people apart. Shoulder-to-shoulder we stood against others. There were no seats, so both Zach and myself were forced to stand and hang on to a pole for dear life! I also believe we were technically supposed to pay, but there seemed to be so many passengers getting on and off that we never even got the opportunity to do so.

The doors to the bus swung closed, and the bus took off like a drag racer. Twisting and turning through the streets of Rome, the bus raced from stop to stop. With so much happening, I lost my bearing and was thankful that Zach had managed to keep up with where we were. It also probably helped that he was a head taller than most other passengers.

"TIM!" I heard Zach yell over the noise to me after several stops. I looked over at him on the other side of a few other people. "I think the next stop is ours!" There was no sense attempting to yell back to him, so I simply nodded the confirmation that I heard him and positioned myself to make an exit. I didn't want to find myself separated from Zach and dropped off at the next stop and have no clue where I was!

A few minutes later, the bus came to another screeching halt and the doors swung open. Zach and I pushed past people still on board and got off before the bus flew away again on to its next destination. Zach and I consulted our map again to see that we were in fact not far from our hostel. We were both relieved in this conformation. After a five or ten minute walk, we managed to find our hostel.

Zach and I made our way to our room while talking about the day's adventures. We further decided that since the Vatican was our last item on the agenda, we ought to take a chill day tomorrow.

"We could still get out and walk around a little bit, but super casually, nothing exuberant." I suggested. Zach agreed.

However, I knew that "chill days" rarely stayed "chill."

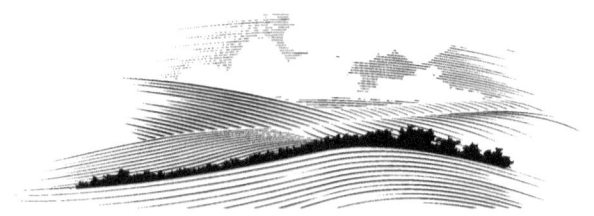

The City Of Gaud

Thursday, July 3rd

Zach and I woke up to realize we had more energy that we were expecting. We knew that we wouldn't be able to "go hard" like we had been doing, but if we took things slow, we could make it.

"So, what about a casual tour of the Vatican?" I asked

"Yeah, I think that could work. We can take the subway rather than walk to conserve energy." Zach suggested.

"Sounds like a plan to me! I replied.

From here, Zach and I made the short trip to the train station where we caught a bus to the subway station. Within a few minutes, we were a short walk from the Vatican City.

As we approached the outskirts, Zach and I heard an American accent and headed in the direction of where it came from. We came to discover that it was a guy selling tours. He ended up being a nice guy who got a kick out of our story about meeting Conan.

"So, this may be super random, but,…do you know Christine? She's German and is apparently a manager of one of the tour groups — like the one we used for the Colosseum tour." I asked candidly.

"I do!" He exclaimed laughing at the coincidence. "She's my boss!"

"How about that!" I replied. "Well then,…considering this, what are the odds we might get a discount on the tour?"

"Haha, no, sorry." He said. "But if you're students, you can get a discount."

"Do they have to be current?" Zach asked slyly.

"If you don't tell me, I won't ask." The guy replied.

"Excellent! So we're both students then!" Zach said giving me a smirk. Zach and I pulled out our University ID's and showed him. This granted us a tour purchase for €35 instead of the full price of €50! I was happy make the deal. After making our purchase, the guy instructed us on where to meet for the tour, then we said farewell and made our way into the city.

Zach and I only had to wait in the designated area for around 20 minutes. The guide then appeared who was again a native Italian. This guide, while very knowledgeable, never stopped talking nor paused to field questions. This got a bit annoying to say the least. Yet again, despite this, he did an excellent job — far better than the last one who insisted the Jews built the Colosseum.

The guide took us first to what was called the "Pine Cone Courtyard" which was simply a large courtyard with a giant ball in the center. I never really understood the hype. Next, the guide led us through a museum which featured statues, photos, and paintings. I couldn't help stop and get a few photos with the heads of notable characters (e.g. the Roman god Jupiter which is the Greek equivalent of Zeus). Next, we were led to the Sistine Chapel.

Walking in, my eyes were bombarded with colors. To be honest, it was kind of intense. Literally, not an inch of space in the room was left without some sore of artistic design. Every corner had an accent, every square a design. From the floor to the walls to the ceiling, there was color, design, and intention. Brilliant paintings depicted scenes and/or Biblical characters which lined the walls. The ceiling alone told the whole story of creation in paintings, all using the Golden Ratio through boarders. To call such an artistic feat impressive would be a vast understatement. I was overwhelmed.

Meanwhile, there were security guards everywhere whose job it seemed to be to usher groups in one at a time. The groups were very large, but were required to be silent going into the chapel out of reverence. This was fine, but it seemed the primary reason they were there was to ensure no one attempted to take photos. I witnessed a few people attempt to snap a sneaky shot, but were caught, yelled at by security, and immediately escorted out. I felt like this was a little unnecessary and thus felt rebellious. In turn, I found a hidden place, very carefully slipped my phone out and grabbed a quick shot of the ceiling before quickly shoving it back in. The picture ended up not coming out very good, but that wasn't the point. If I wanted a photo, there are plenty on the Internet for free.

After being ushered out again by security, our guide led us inside St. Peter's Basilica where the tour concluded. I had a similar feeling about this Basilica as I did the chapel — super intense. Near-ancient stone and white marble made up the floor, walls, and ceiling of the church. White, gold, and bronze seemed to be the structure's theme with high ceilings and tall pillars. Colored marble intentionally made designs across the floor as the sound of bustling tourists echoed through the hall. Everywhere I looked were artistic designs carved into the marble or stone with gold trim everywhere. The lighting from small lamps or ceiling lights shone perfectly in the right direction to lure your eyes to certain points, and reflected gently off surrounding objects.

Something else I noticed were statues, like, SO MANY STATUES of former Popes all over the walls with a few Biblical references here and there. It appeared as though every former pope had his mark. To be frank, the church seemed much more concerned about honoring popes than God as the dedication to popes far outnumbered dedications to God.

In the center of the Basilica was what appeared to be a great throne area (but without a chair). With four bronze pillars shooting up 3/4 of the way to the domed ceiling, then coming to an artistically designed point with golden crosses at the top — it was hard to miss. Underneath was a small table (I assumed was an alter) with candles.

"We're in the palace of the Pope." I thought. "Avignon's got nothing on this." Looking at the incredible number of busts of former popes, I couldn't help consider that while this was supposed to be "God's house," it didn't seem to be that way at all. Speaking as a medievalist with no offense toward modern popes, Jesus seemed to be a means to the papacy's own power and glory. My mind then wandered to my experience at the train station and all the beggars that came out of nowhere. Considering all the value in marble, gold, bronze, etc this building contained, if the Vatican took down a 100th of the material for the poor, poverty in the city of modern Rome could be drastically improved — if not perhaps resolved.

What would Jesus do? Sing in Latin while strolling around in his great, big, white, house made of gold, marble, and bronze? Or would he tear it down to nothing, sell it all, and use the money to take care of starving people? You don't have to believe in a divine Jesus to know what he'd do. Whether one believes in his divinity or not, Jesus was a compassionate person and a leader. His character is expressed in the Covenant of the New Testament which highly suggests what he would do and say in this instance.

After looking around for a while, Zach and I started making our way toward the exit when something suddenly started happening. We looked and quickly moved in the direction of the commotion while it seemed many others were doing the same. As we neared, we saw Swiss guards had set up barriers. Through the newly created isle, Cardinals dressed in all red processed through toward the previously described structure in the middle.

"Uh, sorry." I said to a woman standing nearby. "What is happening?" I didn't even think about asking if she spoke English. Fortunately she did.

"The hour just struck and it is time for Eucharist. If you're willing to wait, you can participate." She explained.

It was tempting to stay. It might be really cool to tell others back home that I had the opportunity to partake in the Eucharist at St. Peter's Basilica in Rome. However, aside from the fact that we were both protestant and would not be allowed the elements, Zach and I chose to move along instead.

As we made our way down the road back towards the subway station, Zach and I discussed what we thought of the Vatican. Zach said he was really impressed with it. He said his own religious beliefs were strengthened because of it, and seeing the Basilica really felt to him like, if God were to live on earth, the Basilica would certainly be his home.

The city and Basilica were indeed incredibly impressive, and in some respects, even intimidating. On this, Zach and I could both agree. However, my overall impression was different from his. On the contrary, I honestly felt like it was gaudy. It's (quite literally) art on top of art on top of art. Each piece individually was certainly beautiful and extremely impressive. Yet everything thrown up from the floor to the walls to the ceilings was simply overkill. It reminded me of a time where I was at a sports pub in the United States watching a football game. On another tv (because there were many), was a Hooter's Girl pageant. As I happened to look up from the football game, I saw it and couldn't help notice that while the girls standing alone or in a small group were very attractive, when they were all bunched up together in a giant group, they were not. Looking at the large group, it just looked like blond (hair), orange (spray-tan skin), and bleach-white (teeth) blotched together. In the same way, this is how the art in the Vatican seems to me. Beautiful, immaculate paintings all over the walls individually, but all together, all at once, honestly......just gaudy.

After returning from the City of Gaud, we went immediately to the corner grocery store to grab more food, some beer, and snacks. Once back at the hostel, we made dinner: chicken and peppers in tortillas with salad. It wasn't an amazing dinner, but it was good and somewhat healthy. During this time, an American guy our age appeared in the common room. We started talking with him and invited him to join us as we had plenty of food. The guy's name was Josh and he was from Michigan. He was honored that we would invite him to share in our meal.

After dinner, Zach and I decided to go out for a few drinks at a nearby Irish pub. We ended up making some friends at the pub who suggested we go for a walk. They were cool, so we obliged.

After grabbing a €1.50 40oz beer to sip on, we all strolled through the streets without much of a heading. Somehow, we ended up at a spot looking towards the Colosseum and chose to have a sit. Here, the evening took an interesting turn.

While sitting here talking, an incredibly attractive girl came walking by. By the look of her, she appeared to be Italian.

"Hey! What's up?" I called somewhat impulsively. "Do you speak English?"

The girl stopped and replied in good fun. Her name was Sasha, and she was Russian, not Italian. She did, however, speak English. Sasha stayed and chatted with us for a few minutes, but then confessed that she needed to continue making her way to her hostel. She had plans for the following morning and it was getting late.

"Are you staying near by?" I asked. Perhaps I could walk with you?" I wanted to keep talking with her, but was also genuinely concerned about a young, attractive girl walking the streets alone at night.

"Yeah, sure!" Sasha said happily. She said she wasn't going too far and I was welcome to walk with her.

"I'll be right back, guys. Just want to make sure she gets home safe." I told the group, then hopped off the rock I had been sitting on and joined her.

Sasha and I walked, chatted, and shared some great laughs. We exchanged stories about what brought us both to Rome and discussed cultural differences between the United States and Russia, and between Italy and our home countries. The conversation never became stale, and I gave her several opportunities to dismiss me in case she felt the least bit uncomfortable. Her response to these opportunities were always cheerful, and kept the invitation to walk with her open.

As we walked, I kept hoping that around the next corner would be pub where we might stop and continue chatting over a drink. Yet, this never happened and soon I found myself at her hostel's doorstep. She thanked me for walking her and said goodnight with a hug and a little kiss on the cheek, then turned and went inside. As I watched her go in, I couldn't help blush a little.

I then looked down at my watch to realize we had been walking for THIRTY MINUTES. It certainly hadn't felt like it. Worth it. I really enjoyed her company and she seemed to have really appreciated mine.

As I turned around to head back, it donged on me that I had absolutely no idea where I was. I had been so busy enjoying the conversation with Sasha and looking for a pub that I hadn't been paying attention to where we were going! I started trying to retrace my steps as best I could.

Somehow, I managed to find my way back to the Colosseum, but it was nearly impossible to figure out where Zach and the others were! It also didn't help that everything seemed to look the same at night — it was after 2am! And I had gone off without a map!

"Ok, Tim. Think." I told myself, straining my brain to remember and problem solve. "Zach and them seem to have disappeared so I can either continue searching for them or try to find my way back to the hostel." I chose to try to find my way back. I had no intention of spending the night out on the streets of Rome. I further considered the fact that trouble was more likely to find me if I appeared to be lost. With this in mind, I made every effort to appear as if I knew exactly where I was and where I was heading. I even jogged a good bit to keep up that appearance….because it's normal for people to go for a jog at 2am, right?

I fortunately happened upon 2 American girls whom I greeted with a friendly "hi!" and kind smile. I slowed my jog to a walk and approached them. I asked for assistance and they helped me find the direction I needed to head in. It turned out they were temporarily headed in the same direction, so they allowed me to walk with them for a minute while I caught my breath. I entertained them with the story of following Sasha then realizing I didn't know where I was. They naturally gave me a hard time and we all had a good laugh at my expense. After a short while, their path diverged and we went our separate ways.

After asking a few other random people walking around at night for directions, I eventually managed to find my hostel. I came in the door at 3:30am to find a somewhat concerned Zach waiting in the lobby.

"DUDE!" He exclaimed in relief. "Where did you GO? We waited forever for you to get back, but gave up. I figured maybe you decided to spend the night with her and would message me on Facebook so I came back here."

"Man I'm sorry!" I said. I then told him the story. He had a laugh at my expense and he was relieved that I wasn't dead. With everything wrapped up, we retired for the night.

"So much for a 'chill day,'" I thought as I pulled the covers over my head. Tomorrow we had zero plans and zero things on our itinerary. "Tomorrow will be a chill day. There's no way it can't be."

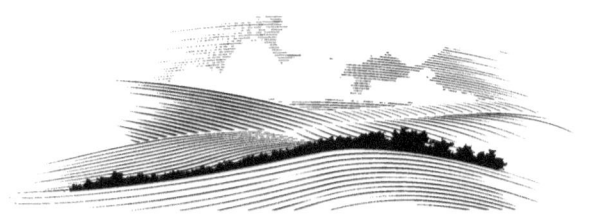

Tanja, Don't Kill Me

Friday, July 4th

Zach and I woke up and briefly discussed possibly visiting Pompei, where Mount Vesuvius rocked the ancient Roman world in 79AD during the reign of emperor Titus. Zach and I had done a study on the area at University and translated an eye-witness account of the event from Latin to English. As great as it would be to visit the city and possibly even Naples, we still agreed that we needed a day to take it easy. Our spirits were willing, but our flesh was very weak.

After getting up and moving into the common room, we downed a few boiled eggs for breakfast. About this time, Josh appeared. He ended up telling us about his agenda for today and asked if we would join him.

"Well," I said. "Zach and I have been going pretty hard the past few days and were planning to have a chill day. We need it." Josh completely understood, and assured us that if we came, we would take things slow and easy. I knew from personal experience that while traveling and exploring alone is fun, having companions makes the adventure much more enjoyable.

"Ok." I said. "As long as we take things slow and easy, I'm down." Zach concurred.

"Awesome!" Josh exclaimed, happy to have someone along for the experience. Once we were finished with breakfast, the three of us gathered a few things for the day and headed out.

Josh led us by a few small destinations he wanted to see that weren't crowded, then the one big one, which was the Pantheon. Since Zach and I had done the tour with Amanda, we shared with Josh all that Amanda had told us.

After visiting the Pantheon, we realized how hungry we were. There were plenty of places to eat nearby, but we knew that these options would be expensive due to their proximity to the tourist attraction. Instead, we wandered away from the area and down a couple allies until we came across a small restaurant that appeared to be local. We walked inside to find that it was a cafeteria style restaurant. We grabbed a tray and started down the line.

Perhaps because I had taken my glasses off or perhaps because I didn't look too closely, I chose my main course which I thought was some sort of chicken salad with noodles. However, after sitting down and preparing to eat, I made an unexpected discovery. What I had chosen was not chicken. As I combed my fork through the salad, I realized that what I had thought were chunks of chicken had tentacles, heads, and eyeballs!

"Holy shnikies!"[Pronounced shn-eye-keys] I exclaimed. "I've got a *squid* salad!"

"You didn't look at your plate before you got it?" Zach asked grinning. I told him I hadn't looked closely and made somewhat of an assumption. Both Josh and Zach had a laugh. "So whatchya gunna do, Tim?"

"I doubt they'll take it back," added Josh. "And they don't speak very good English."

I thought about it for a moment. I was actually a little excited. My adventurousness was coming out. On one hand, I could eat it and it might make me sick. On the other hand, it might be awesome. I knew I had a pretty strong stomach and like sushi, so…

"YOLO [you only live once]!" I said as I stuck my fork into one. I made a face as I took a fork full of tentacles in my mouth. Josh and Zach gave disapproving, yet anticipated looks.

I expected this squid to be rubbery with very little taste, like I had eaten in the form of sushi and tentacle and sea weed salad at a Japanese restaurant back home. However, *this* meal was surprisingly delicious! The squid were very well seasoned and covered in some sort of olive sauce with other herbs and peppers. In a matter of minutes, I had cleaned my plate. I considered actually going back for more, but didn't want to spend the money for a whole second meal.

After eating, Josh concluded that he had seen all he wanted to see for the day. Zach and I then told him about the Santa Maria Square that Amanda and Christine had taken us to. Josh said it sounded really cool, so we picked up a few drinks to sip on and headed in that direction.

We found a seat at the fountain just as Zach and I had done with the girls. There were people walking around, shopping, and eating casually while others could be heard from the outdoor dining areas talking merrily. We talked casually while people-watching for a while until I made a sudden realization. Once again, I needed to pee and there were no public rest rooms. Was I prepared to pay in order to use a restaurant's facilities? Hell no!

Just across the way was a large, very busy looking restaurant. I set down my beverage and walked over near the entrance. I tried to look very inconspicuous as I passed by and peered inside.

Judging by what I could see from outside the entrance, upon entering was an inside area which seemed to continue out of my line of sight to the right and around a corner. To the left was another corner that, judging by the size of the building, might be the direction of where the restroom should be. Immediately to the back from the entrance, I could see an open door leading to an outside seating area. I made an educated guess about which staff members were managers and felt sure that the regular, busy waiters would be less inclined to pay me much mind than the managers. After canvasing the target, I formulated a plan with an exit strategy should my plan fail and made my move. The game was on.

Swiftly yet nonchalantly I strode through the entrance. No one at the host podium – one barrier down. Quickly I moved beyond the podium to confirm that there was a large dining area to the right with people sitting around covered tables with wine in hand. Suddenly, I saw a waiter coming from the corner of my eye. I instantly constructed a casual yet believable cover story in case he stopped me.

"I'm trying to find my family." I planned to say. "I believe they are outside."

"Do you need help finding them?" I figured he would ask.

"No, I don't need any help. Thank you." I would reply. I would then proceed outside. If he were to stand by and watch me, I planned to look outside his field of vision and wave in that direction and say "hey!" — similar to what I did in England with the homeless "traveler".

As he came by me, I attempted to seem confident as I acknowledged his presence with a nod. I intentionally did not make eye-contact. Fortunately, he continued past me without pause.

I followed him with my eyes as he walked down the hallway and took a turn into a door with a small, circular window. From here, the hall turned a corner to the right.

"EUREKA!" I thought to myself. "This HAS to be the way to the rest room!" I then began walking in that direction, but just as I turned reached the kitchen door, I saw another waiter noticed me out of the corner of my eye. I had been standing by the podium for a few seconds, so he must have been on to me. He began walking after me. My destination was most likely just around the corner. As quickly and nonchalantly as I could, I made a b-line. I tried to maintain a casual stride with yet a swift pace. I could hear him gaining on me. He further started speaking in a questioning tone. I knew that until he spoke English, I had plausible deniability, so I ignored him. As soon as I rounded the corner, I saw the male rest room sign on the door a few paces forward and to the left. I took a few larger-than-normal steps towards a door, jumped a few paces, pushed open the door and strode in. Mission accomplished!

I half anticipated the door swinging open behind me and the guy coming in after me. He didn't, and I was able to relax and conduct business casually. I then exited the same way I had entered, walking now with a bit of a strut and wearing a smile. This had been a more complex venture than the last, and I had succeeded.

Shortly after rejoining Zach and Josh, a few girls came by and joined us. I initiated contact with them by giving a friendly "hello!" We instantly realized they were American by their accents. We connected on those common grounds and the conversation took off. Initially, it was Zach and I primarily involved in the conversation until they mentioned being from Michigan — Josh's home state. Josh then jumped in and I took a back seat as he took over the conversation. I turned to the one girl's friend and began chatting more with her, but would occasionally jump back into Josh's conversation for a positive comment or two in Josh's favor before returning to the other. Zach took a back seat to this conversation between me and the other girl's friend. He was already engaged to a wonderful woman and thus wasn't concerned about talking to cute girls.

After a while of talking, the girls both said it was time for them to head back to their hostel. Before parting ways, Josh suggested we meet up later. They agreed and Josh exchanged information with the girl he had been talking to.

Not long after the girls left, we too decided to head back. Despite the day being quite chill, or at least compared to days prior, we were still in need of showers before meeting up with the girls. Once we had returned to the hostel and freshened up, we chilled until Josh received word from the girl. We then grabbed a few things and headed out. I'm not sure I really had a reason other than simply *feelin'* it, but I also chose to bring along my guitar.

During our journey to meet the girls, we somehow ran into some other Americans. One was a really cool girl whose companion was a comical gay guy. They wanted us to come hang out with them, but we explained that we already had plans. Otherwise, we might have joined them. Meanwhile, it turned out that Zach had run out of smokes and had no idea where to buy any. The couple told us that they had some he could have. Zach was very interested. However, he didn't notice that the guy was hitting on him.

"Should we tell him?" Josh quietly said to me with an uncertain grin.

"No, he'll figure it out." I said chuckling.

"So I'm gunna run down the street with them real quick and grab a pack of smokes, but I'll meet yall down there right after. Sound good?" Zach said.

"Are you sure you feel ok about that?" I asked questioningly. He assured me that he did. "Alright man, well, please be careful. Keep your wits about you, and if at any moment you start getting a sketchy vibe, get the hell outta there."

Normally, I would say 'absolutely not.' I'm not quick to just let my friends go off with some people neither of us know late at night (it was around 10:30 at this point) by themselves. BUT, Zach is a pretty big guy (tall and in shape). The two he would be going with was a petite girl and a skinny gay guy. They would be catching a cab, so if they got to a destination and Zach got a bad vibe, he could simply stay in the cab and be driven elsewhere.

"I will Tim, I promise. And I mean," he said with an air of humor and an elbow to my arm, "I'm pretty sure I could take'em if I needed to." I laughed.

"Well, I mean, it's a skinny gay guy and a petite girl, so I'd hope so. But I'm just saying. I don't want to have to use my particular set of skills if you get *Taken!*" I concluded. I shook his hand, made sure he had his phone on him, then left him with the two Americans. Josh and I then pressed on to meet the girls as planned. "If something happens to him," I couldn't help think, "Tanja is going to KILL me."

The area we were meeting the girls wasn't much further according to Josh, and soon we found ourselves in a large courtyard with bars and restaurants all around. We wandered around for a minute until we came upon the restaurant Josh said we were meeting them at. She then appeared after Josh messaged her to announce our arrival, but our *buzz* was instantly killed. With her was a guy holding his arm around her. Thus, she had apparently either failed to mention to Josh that she had a boyfriend with her, or she had found a guy before we had arrived. To add insult to injury, her cute friend wasn't even there! Further, she seemed to be quite involved with the group of people she was with and they had all clearly been there a while.

Josh and I had expected it to be just the five of us hanging out. Now it was her, a dude, and a bunch of people we didn't know who had already started throwing down. It was not the chill night we were looking forward to at all. Yet, we politely talked for a little while before ultimately taking our leave disappointed.

Before we had exited completely, Josh said he needed to use the rest room, so I told him I would wait for him at a nearby fountain. He then went on to find a rest room as I swung my guitar from across my back and into my hand.

I then sat on one of the steps in front of the fountain. It was a beautiful night. The stars were out, people seemed merry, and my guitar needed to sing.

As I played into the cool night air, it felt great to receive approving looks from passerbys. A small group of guys collectively ended up moving closer in my direction. As one jam ended and I was transitioning into another, they approached me. They smiled and a couple said something in Italian. I returned the smile and said, "English? Sorry."

"Oh! You sound awesome!!"The guy said enthusiastically. The others echoed this sentiment.

"Oh, thank you so much!" I replied graciously. "I'm so glad you're enjoying it."

"Absolutely!" Another replied. "We love how you're just sitting here jamming out by yourself, not trying to get money or anything — just because you like to play and sing."

"Yeah, I'm just waiting on my friend to return from the bathroom. It's so beautiful out here, I couldn't help take the opportunity to play. Thank you again!"

Soon, Josh returned and said he had just met some really cool guys who had invited us out. I thus stopped playing and stepped away. I was both humbled and honored when a few people who had been listening to my music applauded me. I laughed appreciatively and thanked them kindly.

I followed Josh to where the said guys were, and it happened to be the guys who enjoyed my playing earlier.

"Guitar man!" They said excitedly. "You're coming with us?!"

"If you'll have me!" I replied. They all cheered as we began walking. I casually picked my guitar as we went, having no clue where we were going or where we would end up. I was letting Josh have the lead. I was just along for the ride. I just assumed it would be an adventure regardless. I only hoped Zach would be alright.

After a short walk, we arrived at a pub. It was simple, but a cool looking place. There was loud music coming from within and lots of people could be seen through the windows. We walked up to the entrance and started showing our IDs (it was a 21+ place). Things were going as one might expect until the man checking IDs came to me.

"You can't come inside with that." He said, referring to my guitar. Why this was a rule, I had trouble comprehending. Unfortunately for him, I was not ok with this and was feeling surprisingly bold. This feeling was particularly due to the fact that there was nothing I could do with my guitar and was certainly not simply going to leave it outside the bar for someone to steal.

"Um, yes. I can and yes I will." I replied sternly with a 'matter-of-fact' tone. Without another word, I walked straight past him and that was the end of it. I didn't stop until I got at least to the center of the bar. I was a little afraid he might come after me, but I was absolutely hell-bent on being at the bar WITH my guitar. Fortunately, he must have realized how unrelenting I was and didn't. Honestly, I felt pretty savage. Low-key flex.

Once I felt my presence was secure inside the pub, I connected to the free wifi to check and see if I had any messages from Zach. There was nothing, so I sent him an update on our recent developments. I was relieved when he replied not long after to confirm that he understood and was alright. We planned to meet back at the hostel.

Now that I was inside and knew Zach was alright, I was able to completely relax. The music being played by the DJ was fun, and we all had a great time. The coolest thing I thought was the fact that there were actually 2 bars in 1. On one side was the DJ playing loud music and where people were dancing. On the other side through some thick doors was another that was more chill and quieter. I ended up meeting some really cool people in both, including a group of Americans and Canadians. After getting to talk to and dance with a few super cool and cute girls, Josh and I decided to head back. After all, it was now extremely late. We bid our new friends adieu and headed back to the hostel.

During our journey back, we passed a really pretty fountain where two, very cute, girls were sitting. I had been picking casually on my guitar, which got their attention.

"Hey! You play the guitar?" One of them said in a Spanish accent. We must have *looked* American.

"Yeah, a little bit!" I replied. I stopped to join them and Josh followed suit.

Both girls ended up being from Spain and had lovely accents. I had actually never met a Spaniard, so it was a nice experience. One of them, the beautiful Verginia, seemed quite taken with me. She had lovely golden skin, brown eyes, and long, dark hair. The four of us enjoyed a fun conversation full of travel experiences, differences between Spain and America, and other interesting topics. Our time together concluded with them requesting I play a song for them, which I happily obliged. After the song, we exchanged contact information and made a plan to get together again the next evening for dinner.

By the time Josh and I made it back, it was after 4am! We obviously both expected to find Zach inside, but he wasn't there. I became a bit worried at this point. Where could he be? What could have happened? Tanja was *definitely* going to kill me.

I checked my messages, but hadn't received any from him. I messaged him, but no response. I felt sure he could take care of himself, but still, I knew I wouldn't be able to sleep until I knew he was back safe. Therefore, despite getting into bed, I restlessly waited. 4:30am came and went. 4:45, 5am, 5:15, 5:25, nothing. No messages, no Zach.

Suddenly, at 5:30am, a key was inserted into our room door. The door opened, and a tall silhouette appeared in the doorway and attempted to come in quietly.

"DUDE!" I exclaimed, half-laughing in relief to see my friend alive. "Where the HELL have you been?!" Zach, now realizing I was fully awake flipped on the light. I could instantly tell he was tired and out-of-it, but clearly alright. He laughed as he began to explain.

"Man, I ended up in the gay and lesbian district of Rome. I didn't even know they had those!" He said.

Unfortunately, I failed to write down how on earth he ended up there. It was extremely late and I was exhausted. I figured I would remember, but didn't.

"I managed to get them [the couple] to drop me off on the other side of the Vatican and I had to walk the entire way back." He explained. From the Vatican itself to the hostel was a little over 4 miles! "The buses weren't running for some reason, and then my phone died, which is why I couldn't message you. It took me forEVER to get back. I'm absolutely exhausted."

"Man, I bet!" I replied. "I'm just glad you're alright. Tanja would have KILLED me if something had happened to you!" We both laughed at this reality. "Did you at least get your smokes?"

"……..No." Zach replied, which made the entire story that much funnier. After this, we said goodnight and Zach flipped off the lights.

"So much for a chill day," I thought to myself once again. "Tomorrow. Tomorrow HAS to be a chill day."

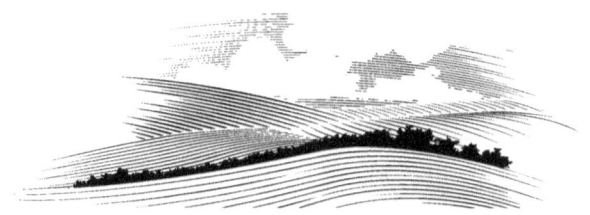

A Time To Chill

Saturday, July 5th

This morning, Zach and I both rose quite late, which was expected (though I don't recall the time). We eventually got up and took showers, then ended up in the common room where we met up with Josh again. We enjoyed each other's company for a while before realizing we were all a little hungry - but not enough to have a full meal.

"Yo!" I exclaimed suddenly with a brilliant idea. "Let's go get some gelato!" It was the perfect in-between hungry and not-hungry snack, which would carry us over to lunch. The other two guys agreed that it was a great idea, so we decided to set off in search of some.

Fortunately, it didn't take us long to find a place. I of course got pistachio flavor. It was delicious. The three of us sat and enjoyed our treat while Zach recalled for Josh his adventure from the previous night.

"So what are we gunna do for [late] lunch, boys?" Zach asked after Josh and I had made sufficient jokes about his story.

"No idea," I confessed. "But if we do something tonight, I'd prefer to spend as little as possible."

"I was thinking the same thing, actually." Zach replied.

"I think there's a market down that way," Josh pointed out.

"Since you were both so kind to share your meal with me last time, how about we throw in for some pasta? I'll take care of the meat if you guys want to supply the rest."

"Wow, that's a great idea, Josh!" I replied, "And a very kind offer. I'd be down with that. Zach?"

"Sounds like a plan to me." Zach replied through a yawn, which essentially embodied this group's current state.

We left the gelato shop and casually walked around for a little bit in an attempt to wake up before circling back around to pick up supplies from the corner grocery. Shortly after arriving back at the hostel, we pulled our supplies together and begin cooking. Meanwhile, I sent a message to Verginia to touch base about dinner later.

It didn't take too long for the food to cook, and unlike my last experience in Nice, we chose to purchase pre-made sauce rather than try to make it from scratch. After the food was prepared and we finished eating, I still hadn't heard back from Verginia. We then simply relaxed in the common room for a while listening to music and talking casually until Josh suddenly had a realization.

"So guys, I don't know if you two are much into soccer, but Germany is playing France in a World Cup match tonight. Would yall be interested in going to the Irish pub down the road and watching it?"

"Absolutely!" I replied. Zach agreed.

I checked Facebook one more time to see if Verginia had responded, but she had not. I assumed she must have changed her mind or was busy. I was a little bummed because I was really looking forward to seeing her again, but it was what it was. Zach, Josh, and I then strolled down to the pub and enjoyed a couple beverages as we cheered on Germany against France.

It ended up being a great game with a victory for Germany. If they keep this up, they'll go far! Once the game was over, we decided to head over to the same square as we had the previous night. I used the pub's wifi to check my messages again, but still no word from Verginia Along the way, we passed by a couple ancient statues of some of our favorite characters in Roman history such as Julius Caesar. Zach and I both of course had to get photos with them. About the same time, two American girls came walking along who we ended up talking to. They were both headed to the same place we were, so we all decided to head that way together. They were really nice and a lot of fun to talk to.

We got down to the square and found a nice looking restaurant and had a seat while Zach went and alerted a waiter of our arrival. We ordered a few drinks and ate light (the guys and I had of course eaten "lunch" only an hour or two prior so we weren't real hungry). We enjoyed each others' company and shared some laughs. However, at one point while I was talking, I wasn't paying attention and accidentally knocked over my drink. The girls' reaction told me what they were thinking despite having had only a couple. This made me quite subconscious, which hindered some of my enjoyment the rest of the evening.

After another hour or so, we all decided it was time to head out. The two girls, Zach, Josh, and I left together, then parted ways around midway back to our respective hostels. Once back at the hostel, I checked my phone via the Internet and realized I had just missed Verginia and her friend after leaving the pub!

Apparently, she had responded to me not five minutes after we had already left the pub! I felt so bad! I apologized to her and she responded to me. We both expressed that we hated we missed each other, but it was what it was. She suggested we try again the next night. I told her I wished I could, but this was my last night. However, I must confess I was slightly tempted to stay one more. Would it have been worth it?

Verginia and I regretfully wished each other good travels moving forward with the hopes that perhaps one day our paths would cross again.

Zach, Josh, and I sat in the common room discussing our plans moving forward. I simultaneously attempted to find rooms in Venice, which was where I had originally intended to visit next. However, it seemed impossible to find an economical room! They were all single to 4-bed rooms, but to book the room, all beds had to be paid for! Twenty to fifty euros per bed per night just wasn't going to cut it for my budget. As I expressed aloud my frustration, Josh made a suggestion.

"Hey, I'm actually planning to go to Florence tomorrow, then to Greece before heading to Spain for the Running of the Bulls. I'd love if you came along." He said. I have a buddy from Greece I plan to stay with who lives on the beach. I'm sure he'd be cool if you came along. What do you say?"

This was an interesting offer. I hadn't been to Greece and had not originally intended to visit. I also was familiar with Florence through Ubisoft's Assassin's Creed II, but had not planned to go there either. This was also another opportunity to travel with a companion rather than by myself, and Josh had become a cool, new friend. What did I have to lose? As long as I could get to Bon, Germany within a week to stay with Zach & Tanja as panned, I was good to go! And thus my plan was made. Usually, I would look for a hostel, but I was tired and some time in the morning so there was no rush to make it happen tonight.

Shortly thereafter, we all headed to bed.

Last Minute Decision

Sunday, July 6th

When Zach and I woke up, neither one of us were interested in breakfast. Instead, we decided to simply go grab coffee and bring it back to the hostel. It wasn't until lunch time that we felt like eating. We then chose to return to the pizza place we had gone to upon arriving. He and I reminisced about the craziness of the week and what all we might get into when I got up to Germany.

Upon returning to the hostel, we found Josh in the common room. Zach went to the room to pack while I stayed behind. Josh and I chilled until Zach returned at which point we said our goodbyes.

After Zach left, Josh and I realized we had better get busy finding a place to stay for the night. Worst case scenario, we *could* stay in Rome another night, which would give me another chance to see Verginia, but at the same time, we were both pretty tired of Rome and ready to move on. Therefore, we searched for hostels in Florence.

It seemed that most places in Florence were more hotels than hostels. After nearly an hour of searching, however, we settled on a place called The 7 Santi (or *The Seven Saints*). It cost a little more than we wanted to pay, but it was one of the cheaper options that wasn't too far from the city center. Considering that it included an in-room shower and two 2 beds, it wasn't a terrible deal. As soon as we had booked it, we packed our things, checked out, and headed to the train station.

The ride from Rome to Florence was extremely long. The only redeeming factor was the absolutely beautiful scenery provided by the Tuscan countryside. Rolling green foothills, small, quaint villages, stone-arched bridges over small rivers, and ruins of what appeared to be medieval castles whizzed by. Such things as this never get old and pictures simply cannot do them justice.

We eventually pulled into Florence a little after 6pm. After leaving the platform, we picked up a city map provided at the station and followed it to where the hostel appeared to be. However, despite the instructions provided by the hostel and our map in hand, the hostel seemed nowhere to be found. Was this like Sirius Black's house in Harry Potter? Was there some sort of magical incantation we had to recite in order for it to appear – which we did not have?

Before us stood a tall cathedral on the corner of two streets. Immediately next to this cathedral was a series of shops that ran into a gas station. Josh and I walked around the cathedral and down to the gas station, then back. This time, we happened to notice a sign attached to the black, iron bars of the cathedral's entrance that read, "Hostel 7 Santi." There was a concrete path leading along side the hostel that we had assumed was merely a part of the church. We had both technically seen the sign, but had not actually read it, assuming it had something to do with the cathedral (seeing as it was attached to the aforementioned bars).

We followed the concrete path around to the side of the cathedral where the back of the shops were located. Tucked away, unseen from the street, was an enclosure separated from the outside by metal bars similar to those in front of the cathedral but with fake leaves hanging on it creating a man-made hedge-wall. The entrance opened up to a beautiful courtyard with plenty of outside seating, filled with lush greenery, an outside bar, and large tent coverings with tables and chairs set underneath. The ground was made up of red, clay brick with gray stone going down the middle, splitting the red brick like a river towards a narrow, green, arched walkway canopy bearing the text, "Hostel Dei 7 Santi," on the front. At the end of the canopy was the front door of the hostel.

Josh and I got checked in quickly at the front desk and were informed that breakfast was served inside at 7am though I failed to note the price (very cheap though, I'm sure). In addition, a buffet-style, all-you-can-eat dinner was served outside every night along with your choice of drink (a house-made sangria, a beer from the bar, or a water/soda) included in the price. The cost for this complete dinner was only €7, which was €5 cheaper than what I had budgeted! The outside bar would be open each evening as well.

Josh and I continued to our room to get settled in. We found it to be small, but had enough space to manage. The only odd feature was the shower. It was placed in the corner near the bed that Josh chose. It was a sliding door shower with clear glass. The shower itself was nice, but it was not located within its own separate space ergo zero privacy. Aside from this drawback, I was very satisfied so far.

After dropping off our things, we went back down to the patio area where we were met with amazing smells of covered dinner. I couldn't wait to dig in! We found a place to sit at a covered table and began talking to other people as they also sat down. By the time our table's seats were taken, Josh and I were sitting with a few Germans, a couple Ausie girls named Maddy and Indie, another Ausie guy named Riley, and two girls from Holland named Paula and Kelly. Soon after we had all gotten acquainted, the hostel staff announced that it was time to eat. Our instructions were very simple: go up, grab a plate, fix it, and enjoy!

The spread the hostel provided for only €7 was so much more than I was expecting, and SO good! I honestly can't even describe how delicious it was! Breads, potatoes, pastas, salads, seafood, veggies, fruits, and things I'm not even completely sure what they were but tasted incredible! Never had I eaten at a restaurant, much less a hostel, where the food provided was this good! I turned to Josh in between bites and expressed that I was now completely fine with the price we paid for the room. He felt the same.

The table of new acquaintances ate and drank together merrily, enjoying the food and fellowship. It's funny how people from completely different cultures and parts of the world can come together with one commonality (being travelers) and so quickly become friends. This was the case for our table, having only met for the first time ever this evening.

As we ate, I couldn't help but notice Paula from Holland who was sitting near me. She wore shoulder-length brown hair, had big brown eyes, and a contagious smile. She smiled and laughed a lot, but didn't speak English real well, so her friend, Kelly, had to help her.

Kelly was really sweet, not to mention lovely. She spoke near perfect English, though with a strong Dutch accent. She wore blond hair with bright, blue eyes and fair skin. She would occasionally pause to fill Paula in on something we said or a joke I would make. She herself also had a fun personality and kept up quite well. She explained that her and Paula were on holiday for a couple days, and randomly chose Florence to visit.

Riley was tall, dark headed, and tan. He had a thick Ausie accent and a great sense of humor. He and I connected well. Like Kelly, he also managed to get most of my jokes and references. I inquired about Australian culture and (naturally) about Crocodile Dundee and (R.I.P.) Steve Irwin.

"Dundee is actually sort of a joke in Australia. Steven Irwin, though, is a national treasure." He explained at one point.

"Ah, as he should be." I replied in reference to Irwin.

The table spent the next few hours enjoying one another's company and discussed possibly exploring togeter the next day.

"I'll be honest." I confessed. "I'm not sure what time I'll be up, but if I manage to catch yall, I am down."

Soon, we all begin retiring one-by-one. Riley, Josh, and I were the last of our group left when we finally decided to turn in as well. It had been quite a day, and ended on a beautiful evening. I was very happy with my decision to join Josh on this trip and looked forward to the possibilities of tomorrow.

As I was heading past the front desk, I passed a cute girl who was checking in late. She had a dark complexion, was around two heads shorter than me, and wore big framed glasses. Being in a fun, happy, confident kind of mood, I spoke to her with a silly off-hand comment referring to her glasses. This became a joking conversation between us that led to me learning her name was Angelica and she was from Colombia. I mentioned looking forward to seeing her around, but she said she was only visiting for one day.

"Oh, well, I hope I run into you tomorrow, but if not, I hope you have a great visit!' And with that, I bid her a good night and was off to bed.

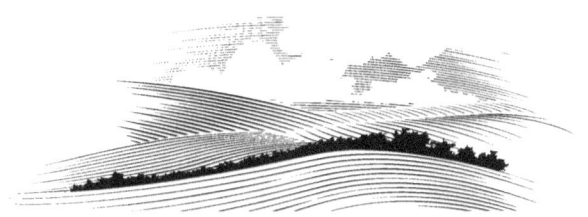

Don't Follow The Germans

Monday, July 7th

This morning I woke up to find Josh checking his phone. I asked him if he wanted to go grab breakfast.

"Na, I'm sleeping in today." He said. I, on the other hand, felt well rested. I therefore got up, threw a shirt on, slipped on my flip-flops, and headed down stairs.

When I got down, I saw that the breakfast spread was almost as good as the dinner spread. Fruits, breads, butter, cereals, cold breakfast meats, tea, juice, and coffee were set atop a table. After fixing myself a plate and a cup of tea, I looked over and saw the two Ausie girls from last night. I went over and asked if I could join them to which they were happy to oblige.

The conversation was pretty slow moving, partly because tea doesn't wake me up like coffee does, but European coffee doesn't wake meat all. However, we did talk and enjoyed our breakfast together. I was intentional about enjoying this time with them as they were leaving after breakfast. It turned out that their mom was with them as well whom turned out to be really nice. I unfortunately didn't get to talk to her very long. Suddenly, a minute or two after the Aussies' mom had joined us, we were interrupted by Paula who came bustling in looking for me.

"Tim!" She exclaimed. "Are you coming??"

"What?" I asked, still a little foggy.

"We are going to explore, remember?" She reminded me. Technically, I hadn't actually forgotten. I just hadn't expected them to have quite such an early start.

"Oh! Yeah, yeah, yeah! Sorry! I'm still waking up!" I replied.

"Ok. We are leaving in a few minutes! Hurry!" She said insistently then retreating back into the courtyard.

I hated to rush and not enjoy the rest of breakfast with my two friends — especially since their mom had only just joined us and she was hilarious! Yet, I didn't want to miss the opportunity to explore the city with these other friends. Therefore, I finished my breakfast with haste and apologized to the two Ausie girls and their mom — who were very understanding. I bid them a farewell and ran out of the door.

Waiting in the courtyard were Paula and Kelly as expected, Angelica from last night, and a guy I hadn't met named Gustavo from Mexico. The girls of course gave me a hard time about being late and making them wait, but then we all headed off.

First, we stopped at the Piazza Del Duomo (*The square of the Church*) which featured Santa Maria del Fiore (*Saint Mary's Cathedral of Florence*) and Campanile di Giotto (*Giotto's Bell Tower*). The top of Santa Maria's dome could be seen at a distance high above the other domestic buildings lining the streets. This large church towers over the city at 375ft, which is 60ft higher even than Big Ben. Needless to say, it was very impressive. The church's exterior polychrome, marble panels with traces of its original coloring still yet visible through the white bordering took my breath away. Everything about this building popped like a great work of pure art. Having taken over 100 years to build and completed during the early part of the Renaissance (c.1436) anyone can see why this beauty is clearly a national icon.

I knew mere words would not be enough to capture the magnitude of this structure, so I took out my camera and did a "Mission Log." This was (selfie-video as described earlier). As I did this, the girls took note and unapologetically made fun of me for it. I of course shot back with jokes of my own — all in good fun. I then explained my reasoning for doing this, which they admitted was actually a good idea, though still goofy. I couldn't argue there.

The duomo was unfortunately closed when we arrived at the entrance due to interior construction/renovation but would be open later. We therefore decided to visit the great bell tower of Giotto which was located just to the side of the massive church.

The bell tower was perfectly square and narrow all the way up to the top, which was said to be 278ft. As one might imagine, there were no elevators, so we were required to climb 414 steps. Round and round we climbed with 2 levels that broke up the climb. Once we made it to the top, words could never do the view justice. The entire city and beyond to the countryside could be seen from this vantage point. We peered down to see the Spanish tile roofs on every structure, the narrow streets between them, and the rolling foothills of the Tuscan Apennine Mountains beyond. It was pretty incredible.

As I looked across the city, I was unable to resist recalling the hours I spent playing the Assassin's Creed game as Ezio. In fact, I led Ezio through this part of the city countless times and climbed to the top of this very church. There was a sense of nostalgia, and having visited this place in the game, I had a deeper appreciation and respect for the designers of the game. To say they did a fine job would be a vast understatement.

Again, I pulled out my camera and started filming a Mission Log. Occasionally, I would have to pause to let other visitors by because the walking space was so narrow. While I was doing this, the girls came over and got a kick out of watching me. This time, they expressed interest and wanted to be in one. I was happy to feature them, especially since I had forgotten Angelica and Gustavo's name! Just like with Lilly back in Nice, I cleverly had them each come on and introduce themselves. We had a great time doing this and I was able to get Angelica and Gustavo's names again without them knowing I had forgotten. Win-win!

We exited the tower and started off in the direction of Piazza Della Signoria, which featured the replica of Michelangelo's statue of David (along with other statues and things). As we were walking, however, Angelica stopped. Her attention had been drawn to some paintings being sold by a street merchant. I had learned previously that many (if not most) of these merchants sold these paintings as if they were their own, but they were actually painted-over prints. Still, they did a good job painting over them and they looked really nice.

While Angelica was looking, the man came over and encouraged her to buy one. She considered it for a moment, but then seemed to decide against it. She then kindly told the man, "no, but thank you." Unfortunately, the salesman would not be taking the rejection so humbly this day. Instead, he persisted in trying to convince her to reconsider. She again said "no thank you," and started to move away. The man followed and began attempting to make her feel guilty for stopping to look without buying anything. Judging by her reaction to this, it seemed to be working. As she continued attempting to move away, the man continued to follow. He was not giving up! I couldn't sit by any longer.

"Hey, you ready to go?" I asked, casually walking over.

"Yeah," she said, but was interrupted by the man. She again politely said "no," yet the man was unrelenting.

"We're good, man." I told him. "She obviously doesn't want anything." I said this in a polite, but strong tone. The man, however, ignored me and continued to implore her, which at this point I felt was definitely harassment, As he continued, she looked up at me. Although she didn't say anything, I could see the cry for help in her eyes. That's all I needed.

I stepped forward so that I was in front of Angelica facing the man. I positioned myself to have Angelica just behind me and to the immediate right so half of her was behind my body and the other was safely behind my right arm that I had outstretched as an extension of my bodily barrier. I was now clearly taking over the situation.

"She said no." I stated very sternly, with a commanding tone in hopes he would now back off.

"I'm not talking to you!" He shot back defiantly and with some aggression in his voice. "I'm talking to HER."

At this point I was done. She and I had both tried to be polite, but now he was starting to *piss me off.*

"No-no-no. You're *done* talking to her. NOW you're talking to *ME.*" I said loudly and aggressively with a scowl. "And I **swear** if you say **one more word** to her or me, I'mma whoop your ass right here in the street! So what's it gunna be, huh?!"

Honestly, I didn't *want* to fight him. I was hoping to simply scare him, but Angelica was now under my protection and if this harassing joker didn't step off, I was ready to throw hands.

After I finished speaking, this nucklehead actually started to say something back. I didn't even think about it. Rolling my right hand into a fist, I lunged hard as if about to throw a blow. This motion caused him to jump and stumble backwards. Finally, he seemed to get it. I wasn't joking.

"Woah, woah, ey, hey!" He cried, moving away. "I call the police!" I then took another two steps forward with a look of angry intention, both fists now balled. At this, he turned tail and went swiftly away. We never saw the police.

It's weird. I'm usually not that aggressive in nature. Something about this trip, however, woke something inside of me — something wild, fearless, dangerous,… and I *really* liked it. Angelica thanked me for coming to her aide and walked with me as we rejoined the others who had been waiting.

We made it to Piazza Della Signoria and found the square to be crowded. We walked around looking at statues of different icons along with the expected replica of David. I attempted to get a selfie in front of David, but somewhat failed. Somehow I had managed to cut David off at the chest while my head was awkwardly positioned next to his groin. I showed the others this awkward photo and after having a laugh at my expense, Kelly helped me take a better photo.

Just as we were getting ready to leave the area, I see a tall, dark haired guy walking past out of the corner of my eye.

"Riley!" I called. Riley turned abruptly in surprise. He then came over. "What are you doing?!"

"Uh, well," he said chuckling. "I woke up late and waited a little while for someone to come out but when no one did, I figured you guys had already left." He was thereby walking around alone and we couldn't have that so we invited him to join us. He of course was happy to.

We then left Piazza Della Signoria and found a nearby strip along a river with several shops and places to eat. The girls all wanted to find and eat gelato while Riley, Gustavo, and I meanwhile needed something more sustaining. The girls, therefore, left to go find gelato while the guys and I found a pizza shop. The guys and I split a pizza which ended up being absolutely delicious (better than the pizza in Riomaggiore)! After lunch, we regrouped and journeyed back to the Santi Maria's.

The church was now open to visitors, but only for climbing to the top for a view. The inside of the actual church (sanctuary, etc.) was still unavailable. In any case, we all entered in through the designated area and climbed the steps to the top. When we made it, the view was not much different from that of Giotto's Tower, but still beautiful all the same.

Not long after catching our breath from all the steps, we began making our way back down. Between the Italian sun, the amount of walking, and of course the hundreds of stairs we had climbed, we were all pretty exhausted. Considering this, along with the fact that the girls were all leaving today, we decided to head back to the hostel. Angelica, who had brought her things with her and already checked out, walked with us until she had to part ways. We said goodbye to Angelica before continuing back to the hostel.

Once back at the hostel, Riley, Gustavo, Kelly, Paula, and myself reclined at our dinner table under the tent. We talked here for a while, but soon exhaustion began overtaking us. One by one, we all retired for a nap with the plan of returning later.

An hour or so later, Riley, Gustavo, and I were back on the patio. Josh, who had returned from site seeing while I was napping was also with us. As we sat, a large group of German high school students came into the area. Apparently, they were on some sort of school trip. They were excited to meet our small, eclectic group representing different parts of the world (Gustavo of Mexico, Riley of Australia, Josh of the northern United States, myself of the southern United States). The students appeared to be instantly drawn to us and engaged us in conversation. To be honest, it got to be a little much sometimes. Josh in particular became annoyed due to a couple of them constantly asking to bum a smoke.

Eventually, Paula and Kelly appeared with their backpacks on.

"You're leaving already?!" I exclaimed, having not expected them to just up and leave like this.

"Ya," they said in their cute, Dutch accents. "We've got to go get dinner before our plane leaves."

"What?! We figured you'd stick around here for dinner! Dang, that sucks." I replied disappointedly.

"No, I'm sorry!" Kelly said frowning. "But if your travels bring you through Holland, let us know!"

The guys and I began saying our goodbyes and giving hugs. Then, I had a sudden realization.

"HEY!" I exclaimed. "Holland is right near Amsterdam, right?"

"Yeah!" Kelly answered." It's not too far. Not much more than an hour on the train."

"Well,…I'm actually planning to visit Amsterdam later this month. Maybe I might drop by for a visit?" I suggested with a hint of jest in case they thought it was a weird idea.

"Oh yeah!!" Paula exclaimed excitedly. "You SO should! That would be SO much fun!"Kelly echoed this sentiment. The girls made sure we got connected on Facebook right away.

"Let us know when you're coming and we'll plan a whole day to show you around our town!" They said, already excitedly half-discussing it with one another in Dutch.

We said final goodbyes with me promising to stay in touch until I made it up to see them, then they were off. I was excited for the opportunity to see them both before returning home. They are both SO much fun to be around, and I knew we would become good friends. On top of this, I couldn't help feeling an interest in Paula. I felt like we had developed a positive connection between getting to know one another over the night before and throughout the day this day, and was glad for the opportunity to spend a little more time.

After the girls left, the guys and I sat around the table. It was a funny feeling that can't really be described. However, we all felt it. The sentiment can only be explained as an unspoken notion of, "Now it's just us, men. What shall we do?" As if all being on the same wave link, it was unanimously decided that we would have a chill night. Yet up in Heaven, God laughed.

As we grabbed drinks from the hostel bar, the German students started appearing and surrounded us once more. They started telling us about this place not far away that their teacher planned to bring them to. Naturally, they wanted us to join them. The way they talked, it did sound great, and very chill. The guys and I discussed it, and decided that since it was not far — though they didn't know exactly where it was — we would go and hang out for a little while. It would essentially still be a calm evening, so we agreed to join them. They were very excited to have us join them.

A little while later, we followed the large body of German students. We were led by their teacher away from the hostel and down the street. Assuming we would be walking a short distance, I was wearing my casual clothes and flat-footed Sperrys (aka "boat shoes"). It was fun at first. One student brought a guitar and would strum and sing silly songs as we all walked. A few of them were in English and were songs I recognized from the radio. We joked and talked while we walked, but soon it became evident that our destination was not so nearby.

As we pressed on my feet began to hurt, and I was sweating from the warm air in my good, casual clothes. Multiple times, I considered turning back. Yet with each time I asked a student how much further it was, it was always the same answer: "we're nearly there!" The only reason I did not turn back was for my poor feet. It would have surely taken longer to get back at this point than it would to carry on reluctantly, so I stayed the course.

After an hour of walking down the Italian roads, mostly made of stone or uneven brick pathways, we finally arrived at this glorified spot. To my grave disappointment, I found it to be severely wanting. This was especially due to the length of time it took to get there, and the tole the journey had taken on the bottoms of my feet! In other words, this spot was SUPER LAME. It was a large square with a lot of people (some with dogs) sitting around drinking, and 3 Spanish guys playing guitar and singing together as a performance for the crowd. We stopped at a corner store to grab a drink, then promptly went and found somewhere to sit. I could not have been more thrilled just to sit down and get off my feet.

The guys and I all sat together, and a few of the German students joined us. They were all super enthused about *the culture* they were experiencing. I, however, was not amused. It actually turned out that Gustavo felt the same way I did. We were both tired and not into what was going on at all. My concern was that I wouldn't be able to find my way back. Gustavo, however, felt confident he could. I was so ready to leave, I decided to take the chance. The others said they would be along later, but weren't quite ready to leave. Without further delay, Gustavo and I headed out back down the road.

After a long walk, but at a quicker pace this time, Gustavo was able to navigate us back to the hostel, even though we ended up getting there a slightly different way (took a few wrong turns but knew the general direction). By the time we made it back, it was after 4am! So much for a chill night. Gustavo and I wasted no time wishing one another a good night before hastily parting ways toward our respective rooms.

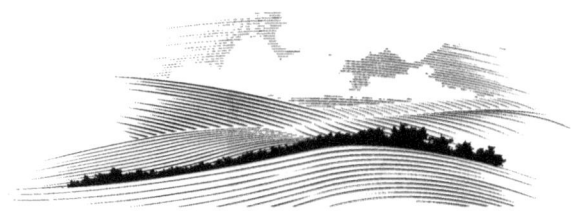

Still Just Guys

Tuesday, July 8th

Josh and I both woke up early this morning in order to run down and grab breakfast just before the closed. I rolled out of bed and stood up. My feet were still sore from last night's miserable adventure. I beared the soreness long enough to get down to the common room and eat before immediately returning to bed. Josh and I had every intention of sleeping in after this. Besides, the only thing to do on my to-do list was getting a final bit of laundry done.

A few hours later, I awoke slowly from sufficiently sleeping in. It felt like a much needed accomplishment. I then threw a load of laundry into the washer before again returning to my bed. I pulled out my tablet and looked for open hostels in Venice. I had hoped the pricing had changed, but it had not. This situation now provided an interesting opportunity. I wasn't expected in Siegburg for another week. I therefore simply needed to choose anywhere else to go before heading to Zach and Tanja's. I hadn't the slightest clue as to where I might go, but since I had time, I put off finding a place. I laid back down and closed my eyes. Today would be a chill day for certain.

Josh and I eventually both got up and took turns using the shower while the other kept a turned back to provide a little privacy. It was a bit awkward showering in the clear-glass shower with the other guy in the room, but we made it work. By the time we had both had the chance to shower, it was nearly 3:30pm. We had slept in and taken so long to get up that we hadn't had lunch! It suddenly donged on us how hungry we were.

"Dude, let's finish cleaning up a little and go get some food." I suggested. Josh agreed.

"I need to get some cash first, but after that, yes." He said.

Josh then used his phone to find a place that did exchanges. The only problem was that it appeared to be half way across town. I agreed to go with him, but only because the rates at this place were unbeatable.

By the time Josh and I had arrived at said exchange place, it was 5:25pm.

"CLOSED?!" Josh exclaimed in frustration as he saw the 'closed' sign. "We just walked across the freaking city and you're telling me your closed?" I should have been frustrated too, but somehow I found it hilarious. The best part, however, was another another small sign that read in big, bold English print: ***OPEN EVERY DAY: 8:30AM - 7:30PM.***

Not only had we now walked half way across Florence to get to this exchange place, but the sign clearly said it was *supposed* to be open! I couldn't stop laughing at the situation in contrast with Josh's frustration. Josh was now super pissed and very hungry. We have a term for this in Mississippi: *hangry*.

"You want to try and find another place?" I asked still chuckling at his poor luck. I could pay for his dinner if I needed to, so it wasn't like he would go hungry.

"Forget it. I've got enough cash to get dinner, but I'll have to find some later or first thing tomorrow. Let's go find food."

"Why don't we just go back to the hostel for dinner?" I recommended.

"Yeah, let's do that. I could smash on some buffet." He agreed.

"Me too." Said I.

On the way back, we stopped at a smoke shop. Josh grabbed a pack of smokes. I ended up noticing a Cuban cigar. I pointed this out to Josh as well. Cubans are illegal to sell in the USA due to an embargo against Cuban goods, but are known to be high quality. Josh and I both therefore bought one. Next, we stumbled upon a wine store and decided to purchase some fancy wine to go with dinner. Fortunately, pretty much all wine in Italy might be considered "fancy" in America so we didn't have to spend a ton of money.

Josh and I arrived back at the hostel to find people already eating. Josh carefully placed the bottle between us to sneak it inside and swiftly found a seat at our usual table. We next went and grabbed our complimentary sangrias along with a plate for food. I carefully poured my sangria out into the bushes when no staff member was looking. Josh then grabbed my glass and covertly poured me some wine under the table.

I took a swig and was blown away. This wine was the perfect choice. Absolutely incredible! It was sweet, but with a nice oaky finish, which offset the sweetness. The wine was much better than the sangria in this way. I don't mind a sangria, but the ones here were too sweet for me.

Riley suddenly came walking out of the hostel as I lit up my cigar. He joined us and received a pour of the wine. Gustavo also came out a short while later and was also given a pour. For the rest of the evening we relaxed. Josh and I enjoyed our Cuban cigars as the group of us talked. When we had finished the wine, we switched to pints.

It's amazing how I had only known these guys for such a short time, yet we had such a connection. I had only known Josh a couple days more than Riley and Gustavo. Yet, in just a couple days, we had become great friends. We each came from different parts of the world. Our cultures were very different. Our accents were very different. Yet, at the end of the day, we were just 3 guys drinking beer, making jokes, telling stories, and enjoying the night. I hated this would be our last night together, but felt sure we would remain connected thanks to social media.

The next morning I would be leaving, yet still had no idea where I would be headed. I was a little scared to be honest. I could hear the voices of doubt in the distance, but remained confident in myself. I believed that I would be able to figure it out and it would all be fine. Contrary to one of the voices, God had not left me yet.

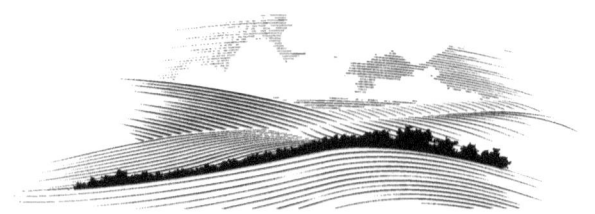

A Series Of Fall-Through Plans

Wednesday, July 9th

*K*nock, knock, knock! "Haskeeping!" A voice suddenly came from behind the door. Then with a crack it opened. "Haskeeping!"

Josh and I had overslept after carrying on late into the previous evening. We both immediately stirred; both still both half-asleep.

"Late check-out!" Josh called instinctively. "I think it's an extra €30, so €15 a piece. Cool?" He said. I nodded in agreement. Josh then stumbled out of bed as the housekeeping woman left. I rolled back over and fell into sleep again.

After what had only felt like 10 minutes, the sound of our door unlocking again woke us. The housekeeping woman shuffled in. She seemed surprised to see us still in our beds and looked displeased.

"You are supposed to be gone!" She said in a thick Italian accent. "You have to go!"

"Sorry! Sorry!" We replied.

"You are supposed to leave!" She said insistently.

Josh and I started pulling our things together, The woman was clearly annoyed, but left us to gather our things. As soon as the door was closed, however, we laid back down in our beds.

I grabbed my tablet and started looking up places to stay in Venice. I hoped again that perhaps the prices had changed. This was not the case. Everything was still so expensive and the requirement to pay for a minimum of 4 beds remained. I considered stopping in Bologna instead, which looked beautiful in the photos. I was disappointed when I saw that the prices and requirements in Bologna were similar to Venice.

I wasn't sure what to do! I could either reach out and see if Zach would allow me to come early, or I could pick a random city along the way and simply hang out. It was a quagmire. Going to see Zach and Tanja early could potentially cause me to overstay my welcome. Trying to find somewhere along the way carried the risk of not finding anywhere economically reasonable. I shared my dilemma with Josh.

It turned out that Josh had a similar dilemma on his hands. He had planned on flying to Spain to participate in the Running Of The Bulls, but it didn't start for another few days. He also happened to have a friend living in Greece whom he intended to visit. They had apparently spoken briefly about him visiting but never nailed down exactly when. It seemed now would be the perfect opportunity for the visit.

"Why don't you come with me?!" He suggested. "I'm sure my friend wouldn't mind. He's a cool guy."

I felt a little uneasy about it, but he ultimately convinced me to join him. My greatest concern was intruding on his friend so I insisted that he make every effort to touch base with him first — for this reason along with making sure we did in fact have somewhere to stay when we got there.

"*BANG, BANG, BANG!*" Came the woman's fist against the door. She then opened the door and begin cleaning as Josh and I scrambled to get our things together. "YOU ARE SUPPOSED TO LEAVE! SECURITY WILL KICK YOU OUT!" She shouted.

Once quickly out of the hostel, narrowly escaping a security call, we made for the train station. In order to get to Greece, the easiest option was to take a ferry across the Adriatic Sea. This required getting to the port located in Ancona. We arrived at the train station to discover that the next train stopping at Ancona would not be leaving for one-and-a-half hours. We didn't have any other choice but to sit and wait. The good thing was that it seemed like a pretty straight forward trip so we didn't mind waiting a little while. We knew it would be worth it.

An hour and a half later, we boarded our train and were soon at the port of Ancona. So far so good. We then went and inquired about tickets for the ferry. This is where things took an unexpected turn.

"SEVENTY EUROS?" I exclaimed to Josh. And the price wasn't even the worst part! The ride was a 15 hour, over-night trip! On top of that, the ferry was apparently full, so it was standing-room only (no bed, no seat, no pillow, nor blanket). Then, just when it sounded like it couldn't get any worse, a STORM was brewing, so they were expecting rough waters!

I thought about it. I really did. I carefully weighed the pros and cons; the adventure verses an alternative route — which neither of us presently had. I didn't want to bail on Josh who was less deterred, but also felt very uneasy about the idea. I had experienced rough seas on my journey across the Irish Sea. I recalled how rough those waters were, and it wasn't even storming — just real windy. Imagining seas this bad or worse for 15 hours over night without the minimal comforts of a bed, a seat, a blanket, or a pillow sounded very unpleasant and potentially a bit scary. I knew I would get absolutely zero sleep and be miserable throughout the experience and beyond due to lack of sleep. It was now after 5pm and Josh had not been able to get in contact with his friend. Therefore, even if I were to chose to go for it, where we would stay upon our arrival was very uncertain.

"Man,...I can't do it." I finally confessed after mulling it over for several minutes. "I'm sorry. I have no idea what I'm going to do, but taking the ferry under the present circumstances sounds like an absolutely miserable experience." He was very disappointed to hear this, and asked what I was going to do instead. "I guess I'm just going to catch the next train headed north and see where I end up."

I thanked my friend for inviting me to join him for the Florence adventure and for the opportunity to join him again in Greece, but concluded that if he planned to stay the present course, this was where our ways would be parting. "I hope we can maybe meet up again back in the States." I said, then shook his hand before heading back to the train station.

I sat down on a bench inside the train station and put my head in my hands. I had absolutely no idea what I was going to do. I then pulled out my tablet and used the station's wifi to search for cities to the north and respective hostels. It seemed that the further north one went, the more expensive hostels became. They all also seemed to have the same deal as Venice.

"Can I even afford to drop €80 for a single night, and if I can, would there be any place still open by the time I arrived?" I thought to myself. I was scared. I wished I wasn't alone in this situation. At least if there had been someone with me, it wouldn't have been quite as scary. My heart beat hard as my mind raced. I tried to hold onto the faith that God was still with me; that he would somehow work things out. I thought about my buddies back home and wished an impossible wish, that one would somehow magically appear. It is interesting that when you're in very uncertain and scary situations, you wish for ridiculously impossible things.

But no one was coming. I was alone, and the voices of doubt and fear were returning:

"You don't have what it takes....you're not gunna make it...God isn't with you..."

As I'm trying to stay sure of myself while battling the voices of doubt and fear, looking for possible cities and hostels to stay in, I notice someone approaching out of the corner of my eye. I ignored them. The person then plops down next to me. Trying not to appear too concerned, I look up to acknowledge their existence out of politeness. I was absolutely shocked to see that it was Josh looking back at me.

"I couldn't do it man." He said with a big sigh. "You're right. I tried to convince myself to go though with it, but I agree. It would be miserable and I don't know if I'll have a place to stay." Words could not express the joy and relief I felt in seeing him! I instantly felt 10 times better. I was no longer alone.

"So what now, bro? What should we do?" He asked as much to me as he did to himself.

I told him the trouble I had been having with the availability and pricing style of hostels. He could tell I was frustrated, concerned, and frankly lacking in creative ideas.

"Ok," he said. "Let's just chill and worry about catching a train right now." He pointed to a train route in the app I was using. "This one's got the longest run heading north. Let's just worry about catching *it*, then figure out what to do along the way." I agreed that this was a good plan. No need to stress so much now. We could get a beer on the train and look at the map while we traveled.

Josh and I boarded the decided upon train at 8pm. We sat down, ordered much-needed beers for the ride, plugged in our devices, and went to work looking for a reasonably priced place to stay for the night. One of us pulled up a potential city while the other looked up hostel options in the area. Most hostels we found seemed to be booked out or really expensive. With each passing city, our options became fewer and more expensive. Eventually, the train would stop, and we could find ourselves spending the night on benches. It seemed hopeless.

"There's a hostel with availability in Milan." Josh said at one point. "After that, there's pretty much nothing. It's a little expensive, but we're running out of options." He was right. The train only had a couple more stops before the end of the line. Neither of us were interested in sleeping outside.

"Book it." I said.

"2 beds, €40 each." He replied. I confirmed my acceptance.

Despite not being particularly happy with the pricing, we both sighed a big sigh of relief. We had a place to rest for the night, a new adventure awaiting us tomorrow, and a friend to share in the experience with. God is good, and hadn't left me yet.

Josh and I were now able to relax. Our fate seemed taken care of so we could sit back and enjoy the remaining long ride to Milan. It was during this trip that Josh and I began a deep discussion. We talked about our personal backgrounds, life experiences, and faith journeys. I ended up sharing with him some very real pains in my life regarding my poor self-esteem and self-confidence growing up; the belief that I was both stupid and ugly (made worse by having terrible luck with girls while my friends somehow seemed to get it right). While I often wore a face of confidence on the outside, the truth was that it was like a balloon — nothing but hot air. I shared how I had a tendency to imagine myself as tv and movie characters who had confidence and mimic their behaviors which probably made me seem weird. Only recently before leaving on this trip had I really attempted to accept myself as I was and tell myself that these two things were not true of me. It was much easier said than done — like looking at the sky and trying to convince yourself it is green.

Josh and I delved into this topic for the next four hours. He shared different but relatable experiences and challenges he had faced in his own life. He gave me new perspective. He showed me a more real and positive way of looking at things. He helped me see that these things I struggled against, which no one else had ever seemed to understand, were purely lies. Furthermore, there was plenty of evidence in my past to back up the fact that I wasn't stupid — this trip being one of them.

There is much more to this conversation as so much that I could probably write a book on it. However, I won't linger long on the issue. The important factor was that this friend, who I had only known for around a week, who I did not expect to see again after parting ways at the port, returned unexpectedly and ended up having a conversation with me that literally changed my life. Had I not taken this trip that I was convinced I would die on, that I was scared God was against me on, that I wasn't sure I would have what it took to go through with, I would have never met Josh and had this conversation. I had spoken to others about this issue before, but they either didn't believe me because my outer projection suggested otherwise so they thought I was joking or maybe being dramatic or they were unable to help me see through it. Yet, over the course of 4 hours, Josh set me on a new mental track by which I would be forever changed for the better. I am eternally grateful. [So Josh, if you're reading this,…thank you.]

The train pulled into the station at Milan, and after a short walk, we were at the Zebra Hostel. We expected to get inside, check in, and be shown to a room. We were taken aback when we realized Josh had somehow made a grave mistake.

"Oh,..we weren't expecting you tonight." The hostel worker said.

"…..what??" Josh and I both said concerned.

"Yeah, it looks like you're booked for tomorrow night and the next night. We're all full tonight." The guy explained.

Josh and I stood dumbfounded. Staying here was the plan. It was our *only* plan. We literally had nowhere else to go. Sleeping outside became a very real reality in my mind. Josh was thinking the same thing (he told me later). All I could do was take a deep breath and accept it. I hoped it would make a good story at least. I was grateful again that I was, in the least, not alone. The voices of doubt and fear still begin stirring.

We had made a mistake. It was no fault but our own. It was late, and our tired minds had confused our dates. The hostel was booked, and had no obligation to help us in any way. By all rights, they could have justly said, "tough luck, guys. Hope you find a place for the night," and sent us on our way. Yet to our astonishment, the hostel staff did not. Instead, they did something unbelievably kind and completely unexpected. After some conversation between them and some running around, we were instructed to follow. Uncertain as to what was happening, we did.

The guy led Josh and I through the hostel, up some stairs, and opened the door to a room full of bunk beds — all of which were clearly occupied. A moment later, two other guys came in carrying single-bed mattresses which they laid on the floor. Another staff member then came in with an arm full of clean blankets and pillows which she placed on each bed.

"I'm sorry." The lead worker said apologetically as the places were being set. "This is unfortunately the best we can do for tonight. Tomorrow though, you can have one of the regular beds."

"What?! No, man! Thank YOU!" Josh and I both replied shocked. We were absolutely grateful for this unbelievable act of grace . We both thanked the staff profusely for this accommodation. Then, as if we couldn't have been happier, the manager further comped us both a FREE BEER at the hostel bar downstairs! I couldn't believe it! God came through yet again, and made the otherwise impossible happen. Praise God!

After getting settled in and placing our things safely in storage, we went and found a nearby kebab place for a late-night dinner. We then returned to the hostel for a couple beers where we met a few interesting people. Soon, however, we retired for the night. It had been along and stressful day, so sleep came easy.

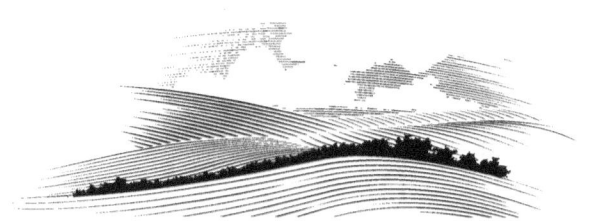

Ride On The Wild Side

Thursday, July 10th

Josh and I woke up this morning thankful to have had a bed to sleep on. The night's guests were already getting checked out and beds were being stripped. After getting showered and dressed, Josh and I selected proper bunks and settled in. Once this was done, it was time to get brunch — as it was around 10am.

After setting off in search of food, it wasn't long before stumbling onto a sushi place. The sign advertising its "€10 all-you-can-eat" immediately caught our eyes. With one look at one another, we knew we were both thinking the same thing and immediately went inside. We sat down and looked over the sushi menu. Within minutes we had ordered our first round. Those poor workers were not expecting two hungry Americans to come in this day. One plate after another, Josh and I chowed down on several plates of sushi. The chef behind the counter broke a sweat as he tirelessly chipped, rolled, and prepped sushi for Josh and I who placed our next order upon receiving the previous. We ate so much that the couple other people in the restaurant couldn't help sneak glances in our direction.

By the time we finished, Josh and I were stuffed to the rim. I think the chef was relieved. We were both extremely satisfied and expressed our gratitude to our server as well as the sushi chef who was still sweating from his relentless preparation. We further tipped the chef a little extra for his efforts.

We next returned to the hostel where we rented bikes. This was partly to save time and money, but also to burn off some of the carbs we had just inhaled. Renting bikes from the hostel was easy. Riding them to our destinations, however, proved to be quite hazardous!

As we turned onto the busy street, we realized there was hardly a sidewalk. We were therefore forced to ride along the side of the street! Cars, motorcycles, big busses, and scooters raced by us as we rode. The wind from the busses shook us, and occasionally forced us to swerve away. Our bike path was almost as narrow as the wheels of the bikes themselves, and the vehicles passing us were mere inches away. To make matters even more hazardous, there were obstacles sticking out into the bike lane from the side that forced us into traffic to get around. A couple times, we even had to stop and go around the other side altogether. Such obstacles included leaning street lights, jagged curbs, trash, poorly paved spots, and potholes (among other things). I have always enjoyed a good bike ride, but this was a nightmare! I prayed the whole time I would simply make it through alive.

After only a few near-falls into traffic, we arrived at the *Duomo di Milano* (Cathedral of Milan). Josh and I approached the massive church, which happened to be the biggest in Southern Europe. It was an impressive site. We then continued inside which looked like most every other cathedral I had visited so far, except for one thing. Located all over were the final resting places of different individuals (I assumed notable priests and such). What made these different from the others was the fact that they were not in stone tombs like others I had seen. Instead, they were in glass cases! Yes, dead bodies behind glass, some of which had visible rotting flesh! Whoever thought this would be a good idea was clearly nuts! Yet, I have to admit, it was kind of cool,…but still absolutely disgusting.

After leaving, we hopped back onto our bikes and road a short distance to Castello Sforzesco (Sforzesco Castle). The castle was unfortunately closed this day, so Josh and I simply took a rest at the lovely fountain on the grounds. Behind us was a gorgeous clock tower rising up from the castle walls with multiple levels of artistic design. Not long after arriving, Josh and I noticed ominous clouds starting to move in. We then decided to take our leave before getting caught in a storm. Neither of us fancied being on a metal bike if it were to start lightening.

We chose to take a different route back which proved not to be as bad as the one we took to arrive. Soon we had arrived safely back at the hostel, and had time to run out for some sandwich fixings at the nearby grocery store. After eating, Josh and I retired to the bar in the common area where we could see the rain coming down through the windows. It was here that we learned of the hostel bar's happy hours pricing. For a full liter of quality beer, the price was only €6! My day was made.

Josh and I stayed at the bar for the rest of the late afternoon and evening. We met some interesting people including a girl from Brussels, a Belgium guy from Naples, Italy, and 3 cute posh girls from Essex, England. They were all really cool and we had great conversation. We loved one another's accents and learning about one another's cultures. Later, the Holland vs Argentina match of the World Cup games came on and we all watched. Since it was Holland playing, I couldn't resist pulling out my tablet and messaging Paula.

"Are you watching the match?!" I randomly messaged her. I was excited when I saw the indication that showed she was responding"

"Of COURSE!" She replied.

She and I talked throughout the match, commenting on the game here and there. It turned out that she wasn't a big soccer fan outside of her country playing in the World Cup. This meant the bulk of our conversation was about other things. I made plenty of jokes and kept her sufficiently entertained throughout. The match ended in a shootout with Argentina winning. Despite the match's conclusion, Paula and I continued messaging back-and-fourth for some time after, until she confessed to being "an old person," meaning she was tired early. I attempted to convince her to stay up, but she couldn't, so I wished her sweet dreams and promised we'd talk again soon before I made it up to visit.

I looked around to notice Josh chatting it up with a few British girls on the couch nearby. Just about this time, he came up to the bar to grab another drink.

"Dude, they want me to come to Nice, France with them. I'm not sure what I should do." He said.

"What about Running of the Bulls?" I asked.

"It's not for a few days." He replied.

"Oh, then dude, you should definitely go with them!" I exclaimed.

"You think so?" He asked.

"YES!" I said enthusiastically. "Those girls are cute, and Nice is awesome!" I then told him about the water fall, the beach, and the strip. By the end of our conversation, I had convinced him.

He then returned to his seat with the girls. They sounded enthused when he announced that he would indeed join them in Nice. I didn't feel like chatting it up with girls, so I remained at the bar until I finished my drink. Then, I bid those left at the bar, as well as Josh, a good night.

As I laid down on my bed, two drunk girls came in. One seemed to be crying and acting really pathetic about something silly. We've all been there though, haven't we? I unavoidably listened enough to gather that the one crying was struggling with feeling inferior and inconfident. I couldn't help empathizing with her as I am all too familiar with similar struggles. I said a silent prayer over her that she would find a way to overcome these issues and that *her* friend — like Josh did for me — would help her see that she is of far greater value than she presently realized.

After a while, the girl seemed to calm down and both girls quieted. Once they were settled, I rolled over myself and drifted off to sleep.

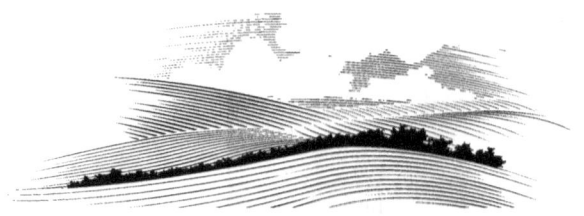

Interpreting Squiggles

Friday, July 11th

Iwoke up this morning thrilled for what lied ahead. Today I was heading to Germany! I planned to stop for a couple nights in Munich before traveling North to see Zach and Tanja in Siegburg! I hopped out of bed, went down and grabbed a quick breakfast, then returned to the room. As I climbed onto my bed, Josh stirred.

"Good mornin'!" I said with a tired but cheerful voice.

"Mornin'" Josh replied lazily.

I pulled out my tablet to look up hostels and train times. I was glad I had already decided to stop in Munich because a ride from Milan to Siegburg was apparently 15 hours long! Stopping in Munich would not only allow me to visit a major city in Germany, but also to break up the long ride. After selecting my train and booking a hostel in Munich, I went ahead and looked at available attractions. By the time I had written down my train and taken a short list of possible attractions, Josh had also gotten up and had his things together.

"You ready?" I asked.

"Yeah, let's head." He replied, still a little groggy.

Josh and I went down to the train station together. The mood as we walked was a little somber. We had been through a lot together and had become great friends. We both knew we may never see each other again, but were excited about our next adventures.

After we arrived, we parted in order to get our tickets. As if to foreshadow my poor luck that was coming, I learned that the train I had originally chosen was full. I therefore had to quickly choose another one.

"The only one leaving sooner than the next several hours is one leaving in a few minutes." The train worker said. I didn't even think. I paid, took the ticket, and raced in the direction of the train's platform. I managed to make it to the train and grab a seat with about a minute to spare. As I sat down, I couldn't help be a little upset. I had to leave in such a rush that I wasn't able to look for Josh and say a proper goodbye — much less explain my situation.

"I'll just message him to explain what happened." I resolved. It was all I could do.

I looked down to review my ticket information. I immediately realized something that made my eyes widen. This train was not heading to Munich, but to Verona! Verona was north, but obviously not north enough! This meant I would have to get off at Verona and *find* a train headed to Munich. If I was unable to find a train to Munich from Verona, I would have to settle for staying in Verona for the night or dropping the Munich plan altogether. To make matters worse, this train did not have wifi. I was therefore unable to look up hostels in Verona or look up trains leaving from Verona to Munich. Needless to say, I was anxious. The voices of doubt and fear started again, but I resisted giving them audience. I took a deep breath and said a prayer. After all the times God had come through for me thus far, I knew he could do it again. However, there came a new voice I was now forced to reckon with.

"Geez, why are you now CONSTANTLY hoping God will save you in these circumstances? He's going to get tired of doing it. It's YOUR fault, why should HE intervene? You're annoying him." It said.

"You don't have what it takes, so you are constantly having to hope God will bail you out." One of the familiar voices whispered.

Were they right? Was God annoyed with me? Was this an indication that I indeed didn't have what it took? Would God get tired of being there for me whether these circumstances were my fault or not (many of them certainly were)?

I wrestled with this for the next 3 hours until my train arrived at the Verona station where I had to put my thinking on pause. I immediately went to the ticket booth to inquire about trains to Munich. To my great relief, there was 1 train headed to Munich from here. The only problem was that it wouldn't be leaving for 1 hour 15 minutes. It was also a slow train, meaning it was going to take 5 hours to get there! I wasn't happy about it, but there were no other options. I purchased a reservation, then found a place nearby to get some food.

Having secured a train to Munich, the voices quieted, though the questions of the one still haunted me. I didn't have an answer. God wasn't responsible for me. By all rights, he could allow me to perish. Yet, he had come through and made a way for me numerous times since I had left home — whether I recognized it at the time or not.

"God is love." Came something.

I paused. It was not a voice nor a thought that I heard. It was more like a feeling; a sudden and immediate understanding. A simple truth that somehow had been locked out of my conscious mind. God is love. These three words that suddenly manifested in my soul forced the voices that were distant yet still present in my head to pause, then remained silent. To this notion, they had no answer.

My circumstances hadn't changed. With each passing moment, the more anxious I became. It was looking like I wouldn't be arriving in Munich until around midnight. Would the hostel be open? Would I have a place to stay? I sat back in my chair in the restaurant near the station and took a deep breath as the voices of doubt and fear seemed to make an attempt to regain traction.

"God is love." I whispered out loud, and again they were silenced.

About this time, I looked at my watch. The train would be leaving in about 15 minutes so I needed to go ahead and board. I left the restaurant and found my platform. Despite being the slow train, I was thankful that the seats were actually very comfortable. In fact, this train was nicer than most I had ridden yet. It was compartment style — exactly like The Hogwarts Express, complete with sliding doors.

Only a few minutes after the train pulled out, the countryside opened up to the Alps in absolute brilliance! The mountains jumped up out of nowhere, climbing over one another. Some had grass growing over top, others with white rock peaks. All along the way, the train passed villages, farm houses, medieval-looking buildings and a few small castles, clearly once inhabited by nobles long ago.

Five hours after initially pulling out, the train arrived in Munich. It was now 11:35pm, and I still had to find my hostel. I wandered around until I found the metro. I followed the instructions provided by the hostel to get on the metro train. However, as soon as this train started moving, I got the odd feeling that something was wrong. I looked around to see a woman who looked to be a nice person.

"Um, hallo," I said with an uncertain smile. The woman looked at me. "Sprichst du Englisch?"

"Yah." She replied politely

I explained my concern in English which she was easily able to understand. In turn, she confirmed my feeling. It wasn't that I had gotten on the wrong train exactly. It was just that this train changed directions. I was therefore now heading in the opposite direction I needed to go! I placed my hand over my face in frustration, which was exacerbated by my weariness.

"Don't worry! It's ok!" The woman said in response to seeing my frustration. "Here, this is what you need to do.."

The woman pulled out a metro map. She pointed to the routes and explained what I needed to do. In addition to this, she got off at the next stop with me. She pointed to where my train would be coming in at and reiterated what stop I would need to get off on. A few minutes later, another train came screeching in. She double checked that I knew what train I needed to catch. I confirmed and thanked her for her help. She then boarded and was off. I will be forever grateful for her help.

I sat there in the station for what seemed like forever. This metro had available wifi, so I took the opportunity to look up hostels nearby in case mine was closed.

I figured Munich would have plenty of hostels, so I was surprised when I was unable to find any…at all. It was now 11:50pm. My hostel closed at 12am. I felt sure I could make it if the metro train arrived and I made a mad dash from the next station to the hostel. Yet, it seemed I had the very real potential of sleeping outside, which was a scary thought.

I began putting a plan together as I continued praying the train would arrive soon. I figured I might could find a bench to sleep on or some bushes to lay near.

"I guess I could just cuddle with my travel backpack, use my electronics backpack as a pillow, keep my arm through a strap of my guitar case, and have my knife in my pocket for protection." I thought.

The only relief was the fact that guns were not as prevalent in Europe compared to the United States. Bad guys could obviously still get them, but the typical mugger here would be much more likely to carry a blunt object or blade than a gun. I also figured that a criminal wouldn't likely attempt to murder me in my sleep over a bag. Still, I hoped and prayed I wouldn't have to find out; that I would somehow make it to my hostel in time.

"SQWERRRRRR!" I suddenly heard coming from the railway. I jumped up with my things, and prepared to board. Within minutes, I had boarded the train, gotten off at my stop, and was racing up the steps of the metro. I had my tablet in my hand looking at the Google Maps screen shot I had taken in Milan. After climbing the last step of the station, I glanced at my tablet and bolted in the direction of my hostel. I noticed as I raced down the street that there were no visible street signs. I even looked at the sides of buildings as I had learned in Rome, but saw nothing.

I ran into a couple guys walking who appeared to be friendly and asked them for help. I told them my hostel name and showed them my screenshot. From what they could tell, I needed to take the next right which was a little ways further down the street. I thanked them and continued walking, following their directions.

I attempted to keep my wits about me as I walked. I was in a foreign country, a little bit lost, very late at night. I maintained constant awareness of my surroundings, and stayed near the lights. Before I made my turn, I took a moment to look for any activity I ought to be mindful of. As there was none, I pressed on.

A few minutes later, I made it to the correct area of the correct street. It took me another couple minutes to identify a building labeled as "20." I found it, but was in disbelief. Surely, the building I was looking at was not it. It couldn't be!

The building in question was surrounded by a gate, had several windows, no lights in or around it, and nothing to indicate that it was a hostel. The building looked very residential — just like the others surrounding it in the neighborhood. If this *was* my hostel, it was very clearly closed. I was scared.

It was fairly cool outside and a misty rain gently drifted down from the sky. All my things were beginning to get a damp glaze from the moisture. I looked down the street. I could hear people carrying on at a small restaurant bar.

"I guess that will be my first stop." I thought, starting to consider possible options. "Maybe I'll go there and have a few drinks. Then, if the rain has stopped, maybe I can find a place to sleep. Or maybe I could go there for a few drinks, ask people there about all-night places and pull an all-nighter." Neither one of these options sounded pleasant.

"Excuse me!" I said to a friendly-looking man riding by on a mountain bike. I wasn't sure why someone would be riding this late at night, but he looked like a serious cyclist (as opposed to a homeless person).

"Ya?" He asked.

"This is 20, right?" I asked desperately without considering the fact that he might not speak English. Fortunately, he did.

"Yeh, yeh, that's 20." He replied.

"I'm trying to find my hostel, and it says the hostel number is 20, but I'm confused." I explained, showing him the screen shot.

"Ya, this doesn't look like much of a hostel, does it?" He replied with a tone of humor and confusion. "Let me see if I can pull it up on my phone to see that you're at the right place. What's it called?" I told him the hostel's name. He looked it up on his phone, and sure enough, he got the same result.

"Well," he said, "have you knocked?" We both looked awkwardly at the dark building showing no signs of life.

"No." I said. "But I guess that's all that's left to do. Thanks."

"No problem." He replied, slowly starting to continue on his way. "Best of luck to you!"

I think he felt bad for me, but there was nothing else he could do. As he rode off, I approached the dark building. I knocked on the large, wooden door. I looked into the side windows hoping to see some movement or for a light to come on — anything. There was no answer, no movement, no lights — nothing. I knocked again, this time while praying that somehow, some way, God had this handled. Not a stir followed.

I knocked again, this time BANGING on the door. I was now feeling complete desperation coupled with anger that my poor luck was about to have me spend the night out on the street in the cold and rain, or drinking Red Bull and Vodka (which I NEVER do) all night to stay awake and (hopefully) not be absolutely miserable for the next 7 hours. I banged loudly one more time, speaking in a raised voice. "HELLO!?" I waited. No answer. No light. Nothing.

I stepped back from the door defeated. I turned around, peered out into the night, and…smiled? Yes, I smiled. I couldn't help but smile. Was I defeated? Yes,… but no. I didn't have a place to stay, sure, but this opened up two options that were as absurd as they were unbelievable. I smiled because in that moment, my mindset was forcefully changed. I smiled because I knew the only thing that could possibly make what I was about to experience endurable was to think, "Damn. This is going to be one Hell of a story to tell."

Going to the bar I saw earlier for a drink still seemed like the best place to start. I would then decide what to do for the next 6 or 7 hours — whether trying to pull an all-nighter (having to also keep up with all my things) or attempting to sleep outside in the rain. It was a tough call, but I was somewhat leaning toward the all-nighter idea for the sake of the story.

I had just made it to the curb of the property headed towards the bar when something stopped me in my tracks.

"Ey! Are you Tim?!" A male voice with an Australian accent called from behind me. I turned around and looked up to see a guy leaning out of the 2nd story window directly above the large door I had been knocking on.

"Yes! Yes!" I called back. "I'm Tim!" The relief that rushed over me was indescribable. I could have nearly cried. Yet, there was a tiny part of me that was a little bit disappointed. I mean, seriously, what a story that would have been!

"Good!" He replied. "There is a note on your door! Go around the side and I'll let you in!"

I thanked God Almighty out loud as I followed the guy's instructions. I found a small door around the side of the building nearly hidden by vines and shrubs. The door then opened to reveal a young guy.

"Hey man! Yeh, come on in!" He said. "The name's [truthfully, I failed to write down his name, so let's call him..] James!" I then followed James up the stairs. "You never showed, so the staff wrote this note on your door and told us that if a bloke by the name of Tim showed up, to let him in. I'm in a room with my wife and mom. Your banging woke them up, who then woke me up, so about that time, I looked out the window and saw you standing there. I was like, 'that's gotta be him.'"

"JAMES. I literally can't thank you enough!" I shouted in a whisper after he showed me around the hostel. His wife also stepped out to see what was going on. I thanked her profusely as well. They were both glad they could help and were glad I as not left outside all night. Then, James handed me the note left by the staff.

Tim. You have room number [squiggly mark]. Your room [squiggly mark] is in this floor. The key to the room is inside. Breakfast is from 7 to 10. Thank you.

This squiggly mark could have been a few different things. It could have been a 5 just as easily as it could have been a 4. It could have been a 4 just as easily as it could have been an *S*. It also could have just been a squiggly line or a tiny drawing of a snake. James and I both looked at it and weren't entirely sure whether it was a 4 or 5. James' mom came out at this point and he asked her to look at it. She thought it looked like an *S*. James' wife, who was German, looked at it next and said it looked like a 5. We all then agreed that it was not clear but appeared to look like a 5, *not* a 4. Just to be sure, James walked over to room 4 to see if it was open, but it seemed to be locked. This solidified that it must be room 5.

I bid James and his family goodnight, and they went back into their room. It was now well after 1am. I meanwhile grabbed my things, which I had set down for a moment, and went to room 5. When I opened the unlocked door, I found a surprise.

As I walked in, a guy suddenly jumped up out of the bed! He very obviously was not expecting anyone else. I jumped back surprised as well. Both of us were very confused. I apologized and explained that the hostel must have somehow double-booked the room by mistake. I gave him a super-short summery of what had happened to me and showed him the note. After looking at it, he also agreed that it looked like a 5. Fortunately, he was 1) a fellow American and 2) really cool.

The room had a small, extra bed in it, so he moved his things to allow me its use. I dropped my things, changed out of my wet/damp clothes, and crashed into a heavy, much needed sleep.

Part VI: Germany

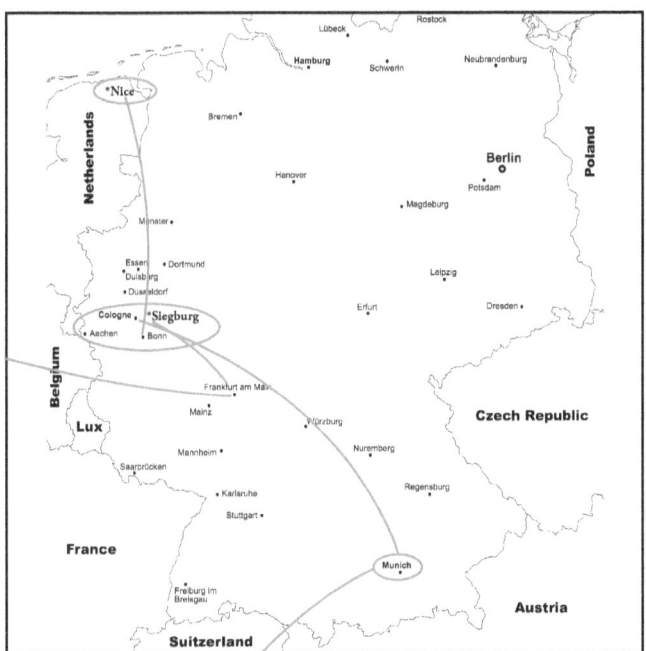

Map of Germany: https://d-maps.com/carte.php?num_car=14453&lang=en
- Lines, circles, and words with asterisks are author's annotations and not on original map

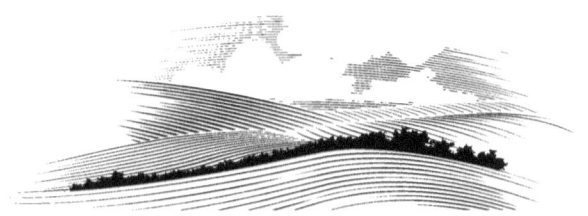

Bayerische Motoren Werke [Aktiengesellschaft]

Saturday, July 12th

I woke up this morning from a dreamless sleep. Rolling over, I was immediately reminded of my current predicament as my unplanned room mate stirred. The previous night had been so bazaar, we hadn't really spoken or introduced ourselves properly.

"Man, I'm really sorry about last night." I said quietly. "I'm about to get up and get it all figured out. Maybe they'll comp us both a night for their mistake or something."

"It's all good man." The guy replied though a yawn while rubbing his eyes. "I'm sure they'll get it figured out."

"I hope so." I replied. "I'm Tim by the way."

"Adam." He said. I responded by stepping out of bed and reaching over to shake his hand.

"Great to meet you." I said. "Now to get all this squared away." And with that, I walked promptly out of the door.

It turned out that despite the efforts of James, James' wife, James' mom, and myself, the squiggly line that we all ultimately came to agree must be a 5 was in fact a 4. I was grateful for the staff's humility and understanding of the confusion. They apologized for the unclear number written and said they would charge Adam and I half price for previous night. I then returned to Adam's room to collect my things before the staff showed me to my actual room for the upcoming night.

"Great news!" I exclaimed. "They're only charging us both half price for last night!" Adam smiled approvingly with a nod.

"Sweet! So they've got you all set up with your own room now?" He asked.

"They did." I replied laughing. And it was exactly as the note they left explained. The only difference was that the squiggly line *was* as 4, not a 5!" I showed him the note they left me again, and he laughed. We then continued chatting as I gathered my things.

Our conversation led to our plans for the day. We coincidently both planned on visiting the nearby BMW Museum and chose to visit the museum together!

"Ok, well I'm going to grab breakfast and have a shower once I get into my room. Meet me in the common room/breakfast area whenever you get ready."

"Cool! Sounds good." He agreed. I then left the room and joined the staff member waiting for me.

The staff member led me to my room and opened the door. It wasn't locked! I had apparently just not applied enough force against the door when I went to open it the night before. My error caused the door to seem locked. I hadn't wanted to push too hard lest an angry guest burst out wondering who was trying to get into his/her room. I didn't mention this to the staff member for fear he might fault me and charge me the full price of last night's stay. The staff member then handed me my key and left me.

I walked inside, dropped my things, and collapsed onto the big, soft bed. This bed was ten times the comfort of the small one in Adam's room. I was still so mentally and spiritually exhausted from last night's series of mishaps and near-outside sleeping arrangements (or likely all-nighter) that I couldn't get up. To be honest, I would have been ok if Adam had given up and left without me. It was this day that I realized what a true introvert I was (introvert as in *one who gets energy from being alone*). Slowly, I felt energy starting to return to me. After 20 minutes, I felt enough to get up and get ready.

I rolled off the bed, got showered, and cleaned up. I now felt refresh and rejuvenated. I left my room for breakfast and found James and his family preparing to leave.

"What?!" James exclaimed with a surprised laugh when I told him about the number. He told his wife and mother who responded in similar fashion. I thanked them again for letting me in and trying to decipher the squiggly line. They were glad to have helped — even if they too had been wrong about the squiggly — and wished me safe travels. I did likewise.

I turned toward the breakfast spread as James and his family made their way out. This spread was nothing like the one I had enjoyed in Florence, but it was enough. As I ate, Adam came out of his room and joined me. Coincidently, he had been feeling tired as well and thought I might have gone on without him. We were both glad it worked out, agreeing that touring with someone else was more fun than touring alone.

After breakfast, we grabbed a city map from the hostel desk and headed out. Once out of the subway stop, the museum was only a short walk. I was thankful for this cool, German weather. In Italy, it seemed to be *hot* ALL THE TIME — kind of like Mississippi, actually. None-the-less, our walk was fairly enjoyable in the breeze, and soon we were at the museum's entrance.

The museum featured automobiles of all kinds such as cars, race cars, motorcycles, racing motorcycles, and bicycles. There were antique models of vehicles still perfectly preserved as well as cars "of the future," that were like nothing I had ever seen before. Each themed exhibit of the museum contained an explanation of what you were looking at and its history. Some exhibits even included moving pieces that showed how they were made complete with commentary. Included in its own section was a theme devoted to showcasing BMW's involvement in aviation development. Adam and I both could have spent hours staring longingly at these incredible vehicles we knew we'd never be able to afford in 3 lifetimes. After eventually taking in all we could handle, we took our leave.

"So what should we do next? Any ideas?" I inquired. Neither of us had anything else on our agendas really.

"I dunno. Do you feel like taking a walk through Olympic Park?" Adam asked.

"Yeah, sure! That sounds good." I replied. As mentioned, it was a nice, cool day, so a walk though a park would be perfect.

The enormous, beautiful park featured a multitude of scenic eye-catchers. A small lake sat in the center with man-made structures springing up to suggest water sports. In the backdrop of our view stood a large stadium in the distance. A wide field next to the water allowed a number of ducks to waddle through the green grass. Hills rolled on the opposite side of the stadium view across the horizon. Adam and I chose to climb one of the hills.

At the top of this hill, we were able to see for miles. All around us were rolling hills and forest. All the grass seemed to be perfectly cut. Rabbits could occasionally be seen racing from one thick bush to another. On one side, we could see the city in the distance, to another, the Olympic Park below. Then suddenly, Adam and I noticed something.

"Look there!"I said. "Big tents!" Adam confirmed he saw it too.

"I think I hear music." Adam replied. I noticed the music then too. It appeared to be some sort of festival.

"What could it be?" I thought to myself. "Oktoberfest is in September. It's only July...."

I immediately wished to go investigate. I couldn't be sure what Adam would want to do. I really wanted an adventure partner, especially for something like this, but he might be ready to head back. I knew we were both a little tired from all the walking we had done, but I wasn't going to pass up a possible festival in Germany. I resolved that if he didn't want to go, this was where we would part ways.

"Dude, it looks like some sort of festival down there. Let's go check it out!" I enthusiastically suggested.

"Psh, man I was just waiting on you!" He said cheerfully. "Let's go!"

Wasting no time, we abandoned the path on the hill and walked straight down toward the festivities. I tried my best to contain my excitement for what I anticipated finding at the bottom of the hill.

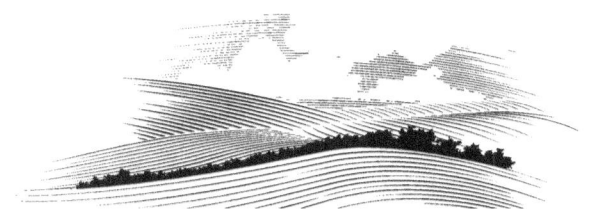

Tollwood

Saturday, July 12th

Adam and I reached the bottom of the hill to find exactly what it had appeared to be: a festival! Only, it wasn't nearly as small as it had looked. We had really only seen the large tent from our view atop the hill. The rest of the festival was blocked by trees.

"What could this be?" I thought to myself.

We immediately made our way to the entrance where they were charging for general admission. The fee was quite cheap so we had no problem paying. Upon payment, we strode through the entrance.

The sights and sounds were typical of any festival or carnival with the exception that there were no rides. Makeshift paths were created like isles between seas of local vendors. Pop-up shops and retail carts lined the paths selling an assortment of local goods. In every direction, people were talking and shouting merrily to one another as children scurried past with prizes won at carnival games. The smell of beer and bratwurst filled the air while sounds of distant music could be heard in the background.

As Adam and I strolled through the scene, we came across a peculiar sight. Among the food vendors, pop-up shops, and carnival games were bars-on-wheels! I for one had never come across such a thing and was intrigued. It was like a cart that contained a full bar complete with attached bar stools and beer taps! Needless to say, Adam and I approached.

We sat down and were greeted in German by the bar maiden. We asked if she spoke English, to which she immediately replied with a merry, "Ya!" She then welcomed us in English.

"So what is this?" I asked after taking a seat on the attached stool. "I know it can't be Oktoberfest because that's in September, right?"

"Yehs." She replied. "This is called Tollwood. It is basically a smaller version of Oktoberfest but in the summer."

"Oh, wow!" Adam replied. "If this is what you consider small, Oktoberfest must be huge!" Our bar maiden laughed.

"It is quite big," she said.

Without another delay, Adam went ahead and bought a beer. I was planning to do the same. However, while she was pouring the beer, she explained how it worked. As it turned out, the beer came in large, German-sized glass mugs. The mugs could be taken from the bar if they were purchased. If we were to purchase the mugs, we could return to the bar and get refills at half price. I considered it for a moment, but decided that since we weren't sure where we would end up, I would hold off. I would hate to have to run back and fourth across the entire festival just for a refill, especially when there were a multitude of "pop-up pubs," everywhere. The other drawback was my concern about getting the mug home if I purchased one. I wasn't sure it would fit into my backpack at the end of my trip. Thus, buying a mug did not seem like the best idea.

After Adam's beer was gone, we went hunting for where the music was coming from. I love sipping on a good beer while watching a live music performance. At one point we turned a corner. We then suddenly found ourselves behind a stage where a band was playing. We followed the stage around the side and to the front where we found the audience.

The audience area was created by a number of different sized tables with chairs. Large umbrellas were also set up to help block the sun. All the tables with umbrellas were taken, so Adam and I were forced to settle with a long table without an umbrella. Once we had settled into chairs, I went to grab he and I a drink while he remained to save our spots.

"Cheers, man!" I said upon returning with our beers. We clung our mugs, took a swig, and turned toward the show.

I surveyed the musicians and realized they were a little bizarre. It was a 3-piece band featuring a drummer, a bass player, and an organist. There was no singer, and the bass player's sound was very unusual. At first I considered leaving, thinking they were going to simply make weird sounds. However, once they got going, they ended up playing some pretty nasty grooves! The sound was still unusual, but I really enjoyed and appreciated it.

At one point, two guys come over to Adam and I. They were friendly and joined us. One of them claimed to be *with the band*. He attempted to sell us the band's merchandise. CD's were €10, so I decided to buy one. The two guys thanked me for the purchase before moving on. They then returned a few minutes later. It was at this point that things started getting weird.

The guy who sold me a CD invited Adam and I to join them along with the band at his place after the show. He said they were going to have people over to pre-game, then go out on the town. It sounded like a cool thing, so I told them we probably would! However, someone who is *with the band* at a show selling their merch does not necessarily mean they and the band are *friends* like I was with Rosco Bandana.

Whenever I see a band that I really like, I most often like to express my appreciation for them in-person. Therefore, when the band had finished playing, I went over to meet them as they were packing their gear. During a short conversation with one of the members, I asked him about his merch guy inviting us out. He said he knew who I was talking about, but they weren't exactly *friends*.

"You guys would definitely be welcome to join us if we were going out! To be honest though, we are going from here back to the flat for a meeting, then plan of having a quite afternoon and evening in. So, I don't think any of us will be going out." He explained.

I told him I completely understood. Having once gone on tour with Rosco, I knew how exhausting it could be. I remember we were all invited to a few house party that the band turned down primarily in favor of napping instead.

Despite the fact that the main guy, the one who sold me the CD, wasn't quite accurate in what he said, I wasn't completely deterred from hanging out. They seemed like alright guys. They were locals after all, and locals are the best types of people to go out with. With this in mind, I returned to Adam where I found both guys engaging him in conversation.

I brought the news from the band and, while disappointed, the guys remained enthusiastic about hanging out. My only concern at this point was ensuring there were actual other people going. The guys seemed alright, but I didn't want Adam and I alone venturing to these random locals' flat. What kept me holding back from a definitive RSVP was the fact that something was fishy. It seemed the longer we talked, the fewer people it sounded like would be there. On top of this, the main guy kept weirdly asking if he could have a sip of my beer. I had to tell him "no" multiple times. Then, I noticed that he kept giving his friend this weird look when discussing Adam and I coming over.

"Dude," I said to Adam quietly so the guys couldn't hear. "I don't know about you, but I'm getting a pretty serious creepy, gay vibe from these dudes."

"Bro, ME TOO…" he replied.

Finally, I asked point-blank how many people were going to be at this flat party and night on the town. I had been hinting and indirectly asking before as not to seem rude, but this time there was no getting around it. The main guy confessed that it would "probably" just be the two of them and the two of us. The plan was to drink wine together, then maybe go out. Between the creepy gay vibes I was getting from these two along with the desire to get a sip of my drink, this revelation sounded like a date. With a single glance at Adam, I knew we were both having the same internal reaction.

After another few minutes, they said they needed to return to the band to help them pack up. The main guy gave us his number and said to call them when we got ready. Adam and I said "ok," but with no intention whatsoever of calling.

Adam and I finished our beers, returned the mugs, and started wandering further into the festival. We passed by many more pop-up pubs, shops, and vendors until we heard the music of a familiar tune. We followed the sound through the festival into a very large tent. Inside, there was a Beatles cover band playing before a large crowd in similar seating fashion as the previous set up! The band played on a large stage facing an audience seated at long tables.

On the far side of the area was another pop-up pub without bar stools. Adam and I went over and discovered that you could buy two for the price of one - but with a catch. The first purchase was a large German-size glass mug. With it, you were provided a wooden token. When you finished the first drink, you would return the mug, hand in the token, and they'd provide the free refill.

Adam and I grabbed beers from the pop-up pub before finding a place at a small table to talk and enjoy the music. The band ended up being REALLY good! I initially thought the band was truly British until they stopped to address the audience. At that point, their British accents disappeared into complete German dialog.

Something I really appreciated about this band, which was the same as the previous, was how they didn't play too loudly. They played loudly enough to be heard and enjoyed without losing any quality of sound or preventing people from having a conversation. Therefore, Adam and I were able to sing along with the classic tunes as they were played — until two cute girls came walking by.

"Hallo!" I said with a big smile at a volume just above the music. "Sprichst du Englisch?" The girls stopped and giggled a little at my attempted German greeting which actually sounded more like, "Spasa ze English?!"

"Hallo," they replied. "Yes we do. How are you?"

"Excellent!" I exclaimed. "We're great! What are your names? I'm Tim from Mississippi and this is Adam from [I failed to note where he was from]." The girls then introduced themselves as Zelu and Terrisa. Zelu was particularly attractive.

The four of us chatted for a few seconds until I saw that they weren't trying to politely move away.

"Well hey," I said abruptly. "Have yall found a place to sit yet?" When they said they hadn't, I invited them to join Adam and I. They happily obliged, but wanted to go grab a drink first.

While they were gone, Adam and I mentioned to one another how attractive Zelu was. It was clear that Adam wanted to win her, but didn't want to make things weird or a competition if I had the same thoughts. Whether because I had Paula on my mind or because I was simply having a ball and feeling quite satisfied with the present circumstances, I had no particular interest.

"Na man, go for it!" I insisted. "I'll wing man for you."

"Are you sure?" He pressed.

"Most definitely." I assured him. "I'm happy as a J-bird right now. I've got a cold beer, a cool bro, we're chillin at the summer version of Germany's Oktoberfest, and a phenomenal Beatles cover band is playing in front of me. I literally couldn't be more satisfied right now, so please, go for it."

"Thanks man!" He laughed.

When the girls returned with their beers, they asked if we could sit in the grass just outside the tent. "Of course!" We said, and followed.

The four of us sat down in the grass together and begin talking. Playing the role of wingman, I made it a point to pull Terrisa into a one-on-one conversation with me so Adam could get some uninterrupted talk time with Zelu. This worked out really well. Adam talked and flirted with Zelu, and I would occasionally jump in and "pump his tires," as Josh would say before returning to my conversation with Terrisa. Despite my conversation with Terrisa primarily being for Adam's benefit, she was really enjoyable to talk to. She had a lovely German accent and was a really nice person. Unfortunately this was all for not. Zelu never seemed very interested despite Adam's valiant attempt. Then we found out that there was a guy she was "sort of" seeing.

About that time, I was starting to lean towards leaving when the girls bid us farewell. Adam was disappointed about his unsuccessful attempt with Zelu, but hey, you can't win every time. In any case, we both decided it was time to head back. It had been a long, exciting day.

As we headed back to the subway station, Adam suggested we get together later and go out on the town. I hadn't been out in Munich, so I said I'd add him on social media and we'd meet up. Yet as I said that, I begin to feel the weight of the day.

Getting back to my hostel after parting ways with Adam proved challenging. I got off at the wrong stop again, then went the wrong way, then got off at the right stop, but made a few wrong turns before finally finding my way back. After dropping my things off, I went immediately to find dinner. As always, there was a kebab place not too far away. After filling my belly, I returned to my hostel room and collapsed on the bed for a while. I supposed it had been a longer day than I thought.

I pulled out my tablet and opened up facebook to find that Paula was online. I said hello to her and we had a fun conversation. During this time, I decided that I wasn't going to go out. I decided I would add Adam tomorrow, but tonight I was staying in. The events of the night prior probably caught up with me. I also spoke to my buddies back home as my conversation with Paula began to wrap up. Once I had caught my buddies up on my whereabouts and most recent adventures, I shut it off and pulled the covers up. The next day I would be headed to Siegburg. I couldn't wait to see where he and Tanja were living and see Tanja again!

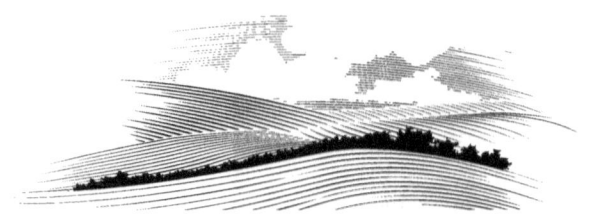

Size Matters

Sunday, July 13th

Iwoke up this morning and chose to remain in bed. My train for Siegburg did not leave until 15:28 (3:38pm) and there was nothing else I was wanting to do in Munich. I could go venture into the city, but with the luck I'd been having, I didn't want to risk somehow missing my train. I thus remained in bed until breakfast was nearly over.

The breakfast spread was the same as before. It consisted of boiled eggs, toast with jams, and assorted cereals, along with tea or juice to drink. Each table featured items that appeared to be short candle stick holders. However, I was tickled when I observed someone else using it properly. These candle stick holders were in fact egg holders. One placed the boiled egg in the holder and proceeded to eat it. Using a German method Zach had taught me, I used the back of my spoon to crack the egg all around. I then pushed my spoon into the cracked shell and essentially scooped the inner egg out. Some people instead cracked the shell and pulled off the top before scooping bits of the egg out of the shell in smaller amounts. I had never realized one could appear so fancy eating an egg.

After breakfast, I returned to my room to gather my things. I showered, packed, and cleaned up a little bit. I next went to reception and checked out. There was no point in actually leaving yet seeing as my train didn't leave for another good while, so they allowed me to set my things at reception until I decided to leave. After doing so, I returned to my breakfast table with a cup of tea.

I sipped my tea slowly and reflected on my most recent experiences. Whether pleasant or unpleasant, it was of extreme importance to me that I fully take in every experience I had. I didn't want to forget, and didn't want to take a single second of this time for granted. I wanted to forever be able to close my eyes and instantly return to these experiences; to see the sights, hear the sounds, smell the smells, and feel the atmosphere. I wanted to be able to reminisce on my experiences in the future and learn from them, or appreciate them again and again.

After nearly two hours of post-breakfast sitting, meditatively reflecting, and journaling, I simply could not sit anymore. I was now fully awake and getting restless. I looked at my watch to see that it was now 1 o'clock. After cleaning my area, I grabbed my things with a friendly "thank you" to reception and headed out the door.

I carried on down the street and around the corner, retracing my steps from the other night. I had to ask for a little guidance from a few friendly locals, but soon found my way to the train station. My only concern was that I was fairly early. This typically meant I would have to find a bench to sit on until the train arrived or began accepting passenger. I was therefore relieved when I saw my train stationed with the doors wide open. Seeing this, I wasted no time climbing aboard and finding a seat. After setting my things in the overhead storage, I once again retrieved my journal and continued writing until the train took off.

Four hours after the train ride and some beautiful scenery, I arrived in Siegburg! Pulling into Siegburg felt like a significant bench mark in my journey that carried mixed feelings. Having the opportunity to temporarily live with Zach and Tanja in a foreign country would be an incredible honor and privilege which I had been looking forward to from the start. At the same time, however, it signified that my trip as a whole was now beyond the half-way point.

I got off the train hardly able to contain my excitement. Within moments, I found Zach and Tanja waiting on me. After a warm welcome and a big hug from Tanja, we discussed dinner.

"We were thinking about grabbing a kebab from a place nearby. Does that sound good to you?" Zach asked. To be honest, I was so hungry, I could have eaten almost anything.

"Sounds good to me!" I replied.

I followed Zach down the road while Tanja and I chatted. Once we were there, I looked at the menu and saw something I wasn't used to. Of all the kebab places I had been to from Ireland to now, kebabs were always the same. Some might be a little bigger, some a little smaller, but they were always around the same size. Here, there seemed to be 3 different sizes.

"Hey man," I asked Zach. "How big are the sizes? I've never seen multiple size options for kebabs before. There is usually only one."

"The big one is pretty massive," Zach replied. "It's literally about as big as my hand." Zach held out his hand as a reference, which was bigger than mine.

"That's what I'm getting," he continued. "'Cause I'm pretty hungry. But you get whatever you're feelin. I've got you."

"Oh man, you don't have to do that!" I said. "I've got money!"

"You're our guest!" Tanja insisted. They weren't giving me any other option, as is the Southern way.

"Thank you," I said graciously. I decided that since I was also very hungry, I would follow Zach's lead and get the big one. We each ordered our food to-go before heading to Zach and Tanja's place.

The journey to Zach and Tanja's place was a short stroll. Having been seated for the last four hours on the train, I was very content with a nice walk. The only down side was my back pack starting to weigh on me. It had been on my back since I got off the train and was becoming heavier and heavier. Fortunately, we made it to their home roughly five minutes later.

Through a door, up a set of steps, and beyond a second door, I followed Zach and Tanja into their home. The second door opened up into a kitchen. Beyond the kitchen was a living area with couches, a tv, coffee table, and a bathroom off to the side. Following this area was a short set of stairs that led down to Zach and Tanja's bedroom. It was a cozy little place, the perfect size for the two of them. Then suddenly, we were greeted by the barks of a little black pug!

"This is Elvis!" Tanja said as she bent down to pick him up. "Are you ok with dogs? If not, we can put him up."

"What?! No! Of course I love dogs! I especially love PUGS!" I exclaimed. :I wouldn't want to have a pug myself, but I love playing with them. They are so goofy and easily excitable." Elvis took a little time sniffing and investigating me, but soon we were pals.

After I was shown around and properly approved of by Elvis, we sat down to eat. Tanja grabbed a large plate for me from the cabinet and I took a seat on the couch. Zach then removed my kebab from the to-go bag and handed it to me. My eyes got wide. I carefully unwrapped it on my plate.

"HOLY CRAP!" I exclaimed! "It's ENORMOUS!"

"I told you it was massive!" Zach said. He and Tanja both laughed.

The kebab took up the entire space of the dinner plate Tanja had given me! It was so big, I wasn't even sure how to eat it!

"Dude, how do you eat this thing??" I asked.

"Just go for it." Zach replied as if that was the best answer he could give. So, I did just that.

I picked up the giant wrap as best I could and managed to take a bite. Pieces of meat fell out onto the plate as sauce ran down the sides. The bread begin to break almost immediately. Continuing the strategy of using my hands quickly became impossible. Thankfully, Tanja was already on it. She brought Zach and I both forks and napkins. After wiping my hands and mouth with a napkin, I continued "going for it" exclusively with a fork.

Zach then turned the tv on and started flipping channels. It occurred to me in that moment that aside from that night in Calais, I hadn't watched regular tv since I left the States! Everything was (as one would expect) in German, but I saw a number of American shows like WB's *Big Bang Theory*. Zach attempted to get the English audio rather than German-dubbed, but without success. Fortunately, the movie, My Best Friend's Girl (2008), happened to be on in English so we watched it while we ate.

By the time the movie had ended, I was sufficiently stuffed. I wasn't even able to finish the gigantic kebab. Being so full, and it being fairly late, it was time for bed. Tanja supplied me with a sleeping bag and pillow which I elected to keep on the floor rather than the couch (easier to stretch out). We all then bid one another a good night and retired for the evening.

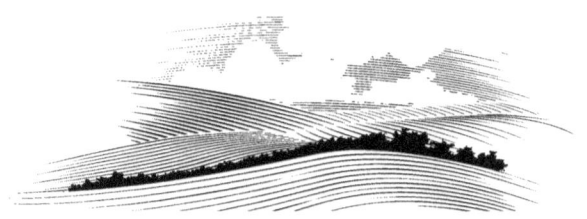

FIFA Weltmeisterschaft 2014

Monday, July 14th

I woke up this morning to Elvis sitting on the side of my sleeping bag two inches from my face. He seemed to be studying me intently.

"G'mornin!" I said quietly with a chuckle. I reached my hand up to give him a pat. He stood up received the pat, then gave me a snort. He turned his tail and started towards the kitchen where Tanja was preparing something to eat. He then stopped and looked back at me with an expression that firmly said, "Time to get up, dude. Let's go." I sat up. Satisfied, Elvis continued toward the kitchen. I laughed. Pugs are so funny.

I made it to the kitchen about the same time Zach came in. We both sat down at the little kitchen table while Tanja finished getting our breakfast ready.

"What's cooking?" I asked. It smelled great.

"It's a type of bread." Zach said. "It's a pretty common breakfast item here in Germany."

"What's it called?" I asked Zach curiously. Zach and Tanja both smiled real big.

"I would tell you" he replied," but I want you to hear Tanja say it first."

"Broyschin." Tanja said through a wide grin.

"Brysechn," replied Zach in an effort to say it.

"Br-bry-brochin?" I also attempted to say.

"BRoys-CHin," Tanja corrected us, attempting to emphasize the phonics.

This went on for a few rounds before Zach and I both gave up. Tanja meanwhile got a kick out of us Americans trying our best to pronounce the German word, *brötchen*. Zach was able to get closer than I was, but we both failed pretty miserably to get it right.

The brötchen bread was similar to an English muffin, but tougher. My hosts also provided me with different toppings such as grape and strawberry jam, along with some sort of delicious cinnamon cookie-dough spread. As we ate and had our coffee, we discussed the plan for the day. I was thrilled that I could simply relax as they both had everything planned out. Tanja was from this area and Zach had been living with Tanja for some time. This meant that I had free, local tour guides who could show me around so I wouldn't have to worry with maps, much less even really think.

As mentioned, Zach and Tanja were living in the city of Sieburg. Nearby was the city of Bon. Zach and Tanja both worked in Bon, and Zach was the pitcher for the city-league baseball team, The Bon Capitals! It turned out that Zach had baseball practice today.

"You're welcome to come, but it will be pretty boring." Zach said. "Tanja was also wanting to show you around Siegburg today."

"It's whatever you want to do though, Tim." Tanja insisted. "If you want to go watch baseball practice, you can, or I could show you around Siegburg, or you could just hang out and watch tv while I run errands. Whatever you want to do!"

I hate baseball, but wanted to attend Zach's practice just to be supportive. However, despite what Tanja was saying, I could tell she was really eager to show me around Siegburg since she grew up in the area and was most familiar with it. I was therefore torn between wanting to support Zach and see him do a little pitching and honoring Tanja who clearly really wanted to show me around her town.

"I actually have a game coming up in Bon soon, so it wouldn't be like coming to my practice would be your only chance to see me pitch." Zach added. A wave of relief rushed over me.

"Oh sweet!!" I exclaimed. "That's perfect then! Yeah, I'll hang with Tanja today and come see you play in the game later!" I saw the excitement come over Tanja despite her efforts to hide it. It's not every day one gets to show off their home area to a friend from a different country. I'm glad I could honor her by making that happen.

After breakfast, Zach left to catch the commuter rail to Bon for practice. A little while later, Tanja and I took the short, five-minute walk past the kebab shop and train station into downtown Siegburg. I couldn't help love how easy it was to get to the area. No driving, no trains. Just a simple, short walk. Tanja showed me all sorts of local shops including a bakery, a produce market, pubs, and other small merchandise stores.

"There's also something really cool I have to show you!" Tanja told me as I was taking in the sights. "That is, if it's open. I'm not sure if it is today, but we can try."

I looked at her intrigued.

"Well what are we waiting for?! Let's go!" I said excitedly.

I followed Tanja away from the city center and up an incline that took us into a wooded area. She began explaining that what we were approaching wasn't a castle, *per se*, but similar. About this point, I started noticing the tops of medieval style architecture further up the hill. My interest increased.

"It's been many different things over time," she explained. "At one time it was a palace, at another time it was a monastery, and at another it served as some sort of fortress. It's really pretty, and since I know you like medieval history, I think you'll like it! I just hope isn't closed so we can go inside."

After hearing this, I couldn't wait! I eagerly pressed on up the path which was now far away from the city. Trees now shot up in every direction while birds could be heard chirping overhead. Finally, the forest gave way to our destination.

"Michaelsburg Abby." Tanja announced casually. The yellow structure broke through the sea of green and brown. A large and most beautiful abby stood tall and proud before us. Laced with stone and rock, it towered three and a half stories high with spires that pierced the sky. I was ecstatic. I regrettably wished I had not run off without my camera.

As we approached the inviting entrance, we noticed a sign written in German and English: "closed to public for maintenance." My heart sunk low. Tanja shared my disappointment. I confessed to her that if I didn't already know she would not approve, I would have climbed the outer wall for a sneak-peak. She appreciated that I would not be doing that as she would indeed have strongly disapproved. Therefore, we admired the building from where we were for a few minutes before turning back.

"There's actually another place Zach and I want to take you to." She said. "It's much bigger too." I was happy to hear this news.

"So where to next?" I asked once we were back in the town square. I looked around and was going to suggest we check out a pub if she didn't have anything specific." Tanja pulled out her phone and looked at the time.

"Oh!" She said. "We need to go! Zach should be back soon and we need to get ready."

"Ready?" I asked.

"Zach didn't tell you?" She replied.

"Tell me…?" I pressed.

"Weltmeisterschaft, The World, Cup final is tonight! We're going to watch it at a bar my cousin owns!" She said.

I had COMPLETELY forgotten! I knew Germany had made it to the final, but had not heard when the final match would be and hadn't even thought about it! I was absolutely floored! I was about to watch Germany play in the World Cup final IN GERMANY. What if Germany managed to win? It would be a night to remember.

Without another delay, Tanja and I returned to the house. Zach arrived a few minutes after we did. Once we had all showered and gotten something to eat, we hopped in the car and headed out. We technically still had plenty of time, but wanted to make sure we got a good seat. If there was ever a night for a bar to be jam packed, tonight was it. Europeans love their football as much as Americans love theirs. This match was like the Super Bowl of Super Bowls for Europe, and Germany had a shot of winning it all. That being said, getting to the bar long before the match started was very important.

We soon arrived at the place in question which was called 8Bar. 8Bar was located on the second floor of a 2-story building. Already, there were people gathered at the bottom waiting to be allowed inside. Tanja's cousin and the staff were still preparing, but we (being family+me) were allowed up. The three of us then climbed an outdoor staircase leading up to a deck with tables and chairs. Near the top of the staircase was a set of glass doors. I followed Zach and Tanja inside where we were welcomed by her cousin. Tanja and her cousin began conversing in German. They stopped briefly to introduce me before we continued into the bar to find a good seat.

The indoor space was long and narrow, but wide enough to be comfortable. The bar eased along the back wall under a chalkboard with hand-written drink choices, written in different colors. This bar stretched from one end of the space to the other and connected to a smaller, side-bar. The dark, tiled ceiling featured dimmer lights which created a cool tone. Deep purple and soft blue lights fell down the walls from hidden ceiling bulbs with an occasional multi-colored spot and laser lights clearly used for dancing. Two enormous screens fell down the opposite side of the bar to face the back. Both were showing the World Cup channel.

Beers were served in bottles or tall, narrow glasses. The glasses were similar to Blue Moon glasses but taller. One could order by the bottle, by the glass, in a mini keg, or a "round" as I called which which was a bulk order of glasses in a large drink holder.

Despite the fact that Tanja's cousin had only let a small number of people inside at this time, I could already feel the excitement and energy growing about the match. We knew that soon, the floodgates would open, and the people outside would come bustling in. Considering this, we went ahead and grabbed a tall table near the back which was directly facing one of the screens. This spot was the perfect distance from the screen, the bar, and rest room without blocking traffic. Once our place was chosen, we noticed more people were starting to trickle in. Zach went and grabbed us a few drinks.

Soon the place was packed with German supporters with face paint, flags, supportive shirts, jerseys, and other fun fan gear. Even Tanja found someone doing face paint and had the German flag painted on her cheeks. The excitement and energy was very evident. This would be a memorable night regardless, "but if Germany managed to win," I thought, "it would probably be a wild night." However, my hosts had to work in the morning, so I decided that I wouldn't insist on staying out any later than they wanted to.

When the match started, everyone's focus immediately shifted to the game. People continued to talk and socialize, but the main focus was the game. Back and fourth, the ball was brought from one side of the field to the other by a player attempting to score. Shot after shot was taken by both teams. Each time, the entire bar held its breath. If Argentina had possession, everyone yelled for the player to be stopped. If Germany had possession, we all sat at the edge of our seats in anticipation of a potential goal. It appeared to be a pretty evenly matched game, but only one could be crowned as World Champion for the next four years.

Drive after drive, shot after shot, the match raged on. Huge cheers were immediately followed by loud groaning as Germany came extremely close to scoring multiple times. Frantic outbursts were immediately followed vy relieved cheers as Argentina made several shots on goal. All were fortunately denied. This continued throughout the match with neither team scoring,...until the 29th minute of the 1st half.

Following a mad drive down field, an Argentina player managed to slip through the German defense to receive a pass. The drive ended with a shot on goal. The German keeper was unable to stop it. It initially appeared that Argentina would be taking the early lead. The Germans yelled and jeered as Argentina celebrated until the camera showed a sideline ref. The player who had scored had been off-sides! The goal therefore did not count, and Germany would get the ball! Everyone in the bar cheered in relief.

Drive after drive, shot after shot, the match continued. Huge cheers followed angry groans; frantic yells followed cheers of relief. Both Germany and Argentina came extremely close to scoring many times. Despite shots taken, it seemed neither team could score. This pattern continued until the 22nd minute of the 2nd half.

Moving quickly and narrowly avoiding a double-team by two Argentina players, a German player drove the ball down the line. A second pair of Argentina players then met him closer to the goal. One come alongside him to steal the ball. He knew that either this defender was going to steal the ball or kick it out of bounds. It was about to be over. He was not at the right angle to score. It seemed like there was nothing more he could do. Then suddenly, he saw an open team mate in the center of the field inside the penalty box. It was a bit of a long shot, but he took it. With a sliding cross, he kicked the ball toward his team mate. The team mate managed to maneuver himself into the perfect position to receive the pass. With profound skill, he trapped the ball with his chest before dropping it down to his feet. Immediately, the player gave the ball a swift, controlled kick.

The bar fell completely silent as the ball flew through the air towards the goal. No one spoke. Eyes were glued to the screen. As the ball came closer to the goal, people rose out of their seats. The goal keeper lunged toward the ball, but he wasn't fast enough! The shot whizzed past and splashed into the back-right corner of the net! Germany had now scored the first goal of the match and secured the lead!

Upon this goal, the intensity of both teams turned up. Argentina wasn't giving up and aimed to respond with a goal of their own. Giving Germany no rest, Argentina came hard. Germany meanwhile put their primary focus on their defensive strategy. Argentina took possession of the ball multiple times, but were unable to secure a goal. Both teams played with every ounce of heart they possessed. Then there came a sound that was the most beautiful sound in the world to Germany: the three-whistle blow of the ref. The match was over, and Germany had won.

The bar went absolutely ballistic! Cheering, screaming, high-fives all around, kissing, chanting, singing, clanging of drinks, and flags waving filled the room. I'd seen and been a part of celebrating the win of a big American football game back home. Never in my life had I witnessed such an intense celebration. This celebration of cheers, yells, chants, and the like just described lasted no less that a solid six minutes!

After a sufficient amount of celebrating, Zach, Tanja, and myself took our leave. As we walked back to Zach and Tanja's place, cheering and chanting could still be heard echoing through the streets. The entire city, the entire country was beside itself. It was without a doubt, a night I would always remember.

Part VII:
The Netherlands

Map of The Netherlands: https://d-maps.com/carte.php?num_car=4121&lang=en
- Lines, circles, and words with asterisks are author's annotations and not on original map

Red Lights

Wednesday, July 16th

*July 15th I slept in while my hosts went to work. I hung out at their place, played with Elvis, journaled, played my guitar, and relaxed until they got off work. Tanja came and got me and met Zach for Chinese buffet in Bon near where Zach worked. Nothing interesting happened.

I woke up this morning very excited. I was heading to The Netherlands — specifically Amsterdam! I had also informed Paula and Kelly of my plans, so we made plans to meet up the next day! I got up and grabbed a bit of breakfast, said goodbye to my hosts for a couple days, and headed out.

Once again, it seemed, my poor luck with trains was striking again! I arrived at the train station to realize I had missed my 10:15 train! The next available train did not leave until 12:15. I could have returned to Zach and Tanja's, but I knew they had things to do. I didn't want to burden them. They would have to provide me a key and such things if I went back. I therefore chose to visit the Subway [sandwich restaurant] conveniently located inside the station.

There was a tv playing inside the Subway [restaurant] showing the news. The World Cup team had apparently just arrived back in Munich and there was a big parade. Huge crowds of people could be seen in the streets cheering and waving German flags. A large Mardi Gras type float carried the team who waved to supporters cheering them on. From what I could gather, they were headed to a specific location for a big celebration. There were announcers set up outside with a stage in the back ground and a crowd facing it. The whole thing reminded me of a *National Football Championship: College Game Day* on ESPN. I enjoyed watching the festivities featured on the program until it came time to board my train.

Three hours after the train took off, I was in Amsterdam! I felt fortunate that it had been a fast train. As I made my way out of the station, I saw multiple small cards advertising things to do in Amsterdam. Each card contained a discount promotion, the attraction's location on a tiny map, and other valuable information. I naturally grabbed a few that appeared to be the most "Amsterdamish" and interesting at first glance. I next followed the directions to my hostel provided by the hostel.

My first step was to catch a ride on the tram #9 then get off at the "zoo" stop. As I rode, I couldn't help notice how lovely the scenery was. I wanted to pull out my camera and record the trip, but chose against it lest I miss my stop. Unfortunately, I still ended up missing my stop! It had looked further away on the map, so I expected to be on the tram longer. Thankfully, I realized it immediately and was able to hop off at the very next one before walking back to the correct stop, which wasn't too far away.

I managed to find the hostel's address and building number fairly quickly without any trouble. However, what I found appeared to be a restaurant! I was confused, but walked inside.

I received a warm and friendly welcome from the host upon entering. Uncertain, I asked about my hostel.

"Yes, yes! This is Hostel Centraal!" The man kindly explained. "The first floor is a restaurant. The dorms are upstairs." He motioned toward a spiral staircase. "Hostel guests also get a special discount at the restaurant!" I thanked him for his help, got checked in, received my key, and found my room on the second floor.

It was 4pm by the time I had settled in. I wondered what I ought to do with my remaining time. My stomach gurgled reminding me that I had missed lunch. I decided to first find food, then go for a walk-around.

After a short walk, I came upon a small restaurant where I purchased a chicken burger. After eating, I strolled down toward the city center where I came upon a small park. Large, green trees overlooked a canal where flowers bloomed. I impulsively entered.

A canal eased through the park, separating it from the city via a short, stone wall. I found a nice place to sit near the water's edge under one of many great willow trees. I sat there while taking in the natural beauty of the park. The lush grass, big trees, and peaceful canal gave an aesthetic that no architecture could ever hope to create. Looking around, I noticed a few small groups of people and a few romantic couples lying in the grass together. It almost made me wish I had someone to share the day with as well. That's when I decided it was time to carry on.

I made it to the city center where I discovered a round courtyard with statues. Near a bench were two guys playing guitars. The talented musicians had drawn a small crowd who threw euros into their open guitar case. While they were taking a short break, I went over and spoke to them. They appreciated my compliments along with the euros I tossed into their case. We chatted for a few minutes until they decided it was time to jump back into it.

I continued by wandering down a road that eventually came to be parallel with a large canal. While walking, I saw a sign for a canal tour! An opportunity to be in a boat? Yes, please! The only thing I couldn't figure out was the name. "Lover's Cruise." Judging by the name, I assumed it had to be some sort of cruise for couples, so I passed it by. I passed a few more similar cruises, but each seemed to get more expensive than the last! I ultimately doubled back to Lover's.

I walked down to the peer where tickets were sold and asked a Lover's Cruise worker about the name. He laughed. Apparently the name is that of the company owner who's last name merely happened to be Lover. He assured me that it was not a couple's cruise. Feeling better about the name, I purchased a €13 ticket.

I climbed aboard the small, oddly shaped vessel. Its long, rectangular shape reminded me of a cross between an air plane and a train, but more flat. The windows started at shoulder-height and extended upward before curving to make a skylight ceiling. This meant we had a 180° view from the inside. The interior was divided into two sides, separated by an isle with booth-style seating with a table in between. I chose a seat toward the back end and sat down. It was actually very comfortable. I slid my window open to the left and rested my arm outside. The breeze felt great as it drifted into the boat. After fifteen minutes or so, the boat set off and the tour began.

Being from the coast, I could not have been happier to be in a boat on the water. I was also excited to simply relax and enjoy the sites from this vantage point. When the tour guide came on over the intercom, I was pleasantly surprised to hear him speak both Dutch and English! I would have been content had he only spoken Dutch, but the added bonus of having the tour in English as well as Dutch was much appreciated!

Under the arches of bridges and through allies of water we went. Unique architecture stood out on either side of the canals with some decorated with flowers. Small boats, houses on the water, and aesthetically designed house-boats lined the sides of the canal with advertisements in both Dutch and English. All the while, our guide provided us a history of the city and our immediate surroundings. He occasionally made joking comments and gave suggestions about places to visit. It was fantastic.

After the boat tour, I chose to head towards the famous Red Light District. I didn't know a whole lot about the area, but it had been highly recommended to me. The funny thing was, the highest recommendations came from church pastor friends. They insisted I see it because the culture was so interesting and wildly different from the States. Considering the blessings of pastors to visit this area, it seemed very important that I check it out.

After a fair walk, I came upon an area that reminded me of the French Quarter in New Orleans. The streets were narrow, and tall buildings lined the sides. Neon lighting jetted out from the tops of doorways as people could be heard socializing inside. I really didn't notice anything too crazy at this point. The most 'interesting' thing I noticed was a man dressed as a woman inside one of the bar windows and an occasional "sexy store." However, this was all about to change. As the sun set and the population grew, I noticed an ally that many seemed to be turning down. Curious, I followed.

Like entering Diagon Ally through the brick wall of The Leaky Cauldron or riding through the tunnel of the It's A Small World ride at Disney World, everything changed. The canal cut through the center of a long strip like a median separating two directions of traffic. Gleaming red lights illuminated the area from red-tented lanterns hung all around. Every twenty feet was a bar, but what lied above the bars in every window was something I had never seen before. Wearing eye-catching bikinis or sexy lingerie, some of the most beautiful women I had ever seen stood, danced, and waved from behind the large windows. I then noticed there were similar windows on the street level. The women behind these windows beckoned to passerbys to stop and speak like siren and mermaids to sailors in legendary stories. I was, admittedly, mesmerized.

More than once, I passed by a beautiful woman on the street level where it was most narrow. One in particular, I passed by only inches from the glass window in a crowded space. Inside was a tall, dark-toned, long-haired brunette with big, beautiful, green eyes, wearing a leopard-print bikini. She came right up the the glass as she caught my eye. As if instantly put under a spell, I was unable to help slowing almost to a pause as I passed. She was breathtaking. Looking me straight in the eyes, she gently scaled her body with her finger tips from top to bottom, highlighting her perfect curves. She bit her lip suggestively, sensually scratched the glass before me, and motioned with one finger for me to come to her door next to the window. I smiled real big, blushed a little, shut my eyes, and pressed on. Another moment's hesitation, and I may have been tempted.

Despite the incredible and undeniable beauty of these women, they were still prostitutes. I had held on for a future wife up to this point, and preferred not to give it up to a prostitute despite what an experience being with this one might have been like.

Continuing on, live sex shows, "peep" shows, porn shops, and sex stores lined the streets next to bars and restaurants with still more gorgeous girls dancing in between. After taking all this in, I started to notice large men in black fedoras. They looked very intimidating. Perhaps they were acting as security for the girls. I noticed some would go over and speak to the girls for a brief moment before returning to their post. I wondered about this phenomenon, at whether they were indeed protective security…or more liken to prison guards. It's impossible to know which girls may have chosen such a career, and which ones may have been tricked into it. Those who get tricked are thus prisoners with no way out. It's a heartbreaking reality.

The idea that many of these woman could choose such a career baffled me. I had trouble wrapping my head around it. All just for money? I took a seat on a bench to collect my thoughts. It was a lot to process. I watched one of the women in a window. She had big blue eyes, black hair, golden skin and wore a zebra-print bikini. I watched as she tried to wave passing guys over to her. Some would stop and approach. She would then open her door half-way and talk. I didn't see any enter this door in particular.

Sitting here in my thoughts, I couldn't help wanting to go over and speak to her myself, though not for the same reasons. I had questions. What was her self-image? Did she know she was so much more than a sex-object? Did she know there was a God who loved her unfathomably? Did she know what real love felt like? Did she have a relationship with someone, and if so, how did this job effect it? These questions and more flew though my head. I probably could have paid her the price for sex, then asked her questions instead of doing the deed, but honestly wasn't sure I'd be strong enough to resist as she was also very attractive. However, I couldn't sit there any longer and resolved to retreat into the bar next to her. As I passed the girl, she smiled at me and waved. I smiled back at her as one person to another.

The bar was pretty cool. It was like any other aside from the sex themed decor. Next to me was a local along with two Canadian guys. They seemed friendly enough, so I turned to them.

"How does it work, exactly?" I asked after getting into the conversation. One of the guys was happy to explain it to me.

"Basically, you pick one out that you like. Then you walk over to the door. She'll open the door to negotiate. You tell her what you would like, and she tells you how much it would cost. Usually, it's €50 for 15 minutes," He explained. "BUT," he continued, "sometimes they will waste time so that right when you're about to finish, your time runs out and they make you buy another 15 minutes to finish. At that point, you'll pay just about anything to finish." He concluded with a laugh. "Why do you ask? Are you considering doing it? If that's what you want to do, go for it! I mean, it's Amsterdam after all, right?!"

"Well," I chuckled, "as truly tempting as it is, especially for how beautiful they are, I'm actually…"

"OH!" He said cutting me off. "Man, wow, well if that's the case, please don't. I've been married and divorced. I'm not doing it because I just don't want to spend the money tonight, but I've done it once or twice. But man, you don't want to give yourself to a prostitute. Go find you a woman to marry. Trust me. But then again, I'm not trying to tell you what to do. Do what you wanna. I'm just saying I think it would be a regrettable decision in the long run."

We continued talking for a bit, discussing how crazy it all was. He then left to head home a little while later. I remained at the bar long enough to finish my drink and settle my thoughts. I then decided to head back myself. I needed to get some sleep and be ready for my adventure to Holland to see Paula and Kelly! However, just before leaving the district, I saw in interesting looking shop. I entered out of curiosity. It turned out to be a coffee shop, and in this coffee shop, they also sold something else. It goes by many names, and in the United States, the stuff is illegal. Here, it is not only legal, but an integral part of the culture.

I don't condone smoking marijuana (in large part due to the legality of it in the States). I especially don't condone smoking anything whatsoever if one is underage. However....here I was an adult, in a foreign country where it was legal and a huge part of the culture. I knew it wouldn't make me hallucinate or trip out or anything — just make me super chill and silly. Therefore, desiring to have the full Amsterdam experience (minus the sex), I chose to make a small purchase.

The guy asked the type I wanted. He rattled off several colorful names, but I hadn't a clue what any of them were. The only name I knew of was completely due to my love of the legendary guitarist, Jimi Hendrix. Jimi wrote a song he called *Purple Haze*. I therefore purchased a small amount of Purple Haze, which came in a small bag complete with rolling paper and matches. It felt really weird buying this, I'm not going to lie, but it was cool buying something legally here where in other places it was illegal. Drugs are drugs however, and people shouldn't do drugs. It was just that I was in Amsterdam, and on an adventure of a lifetime. I couldn't not, as they say, *do as the Romans do.*

I journeyed back to my hostel with my purchase in hand. I figured I would enjoy my Purple Haze after returning from seeing Paula and Kelly where I would have time available to set aside with no responsibilities. I then put my things away and climbed into bed. I couldn't wait to find out what Paula and Kelly had in store for me.

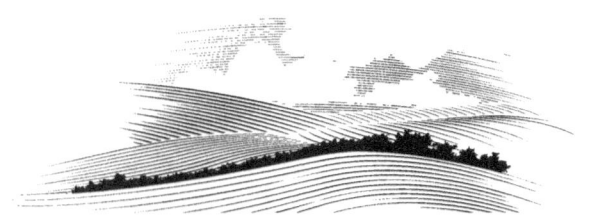

Show Me The Monkeys

Thursday, July 17th

Paula and Kelly were waiting for me at the train station as I stepped off the platform in the city of Apeldoorn. They were both on bikes, and clearly excited to have me there. After a happy greeting, Kelly asked if I had eaten anything. I had actually woken up late and missed breakfast, so they made our first priority to find some food. It was at this point that it donged on me that there were only two bikes and three of us!

"Um,.." I said before pointing this out.

"It's fine!" Paula said coming over with her bike. "You can ride mine. I'll ride on the back of Kelly's."

I objected at first. It seemed dangerous. I also hated to take the bike from Paula — it didn't seem very gentlemanly. However, they insisted it was fine and that they rode together all the time. Considering there didn't seem to be any other options, I agreed.

I was relieved that this ride, compared to my experience in Florence, was much better. It was gentle and relaxing, as well as relatively short. It seemed only five minutes or so before we arrived at a small cafe. We parked our bikes and leaned them against the side of the building before taking a seat.

When the waitress came out, I ordered a simple bagel with cream cheese, a water, and a large coffee. The coffee was called an Americano, which was the largest, but with the least caffeine.

"That's fine." I admitted. "European coffee does nothing for me in terms of caffeine anyway." The girls were shocked. I tried explaining.

"Yeah, for some reason, coffee in Europe gives me what I can only describe as a "background high," as opposed to the "foreground high" I get from coffee in the States. The "background high" wakes up my mind but my body is still sluggish while the "foreground high" gets my body moving even if my mind is still dragging a little.

My coffee Americano came shortly after I finished my explanation. It came in a big cup with fluffy cream and tasted great. My bagel came a few minutes later and soon I had finished.

"So ladies. What's on our agenda today?" I asked.

"Well first," Kelly explained with her Dutch accent, "we thought we would show you the palace where the king and queen of Apeldoorn live. Then— "

"Woah-wait-what?!" I interrupted. "First, there's a *palace*?! Second, there's a *living* queen and king of Apeldoorn??" The girls laughed loudly. For them, it was hilarious to hear someone geek out about something that for them was so common place. I can relate. I'm sure if a United States history nut visited South Mississippi and discovered things I have always known, such as Fort Massachusetts (Civil War fort) on Ship Island or the Biloxi home of Jefferson Davis (Civil War general), they would probably geek out in similar fashion.

A short bike ride brought us through a forest area with tall trees. We parked our bikes at the base of one tree and continued on foot. A quarter mile later we found ourselves looking at a gate between two brick pillars. Standing atop each pillar was a small statue of a buck. Further down each pillar was a small, narrow window.

Kelly and Paula approached one of the pillars at its window. Inside this pillar was a guard, which I didn't notice until the girls had addressed him. The girls spoke to this guard for a moment before returning.

"We have bad news.." Paula said. Despite saying this, Paula seemed to be holding back a smile.

"The royal family is home doing family things, so..the palace is closed today." Kelly finished.

"What?! We came all this way for *nothing*?!" I exclaimed. "This is all YOUR fault, Kelly!" I was very disappointed. However, despite the harshness of my words and tone, I said it in clear jest through an obvious smile. This was why Paula had been holding back a smile despite being disappointed that they couldn't show me the palace. They both knew me well enough to anticipate me overreacting in this way and ate it up. I knew they felt bad, so I wanted to show that I wasn't upset by faining dramatic anger and blame.

"I'm sorry!!" Kelly cried in false lament before laughing. "I should have known the royal family's daily schedule! Ahh!"

"YES. Obviously! Why would you not have known that?" I replied in joking aggression.

We then started moving away from the gate. It was here that the girls got to have a huge laugh at my expense, and where I would have no defense. As we walked through the trees, we ended up discussing the difference of wildlife between Holland and Mississippi. They were fascinated about having to be weary of alligators when near the bayou, watching out for poisonous water snakes, and other such things. I told them the story of how I was once running into my back yard as a kid and a snake happened to be slithering by. I noticed it just in time and jumped as it rose up out of the grass. Fortunately, I cleared it just high enough to avoid a bite. They said that they didn't have to worry too much about venomous snakes there, much less alligators.

At one point while walking, I noticed something interesting at the base of a tree and went over to have a closer look. As I leaned down, my foot gave way a little. Without thinking, I jumped backwards and almost stumbled. The girls erupted into laughter. They knew exactly what had happened. It seemed I had stepped on a branch which lifted up another branch from the brush. I had instinctively jumped back because for a brief second, all I thought was, "snake!" It's not that I had a fear of snakes, but if you step and one stands up, you'd better back out of its range quickly.

Midway through my impulsive reaction, I had regained awareness of what actually happened and joined the girls in their unapologetic laughter. Naturally, even after I had rejoined them and we had continued on our way, they didn't let me live it down. In fact, Two years later, Paula, Kelly, and I did a Skype call to catch up. At one point, one of them said with a laugh, "yeah, like the time you saw that snake in Holland?" I doubt I'll ever live that one down with them, and I have no defense but to laugh at myself too.

Continuing our walk, we ended up stumbling upon the royal pet cemetery. This was apparently the resting place for all royal pets whether they be cats, dogs, birds, or even horses. It was small but well kept. I had not seen anything like this before, so it was interesting. We walked around it for a couple minutes before pressing on.

Next, we came upon a break in the regular palace wall. Still connected to the regular palace wall on either side was a barrier. The barrier was shorter than the rest of the wall, and allowed us to see over onto the palace grounds. In front of the barrier was a pool of water with a center piece of what appeared to be a stack of rocks and shells. The barrier itself was made up of different types of pebbles separated by wood frames. In the center were three artistic paintings of shells. To be honest, it is hard to describe, but was very pretty. Beyond the barrier, we could see a path lined with tall hedges to a large fountain perfectly centered before the large palace building. We stood and enjoyed the site for a few minutes, then continued our walk.

After making our way through the woods around to the front of the palace and getting our picture made, we returned to our bikes. Our next destination was some sort of zoo where Paula worked. They told me it was a zoo only for monkeys, and they didn't have cages. I was extremely interested as I had been to many zoos in my life, but none where monkeys had no cages! I couldn't wait to see!

The name of this zoo was Apenheul. As we approached, it appeared to be like any other zoo I had visited before. The only difference was it seemed to be all monkey-themed. Paula and Kelly spoke to one another in Dutch before Paula scurried off to the ticket booth.

"Where is she going?" I asked Kelly.

"Paula is going to get a discount." She replied.

"Oh, well I need to give her my money then!" I said.

"No, we are paying." Kelly answered.

"What? No, you don't have to do that! I'm fine paying for myself!" I assured her.

"No, no. You are our guest. We will pay." Kelly insisted. There was no arguing.

"Ok.." I replied in surrender. "Thank you."

Paula returned not long after, provided me a ticket for which I thanked her, and we entered. What I found inside was one of the coolest things I had ever seen! Just as the girls had described, there were literally small breed monkeys of all kinds swinging, hopping, and climbing around everywhere! Ropes were strung between real and fake trees that allowed easy travel for the little creatures. At one point, I looked over to see a Capuchin monkey (like Marcel from *FRIENDS*) exploring a child's stroller! Then, a Ring-tailed lemur (long, black and white tail) plopped onto the arm of the baby's mother and appeared to be searching for the crackers she had been giving her child!

I stood there blown away as one of the several lemurs checking us humans out casually took a seat not even a foot from me on the railing of a walking path. I leaned in and got a quick selfie with it, yet while keeping a safe distance. Although the girls said they probably wouldn't try to bite me, there was still a chance they might. I chose not to risk it. I did manage to touch the lemur, however.

Lemurs are known for having long, stripped tails. As the one sat there next to me with his tail casually dangling below him, I carefully reached my hand down and lifted the end of his tail in my palm. He immediately shifted his body and looked at my hand curiously. I couldn't be sure how he felt about it, and I didn't want to offend him so I didn't touch it for long. I only wanted to be able to say I touched a lemur. Feeling satisfied, I politely stepped away from it and continued my exploration of the park.

I noticed there were a few exceptions to the free roam of the monkeys as I walked through the park. The apes, for instance, were separated from the rest, although the smaller monkeys had the ability to visit their areas. Such apes included Bonobos, Orangutans, Gorillas, and a few others I don't know the names of. The funny thing however, was it really seemed like the human guests were the ones who were caged while the animals roamed free around the "caged humans." Despite the fact that the apes were sectioned off, their sections were extremely large compared to most zoos. The animals seemed to be quite happy with their predicament and could be seen playing and socializing casually with one another. In many zoos, the animals are clearly bored and essentially sit around doing nothing. With all the natural trees, brush, terrain, and man-made climbing structures, these animals appeared to be very much at home. This made me feel really good about this zoo. Truly a recreation of their natural habitats (with the added bonus of man-made climbing structures).

The climax of the whole experience was probably the Gorilla "show." I say "show," because it wasn't anything like you would see at Seaworld or other animal theme parks. This was very approvingly different.

The three of us sat in a small set of stands overlooking a large hill filled with trees, brush, and rock. It looked very natural. Between the stands and this hill was a water area that separated the stands from the land. At a certain time, gorillas began coming over the top of the hill and down toward the water. Some came down to sit on a rock right at the edge of the water while others were more cautious, staying back towards the top. There must have been at least a dozen of all ages in total who came out. As they did so, a presenter appeared, and begin speaking. It was all in Dutch so I couldn't understand, but the girls gave me the summery of what he was saying. Then, the presenter began pulling fruit out of a sack he was holding and tossed pieces across the water toward the gorillas.

It was hilarious watching as he threw bananas and apples *to them*. I use the phrase "to them" intentionally, as to say that it wasn't like throwing a bone and watching dogs fight over it. The presenter actually threw the fruit to individuals. It blew my mind how casually and skillfully the receiver gorilla would casually reach up and snag the fruit out of the air, then lie back and enjoy it. They had clearly been conditioned to know what to expect. They were also clearly still fed well as they weren't scrapping for it - even though there might be an occasional tussle over choice fruit. For the most part, it seemed like a pleasant snack or desert time for the animals all while we as humans got to enjoy and appreciate them.

Something else that I found really cool was when the presenter discussed communicating with the animals. I don't remember what exactly he said, but his intention was to try to get a response from one. He seemed to be familiar with a few individuals who he called out. He yelled at one, beat his chest, and made a gorilla sound. One of them looked up at him, acknowledged his call, and returned it with a short gruff and a quick chest beat. The audience naturally awed. After a half hour, the gorillas seemed to decide it was time to go. They casually began making their way back over the hill and the "show" came to a close. The girls and I then made our way back to our bikes. I wondered what was next.

I followed the girls on our bikes first to Kelly's house where I met her parents. They were very nice and spoke a little English. They were naturally tickled that I had stopped by. We then continued to Paula's house where I met her mom and brother. Her dad was on a business trip out of country, but I would be able to meet him later when they did a Skype call. Paula's mom actually spoke very good English as she had spent time in the United States for work.

Paula and Kelly decided they wanted to cook me dinner. I was really exited for this! I love the opportunity to try traditional food from different countries. It was even better that it would be home-cooked, and even better, home cooked by

Paula and Kelly. However, when we drove to the local grocery store to grab ingredients, I couldn't help notice the odd ingredients. There were noodles, ground beef, onion,..

"So what are yall cookin'?" I asked.

"Spaghetti!" Paula said. I laughed. So much for my traditional Dutch dinner.

"It's the only thing Paula knows how to cook." Kelly added with a smirk, "but she still needs help."

When we arrived back at Paula's and her mom saw what they were cooking, she also laughed.

"Kelly, please make sure Paula doesn't poison us." She joked. She then invited me to sit out on the back patio to chat while the girls cooked.

While on the patio, Paula's mom asked many questions. She asked about who I was, where I was from, what I was doing in Europe, what my future plans were, and other things. It almost felt like an interview. Was I being interviewed? Had she somehow picked up on my slight interest in Paula? I hoped I answered well and came off like a good guy. Fortunately, the conversation also included a bit from her life story which was fascinating. She had apparently taught school in the United States for a time before returning to Europe. After around an hour, the girls called to let us know dinner was ready.

"Do you want to sit outside or go in?" Paula's mom asked.

"I'm find out here. It feels nice!" I replied. She agreed. She then called to the girls that we would be dining outside — or at least I assumed that was the case as she spoke Dutch. The next thing I knew, Paula brought me a plate of spaghetti and bread.

The food was great, although it was missing something. I couldn't put my finger on what it was, but it wasn't bad at all.

"I wish there was a little more sauce though." I said as we all started eating.

"That was Paula's job." Kelly replied. She and Paula's mom then teased Paula a little bit for it. She laughed, but I saw the look in her eyes and could tell it bothered her. I knew she had been really excited to cook for me, and the lack of sauce was making her feel bad. Seeing this, I switched gears.

"No, but seriously, yall did a fantastic job." I said enthusiastically. "It's *really* good! I can't thank you enough. I'm honored to be here enjoying dinner with yall." I looked at Paula and gave her a subtle nod to indicating I was being genuine. I think that did the trick.

We all chatted until we had finished eating at which point Paula's mom grabbed her ipad. She opened the Skype app and called Paula's dad. Paula's dad answered and after a moment was introduced to me! He was really nice and welcomed me to Holland.

"I hate I am not there to meet you in person, but welcome to Holland! I hope you have had a great experience." He said. I told him it had been a wonderful experience and I was so thrilled to be there.

After this, I still had some time before I needed to catch my train. The girls suggested we go for a walk. I agreed. We then left the house and headed down the street. During this walk, I heard music. I was naturally interested in following. We discovered that there seemed to be some sort of live music happening in a certain area across the way.

"Let's go check it out!" I suggested enthusiastically.

"No...we can't." Paula confessed. "My mom doesn't want us going because there will probably be a lot of drunk people there."

I was disappointed to hear this. I love any opportunity to hear live music, especially in a different country.

"Ok, but let's at least get a *little* close. Just to have a peak. I wanna see."

Kelly was 100% down. If I went, I knew she'd be right behind me. Paula, however, still wouldn't go for it. I pressed and pleaded, but she wouldn't budge. I was torn. Kelly and I then started messing with her like we were going to go real quick. We ended up pretending to go without Paula. We ran off in the direction of the event and turned the corner, but then stayed there. We assumed Paula would come and protest at which point we would jump out and scare her before going on back to the house. We were surprised, however, when this didn't happen. She instead turned around and started walking back home!

"Wait! Wait! We were kidding, Paula! Come back!" We yelled chasing after her. Paula turned around and I knew immediately by the look in her eyes she was upset. I felt absolutely terrible. She clearly thought we had really left her. I apologized profusely and assured her I never had the intention of leaving, swearing it was a prank.

"We thought you would come after us, and we were going to scare you!" I assured her.

"We were literally just around the corner the whole time laughing." Kelly explained.

I tried to give her a hug, but she wouldn't accept it. She laughed saying she was fine and not actually upset, but clearly was. I felt so bad. I wasn't sure what more I could do now. I just tried to stay up beat and make her laugh as we walked back toward the house.

Once back, we enjoyed healthy servings of ice cream for desert until it was time for me to leave. Kelly and Paula were driving separately because Kelly would be going home after seeing me off. I chose to ride with Paula in her jeep. I hoped I might be able to recover and maybe confess that I really liked her. Unfortunately, nothing of the sort resulted from my choice.

The ride proved to be awkward. I wasn't sure what to say. She didn't say much, and I didn't want to force conversation. I couldn't tell if she was still angry with me or merely deep into her thoughts. Either way, there were few words between us as we drove to the train station. My heart sank.

I hopped out at the station and said goodbye. I gave both girls a hug and thanked them for the amazing day. I then stepped over the gap onto my platform to enter my train. I sat down in the first seat I saw feeling disappointed. I truly regretted the prank and wished it hadn't seemed to ruin our final few minutes. I felt sure I could make up for it in the future if she'd let me. We were still friends, I thought, so I knew the three of us would talk again through social media or video chat. I decided then that the next chance I got, I would apologize again and hopefully gain some clarity around what was going on in her head during the ride to the station.

Back in Amsterdam, I returned to my hostel with the intention of capping off the night with a toke of my legally purchased Purple Haze. However, as I was not a smoker, I didn't know how to roll the contents up into a cigarette.

"Fortunately Youtube knows!" I said to myself.

After getting in, I found that two British guys had claimed bunks in the same hostel room. They were already in bed, but we said hello. I told them about my intention, which they were alright with.

As I got my phone out and attempted to open Youtube, I realized that for some reason, the wifi was not working! It was just my luck. I was thus forced to stick to the original plan.

"Maybe I'll have better luck tomorrow. After all, I will have plenty of time." I thought to myself.

With that, I put my purchase away and got into bed for the night.

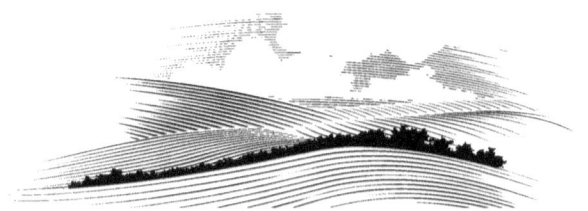

The Longest Night

Friday, July 18th

Upon waking up this morning, I checked train times out of Amsterdam heading toward Siegburg. I saw one that was leaving at 19:00 (7pm) which had a few changes. This would put me in Siegburg around 22:00 (10pm). There was one other train that left slightly later. It was a slow train and had five changes. Taking this train would put me in Siegburg at 1am.

After getting up, having a chat with my two new room mates, then eating breakfast, I decided to take a stroll. I didn't have anything on my agenda, so I wanted to simply take it easy. I eased on through the city to discover a second part of the park I had come upon the other day. This path through the park was wide, with many people walking along enjoying the day. Tall trees sprang up out of the ground to provide shade for people while large patches of grass allowed many to lie on beach towels and enjoy the sun. Those bathing in the sun reminded me of the Royal Crescent in Bath. It was a similar scene. Here, rather than a large hill, the area was flat with flowers everywhere, fountains, statues, and the walking path. I found a place to sit and relax, remaining there until lunch time at which point I wandered around until I found a kebab stand.

After eating lunch, I returned to the downtown area where the guys had played their guitar the other day. I did not find them this time, but enjoyed the scene none-the-less. I sat on a bench to relax while I enjoyed the scene. As people strode by, many stopped to get a photo in front of a large-scale statue of Baruch Spinoza (a Dutch rationalist philosopher of the early Enlightenment age). Others found a place to sit and simply relax. I once again took time to feel, hear, smell, and observe. I reflected on my recent experiences and pondered about life with gratitude.

I sat at the park for a while, then continued walking around casually taking in the sites. At around 3pm, I decided it was a good time to go enjoy my toke. I therefore made my way back to the hostel where I ran into the British guys.

"What's up, guys?" I asked.

"We're just getting back from the museum. What are you up to?" They asked.

"I was actually about to try to smoke again." I said. They laughed.

The three of us went up together and ended up discussing dinner. They suggested we have dinner together, and I agreed. I told them I might need to get dinner a little early to be sure I caught my train.

After getting into the room, I sat down and pulled out my phone again. This time, the wifi worked! I was able to find several Youtube videos on how to properly roll the contents. However, not being a smoker myself, it seemed to be impossible! I tried and tried much to my room mates' amusement. Despite my valiant effort, could not make it work! I probably spent a solid half hour - maybe 45 minutes - trying to get it done. No luck! I eventually became so frustrated that I gave up. It seemed my purchase had been for nothing.

"So what are you thinking?" One of my room mates later asked in reference to dinner.

"I'd like to do something kind of quick. Like a burger or something." I said. They agreed. However, they were planning on going out afterwards and needed to get showers, then we could head out.

After they had gotten showers, I grabbed my things, checked out, and we started down the road. My plan was to eat, then go immediately to the train station to catch my train. I had plenty of time, so there were no issues I expected to encounter. Yet, wasn't this how all my interesting experiences seem to start?

The three of us found a burger place and sat down. We ordered our food and were soon eating and chatting. It was great getting to know these two more, and I made a mental note to be sure and grab their contact info before leaving. As I casually took the last bite of my cheeseburger, I happened to glance at my watch. Somehow, I had lost track of time and was already running a hair late! It was ok though. I was sure I could make up for it. I would just have to move at a little quicker pace than I was intending. No problem. However, I needed to leave immediately. I therefore said a quick goodbye and good luck to my two friends, grabbed my things, and went quickly out of the door.

As I ran toward the tram stop, I wondered if it would be better to journey on foot to avoid traffic or trust the tram would get me there faster regardless. I ultimately wagered that the tram would be faster. Arriving at the tram stop, I jumped on board with around 20 minutes to spare. The tram normally took 10 minutes to get back towards the train station so I figured it might take an extra 5 minutes if there was traffic. Yet, in true form of my luck, the tram was constantly forced to stop. People getting on at every stop, off at every stop, stopping for traffic, hitting *literally* every red light, and other annoyances. I wondered several times if it would be worth it to hop off and run for it. I just kept thinking, "once we make it a little further along, things will clear up." Long story short,..it didn't.

The tram pulled up at the station stop at exactly 7pm, a whole 24 minutes after leaving my stop. I full-on sprinted from the tram stop, across the street, and down the road a little ways before finally entering the station. I raced around to find my train. It was now 7:03. I spotted what I believed to be my train. I noticed it's lights were flashing for some reason which I interpreted to be a bad sign. As I begin making my way towards it as quickly as I could, it suddenly donged on me that I didn't seem to be getting any closer. The train was moving. I finally stopped running, glanced at my watch, and stared as my train slowly pull away at exactly 7:04.

For several minutes, I was in denial. "Surely this was the wrong train and I hadn't actually missed my own," I thought. Unfortunately this was not the case and I had to accept reality. I had missed it by *that much*. I sat down on a nearby bench and weighed my options. I could book another night in Amsterdam (if they had any rooms available) and catch a train out tomorrow, or I could get on the next train that I knew would take me 5 hours and would not get me back to Siegburg until 1am. I considered the inconvenience to my hosts getting in so late, but at the same time, I wasn't really enjoying Amsterdam all that much. I felt like it might have been more enjoyable had some buddies been here to experience it with me.

Experiencing this city alone for some reason felt a little depressing. I also couldn't help feel this odd and eerie fog that seemed to be about the place that manifested in sadness and depression. I'm not sure I can explain it, but I know it's not simply because I have no friends to hang out with. There is something else. In any case, I chose to go ahead and catch the next train out. I tried to contact Zach & Tanja via Facebook, but was unable to. This was most likely due to them being at work. I therefore simply left them both a message explaining what happened and when I expected to be back.

I then boarded my slow train, which was taking passengers already, still frustrated. Sure, I could have left dinner a little earlier, but I still should have had enough time to catch my tram with time to spare (based on previous experience). I had ridden from the station to my hostel upon my first arrival, left from my hostel for the station in order to visit Apeldoorn, then rode back to the hostel from the station upon returning from Apeldoorn. Each ride only ever took 10 minutes or less on the tram! By all accounts, it should not have been any different this time! Yet there was nothing I could do now. I accepted that I would be traveling for the next *5 hours* instead of 3, and making *5 changes* instead of *maybe 2*. These things happen sometimes, and there are a lot of people who would let themselves become angry. I chose to laugh. It was the best attitude I could have for the journey ahead.

Despite being a long ride, the trip was very pleasant. The scenery was quite lovely and the people who sat next to me were all friendly. Each change went smoothly and I had no trouble or difficulty. In fact, it appeared that I might actually manage to arrive in Siegburg sooner than expected! Things were looking up.

I arrived at my final stop where I would board a train directly to Siegburg. At this point, it was very late and I was ready to be back. My sleeping bag at Zach and Tanja's was calling to me. I was so close now. After boarding my next and final train, I would be back in only around twenty minutes. However, upon exiting this train and finding my last, something seemed....off.

The doors to my final train were not open. There didn't seem to be any signs of a train staff or conductor. The lights inside the train were on, but no passengers. I thought perhaps the conductor had simply stepped out for a smoke. I then walked around a bit and discovered a train worker in fact having a smoke. This confirmed my thoughts, so I returned to the train where I assumed he would be returning to soon and thus we would be off. However, after several minutes, no one appeared. I checked back around where I had seen the train worker, but he had gone. I now realized that my final train would clearly not be leaving the station this night, and I, once again, had no idea what I was going to do. To make matters worse, the wifi was not working.

I returned to the train where there were six other people waiting around. I attempted to communicate with them and was thankful they spoke English. It turned out we were all in similar boats. This was supposed to be our last train and no one knew why it wasn't leaving. One among them was a young black guy named Jesse. He spoke with a heavy accent, but was very nice and had a good sense of humor. It was really good to have someone around like Jesse because the more frustrated I become, the more jokes I tend to make about the circumstances. This circumstance was obviously very frustrating, which provoked me to make continuous jokes, causing Jesse to laugh non-stop, which made me laugh and thus helping us both to better cope with the situation.

Jesse fortunately ended up having a cell phone with data so he could access the Internet. He was able to figure out that there was another train scheduled to arrive in a little while that we could both take. This train would take me to Cologne where I could then take another train to Siegburg. In all, that makes 7 changes from Amsterdam to Siegburg when it was originally going to be only 3. I felt fortunate to have found a friend in Jesse for this less-than-desirable circumstance. No matter how bad or frustrating life can get, having someone to get through it with you makes a world of a difference — especially when they have the key to help move you both forward (in this case, Internet access).

Jesse and I waited together until the next train arrived and boarded. We chatted, joked, and got to know each other the whole way until the train stopped in Cologne. As this was my stop, I stood up, shook his hand, thanked him for all his help, and for his good sense of humor. We then said goodbye and parted ways - he had a little further to ride.

I believe it was J.K. Rowling through Dumbledore who once said, "Happiness can be found in the darkest of times, if one only remembers to turn on the light." Jesse, if ever this story finds you, thank you for helping me to find the light. Cheers.

I stepped off the platform with a final wave goodbye to Jesse and went directly to the ticket booth. It was now a little after one o'clock in the morning. I somehow managed to walk up to the booth just as it was about to close! I practically had to *beg* them to stay open just long enough to help me get back to Siegburg! The guy behind the window was obviously ready to go home himself.

"Please sir!" I requested. "I just need to get back to Siegburg! I've had such terrible luck tonight. Please help me!"

The man drowsily pulled up his computer and did some typing. I hoped for goodness sake that I could simply jump onto another train within the next half hour or so and continue my journey without another pause. To my great dismay, however, this would not be the case.

"The next train out of Cologne headed for Siegburg will be leaving at three." He said conclusively, then handed me a slip with necessary information.

"THREE?!" I replied. The man gave me a nod before closing his computer and shutting the window. I cannot begin to express how I felt at hearing this. There was nothing I could do. I was stuck. Fortunately, I was stuck in a relatively safe area. My options now were to either wait inside the train station or go sit in the courtyard in front of the giant Cologne Cathedral. The courtyard was a wide-open space and pretty well lit. With my limited options, I chose to make the most of it. I left the ticket booth and stopped at a small convenient store inside the station. There I bought a cigar and two tall boy cans of Becks beer. I then made my way over to the courtyard where I sat on the steps before the enormous cathedral. As I lit my stick before popping open my beer, I let my mind wander. It was the only thing I could really do.

"Could I walk around and perhaps find a hostel?" I thought to myself. "I could, sure, but there was no guarantee there would be availability, not to mention the fact that I wouldn't know where to begin looking. Besides, even if I did, would it be worth spending the money for a whole night when I would only be there for a couple hours? And if I fell asleep, which seemed a likely scenario, would I wake up in time to catch the train? How concerned were Zach and Tanja who had been expecting me to arrive at 1am?"

In the end, I decided to merely sit for the next two hours and try to enjoy the fact that, despite my frustration and extreme exhaustion, this experience was going to make a great story. Just like in Munich, the thought of what a great story the experience would make gave me the mindset to smile through it. I sat back and chuckled to myself at the faces I was sure my friends and family would make when I recounted the tale.

While perched on my steps, I noticed a few homeless people around, but also a surprising number of non-homeless individuals hanging out. One guy in particularly caught my attention. He kept singing proudly into the night in a meter that sounded like those sung at European football matches. Had he been alone, I would have thought him maybe a little crazy. However, there was another guy with him who was not singing, but laughing. I deduced that they had just had a night out. The guy singing kept cracking me up, proving to be surprisingly entertaining. Eventually, my curiosity got the better of me. I carefully stood up and walked over.

"Hallo!" I said to the presumed friend of the guy singing. I asked if he spoke English, which he did. "What is going on?" I then asked with a smile.

"He's trying to be a hooligan!" His friend replied to me laughing as the aspiring drunken 'hooligan' launched into another chorus in German.

I don't recall if he had any connections to any teams, but he was dead set on being a hooligan. I had a good laugh, then wished them a good night before returning to my spot on the steps. It was turning out to be a nice night, all things considered. The only drawback was discovering that Becks beer and cigars go horribly together. I ended up putting the cigar out and simply sipping the beer.

After what seemed like forever, it finally came time to catch my final train. I returned to the station and boarded a train I thought was it. I then triple-checked my slip of paper to confirm it was the right one.

"God help me if I somehow get on the wrong train." I thought before also checking with a member of the train staff that it was indeed the correct train.

The train took off not long after I found a seat. A short ride later, I was relieved to see the familiar station of Siegburg. I hopped off and racked my brain. I stopped outside the station to recall landmarks that would help me navigate back to Zach and Tanja's. Thankfully, I had a rough idea. Doing the best I could, I made my way through familiar territory using recalled landmarks to guide my way. After a short walk, I managed to find their place! I was home free! Or was I?

The front door was naturally locked, so I would have to jump the tall, wooden gate. In order to do this, I had to climb atop the trash can in front of it. The trash can wasn't exactly steady, but I managed. As I stood on the top and began climbing atop the fence, the neighbor happened to come outside and saw me. I of course appeared to be trespassing. I explained that I was a friend, and assured the neighbor that Zach and Tanja were expecting me. The neighbor could tell I was genuine, and everything seemed fine. I then continued over the gate before jumping down onto the concrete drive below.

I went over to the back door which was the entrance to Zach and Tanja's bedroom. I knocked, then heard them stir inside. They were understandably surprised and a little concerned. The door cracked opened to reveal Zach cautiously looking out.

"Hey! It's me!" I whispered. Zach then opened the door fully, looking dazed and confused. "You won't believe what happened to me. I'm SO sorry I'm so late. I promise I'll tell you the whole story in the morning."

After getting in, I went straight to my sleeping bag and laid down. What an adventure this had been. It would certainly be one for the books.

Part VIII: Germany (Again)

Map of Germany: https://d-maps.com/carte.php?num_car=14453&lang=en
- Lines, circles, and words with asterisks are author's annotations and not on original map

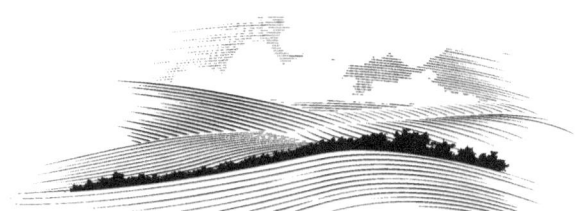

Beer Serious

Saturday, July 18th

"You sat in front of the church for TWO HOURS drinking beer and watching drunk people!?!" Tanja exclaimed through her thick German accent with notes of both concern and amusement.

Zach and Tanja had been at work all day leaving me to feel what it would be like to live in Germany. I spent the day playing with Elvis the dog, writing, and playing my guitar. When my hosts returned from work, the first thing they wanted to talk about was what happened to me.

"Yes!" I confirmed with a grin. "I was SO exhausted and SO ready to get back, but the train didn't leave until 3am and I couldn't get Internet on my phone or tablet anywhere. I also wasn't familiar with the area so I didn't want to get lost and potentially miss the 3am train out."

Zach essentially laughed throughout my entire story. He had been a little concerned, but felt confident that I was alright. Tanja thought the whole thing was funny, but was relieved to know I was ok.

"We were worried about you for a minute," Zach confessed. "But I told Tanja you were capable of taking care of yourself and were probably fine. I told her that you might have ended up getting laid. Who knew?" He concluded with a wink.

"Yes," Tanja agreed chuckling at Zach. "We were worried, but glad you're back safe now."

After recounting my tale, Zach suggested he and I go out in Siegburg for a few beers and an early dinner. Although Tanja had taken me into town for a bit, Zach hadn't had the pleasure of showing me around himself and wanted to take me to a few cool spots he enjoyed. This trip, in contrast to the one Tanja took me on, would be more of a casual experience of being local as opposed to a site-seeing adventure.

Upon arriving back to the area of the city that Tanja had taken me, I followed Zach to his favorite local watering hole. As it turned out, Siegburg had its own Brauhaus. Zach explained that *brauhaus* essentially translated to *brew house*. This meant that it was a brewery that also functioned as a bar-restaurant. Learning this, I was excited for some local beer, food, and flare.

The Siegburg Brauhaus was a large venue with long tables in the center. The place looked very old yet well maintained with notes of modern technology. The bar man who was drying out a glass greeted Zach and I as we found a place at the long oak bar.

"Was wirst du haben?" The bar man asked with a friendly smile.

"Zwei Kilsh." Zach replied, holding up his index finger and thumb. He and Zach had a short conversation in German during which I interpreted Zach had referred to me in some way. The bar man looked at me in a welcoming way. I greeted him in English.

"Welcome to Siegburg!" He replied cheerfully. "Have you had bratwurst yet?"

"None that I've been impressed with so far, but I probably just haven't had it from the right place yet or cooked the right way." I replied. We continued talking for a minute or so before he asked if we would be eating. I ordered a beef tip stew. I wasn't all that hungry, so nothing on the menu really jumped out at me - but not to say that it didn't sound good. Beef tip stew was simple and at least somewhat traditional for Germany.

Shortly after this, the bar man brought us our beers. Zach explained that *Kolsh* was a type of beer brewed in Germany made from yeast. He further specified that it was a yeast beer for a specific reason.

Apparently, Germany has a beer purity law established in 1516 by Duke Wilhelm IV of Bavaria. Zach explained that this law allowed only water, hops, yeast, and barley hops in every stein. I knew Germany had been brewing for hundreds of years, but I had never heard of this and found it fascinating.

"Also, did you know that Germany has 1,300 breweries around the country with more than 5,000 different kinds of beer?"

"WOW." I replied astonished. "That's wild. I knew Germans loved their beer, but I didn't know all of this. I guess they're even more serious about it than I realized."

"Oh yeah." Zach replied. "In fact, they take it so seriously, they even have a special word for it: *Bierernst*. It means "beer serious." So like when we say 'I'm dead serious,' they might say, '*bierernst.*'

The bar man grinned real big and chuckled overhearing our conversation.

After this conversation, I had a whole new appreciation for the Kolsh beer in my hand. I held up the glass that had been brewed not 30 feet from where I sat and took another savory sip. The taste almost reminded me of the Heineken I've had in the States, but with a slightly heavier and more preferable flavor. It felt like I was drinking history an loved it.

Zach and I stayed at the bar chatting for the next couple hours. during which time I finished the Kolsh, and also tried Siegburg's city beer along with a Hefavison - both were very tasty. My stew also ended up being very good and I finished it quickly. Eventually it came time to leave and Zach insisted on paying the bill. I assured him it was not necessary, but there was no arguing because that's how us southern folks are. After leaving this local brauhaus, Zach and I returned to he and Tanja's for the night. There we watched a little tv before turning in.

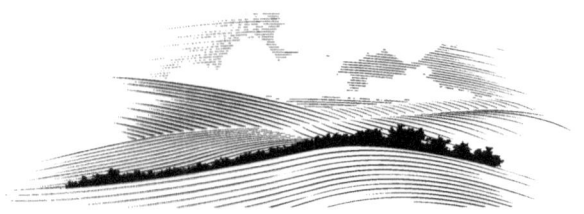

"Don't Knock It Till You Tried It!"

[Date Uncertain]

I ended up spending a couple weeks with Zach and Tanja. Much of this time was spent simply hanging out and living in Germany. It was a really cool experience, but a lot of the time wasn't worth mentioning, so I lost track of the days. However, there were a few tales worth telling. Here is one.

It was a day just like any other. The three of us woke up, ate breakfast, showered, and sat on the couch to watch tv. Zach then turns to me.

"So what do you want to do today, Tim?" He asked.

"I don't know, man." I replied. "I'm not feeling like doing anything crazy today. I kind of want to chill, but I'm up for something casual."

"Well, you wanna go out to Bonn?" He suggested. *Bonn.* is a small city near Siegburg pronounced *Bah-n.* "My American buddy, Sanner, wants to meet up and hang out with us."

"Yeah, sure!" I said.

Not long after deciding this, Zach and I walked down to the train station. Rather than boarding a train, we simply hopped on a tram which took us on a ten minute ride into the city of Bonn. Bonn was not a large city, but appeared to be bigger than Siegburg. As we got out and walked around, there certainly seemed to be more of a hustle and bustle than what I felt in Siegburg. Despite being the oldest town in Germany, it seemed very modern. It is home to Bonn University, a nice history museum, and the legendary composer Ludwig van Beethoven.

As we walked around, I noticed a few interesting spectacles. One was a large shop dedicated to the lego CHIMA series - which I knew nothing about. In the shop's window was a 3 foot tall lego character complete with helmet and brightly colored armor. Around the character were smaller-scale lego toys of the same theme.

The other spectacle I discovered made me stop for a double-take. We passed by this shop with a display window in the front. What made it interesting was the fact that the display was full of *guns*! Having been born and raised in the south, seeing guns at/in a store was nothing new. The difference was that in my experience, guns for sale were typically located near the clerk, locked into place, under a thick-glass counter, or mounted on a wall behind a clerk counter — all this to say not easily accessible. I looked over the weapons displayed to notice another things that seemed very unusual: the *price*! €23 for a serious-looking pistol?! That's it?! Also, I thought the casual purchase of firearms was illegal in Germany - or at least not easy to get as the Brit on the train told me.

"What's the catch?!" I wondered. "What am I missing here?" I was very confused. Then it all made sense when I noticed containers with small yellow spheres being sold alongside several of the weapons. I started laughing to myself as I said out loud, "Arisoft!" I hadn't considered the fact that they were Arisoft because I was used to seeing a bright orange piece at the end of Arisoft gun barrels. Now that it all made sense, I was able to continue with Zach in search of anything that might catch our interest. Soon, we did.

Not far from the lego shop was a Mexican restaurant called *Taco Mexican Bar & Restaurant*. I couldn't help chuckle at how campy and un-Mexican the place looked, not to mention seeing a "Mexican" place in a small German town. It seemed kind of random. The restaurant had the ambiance more to the liking of a themed Disney World diner than any Mexican restaurant I'd ever been to. However, they advertised a half-price margarita, so we naturally made our way inside as Zach sent Sanner a text letting him know where we were.

We were quickly seated at one of the small tables and provided with a menu. I didn't see anything that sounded particularly good, but ultimately ordered a burrito. The burrito came with a side of potato wedges which seemed oddly out of place (usually you'd expect rice and/or beans and/or a taco). What I was pleasantly surprised to see on the menu was sweet iced tea! Seeing it, I even decided against the margarita in light of the tea. Even though it was bottled Arizona Lemon Iced Tea (I prefer plane Lipton + sugar), the restaurant scored points with me for even having a sweet tea option.

When the food came, I was quite pleased with the quality. It was less Mexican and more like a Southwest Burrito you might order at an American chain restaurant like Applebee's or O'Charlie's. In any case, it was very good and I left satisfied with our choice. It was about this time that Sanner arrived.

Zach, Sanner, and I then walked around the city site-seeing. Zach would point out notable buildings to me and provide a little history of the city. After a couple hours of this, we stopped in at a local Bonn Brauhaus. Over the course of our time there (a couple hours), I had the pleasure of trying a Rissendorf Kolsch,

Gaffel Kolsch, a few different "Pils" beers (which is short for Pilsner) such as one called Krombocker (which reminded me of Guiness), and a couple Weizen aka wheat beers.

We also ended up having dinner here. My dinner experienced proved to be unexpectedly interesting. As most people know about me, I typically don't like sauerkraut. Unless it is a small portion on a Reuben sandwich or on one of my buddy James' famous beer-braut sausage dogs, I'm not having it. You couldn't pay me to eat it, certainly not a whole scoop of it by itself.

Well, when my small dinner arrived, I saw a healthy portion of sauerkraut next to the other items on my plate. I must have overlooked it when I ordered from the menu. However, it was possible that in Germany they cooked it differently than what I was used to. I was on an adventure after all, wasn't I? Therefore, with an adventurer mindset, I decided to go for it. I stuck my fork in, picked up a big scoop, and stuck it in my mouth half holding my breath.

I expected it to be absolutely gross. My goal was to simply chew and swallow, then be done with it. I could then at least say I tried it. My dad always says, "Don't knock it till you tried it!" That is, unless he is offered a roasted goat's head for dinner while in Saudi Arabia…but that's a different story.

Yet to my incredible surprise, a smile came across my face as the warm, sweet substance erupted my taste buds. I can't explain it. I couldn't compare it to anything else I'd ever tried before. The name sauerkraut suggests that it's going to be sour. This is typically the case in my unpleasant experience with the item. *This* time, however, it was very different. There was still a very slight sour taste, but the overpowering flavor was that of something sweet and savory. Was there some sort of wizard in that kitchen? I couldn't get enough of it! Despite wanting to gulp it down, I forced myself to take my time enjoying this manna of the gods. Zach and Sanner made fun of the way I was acting.

"Have you never had it before?" I asked them?

"I mean, I've had sauerkraut before, but not from Germany." Sanner said, to which Zach agreed. They clearly couldn't understand. Unless they were to order some (because I wasn't sharing), they weren't going to understand. They never ordered any for themselves, but that was ok. I will forever cherish the memory of that taste until I return one day for another round.

We made the next hour or so a merry time and I got to know Sanner a lot better. It seemed that he was an atheist/borderline agnostic and somehow we got on the topic of religion. I was very appreciative of how considerate he was in sharing what he thought and asking to better understand what and why Zach and I believed what we believed. Some people ask questions but not with the intention of getting an answer but rather in an attempt to show you that you can't explain it or make it make sense. Sanner genuinely wanted to understand. He was a classic case of religion being shoved down his throat as a kid and therefore rejected it when he became old enough to choose for himself. I eventually shared with him my upbringing and the difference between mine and other denominations. He appreciated this, and said it gave him a broader perspective. I hope he'll find his way to God and discover who He really is.

When 5pm came around, we decided to call it a night and parted ways. I was really excited about the days to follow. Zach and Tanja were planning to take me to a palace, then Zach had his baseball game in Bonn, and there was a chance we would all go out again. I couldn't wait.

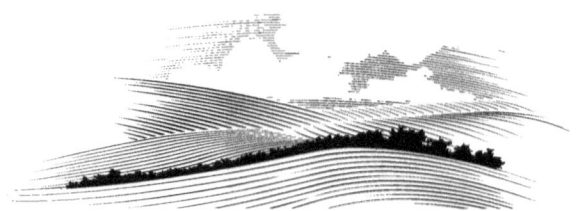

Palace Rules

[Date Uncertain]

Today was the day Tanja and Zach were going to take me to the palace. However, there was an issue that had to be resolved. Tanja's car was in the shop. Her mirror had apparently come off and she had taken it there to get fixed. The problem was that this was the 2nd time she'd taken it because it hadn't been fixed the first time. So after my typical breakfast consisting of brotchen bread, jam, milk, and coffee, the three of us set out to get Tanja's car.

We went inside to get the car expecting Tanja would be handed the keys and we would be on our way. This was not the case. Tanja and the shop guys engaged in conversation. I was unable to understand because it was all in German. I looked at Zach.

"Tanja paid for the repair last time, and it broke again after they gave it back. They are wanting her to pay again." He explained.

Tanja is a very mild-mannered, easy going type of woman. One would likely not expect her to be confrontational at all. Hearing her and the men going back and fourth, interpreting from her tone that she was very dissatisfied was impressive.

"NO! I brought it here and you said you fixed it but you didn't. I'm *not* paying you to fix it *again!*"

All of this was in German of course, so I didn't actually understand what she was saying. What I did understand was her tone, and Zach translated the gist of what she was saying for me. Seeing that Tanja had the situation clearly handled, I chose to pull a soda (called "Mezzo Mix: colakusstorange") out of the drink machine and wait outside. Tanja soon came out victoriously. The guys had agreed to fix the car another day free of charge. Word to the wise: don't try to rip Tanja off - she's not going to have it.

A half hour's ride later, we pulled into Augustburg Palace in Bruhl located to the north of Siegburg and west of The Rhine. The palace itself was not immediately visible from the parking area. We exited the car and begin walking. As we rounded the corner of a white building, the Palace was in clear view.

A wide, diamond-carved stone drive led up to the palace through a gate surrounded by light-gray, stone brick giving way to a rectangular courtyard. The shape of the palace formed around us resembled a horse shoe, but more squared off. This formed the courtyard in which we stood. The middle of the horse shoe shape facing us was 7 windows wide. The sides of the palace stretching out around us was 7 windows long and 3 windows deep.

To the right was a door which, according to Tanja, indicated where tickets were purchased. We walked inside to find a room with a desk and a few women behind a desk. They soon were explaining to us that the fist tour would begin shortly and allowed us to purchase tickets. However, I was surprised to find how impersonable and unfriendly these women seemed to be. I simply assumed they must not be having the best morning for some reason.

One of the women explained the rules for the tour as we purchased tickets. She said we were not allowed to tour the palace alone and thus required a guide. No problems with this. She next explained the tour was not in English, but a prerecorded English-speaking tour with headphones was available without charge - but it was only for the second half of the tour, not the first. We were further not allowed to take any pictures or video and were therefore required to surrender our cameras and/or phones for the duration of the tour. I was pretty unhappy with this rule. I get the concern about flash photography somehow affecting things, but still. I surrendered my camera, but kept my phone in my pocket thinking I might could sneak a few stealthy photos like I did in the Sistine Chapel. The final rule was that we were not to touch anything at all. Violation of this would result in getting kicked out with no refund.

"What is this?" I thought after learning that no touching whatsoever was allowed. "Are we about to enter *The Cave of Wonders*? If I touch something other than a magical lamp containing a genie, will it all melt away into a giant sea of gold lava? Should I be on the lookout for a magic carpet just in case?"

It wasn't long into the tour that I couldn't help closely examine a beautifully designed wallpaper. As the guide carried on in German, without even thinking about it honestly, my finger drifted up to just barely touch a single spot of the wallpaper. Suddenly the guide stopped talking. I returned to face the guide innocently to notice everyone glaring at me. Looking around, my eyes widened. The woman next to me leaned in and said something in German. I looked at her confused and whispered back,"English?"

"Oh," she said smiling, now slightly amused. "We're not supposed to touch."

"Oh, sorry." I replied. The tour then continued. I imagine the guide simply picked up where she had left off.

The next space we entered was magnificent. It had a beauty no description could do justice. Every square inch of this area was artistically decorated with patterns and colors like I had never seen. From the floor to the walls, from the windows to the ceiling, shapes and colors swirled together in tile, marble, curves, and waves. Forget the Vatican! If God Almighty had a palace on Earth, this would truly be it.

This time, I truly couldn't help myself. I *had* to connect with this space and wasn't allowed a camera. It wasn't enough just to take in with my eyes. I inconspicuously moved toward a tall column facing the guide who carried on talking in German. I slipped my hand around the the side of the column where no one could see and carefully touched the decorated marble. I slid my finger, feeling the smooth surface and colorful pattern that danced around it.

"TIM." Came a sudden stern whisper from Zach. "*STOP TOUCHING. STUFF.* You're gonna get us kicked out."

"Ok, ok! Geez." I replied. But it didn't stop there. Twice more it happened, partly for the same reason as before, and partly because I was annoyed, bored, and thus feeling a little rebellious. Eventually I gave it up, not wanting to anger my hosts.

All the rooms eventually started to look the same anyway so the desire to connect with it diminished. I became tired of listening to the recorded tour, so I merely walked around half-heartedly looking at things and doing my best to appreciate it despite knowing that I'd forget most of it without a photo/video.

When the tour ended, although I was very grateful that Zach and Tanja were so kind to bring me, I was relieved. I took one last look as we headed back down the stone drive toward the car. I felt confident I would be able to remember the face of the palace, the first room with the wallpaper, and the really decorative one. Beyond that, I knew it would unfortunately all fade away.

We got in the car and drove away with our next stop being Zach and Tanja's to grab Elvis the dog, then travel to Bonn for Zach's baseball game.

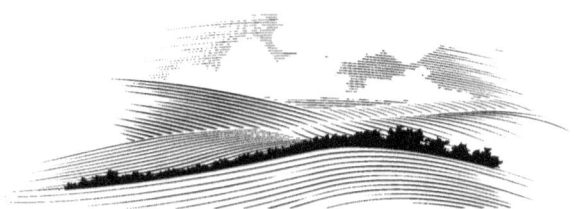

Bonn Capitals

[Date Uncertain]

We arrived in Bonn with Elvis the dog and immediately took him on a walk. We passed through a park where trees seemed to grow upside down, then on to a big field looking toward the city. Zach and Tanja pointed out the main Bonn University building to me which apparently has other academic buildings scattered throughout the city. I was glad American universities weren't that way. Walking to different buildings on campus could be taxing enough, so I couldn't imagine having to drive all over town between classes. Soon, it was close to Zach's game time. Tanja unfortunately had some errands to run so she and Elvis took off while Zach and I made our way down to the ball park.

The Baseball Park was a familiar site having spent plenty of time at my local ball parks growing up. I actually played through the beginnings of kid-pitch until I realized how terrible I was at the sport and hung it up. I spent the remainder of my childhood focused on soccer.

Zach left me to find his team and get changed into his uniform. I meanwhile found a place on the bleachers to sit behind Home Plate. Zach's team, The Bonn Capitals, arrived first and took the field for warm-ups. Zach took the Pitcher's mound to warm up his arm. As the stands began to fill, the opposing team arrived and was given some time to warm up. Soon, the umpire called for the game to start. The Capitals were met with cheers from the stands as they emerged from the dugout. Zach then took his place on the mound.

It was funny to me being in a small German town watching "America's favorite past time." Unlike what I was used to however, there wasn't any chanting or talking from within the stands. Attend any local American (non-professional) baseball game of any age group and you'll hear people shouting things like, "3 up, 3 down," "atta boy," or "good eye, good eye!" The spectators around me were pretty silent aside from clapping, so I took the liberty of doing some. All my shouts were positive and supportive except for this one time when one of the Capitals pitched a fit and slammed his bat down like a child after striking out. I was a little shocked at this behavior. I actually jerred at him, yelling out that he was being immature and unsportsman-like. He was a pretty big guy though, so I didn't want to make too big a deal about it lest he come find me after the game.

In between one of the innings, I took the opportunity to see what was available at the concession stand for lunch. I could smell bratwurst being grilled from where I was and it smelled pretty good. Something happened to where I closed my eyes, then was suddenly in front of the person grilling the brats. *I swear I have no idea what happened...*In any case, he asked if I wanted a bratwurst or currywurst. I had never heard of a currywurst, so I decided to get both along with a beer! I was not disappointed with either, though I did decide that I preferred the currywurst.

With two brats in hand and a beer, I reclaimed my seat for the remainder of the game. About that time, Tanja returned from running her errands with Elvis.

Zach ended up having a really good game! He shut out several innings, knocked a few balls into the outfield while batting, and represented America well overall. I was proud.

After leaving the ball park, I decided I'd like to try to find a genuine German stein before leaving Germany. As we walked through the city, my eyes darted into each little shop we passed. It seemed that they were all upwards of €100 or more! I felt hopeless in finding one. Eventually, I gave up and simply walked.

Once back in Siegburg, Zach and Tanja had to run by the post office to complete Tanja's final errand. While my hosts were taking care of business, I casually took a look around. Suddenly, I just happened to notice a stein on a shelf featuring what appeared to be Michaelsburg (the monestary in Siegburg that was closed when Tanja and I went) carved into the front. I picked it up carefully for a closer look. It didn't have a *for sale* sticker anywhere, but I decided to ask anyway. I was willing to pay up to €50, but no more.

"Hi, excuse me." I said to the clerk who was very nice. "What would it take for you to sell this to me? I'm from Mississippi and I would LOVE to bring home a real German stein. All the ones I've found have been super expensive."

"Is that the one from Michaelsburg?" The lady asked.

"I'm not sure." I looked at the picture. "Maybe?" I held it up for her to see.

"Oh yeah!" She said. "That was made by the monks there years ago."

"Wow!" I exclaimed. "It's beautiful." The lady looked at me thoughtfully.

"Thirty euro." She said with a smile.

"Really!?" I exclaimed.

"Yes." She said. I pulled out my wallet and counted out €30 and handed it to her.

"Enjoy!" She said cheerfully.

"Thank you SO MUCH!" I cried. I could not have been more excited! Finally, a REAL German Stein MADE BY MONKS! This is far better even than I could have hoped for in finding one at a shop! And at such a most unlikely place! God clearly heard my heart and mysteriously provided.

The three of us stopped by a grocery store on the way back to the house and picked up some stakes for dinner which Zach grilled. By the time we had finished dinner, we were all exhausted from the day. Needless to say, we all turned in early. Zach and I planned to visit the city of Koln in the morning. I couldn't wait.

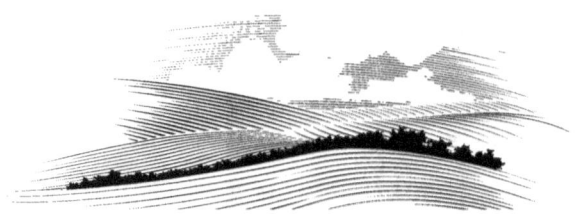

The Scented City

Tuesday, July 22nd

I awoke this morning to Zach already cooking breakfast. We had a big day ahead of us and I was filled with anticipation. Today we would be visiting the city of Köln or *Cologne* as we say in English. We didn't have any specific plans, only to explore the city, enjoy some great local food and beer at the Gaffel Kulsh Brauhause, and visit the enormous cathedral I sat in front of that night. The fact that I had Zach who was somewhat familiar with the area and spoke the language made it all the better. Thus after a hurried breakfast, we strode over to the Siegburg tram and rode it a short while to Köln.

The church I mentioned was one of the first things that came into view as we entered the square. I was grateful to now see it in the daylight as opposed to the darkness. Before, I could only see its towering magnitude. Now in the light, I was compelled to take pause in admiration. Its color and artistic design from bottom to the very tip tops was now clear. The decorated arches standing under artistic spires were carved into the front. Uniquely designed columns shot out from the ground which seemed to climb up the face of the structure before shooting up towards the sky.

Zach and I then continued on inside the church. There really wasn't anything unfamiliar to me at this point having seen so many cathedrals. However, there were still plenty of beautiful paintings, stone statues, enormous stain glass windows, and gold-trimmed religious relics. There were a course a few tombs similar to that of Strongbow in Dublin, but I was thankful that there weren't any rotting bodies. The one thing that did stand out to me was a center space lined with tall, enormous columns and a high, artistically domed ceiling. I say "domed" but it wasn't truly domed as you might imagine. It wasn't spherical. Rather, it was triangular with rounded tops. If there is a word for this, I'm afraid I don't know it.

After wandering around for ten minutes or so, we chose to move on to the entrance of the tallest spire. As Zach had made this climb before, he took the lead and I followed. Out and around the corner of the church I followed Zach. Then through a small archway there was the entrance which suddenly became a spiral stair case.

I can't explain why, but I love spiral stair cases. This one however was very steep and very narrow. It was so much so that my face was directly behind Zach's rear end.

"I really hope Zach doesn't experience indigestion," I couldn't help think to my self as we climbed.

According to the information pamphlet Zach had picked up inside the church, the climb was 475 feet to the top. The number of steep steps required to get there was 533. This made it the tallest in Western Europe. In fact, during World War II, American Air Force pilots used this church as a landmark because it could be so easily seen from the sky.

Sweating hard, the two of us climbed until the steps came to a halt. I thought we had reached the top. I quickly realized this was not the case and we had only just arrived at the Bell Tower. Zach and I took the opportunity to have a short rest before moving on. During this time, Spanish (or maybe Portuguese?)-speaking black girls who were present apparently found Zach very attractive. We knew this because they told us so and asked if they could get a picture with him. Neither of us could contain our laughter. He was both humored and flattered, and kindly obliged them. I told him afterwards that he just obtained "hot American" status. Suddenly, the bells began to chime announcing the turn of the hour and we took it as a cue to move on up the next set of stairs.

Once at the top, Zach and I found a maze of narrow walk-ways and arched entrances with signs indicating which way to walk. Just as I described the outside of the church, no corner here was left untouched by an artistic hand. Every ending space started a new design or a return to a common theme already used.

"Wow," I thought. "The time it took to construct something like this with such consistent and intricate detail is a feat worthy of eternal celebration." With that being said, one can therefore imagine my disgust with the amount of modern graffiti that completely disrespected the magnificence of this church. Everything from people signing their names or 'so-in-so [heart] so-in-so' to profanity and sexual images like one might find in a porta potty

On the ground, green arrows guided us to a lookout point with an incredible view. Looking out, we could see for a hundred miles or more. It reminded me of the view at the top of the Arch of Triumph in Paris, but even higher. We remained here for a while taking in the view and enjoying the breeze.

After returning to the ground and exiting the spire, I noticed a "Römisch-Germanisches Museum (Romano-Germanic Museum) to our immediate left.

There in the window was a full-body sculpture of my hero: The man, the myth, the legend, Gaius Octavian Caesar Augustus! With his outstretched hand, he beckoned me to enter. My heart filled with excitement, joy, and the desire to enter immediately. Fortunately, Zach enjoyed Roman history as well. After pointing it out to him, we both charged forth into the building. I naturally immediately got a selfie with another sculpture of my hero which was painted. We then quickly purchased tickets to the museum. We learned that there was no tour, but all the descriptions included an English translation.

The museum was absolutely incredible! It was even better than the Louvre! I think what was so exciting for me were the little things - the small details. While the Louvre was great and featured large items and relics, the RG featured not only large pieces, but tiny, more personal items as well. What I mean is, it's so easy to study history and see great memorials to the deeds of the people who lived. Things like great statues, arches, carvings, et cetera, et cetera while at the same time not really feeling connected with the humans who lived at the time. That's where the little things come into play.

In the past just as in the present, there were children, teens, young adults, adults, and elders living in the ancient Roman period. These people by nature weren't really so different than we are today. Seeing great stonework is marvelous, but feels at the same time so distant. When I walk through a museum and see small items such as a hair brush, jewelery, children's toys carved from marble and stone, bowls, common tools, and other common yet recognizable materials, I feel a real connection to them. They weren't some alien race. They were just like me. Kids played with toys, women spent time in front of mirrors combing their hair, they ate cereal or grain out of bowls, and they took pride in what they wore. The only thing really separating us today from those who lived then is the amount of time we have spent further developing these items. Kids still play with action fig-ures and animal toys, only instead of carved marble and stone, they are made of rubber and plastic. Now instead of combs made of bone or wood, they are made from plastic. Looking at all of these incredible, both big and small artifacts, took me out of the 21st century and dropped me into a time-lapse spanning nearly 1,000 years. By the time I had gotten three quarters through, my cup was over-flowing. I could hardly appreciate or handle much more. I did my best to take in the final quarter (there was SO much), and was relieved when I came to the end. I left the museum feeling so fully satisfied, I could not express it in words. I needed to celebrate such a wonderful experience, and Zach knew just the place.

By the time we left, it was well after noon and neither of us had eaten since breakfast.

"We could go eat at the Gaffel," Zach said, pointing to a brauhaus called "Gaffel am Dom." It was across the street and just to the north of the great cathe-dral. It looked like a nice place from the outside, so I agreed.

As we entered, I was immediately blown away by the aesthetics. The res-taurant had tall ceilings with large, square beams. The entire interior featured a darkened oak Wainscot paneling to bring a classy feel. Warm lighting hung from the walls reflecting off many signs, photos, metals, and golden beer drums which easily caught the eye. The ceiling featured decorative stain glass which captured the warm hew of the light. I inhaled the aroma of delicious-smelling food drifting from the kitchen as my stomach grumbled. Looking around, I chose a smaller table next to a pillar and the two of us sat down. Zach had funny look in his eye that told me this was going to be an experience to remember.

A waitress came over shortly after we sat down and handed us a menu. She initially addressed us in German. I obviously wasn't sure what she said, but I could have guessed based on the setting. Zach replied in German.

"What can I get you to drink?" She asked in English with a friendly smile.

"How about a round of Gaffel Kolsh?" Zach asked. Seeing as we were in the Gaffel Brauhaus, it seemed the most reasonable thing to order, but I wasn't sure what he meant by "round." The way he said it sounded like it was different from the mere ordering of a drink for the both of us. "It's an order of several small glasses that come on a circular holder." He tried to explain. I couldn't exactly visualize it, but it sounded like a good option so I agreed. The waitress nodded with understanding before leaving us to get the round. A couple minutes later, she returned. I then understood why it was called a *round*.

There was a handle at the top which fell down to the center. Eleven beers were encircled around the center handle which was on a spindle. After the waitress sat it down, Zach spun the round so that it rotated 360 degrees. Each glass was tall and slim rather than a full 12-16 ounces which is the norm. If I were to guess, I would say each glass held around 8 ounces of the liquid gold. Without wasting any time, Zach and I clanged a glass and took our first drink. Then we had another, and another, and yet another. Truly, I didn't typically drink that fast. I was simply trying to keep up with Zach! Soon after we started, we had nearly finished the whole round.

"What can I get you to eat?" The waitress came over to ask as we were getting ready to polish off the last couple drinks of the round. Although I had looked over the menu, I had been so focused on keeping up with Zach in the drinking department that I failed to decide. I gave an undecided look.

"I think you aught to go with the traditional German Schnitzel." Suggested Zach. "It comes with potatoes, [pureed] spinach, and a fried egg. It's good. Get whatever you want though! That's just what I'd recommend."

"Sure!" I replied. "I'll trust your advice." So I ordered the Wiener Schnitzel along with French fries. After she had taken both of our food orders, we also went ahead and ordered another round of Gaffel Kolsh.

When the next round came, I decided to slow down and not try to keep up with Zach. He had been living in Germany for a while now, which gave him an advantage.

"Dude, I'm already a little bit buzzed!" I confessed with a chuckle. "I better slow down or you might be carrying my out of here…"

"Man look, I want you to just enjoy yourself." Zach replied. "You're in Germany, the brewing capital of the world. You're also with a buddy who lives here and can guarantee you get home safe. If you want to slow sown, that's fine, but if not, know I'll take care of you either way." He further went on to assure me that I was also fee to make stupid mistakes and jokingly reminding me that, "you've got a lawyer in your corner," and even did some hilarious courtroom defense scenarios where he defends me. I laughed and chose to take him up on his offer. I knew I could trust him. Besides, when might I ever have this opportunity again? As they say, "when in Rome!"

By the time our food arrived, we had already finished a second round and had started on a third. The Wiener Schnitzel was very good, though I had a little trouble cutting through it. Zach of course jokingly blamed this on the alcohol. Somehow acquiring the hick-ups didn't help my case any. The eggs and spinach was also very good, especially when I mixed them together and dipped the Schnitzel in it. I ended up only nibbling at the French fries because the traditional German food was much better.

After finishing our dinner along with our third round of Gaffel Kolsh, I was feeling pretty good. We then paid our waitress and made our way back outside and into the courtyard of the church. Here, we found a place to sit and watched people for a while which is always interesting. Within the courtyard was a guy playing a digeridoo and a box drum (called a cajon). Sitting beside him was a guitar. People would stroll past and occasionally drop a euro or two in the box he had next to him for tips. I then got a funny idea.

"Hey," I said to Zach. "Watch this." He looked at me questioningly. I jumped up and walked over to the digeridoo guy while he was taking a short break. I asked him in German if he spoke English, which he did. I complimented him on his playing, which he appreciated, then asked him an unusual question.

"I actually play the guitar!" I said. "I was wondering….could I play your guitar while you play the doo and cajon??" He looked at me for a moment before taking me by surprise.

"Sure!" He said, and motioned to his guitar! I couldn't believe it! I didn't think he'd actually go for it! I figured I'd go ask, then after he turned me down, I'd go back and have a laugh about it with Zach. This just got 10 times better.

I picked up the acoustic guitar and he begin to play. Without hesitation, I started strumming a chord progression in the key of G to the tempo of his drum. Zach realized what was happening and quickly pulled out the camera and started filming. I looked over as I played to see Zach smiling from ear to ear, hardly being able to believe that this was actually happening. To be honest, I felt the same way! I was in Germany, playing guitar with an Aborigine, who was playing the digeridoo and cajon as a street performance. Had Zach not been recording it, I felt sure no one at home would have ever believed it happened. How funny must it have also looked to other people passing by, many of whom met my eye and couldn't help but grin.

The Aborigine and I played together for about two minutes until he quit. I didn't try to keep it going any longer. I thanked him for allowing me to play with him, told him it sounded great (might have been exaggerating a little), then put the guitar down and returned to Zach who was falling over himself laughing. To be clear though, neither I nor Zach were attempting to make fun of the digeridoo player in any way. The humor was me, a random American, playing the guitar with a guy playing the digeridoo.

After we'd had our fun, Zach and I decided to return to the train station and head back to the house before we got into any trouble. It had been a fantastic evening. I looked forward to the next adventure.

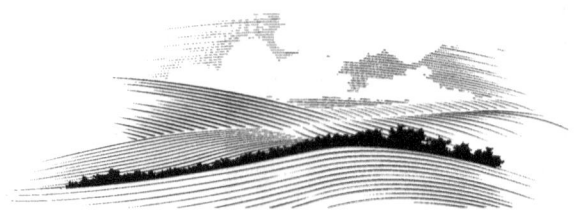

Farewell Zach & Tanja

Date Unknown

Idon't recall how long Zach and Tanja had been living in Germany, but I want to say it was at least a year. He had moved there not long after finishing at University. However, after Tanja had completed her degree program in Germany, they planned to return to the United States to get her PhD and get married in Mississippi. That being said, Tanja's family and friends (along with some friends Zach had made) wanted to throw them a farewell party at their house. This was that day.

Preparation for the party began early that afternoon. Zach, Tanja, and I went down to the beer store where we got a few cartons (24pk cases) of Kolsh beer. Upon our return to the house, we unloaded the beer into multiple coolers. Next we went out and cleaned the grills (there were a couple) in the back yard before setting up tables.

To my delight, the garage had actually already been converted into somewhat of a beer hall. It only lacked tables and seating, which we brought in. It featured a full-size bar on the far right side complete with a couple beer taps and workable sink. Colored lights were strung around the garage and out onto the front patio. It was a typical festive atmosphere with one unusual site. This was a tripod set up just outside the garage on the patio. I considered asking what it was for, but ultimately decided to simply wait and see.

Around 5pm, friends and family of the couple begin to arrive. Many of them brought extra beer. By the end, we had acquired 3 coolers, 7 (24pk) cases, and 1 mid-sized keg which was hooked up to the tap on the bar. The types of beers I recall included Gaffel Kolsh, Reissdorf Kolsh, and Lion Kolsh.

I was glad to already know some of the guests such as Tanja's brother and sister whom I had met briefly during the World Cup match along with Sanner, which was Zach's work friend who had joined us for dinner that night. I felt very blessed to be a part of this happy-sad occasion. I was also happy to meet several friends and members of Tanja's family that I had not yet met.

One particular friend of theirs I met was a guy named Manuel. Manuel was a few years older than me, married, and had a young child. His English was very good and he had a good understanding of American culture. He and I connected fairly quickly and bonded over a discussion of American movies and music. Throughout the night, if I were trying to have a conversation with another German whose English was not as strong, Manuel would often jump in to help translate. I very much appreciated this, especially in one incidence.

At one point, I was having a conversation with Tanja's brother about Christian denominations. I'm not sure how we got on the topic - maybe while talking about history and local historic places as European history is strongly tied to religion. Somehow there came some confusion between he and I. This resulted in him starting to get a little heated. I understood what he was telling me, but I was having trouble communicating clearly what I was saying. His misunderstanding of what I was trying to say very much offended him. Luckily, Manuel happened to overhear this and came to my rescue. Manuel joined the conversation and clarified to Tanja's brother in German what I was trying to express in English. There was a classic "OOOOOOOOhhh," moment of clarity and the heat was immediately diffused.

As more people arrived, the grills were lit up. The smell of bratwurst soon filled the air, and it was then that I saw what the tripod was for! A long chain had been fashioned to the top of the tripod which was connected to a round plate hanging down. Under the slowly swinging plate was a small fire pit. The plate slowly swung over and around the flames, cooking the wursts. I found the strategy odd, but clearly effective.

Probably one of the best parts about this party was the fact that Claire from France took a train all the way from Paris (a few hour ride) to be there! It was wonderful to see her once more and spend more time catching up. We were able to have a few drinks together and she humored me by doing a mission log video for me by herself! It was indeed a wonderful and merry time.

At the end of the night, several guests stayed to help with basic clean-up. After that, everyone said their goodbyes. I shook Manuel's hand and gave Claire a big hug as I didn't know if I'd ever see her again. Once everyone had gone, I went inside and searched for hostels in Brussels, Belgium. That was my next planned adventure. There was one I found called "Hostel Generation Europe," which didn't appear to be too far from the city center and seemed reasonably priced compared to some of the others (as is usually the case). I also actually upped my budget for a somewhat nicer stay - it would be my final week in Europe after all! I therefore went ahead and booked the next 5 nights.

I next looked for train times. I found a 2-hour train to Brussels that left Sieg-burg at 3pm. With my hostel booked and my train chosen, I was set and ready. Although I was a little sad about leaving Zach and Tanja, I knew they had a lot to do over the next couple days in order to be prepared to move back to the United States. I also knew I would likely see them again in the relatively near future as they would be in Mississippi. Thus, I went to bed full of anticipation for my next adventure and final week in Europe.

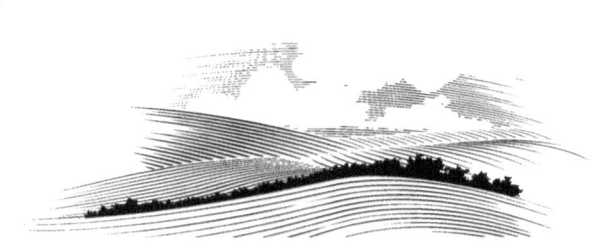

Compulsory Reservations

Monday, July 28th

I woke up fairly early and spent the morning hanging with Zach and Tanja while doing a load of laundry. I did my best to take in my surroundings one last time to remember what it was like to be in a German home. I knew Zach and I would have a blast in the future recounting our adventures during this time.

Since the train station was just a couple minutes away and within walking distance, I didn't stress too much about having all my things together. I packed casually. However, at one point I happened to glance at my watch to realize…it was 14:56 (2:56pm)! I literally had 4 minutes to get there! I jumped up, grabbed my bags, and went to slip my shoes on…..but they were missing! Zach and I scrambled to find them before he eventually called Tanja who had gone to the grocery store. She fortunately answered quickly and said she had moved them while cleaning and had forgotten to put them back. She told us where they were and I quickly went and slid them on before Zack and I dashed out the door.

For some reason, I had thought there was only 1 train at the station. This was probably because the few times I had been, there had only been one. Naturally because I was in a hurry this time, there were a few. I wasn't sure which was which. Zach looked with me at the train menu.

"Um….ah! There it is! Platform 6, I'm pretty sure.! It's right there!" He pointed and moved in that direction. I followed. When we got over to it, I turned and gave him a bro-hug and thanked him again for hosting me. After a short goodbye, I hopped onto the train, literally seconds before it started pulling away from the station.

"Phew!" I thought. "That was a close one." This was the only train headed for Brussels this day, so I was thankful I had made it. Looking around, I found a seat and sat down. Yet after a few minutes, I started to get a concerning feeling in my stomach. "What if this wasn't the right train?" I thought. We had been in such a rush, it was technically possible. I didn't want to think about it. I tried to assure myself that it had to be right because Zach had found it. Still, he said he was 'pretty sure.' This was enough to compel me simply to have this verified for my peace of mind. "There's a train staff person right there," I thought. "I'll just ask to be sure."

"Hallo." I said to the man. "Sprichst du Englisch?" I asked as had become custom.

"Hello, and yes I do. Is there a problem?" He replied.

"Well, I just want to make sure I'm on the right train. I'm trying to get to Brussels." I explained.

"Brussels? Oh no, you're headed in the wrong direction. This train is headed to Frankfurt." He said. My eyes got wide. I took a deep breath. My mind immediately began to race in search of possible solutions. Various options flew through my mind based on what I knew, but none of them provided a desirable outcome. I was at a loss.

"What can I do?" I finally asked. The train man pulled a phone from his jacket pocket and created a route for me to follow moving forward. I took a photo of this route with my tablet (a picture of a picture basically). I thanked the man for his help and returned to my seat. After reviewing what the man had given me, I realized that I went from a 2 hour trip with zero changes to a 6 hour trip with 2 changes. I would thus first have to arrive in Frankfurt (50 minutes) before boarding another train and going back the opposite direction and changing trains 2 times before getting to Brussels.

Despite all this, having every reason to be frustrated or angry, I laughed instead. Getting angry or frustrated wasn't going to solve anything. Besides, it was my own fault for not being ready. The positive was that I had a plan to get where I originally wanted to go , I was safe, and I was comfortable. However, Zach would absolutely have to be given a hard time for putting me on the wrong train next time I saw or spoke to him! So, I laughed and used my excess time to do some catching up in my journal.

My journey went quite smoothly until I got on my 3rd and final train. This train was rather nice compared to most I had ridden before. It had blue, fuzzy seats that were soft to the touch and very comfortable to sit in, and red carpet for an isle. I really didn't think anything of it until the French-speaking attendant came through to collect tickets.

When I showed the attendant my EU Rail Pass, he said "no" and something else in French.

"Pardon," I replied politely. "Sorry. Parlez vous Anglais?"

The man could see the confusion on my face. He then informed me in English that my pass would not work fully for this train. As he explained, this was a privately-owned French train service as opposed to the others I had ridden before which were public. The ticket itself would work, but I still owed a €30 *"compulsory reservation"* charge which "guaranteed" me a seat.

"A reservation?" I asked, looking at him with high eyebrows. I slowly looked around at *all the empty seats* around me then back at him.

"Yes, I know..." He confessed. "But it's the rule. There's nothing I can do. Unfortunately, you'll have to pay it or you will be required to get off at the next stop." I thought for a moment to consider my options. "If it makes you feel any better," he said, "without a Rail Pass, you would be required to purchase a €60 ticket PLUS pay the €30 'reservation' charge."

"It *would* be a French train doing this." I thought to myself annoyed. The train guy was nice though, and leveled with me. He was just doing his job and I didn't hold it against him. "Not really,..but whatever," I said reluctantly handing over €30 from my wallet. I was glad I just happened to have some cash on me to pay for it otherwise I'd be in a real pickle.

I could have gotten off at the next stop and attempted to find an alternative route, but an alternate route this day was not guaranteed. If I did get an alternate train, it might be a slow train which would put me in Brussels a lot later...and I didn't want a re-do of the night I almost slept outside in Munich.

The train man apologized for the confusion and frustration. I accepted his apology and assured him that I didn't blame him personally. I felt the train company was being ridiculous. I could also blame Zach in jest for this too. In reality however, I knew it was really all my own fault. Had I been ready to leave Zach & Tanja's, I probably would have gotten on the correct train the first time and avoided all this.

I finally arrived in Brussels before the sun set. I hopped off the train and immediately began searching for the tram I was supposed to take based on the hostel's instructions. A friendly security guard pointed me in the direction I needed to go to find the trams. Once I found the trams, I became a little confused about which one I needed to take. I first asked an older woman who right next to me. She was very sweet but didn't speak any English. She apologized several times.

"You need some help?" The voice of a man with a French accent came from behind me. He had apparently overheard me speaking with the older woman.

"Yes, please! Thank you!" I replied gratefully. I explained where I was trying to go. He told me which stop I needed to get off at and what tram I needed to board next before getting to my stop near my hostel. "Thank you so much!" I said. "I really appreciate it."

"No problem!" He replied, before jumping aboard his own tram.

I hopped on my tram shortly after this as the man had instructed. However, having been given wrong instructions in the past (most certainly unintentional), I decided to verify.

There was a man standing near the stop who looked like a nice person. I went over to ask him for help. However, just like the woman earlier, he only knew French and zero English. Yet even with this language barrier he was more than happy to help me the best he could! Through a couple basic English words, fingers for numbers, and a lot of charades, he was able to communicate to me where I needed to go. After this I thanked him and started to move on, but he wasn't finished. Perhaps he noticed the still uncertain look in my eyes.

When the correct tram arrived, he hopped aboard and motioned to me to follow. The man spoke to the tram driver who evidently knew more English than my guide. The tram driver explained that the man's own stop was the net one, but he insisted on riding with me to be sure I got off at my correct stop. This would mean he would have to ride around the entire city before getting off at his stop. Wow, what a kind person – or so I hoped. I have to admit that while I hope all people are genuine, there are bad people in the world so I maintained my wits.

It wasn't more than a couple stops later that I looked at him for confirmation. He motioned to me that this was my stop. I looked at the instructions provided by my hostel to verify the name of the street and compared it to the street name that flashed inside the tram. This was indeed my stop. The man then stepped off the tram with me, then made "walking fingers" and pointed to direct me to where I would find my hostel. Again, I looked at my instructions and they matched with his "walking fingers" exactly. I confirmed with a head nod and a grateful smile that I understood. He then shook my hand as I thanked him for his kindness (having the driver translate a thanksgiving for me) before re-boarding the tram. The doors of the tram shut and hauled away with one last goodbye wave from the stranger.

God is so good. My impression of this city after only arriving less than a half hour prior to this was already an incredibly positive one.

I very quickly found my hostel and was impressed by how nice it was. It felt very much like a regular hotel but wasn't. In the lobby were many people of all different ages. Most of them had backpacking backpacks like mine. There were individuals, groups, and even whole families checking in. The lobby itself was very large with several lounging chairs, table chairs, and tables spread across the area. To my left from the lobby desk was an entrance to a fully stocked bar where one could purchase beverages along with a variety of foods. This bar area also featured tables, chairs, and a few pool tables and dart boards. To the right was a hallway where guests could find their rooms. I looked forward to meeting many of them, but after being on a train for nearly 6 hours, all I wanted to do was drop my things off at my room, grab a nice cold beer at the bar, and unwind. That was the priority. If I met some cool people in the process, all the better. I therefore wasted no time after getting checked in and was soon ordering a light logger at the bar.

I coincidently ended up meeting several really cool and interesting people over the course of the evening. I first met a Dutch guy from Holland whose name I can't recall but we'll call him Todd. Along with Todd, I also met a Swiss guy named Tyler. The two of us got to know each other for a while over a couple drinks until I heard the distinctive sound of an American accent coming from somewhere behind us. I felt inclined to politely exit my conversation with Todd and Tyler to investigate the source of the accent(s).

It took me less than 15 seconds to identify two Americans casually playing pool. I immediately went over and said hello! There were two of them - Ryan and Mazzy. The couple were school friends from Philadelphia, but were not dating. As we were getting to know one another, a Turkish guy came up and joined us as well. His name was Fife. The four of us played several rounds of pool together and had an absolute blast until eventually parting ways for bed.

I couldn't believe I had spend so little time in this city and already loved it! I had such a wonderful experience in simply finding my hostel and now despite having only been checked in at the hostel for a few hours, had already made several new friends! The overall mood of the city even felt excited and happy to be alive, and I loved how diverse of a population there was between the locals and the variety of different people/countries/cultures at the hostel. It made things very interesting and refreshing.

"If this is a foreshadowing of what my experience here will be like," I thought as I closed my eyes to go to sleep, "Brussels will likely end up being one of my favorite places in all of Europe."

Part IX: Belgium

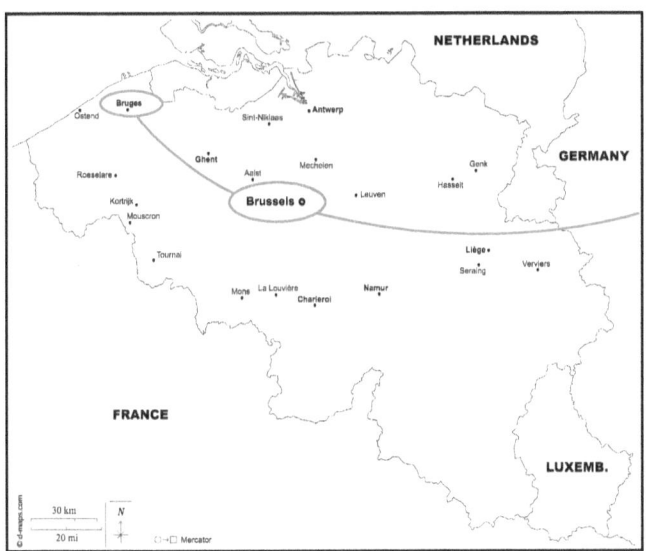

Map of Belgium: https://d-maps.com/carte.php?num_car=5647&lang=en
- Lines, circles, and words with asterisks are author's annotations and not on original map

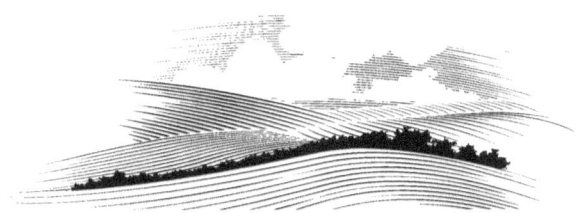

Patron Saints Of Beer?

Tuesday, July 29th

Breakfast at this hostel turned out to be lacking compared to others. For €7.99 the options consisted of yogart, sandwich quarters, cereal (aka dry oatmeal with milk), toast with jam, assorted fruit, and coffee - that's it. For the same price or better, I could have eaten the buffet at Denny's. Needless to say, I decided then that I would find breakfast elsewhere from then on. Also, who eats ham & cheese sandwiches for breakfast anyway???

After breakfast and coffee, I bought a map at the front desk and was out the door by 10am. I quickly found the road leading into town which was called Chausse de Gan.

As I followed de Gan to the Southeast, my eyes spotted a restaurant on the corner of Chausse & Rue Ransfort not far from the bridge over the canal. Above the door were photos of food items that wrapped around the building like a bandanna. These photos featured burgers, wraps, kebabs, fries, and more.

"Wow!" I thought. "If the inside lives up to the photos on the outside, this might be the perfect place to eat having so many options!" With this thought, I went over and peaked my head inside.

The small restaurant immediately reminded me of a little Chinese take-out place. The ordering counter stood at the back wall with a few individuals behind it preparing food. Large pieces of meat were spinning on a spit, cooking slowly and giving off a flavorful aroma. Considering it was still early, none of the customers inside seemed interested in the meat. Instead, they were concerned with the contents beneath the clear counter between them and the workers. Under the clear counter were all sorts of breakfast items including donuts, danishes, small waffles, and other breakfast sweets. Having just eaten, I was not hungry but made a mental note of this place for the future. Looking up at the sign, I saw the restaurant was called *Regalo: Petite Restaurant.*

I continued down Chausse de Gan which took me across the canal before turning into Rue Antoine Dansaert. Directly ahead in the distance was an impressive, white building. I had no idea what this building was, but it seemed like a good first stop in my exploration of the city. Along the way, I passed many nice-looking shops, gift shops, and cafés, though most had not yet opened. The most intriguing of shops were the chocolate shops. Belgian chocolate was supposed to be excellent, so I looked forward to stopping in at one in the near future when they opened.

It wasn't too long before I drew close to the white building mentioned earlier. This Greco-Christian designed structure featured tall white columns and rooftop sculptures along the top and stood up above the other surrounding buildings creating its own square. The road meanwhile was required to fork and lead around the building. Upon closer observation, I discovered that this building, despite looking almost chuch-like, was the Belgian Stock Exchange Building - which was not open.

I followed the road around to the right and discovered a tiny little church that was diminutive in comparison to the stock exchange building. According to the sign, this was *Eglise Saint Nicholas* or The Church of St. Nicholas. The church was open to the public so I went inside. There I discovered large paintings illuminated by natural light flooding in from the surrounding windows as the walls reached up to the high ceilings. The furnishings were old, stained wood with Christian symbols and depictions carved into them. Despite being so small, the church's inner beauty did not fall short in comparison to the outer beauty of the building under whose shadow it stood.

A little ways beyond the church, I found a narrow passage (only a few people wide) and followed it. Through a narrow ally with 5-story buildings towering on either side, I made my way curiously. When I emerged, I found myself in an enormous square. The ground was a sea of gray stone that broke before a raised pathway on which stood impressively massive buildings. It's name was The Royal Grand Palace of Brussels. At every turn I was surrounded by Victorian architecture. Spires, wall-carvings, balconies, and windows continuously drew my eyes. It reminded me of the courtyard of The Louvre Museum, but on a much smaller scale. The Royal Palace of Brussels was surely smaller in comparison to that of the Louvre, yet I felt no less insignificant to the towering buildings around me.

On the bottom levels were restaurants, small museums, and occasional street musicians. The area was bustling with life and energy. My only disappointment came with that of the palace itself. My heart was broken when I learned that the palace would be *closed for the foreseeable future* for reasons unclear to me. Still, I stood in admiration of the area wondering if there might be a next time where I might have the chance to visit the palace.

As I wandered around for closer inspections, something caught my eye. At the bottom of one of the buildings was a sign that read, *The Belgian Beer Museum.* I was instantly intrigued. Belgium had been brewing beer since the 1100's or earlier.

The opportunity to learn about this history in the capitol of Belgium was all too inviting. I therefore made my way in without hesitation.

Upon entering, I noticed a variety of eye-catching features. A large display cabinet, for instance, displayed many stein-like jugs that bored painted labels such as "BEER," "LITRE," and "DOUBLE LITRE." Also displayed were old wooden carvings of what appeared to be Popes. One was labled "St. Arnauld." Near the described display case was an area with many wooden barrels - presumably to represent old beer brewing barrels. Next to this was a poster titled "A Brewery of the XVIIIth Century," with 10 illustrations under it depicting brewing-related images. It was fascinating and grew my excitement for the tour. My only concern was how much it would cost. I was willing to pay up to maybe €15, but if it were much more than that, I would have sadly turn it down.

I approached the attendant behind a counter and requested a tour.

"Just one?" The attendant asked cheerfully?

"Yes sir." I replied.

"Alright. That'll be €5." He said.

"That's it!?" I exclaimed in surprise and joy.

"That's it! That'll cover the tour, a book if you'd like, and a complimentary pint of your choice while you wait [he motioned to a few taps behind him]."

I couldn't believe it. This had to be the greatest value of all time and certainly the best I had gotten anywhere else. I happily handed the attendant the cash and inquired about beer choice. I had never heard of or tried those that he had, but after a short chat about my tastes, he recommended a Fier Op Ons Bier. He then handed me a copy of the promised book before pouring me a pint in a uniquely shaped glass.

"Enjoy!" He said, handing me the glass. "The tour will begin in about 20 minutes."

I thanked him and found a seat nearby next to a side table. For the next 20 minutes, I sipped my beverage while flipping through the book he had given me.

I regret failing to describe in my journal what my beer tasted like, but I recall it being very tasty.

At one point while sipping my beer and reading my book, I realized I could no longer be in the dark about the displays mentioned earlier.

"Excuse me, sir. What are those carvings? Popes?" I asked. The attendant was still minding the counter to help other guests who had appeared.

"No," he laughed. "Those are patron saints of beer." I gave him a puzzled look. I had never heard of such a thing. "There you have Augustine, Arnauld, Jan Primus, Nicholas, and of course King Wenceslas." He concluded.

"That's very interesting. I didn't know there were such things as 'patron saints of beer.'" I explained.

"Yeah,…us Catholics, huh?! We even need a saint for drinking!" The attendant concluded with a big laugh before returning to his duties. I laughed along with him before returning to my book. I felt better knowing what the carvings were.

Just about the time I had finished my beer and returned it to the counter, there was a call for the next tour. I was grateful that the tour was fully in English and very accommodating. It ended up being short, but very educational. They talked about the development of the brewing process, tools used over the centuries, and the culture that surrounds brewing beer in Belgium.

I left the brewing museum feeling very satisfied and looked forward to my next discovery - which came rather quickly. I next stumbled onto a museum detailing the history of the city. This museum featured huge paintings, ancient and medieval sculptures of all sizes, artistic vases and cups, medieval home decor and royal kitchenware, a miniature model of the medieval city and more. There was one display that was both super random yet very interesting. This display featured small, metal statues of babies adorned with material clothing styled to different eras from all over the world. One that really stood out was apparently supposed to be Elvis Presley. "Elvis" baby was clothed in an all-white, studded outfit such as in his later years of fame. I never found out what the purpose of it all was, but it was certainly very interesting.

With plenty of time remaining in the day, I chose to venture eastward to see what I could find. It wasn't long before I came to a Cathedral with towers reaching above the other buildings lining the streets. The sign indicated that this was St. Michael and St. Gudula's Cathedral. There didn't seem to be anything special about it after having seen SO many at this point. Yet, it was open for visitation so I wandered in. The inside was pretty typical although a little smaller than most - with the exception of its high ceiling. I had just decided to exit when my eyes caught something exceptional.

Silver pipes reflected in the light high above me on the wall fastened to wooden faces. Under the large faces projected a balcony where I saw someone moving around. It was a man who appeared to be taking a seat. I looked on curiously. A couple minutes later, music from the great pipe organ began to echo through the church. The beauty of this compelled me to be seated at a nearby pew and listen. The organist did not play full songs but rather pieces. It was as if he were practicing for an upcoming service, a special event perhaps, or possibly doing simple routine maintenance. There was no way to know. Whatever the case was, I was thankful I had chosen to walk in and receive the blessing of this music.

I stayed listening to the organist for several minutes before realizing how hungry I was. I suddenly felt like I would collapse if I didn't eat something very soon. The toast, fruit, and coffee I had eaten earlier was now gone. I therefore left the cathedral and wandered back in the direction of the hostel where I noticed what appeared to be a small burger place. There didn't seem to be many guests and I assumed it would be reasonably cheap so I hurried inside.

I was pleased to find no guests in line upon entering and quickly ordered a burger. After a short while, I was brought a metal plate with fries, a drink, and a burger as ordered. The burger they brought me however, reminded me of what one might see eaten by Scooby-Doo and Shaggy. I mean that this burger was at least 6 inches high! I was very tickled by this but then realized the height was mostly due to the amount of lettuce on the burger. Still, it was fun to bite into and it made me feel like a cartoon character. Also like Scooby and Shaggy, I basically inhaled it being so hungry. I sat in the restaurant for a little while to let my food digest before leaving and heading back to the hostel.

The sun really beat down my entire walk back. It was about a mile from the burger place to the hostel using the most direct route so by the time I made it to the hostel, I was soaked in sweat. I felt disgusting. The inside temperature of the hostel was cooler than the outside, but there didn't seem to be any A/C. This meant that if I were to get a shower too early, I would likely just get sweaty again. I would have to wait until the sun went down. In the mean time, I decided to go drop my things in my room, grab my guitar, get a cold beer from the bar, and find a shady spot to sit in the courtyard.

As I warmed up, I wished there was someone to play with. Having a second musician to play along with added to the enjoyment. Unfortunately, there didn't seem to be any other musicians around.

About the time I started picking around on a blues riff I often toyed with, Fife came walking in. He had just returned from exploring as well. He was tall with long, blond hair, and a wide smile. His body language and eye contact suggested he was digging the groove I was playing.

"Hey hey!" I said greeting him.

"Sounds good!" He said with an accent, stopping to listen. "Can I sit?"

"Of course!" I replied cheerfully.

"You like the blues?" He asked.

"Oh man, I LOVE the blues!" I replied. "I'm from Mississippi so it's kind of my roots, you know? Haha."

"That's awesome!" He said enthusiastically. "I like to play too…but I don't have mine. I miss it."

"You play?!" I answered. "Man, please, play mine a bit." I handed him my guitar.

"Oh wow! Thank you!" He said. I couldn't believe Fife just happened to also play the guitar. I wished there was another he could play so we could play together, but this was much better than nothing.

As he played, I was blown away by his skill. He was able to play a rhythm and then do a lead at the same time. This was a skill I had never mastered. He and I passed the guitar back and fourth a few times until a couple came outside after hearing us. We greeted them and learned that the guy was named Jake while his girlfriend was Emily (actually, I failed to record what her name was so I'm just calling her Emily). At one point, Emily mentioned her hobby of playing the ukulele. I asked her if she had it with her. She did, so the three of us played round and around until the temperature fell enough to ensure I wouldn't start sweating again after taking a shower. I thanked Emily for playing with us and took my temporary leave.

I later returned from my shower feeling very refreshed. I then grabbed another cold drink from the bar as other familiar faces from the night before started trickling in. Within an hour, most of my friends from the night prior were there. We all talked and shared our experiences from the day and had many laughs. After a while, people started talking about dinner. It was then that I realized I was starting to hunger myself.

"What are yall doing for dinner?" I asked Ryan and Mazzy.

"We saw a Chinese place across the way." Ryan explained. "You wanna come?" I appreciated the invite, but for some reason I wasn't really feeling Chinese.

"Na, I'll pass this time. Not really feeling Chinese. Thanks though!" I said.

"Ok!" Ryan said. "We'll catch up here later then, yeah?"

"Absolutely." I replied.

I asked a couple others what they were doing. None of it really appealed to me. Then I remembered Regalo. That was exactly what I wanted. With that, I left the hostel and was at Regalo within 5 minutes.

There was a short line when I entered the small restaurant. I was grateful for the line so I could have time to look over the menu without feeling awkward. In front of me in the line was a young kid, may 13 years old. He wore an old white shirt, dirty shorts, and worn tennis shoes. Out of nowhere the kid turns around and engages me in friendly conversation. His English wasn't great, but he was obviously doing his best and I commended him for it. He asked me where I was from. I told him Mississippi. He was very interested in this. He also asked what I was going here in Brussels.

"Well, this is actually my final stop. I've been backpacking Europe for the past two months and will be leaving soon." I explained.

"Do you miss home?" He asked. Admittedly, I did in some ways.

"Yeah, a little bit." I replied with a homely smile.

He and I chatted all the way up until it was his turn to order. I again reviewed the menu to be sure I knew what I wanted. After he finished ordering a kebab, the cook took my order.

My original intention was to get a burger, but after seeing and smelling the meat still cooking slowly on the spit, I decided to go with a kebab as well. The cooks both worked on our kebabs, asking if we want this on it and that, more sauce or less, etc. It was funny. The process of getting the kebab reminded me a lot of subway. The clear counter described earlier no longer displayed breakfast items. Instead, it now contained things such as lettuce, onion, sauces, and other toppings available to add to the kebab at no extra charge. Fries could also be added for an extra charge and you had the option of having them as a side or being added to your kebab (I got fries inside my kebab and extra sauce).

One thing I really liked was that here, they would gather your meat, onion, lettuce, sauce, and whatever else and mix it all together in a bowl before placing it in the wrap. This made the flavors come together perfectly. All the while that the cooks worked, they chatted in friendly fashion with the boy and I.

They boy's order was obviously completed first with mine not far behind. While the boy was at the register getting ready to pay, he said something to the cook in French. I didn't think anything of it. Then the cook asked if I intended to buy a drink.

"I do," I replied. "I'm just not sure what I want yet."At the moment, I was considering getting a water or something - just not a soda. I then moved along with the cook who had been preparing my food to the register to pay.

"Do you want a drink?"I was asked again. I paused to consider my options, then before I could say "water," something unexpected happened. The boy stuck out his hand, beaming the the most pleased smile I had ever seen. In his out-stretched hand...was a Coke.

"For you!" He said triumphantly.

It's hard to explain, but I could see by the look in his eyes and the expression on his face that this kid wasn't buying me a soda; a Coke-Cola soda that cost him over €2 of his own money. This sweet kid purchased, specifically, a Coke-Cola for me simply because I told him I missed home and he knew that a Coke was a semblance; a taste of home for me.

I was touched. I could tell he was expecting me to be surprised to have a Coke like I might get at home. In response, I acted surprised, thrilled, and humbly honored. The joy on his face was like a kid whose present is being opened at a friend's birthday party and the friend loves his gift.

"Whaaaat?! Oh man! You didn't have to do that!" I exclaimed. "Thank you SO much!" I accepted his gift and he smiled all the more, satisfied with himself for the act of generosity and kindness to a stranger. He then walked with me as I left and asked where I was staying. I told him it was the hostel down the road.

"I live near there! Can I walk with you?" He asked.

"Of course!" I replied. How could I turn him down? Such a sweet kid. We had a really nice chat down the road until he was forced to part ways. I thanked him again for the Coke and wished him the very best. I hope one day he comes across this book (probably as an adult now) and knows how much his gift meant to me.

I made it back to the hostel to find everyone I knew still gone for dinner. I therefore took a seat at a table by myself and enjoyed my delicious kebab and Coke. However, it wasn't long before familiar faces begin appearing. First Fife, followed by Ryan and Mazzy and others. Soon we were all engaged in conversation and enjoying one another's company.

"Hey!" Ryan said suddenly. "Let's get a group together and go out tonight!"

"Yeah, sure!' I replied. "I'm down!"

"Hey Fife!" I hollered. Fife was busy talking to someone across the room by a pool table. He turned with interest. "You wanna go out tonight?!"

"Yeah, that sounds fun! Where to?!" He called back.

"Downtown I guess?" I replied. I looked at Ryan for confirmation.

"Yeah!" Ryan called back so Fife could hear. "There's a few bars down there that are supposed to be cool! Let's get some people together and check it out!"

"Let's do it!" Fife cheered.

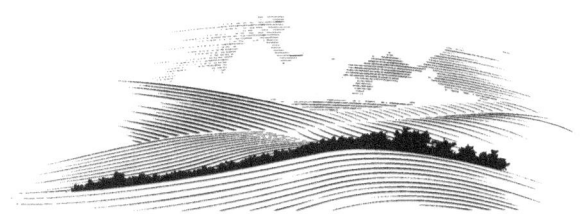

Beware The Delirium Woman In Red

Tuesday, July 29th Continued...

Most people didn't feel up to going out for different reasons. However, we did manage to round up enough for a small group. Among those interested were these two attractive British girls. Hannah, a red head, and Scarlet, a brunette. They had been planning on going out tonight and were already dressed for it. Both girls sported similar low-cut, loose-fitting tops that barely grazed their belly-buttons. Hannah also sported slim-fit designer jeans with her long hair in a half-bun while Scarlet rocked a mini-skirt with a cute shoulder-length bob. Not only were they dressed for the party, but had also already gotten started. I wondered how this night would go.

Hannah kept giving me a hard time, urging me to "catch up," in my drinking. Too bad for her, I didn't intend to "go hard," but did have a couple pre-game drinks while I enjoyed getting to know them both before heading out. By the time I finished, someone had initiated the move to head out so we all went, making our way down Chaussee De Gan. A few of us (myself included) brought a "road beer" as one might say in the States.

As we passed by Regalo, I dropped my now empty road beer bottle into a trash can that sat on the walking path. Hannah, who had also brought a road beer ended up dropping hers on the concrete accidentally. Lest a car or bike drive by and catch a flat, I carefully grabbed the broken glass and transferred it to another nearby can.

The first bar we came to both surprised and excited me beyond belief. I was a little beside myself. To explain, I once visited a restaurant in Atlanta called Taco

Mac which has an insane number of beers on tap. While there, I tried several kinds from all over the world. The one that really blew me away was a Belgian brew called Delirium Nocturnum. This beer came cold and tasted like blueberries. As it warmed to room temperature, the flavor literally changed. This beer was not only delicious, but mind-blowing as well. Thus, it became my favorite of all time. As it turned out, this bar the group and I had come upon in Belgium was called The Delirium Bar and Brewery!

We all walked into a large room filled with tables and chairs. The house lights were out while dim strobe lights illuminated the area enough to see. Music played in the background that was loud enough to dance to, but soft enough to carry on a conversation at a table without having to yell or scream. I truly wish bars in the States were more like this.

I immediately made my way to the bar, inviting the two British girls to join.

"First round's on me, ladies!" I said with a wink and smile. "Pick your poison."

"Ohh! I'll have a Vodka and Coke!" Exclaimed Hannah.

"I'll have the same! Thanks!" Scarlet replied. I then turned my attention to the bar tender.

"Hi! Parlez vous Anglais?" I asked.

"Yeah," he answered, "What do you like?"

"Excellent! I need two Vodka and Cokes for the ladies behind me [gesturing] and I have a quick question." I said.

"Sure, what's that?" He asked.

"So,…my favorite beer of all time is Delirium Nocturnum, and I see that this is called the Delirium bar, so…." I began.

"Yes!" The bar tender cut me off with a laugh. "This is the bar for the brewery which is in the basement." My face lit up even more. Yet, I was still not ready to release my excitement lest there be some misunderstanding.

"And so that means that the Nocturnum you have here…. is fresh from the barrel?" I asked hoping there wouldn't be a technicality involved.

"Yes, that's right!" The bar man replied chuckling.

"AWESOME!!!" I exclaimed with overflowing joy. "In that case, my good sir, I will have one!"

"Coming right up!" He said, clearly entertained by my enthusiasm.

I admit that I sometimes go overboard with my emotions and expressions with people. My intention is for my joy of simple pleasures will rub off onto others so that they feel good along with me. This was certainly one of those occasions in action.

The two Vodka and Cokes were in my hand within seconds. I passed them both back over to the girls. I then promptly received my tasty beverage. When I looked at the check to pay, I realized the Vodka and Cokes were €6.50 each! I was not expecting them to be quite so expensive! Yet, it was alright. I had a Nocturnum beer straight from the brewery in my hand. Nothing was going to extinguish my pleasure in that. Besides I had a feeling that this night was going to be an absolute blast, and that requires cash - especially if one plans to buy drinks for others. To my good fortune, however, when I went to pay for them, I realized there was no charge for the beer. It was of course tempting to say nothing, but I'm an honest guy so I had to.

"Hey sir!" I yelled to the bar man who was fixing another drink near the other end of the bar. "You forgot to charge me for the beer!"

"Oh, no problem!" He called back. "That one's on me! Welcome to Brussels!"

"Wow." I thought to myself. "The friendly kindness of these Belgian strangers just doesn't seem to end! I swear, it's like they are Irish that happen to speak French!"

I thanked him kindly before turning back to catch up with the guys. After regrouping, they and I talked and cut up as guys do. Then suddenly the British girls came walking by.

"Hey, what's up?!" I asked. "Having fun?!" I immediately realized something was not right. Hannah didn't look like she did earlier. She was neither enthusiastic or excited like she had been. She was also walking very close by Scarlet. My enthusiasm switched to concern.

"Is she alright?" I asked sincerely.

"No…Hannah's feeling sick," Scarlet replied sorely. "I'm going to have to take her back. I'm sorry. Thank you for the drinks though!"

"Yeah, no problem! I'm sorry she's feeling bad." I said. "Would you like me to walk back with you or anything?"

"Oh no, it's fine…I promise." Scarlet assured me. "We'll be alright. We've been here many times. I've also got pepper spray in my purse if anyone messes with us. But thanks again." And with that, they sat their drinks down on a table nearby and left.

I felt better knowing she had something to defend herself with should anyone bother them. Brussels did seem like a pretty safe place, but still. I said a silent prayer for their safety.

By this point I had finished my drink and was ready for another. As I approached the bar, I noticed a stunningly attractive girl sitting alone at the bar. She had long, dark hair, lightly tanned skin, perfect curvature, and dawning a slim red outfit. I made it to the bar and slid in near her - somewhat coincidently. The bar tender was busy with several orders, so since I was there, I turned to the woman.

She and I started a really nice conversation. I'm not sure where she was from, but her accent was very sexy. Spanish perhaps? Despite her broken English, she seemed really cool and pleasant to speak with. I was truly shocked when she told me she was out alone and did not have a boyfriend. She further seemed to flirt with me quite a bit as we chatted. After a little while, the bar tender came by and asked if I needed another Nocturnum. I told him I did and asked the woman if she'd like a drink too. She happily obliged, but to my surprise, chose to order a very fancy drink which ended up being €13! I had expected her to order a simple mixed drink or beer or something. I instantly felt taken advantage of and wanted to take my leave. Instead, I decided to stick around to observe her next move for my entertainment. This decision proved to be a good move.

As soon as the free drink was in her hand, she shifted her attention away from me and our conversation - though still turning back to me often enough to keep me "on the line," you might say. However, I was clearly not a priority anymore. I noticed also that she suddenly became chatty with another guy who came up behind her with whom she spoke a different language. I remained there observing. This guy left, so she started chatting with another guy further down the bar, being noticeably flirty.

The expensive drink she ordered was small, so it wasn't long before it was gone. This was the instant I had been waiting for. What would she do next?

She suddenly engaged me in conversation again for a minute before sweetly and flirtingly asking for another drink.

"Interesting." I thought. "I wonder how she'll react if I don't. If she is interested at all, it shouldn't matter, but if her intention is just to play men for drinks, she'll probably let the conversation die before moving to the next guy." I therefore chose to deny her another drink. I did so in a way that was clear yet polite and playful.

"You won't get me another drink?" She said in a surprised and entitled sort of tone like a rich girl being denied extra mocha in her Starbucks Frappe.

"No." I said in a way that invited her to a verbal, playful jouste. "Still want to talk?"

"Why will you not get me another drink?" She asked, ignoring my question.

"I don't want to." I said plainly. I tried to be frank with her, but still playful. I wanted her to see that I wasn't a pushover like other guys she probably talked to. Perhaps if I showed that I had self-respect and confidence, she might take a genuine interest. Unfortunately, it didn't play out like that. As soon as she realized she would not be getting another free drink from me despite her sexy flirts, she dropped her attention from me and focused entirely on two other guys nearby and started her game with them. Judging by their accents, I realized they were Australian. With her back now turned toward me, I tried to say something to her just to see how she'd respond. As I expected, she completely ignored me.

I couldn't help but laugh out loud. I found the whole thing to be hilarious! It was just like something you'd see in a movie. Seeing that she was now done playing with me, I stood up from the bar stool and moved away. However, to spare the poor guy now talking to her, I wanted to give him a heads up. I walked passed the one who was further away and tapped him on the shoulder. He was naturally focused on the beautiful woman as his friend talked to her, so he was slightly reluctant to turn to me, but did.

"Hey man," I said quietly. "I just wanted to let you guys know. Don't bother wasting your time with her. She's just trying to use you for free drinks."

"Huh?" The guy asked. "Her?"

"Yeah." I answered. "She got me to buy her a drink - and she ordered a really expensive one. After that, she basically dropped me until she needed another."

"Oh wow, thanks for that, mate!" He said to me. He then pulled his friend. "Ey, this American bloke here just told me that girl's just after free drinks!"

"For real?!" His friend asked.

"Yeh!" He replied. "She did it to him a few minutes ago, he says."

"Wow, that blows!" He said disappointingly. "She's bloody sexy!"

"Yeah, I know, right?" I said. "But yeah, I offered to buy her a drink, and she ordered one that was €13! Then she asked for another soon after. When I didn't go for it, she turned away from me and that's when she started talking to the both of you. I heard your accents and was like, 'man I gotta let these Aussies know!'"

"Well thanks for looking out, mate!" The first one said. The three of us took one last look at her before laughing as we walked by. I ended up hanging out and talking with them for a while to be sure they didn't think I was just trying to trick them away from her or something. They turned out to be really cool guys.

After hanging with the Aussies for a while, I excused myself to go find Ryan and Fife again. I quickly discovered Ryan who was sitting at a table with a beer in front of him. He didn't seem to be enjoying the night.

"Hey man! What's up? You look glum!" I said.

"Man, I'm just not feeling it." He confessed.

His demeanor and tone was one I knew all too well myself. I'd been there before. On more than one occasion in my life, I've been out, perhaps with friends, where I should be having a blast. Yet for one reason or another, my buzz dies and I get the blues. However, these blues can be overcome with the aid of a buddy if the cause of the blues in uncovered. I made it my mission to cure Ryan's blues.

After talking to him, I uncovered that he had really wanted to meet some girls this night, but wasn't very confident. This news honestly shocked me. Ryan was a very good-looking guy! He somewhat resembled a younger Dave Franco. I couldn't see any reason why girls wouldn't be super into talking to him. He confessed that one of his biggest struggles was walking up and trying to talk to a girl who was surrounded by a group of girls, which was *totally* understandable. Approaching a group of girls can be extremely intimidating. However, using wisdom I had acquired from Josh along with my own applied experience, I tried to give him an encouraging pep talk.

"Dude, you're the MAN!" I assured him. "You are freaking AWESOME! And dude, I mean, I'm not gay, but you're a really good-looking dude." He laughed. "You've got to own that because if she isn't interested in talking to you, she's clearly an idiot and it's 100% her loss. If she can't see how lucky she is that you would pay her the compliment of going out of your way to approach and speak to her, forget her. You're not missing anything."

"Now, as far as groups go," I continued, "I know how intimidating it can be. However, a group is actually what you want."

"What?" He replied laughing, thinking I must be crazy. "How is that?"

"Well," I began..

I basically explained that if he could get up the courage to approach a small group - say 3-5, then there is that much more potential to get a nice conversation going. You can ask about a graphic t-shirt, compliment jewelry, make a connection based on birth-place, anything to get a conversation started. Then, you slowly engage the girl you're really interested in until the two of you are locked into a 1-on-1 conversation all while her friends have approved of you because you also had a nice conversation with them where they decided you seemed cool.

Ryan saw the logic in what I shared with him and was forced to agree, but wasn't sure where to start.

"So what now?" Ryan asked.

"Now, I grab Fife as a second wingman. THEN…we find you a girl!"

I jumped up and quickly found Fife who was buying a drink at the bar. I went and explained the situation with Ryan and asked if he would be willing to be a wing-man with me. He agreed. Fife then followed me back to the table where Ryan was sitting.

"Ok boys, this is what we'll do." I said. "Ryan, you look around and pick out a pretty girl you'd like to talk to. It's best if it is a group of 3 to 5 like we talked about earlier." Ryan looked around for a minute.

"Her." He said, motioning with his head toward a group of four girls. "The brunette."

"Ok. So next we'll all approach them. I can start us off and break the ice. Fife, it will be your job to get a conversation going and pump Ryan's tires - that means talk him up to show how great he is but without being overly obvious about it. Ryan, you will do as we talked about. When she starts focusing her attention on you, " I looked at Fife. "Fife, you and I will draw her friends into separate conversations." I looked back a Ryan. "That's when it's up to you. Just talk to her and remember that you're awesome and good-looking. She'll love you. If not, we'll abort and it will be her loss." I looked at the both of them. "We good?" They confirmed, and the game began.

After approaching his initial choice, we quickly realized that we were nothing like what they were looking for. Despite the fact that I heard them speaking English previously, they pretended they didn't speak the language when we tried to engage them. I thought this was pretty rude, but also telling of the type of people they probably were.

We tactfully retreated and regrouped. I told Ryan to look around again. His eyes quickly fell on another pretty girl in a group of 3. Unfortunately, they were already being chatted up by a couple Aussie guys - the same ones I had warned about the woman in red. However, all is fair in love and war. If that was the one Ryan wanted, we would swoop in. For whatever reason, Americans seem to have a leg up over most other guys while Aussies are a close second. Thus we had the upper hand. Fortunately, Ryan ultimately chose against swooping in and stealing these girls' attention away from the other guys. I was thankful for this and commended him.

Finally, Ryan found the perfect group of 5. They looked friendly and were not being chatted up by any other guys. Without further hesitation, the three of us approached them and were casually able to execute the plan perfectly. Fife and I carefully pulled the friends into a different conversation and slowly created a little bit of physical distance away from Ryan and the girl he liked. The distance was near enough to her friends that they could easily look back to see that she was safe, but far enough away for them to have a private conversation.

After a little while of distracting the girl's friends, Fife and I saw that Ryan was successfully having a great time talking to the girl he liked and her friends weren't attempting to "rescue" her as sometimes happens. Therefore, Fife and I concluded our pleasant conversation with the friends and moved on. We had accomplished our mission. What happened next was up to Ryan.

After this, I decided to try my hand just for fun. I felt like I started with poor luck considering that the two British girls left early, then getting initially duped by the woman in red. I wondered if my luck would change. However, I soon realized that all the girls seemed to be French - including Ryan's girl and her friends. I felt like this would lower my odds further, but it would be fun regardless. I went around attempting to talk to some girls here and there, but none of them were impressed with me. To be honest though, they really weren't very interesting themselves. Eventually, I accepted my poor luck and joined Fife at the bar for another round and good conversation.

Fife and I remained at the bar until we noticed a significant change in the guy-girl ratio and took it as a sign that we should take our leave. Before leaving, however, we needed to find Ryan. We hadn't seen him since we left him with the girl. We of course didn't want to tear him away, but didn't want to leave him without the option of coming back with us if that was his plan. It wasn't surprising therefore when we found him not desiring to leave with us. Instead, he chose to stay behind with the girl and planned to find his way back later. I made sure he knew *how* to get back before wishing him a good night.

The streets as Fife and I walked back were empty and quiet. The only exception was occasional voices from inside bars as we walked along. I checked my watch as we entered the hostel gates to realize it was 3 o'clock in the morning! I bid Fife a good night, said a short prayer for Ryan's safety, and was soon in my bed ready for sleep.

It had been a long and exciting day full of wonderful people and exciting surprises. I couldn't wait to see what the following day would bring.

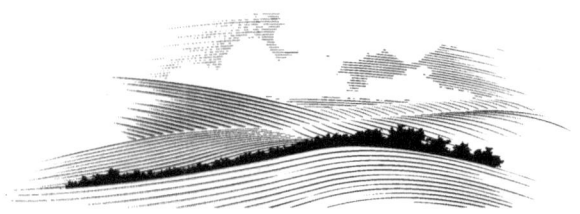

Occupational Adventuring

Wednesday, July 30th

Despite getting in at 3am, I slept in until only 11:30. I got up and went to the bar with my tablet which was a cafe during the day. There, I ordered a cup of coffee and took a seat on the sofa to start planning my day. Ryan appeared not long after I began. By the looks of him, he was hung over.

"Glad to see you alive!" I said with a smile. He shook his head with a smirk.

"Berr.." Was his reply.

"I take it things went well with you and that girl you were talking to?" I suggested.

"Yeah," Ryan confirmed with some difficulty. "Things went really well. I don't even remember how I made it back. I just know it was late....or early?" He blinked hard and rubbed his eyes. "Bruh,...I'm SO hung-over." He said, half chuckling at his misery. "Mazzy's already gone. My own flight doesn't leave until 6pm, but I've gotta be there by 3."

"Well," I said. "Get you some coffee and come with me to get a bite to eat — you don't have to eat. I'm going to have a real Belgian waffle to start my day. According to the map online, the train station is near there so you can hop a train to the air port afterwards."

I had eaten what was called "Belgian waffles" or "Belgian-style waffles" before, but was curious to see how the real thing compared. Would they be the same, similar, or very different?. I felt like I couldn't leave the country without finding out.

Ryan agreed to join me and ordered a coffee as I recommended to nurse his hangover. After he finished his coffee and had gathered his things, we set off for a casual adventure.

The map from the Internet guided us perfectly to the little cafe selling waffles. We found a small table arranged just outside the shop in front of a large window. Looking outward was a small area lined with shops and cafes. People were walking past while horse-drawn carriages came clopping by, all as a street performer played instrumentals of familiar tunes somewhere in the background. It was really a pleasant sight with an unmistakably positive energy. Soon, a waitress came out and I ordered a small Belgian waffle with chocolate syrup and whipped cream from the menu. I had never heard of ordering such things for a waffle and thus seemed different already.

Not long after I put in the order, my waffle came out. It was not at all what I had been expecting! The "small" waffle I ordered was still quite large - in thickness anyway. The thick, fluffy treat was also covered in powdered sugar. On the side was an upside down, chocolate-drizzled cone filled with whipped cream instead of ice cream. A small cup of chocolate syrup was provided on the side.

I poured the thick, chocolate syrup all over my waffle and mixed it around the whipped cream with my fork before taking a bite.

I would be impossible to describe how delicious it was,, but it was indeed delicious, not to mention very rich. I couldn't imagine this being a typical breakfast item as opposed to a desert. Further, this "small" waffle "breakfast" only cost €5. The more expensive version came with actual ice cream and other toppings. However, I was quite satisfied with my choice. No regrets.

Next, Ryan and I explored what I could only describe as a "shopping *hall.*" It was essentially an alleyway nearby with shops all the way down on the other side. I couldn't identify the name for it anywhere, but it featured very pretty architecture.

After walking through the shopping hall, it was time for Ryan and I to part ways. I walked him to the train station and wished him all the best. I also told him to remember that he is awesome, and urged him not to forget what we had talked about the previous night. Then with that, we shook hands and parted.

My first planned destination of the day was The European Union Building. It was only a short subway ride away according to my map. I supposed I should have looked earlier and accompanied Ryan into the train station to hop a subway ride before parting ways. If I went inside at this point and ran into him again, it would have been awkward. So, I wandered around the area for a little while, popping into a comic book shop featuring lots of *The Adventures of Tin Tin* for some reason, then went and hopped onto a subway train.

I got off the subway a short ride later only to realize I didn't know where to go from there. The directions I had weren't real clear on this so I simply picked a direction and started walking. I was relieved when ten minutes later, I saw Brussels' Arch of Triumph in the distance. I felt confident that I was at least headed in the right direction.

As I walked, I slowly begin to realize my need to stop and find a rest room. The only restaurants I could find along the way seemed super classy-looking with people in suits and suitcases dining for lunch. I, meanwhile, was dressed in a sweaty t-shirt, shorts, a hat, and a beard that had not been maintained for class. However, I knew I needed to stop. I therefore approached a place and went carefully inside on of the classy establishments.

The inside was as classy as I imagined it would be judging from the outside and the clientele. All the tables were covered and the waiting staff were all dressed in black and white outfits. The smell of rich wine filled the air. I felt I was in trouble.

"Um,..excuse me?" I asked somewhat timidly to a waitress coming around the corner.

"Yes? How may I help you?" She asked, then subtly reacted to my appearance. I was clearly not dressed appropriately do dine, but perhaps would be allowed allowed use their facilities if I were willing to pay. At this point, I was.

"Hi," I answered as kindly as I could. "Is there any way I might could use your rest room?" I asked. "I will pay if I need to." I hated to pay for the use of a rest room, but it was now situation critical.

The waitress appeared to be a little confused. She then stopped what appeared to be a manager based on his differentiating attire.

"This is it." I thought. "I'm going to be turned away."

The two whispered to one another for a short moment before turning back to me.

"You need to use the toilet?" The manager asked in a tone seeking clarification.

"Yes, if that's alright?" I replied sheepishly. The manager and waitress immediately smiled as if clarity had been restored.

"Oh! Yes, sure! It's right over there!" The waitress answered cheerfully. She pointed towards the back.

I was a little confused by what had happened, but was very grateful for this answer. The only explanation I can think of is that perhaps she somehow misunderstood what I was asking and the manager was able to re-interpret my request.

"Oh thank you SO much!" I replied relieved. "I REALLY appreciate it!" I then made my way to the back. When I returned to head out, I waved and thanked them both again. They returned the wave and smiled, wishing me a good day. Once again, I was moved by the kind friendliness of the Belgian people. I could have sworn it was like being in French-speaking Ireland!

At long last, I arrived at a park that stood before the Arch I had seen in the distance. To my surprise, both ended up being right next door to the EU Buildings! I was therefore able to appreciate the arch and see the EU Buildings all at once! The architecture of the buildings was extremely modern-looking which made them stand out against the surrounding area. I took a photo of the ones I could see most clearly before continuing on through the park toward the Arch.

The park was a bit unusual-looking but absolutely gorgeous. The area leading up to the Arch seemed to be the middle as there were walking paths that shot off in different directions. The center part I was standing before looked to be about the size and shape of a football field. Lush grass met my feet as a concrete walking path paremetered the outside to create a rectangular area. Great, bushy trees lined the sides, directing one's attention toward the Arch. Looking towards the Arch across the ground stood a wall of hedges. The hedge wall, as I discovered later, hid from view a parking lot and parked cars on the other side.

As I strode along the outer walking path towards the Arch, I noticed it extended outwards to form a large crescent such as the Royal Crescent in Bath. Between the arches were pairs of columns carved into the white concrete. Tall and proud it stood, with copper statues positioned at different points both on the ground and at the top of the structure. Largest of all was the depiction of what appeared to be four horses pulling an individual (or maybe 2) in a chariot. From what I had researched, all this somehow symbolized Belgium as being a peace-loving nation. If this is the case, the people (in my experience) are very much living up to that vision.

The information I had gathered on the Arch informed me that there were 3 museums within the Crescent. I searched for the museum entrance only to discovered that they were all closed. I remained in the park admiring the scene for a little longer before moving on. My next destination was Park Leopold.

I was able to find Park Leopold rather quickly and began my stroll through. The park featured tall trees, bright flowers, and a large pond with ducks cruising across the water. The path took me near tall buildings backing up to the park, many of which posed an interesting contrast with its very modern architecture stretching into the natural setting. The end of my exploration took me behind one or two of the EU buildings. As my stroll concluded at the end, I decided to head towards the nearest subway. In doing so, I passed by a small store where a man suddenly and briskly approached me.

"Please," he said desperately in broken English. "I am homeless and need a little food for my family. I have a job, but have not been able to move into a house yet and my job has not yet paid me." He stopped and pointed to a woman not far away who had a child in a stroller.

I don't often simply hand out money to people, especially considering my experience with the beggars in Rome. However, since the man was alone, asking specifically for food and not money outside a grocery store, and had a child in a stroller I paused. I couldn't know if there was a lie in this man's words, but decided to believe him. Therefore, I agreed and followed the man into the store.

As the man pulled food into the cart, I became a little frustrated. What started out as "a little bit of food" and some diapers for the kid became a cart-load of items. Part of me wanted to abandon my decision as I didn't fancy being taken advantage of. Yet at the same time, the better part of me resolved to stay the course. He was still primarily getting food and baby supplies and not reaching for alcohol.

Soon we had finished obtaining the "few" items and were ready to check out. The cashier rang me up for a ticket that was just under €50. The man looked and seemed to half expect me to back out, but I didn't. I paid it as he thanked me profusely. I then helped him carry the groceries out to his wife who also thanked me profusely. There was still no way for me to know for certain if everything was legit or if this was some kind of operation. However, I decided to let it be an act of good faith for the sake of Christ and hoped God wouldn't let the money I spent hurt me later. It wasn't long after this that I came upon a nearby subway and made it back near the hostel.

As I came to where Regalo's was, I decided to stop and grab dinner before making it back to the hostel.

Sitting in the hostel courtyard eating, I calculated how long I had been walking around. To my amazement, it had be seven straight hours! I started to think about this and reflect on my daily life as a traveler. I had never considered it before, but I realized then that I spend as much time exploring as a traveler as I would working a day job. It seemed, therefore, that my job while abroad has been to explore! Considering how much I had to pay to get here, I had to get my money's worth. It was a funny thought. I only wished I could actually get paid to do it. That would be awesome.

As I finished eating, I noticed a few familiar faces and thought I might grab my guitar for a little bit. However, by the time I had gone in, set my things down, grabbed my guitar, and made it back outside, all the familiar faces had gone. I was now alone. Despite being rather tired, I decided to go ahead and play for a while.

At one point while I was playing, a nice girl noticed me and came over. I had not seen her before. She complimented my playing and appreciated it more by going and buying me a beer on her own accord. It was then that I realized how sad I might have appeared being so tired. I wondered if she had misinterpreted my exhaustion for depression and wanted to cheer me up with the compliment and beer. In any case, I thanked her for the beer, but retired once it was finished.

The plan was to get up early the next day and take an excursion to a small village known as Brugges which I had discovered during the process of planning my day earlier. It appeared to be a relatively short train ride away and had great reviews. I looked forward to yet another day of "occupational adventuring."

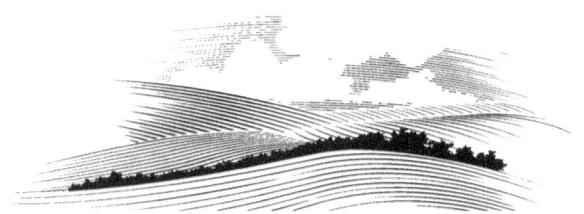

The Half-Man In Brugges

Thursday, July 31st

I woke up this morning at around 9:30 full of anticipation for my excursion. I quickly popped over to Regalo's for a light breakfast (doughnuts) before heading to the nearby subway station which took me to the train station. Without error (for once), I found the right train and was soon flying across the Belgian countryside passing small villages along the way.

When the train pulled into Brugges at around 11, I got out and exited the station. Before me was a parking lot surrounded by trees and no buildings anywhere that I could see. I wasn't sure what to do. The only thing I *could* see reaching over the tops of the surrounding trees was a spire in the distance next to some medieval-looking structure. My best guess was that the spire was attached to a cathedral. Considering this, I decided to head in that direction which would a least get my exploration started.

As I followed the spires, buildings eventually came into view. What I found turned out to be the coolest, most quaint little town I had ever seen! It reminded me a lot of MacClesfield with its narrow, gray-stone streets winding through lines of buildings as if the buildings had been placed before the road. A walking path followed the road like a river bank on either side as it wound around the buildings now clearly visible.

"I've only been here for 30 seconds," I thought to myself, "and I already think I'm in love!" The whole area seemed to have this modernized medieval charm to it that I couldn't help falling in love with.

I noticed while walking that there seemed to be three different buildings poking up above the majority of those lining the street - one of them was the spire I had noticed earlier. I couldn't be sure what the other two were, but they looked interesting. I chose to investigate each one starting with the nearest.

The first I came to ended up being a church. I had somewhat expected this. However, this church had more of a royal look to it than religious. Several towers stretched up to meet the sky with teal-colored, cone tops. The spire I had seen earlier was the same, only much taller. It shot above all the rest as if reaching for Heaven with a cross at the very top. Arches in the shape of spades, both short and tall, were carved into the face at various levels. Stained glass filled in the spades, absorbing the light from the sun. I desired to go inside, but entry was not available to the public this day. I was thereby forced to remain outside to gaze upon it as a horse-drawn carriage clopped past me on the stone street.

The next building turned out to be a museum. This too, to my dismay, was closed. As I walked around the building surveying its unique architectural design, I discovered a small courtyard. Many chairs were being placed in an amphitheater fashion. I asked one of the men setting up chairs what was going on. He then informed me that a music festival would be taking place at 8pm and encouraged me to attend!

I was delighted at the thought of attending. The area seemed to have great acoustics for music and would certainly be worth the time. However, the last train would be leaving at 10. Sure, this would give me two hours, but I was afraid I might get too involved in the festival and lose track of time. I also had a poor track record when it came to catching trains. I therefore resolved that if I had a moment before leaving, I might pop by on my way out.

Continuing my journey, I came across a canal tour. I promptly purchased a ticket and found a seat in the small boat. I realized then that I really liked canal tours. They were really enjoyable and quite relaxing. Of course, I am also one who loves being in, near, and/or around water to begin with. The fact that I was also touring a town at the same time was a huge bonus!

Canal tours allow one to casually cruise on the water and get views that a land vehicle never could. That, and you don't have to walk! One of my favorite parts of a canal tour was going under arching, stone bridges. Something about it was simply fun for me.

As my tour group rode, the captain would point out things to notice and provide a history of the features. I should also note that this tour guide would speak in French, but then also in English. He was also great about making jokes or pointing out humorous pieces of history to keep things fun.

After the canal tour had concluded, I thanked our guide and provided a small tip before re-locating the third and final structure I had seen. I found it and headed in that direction. Unfortunately, as I arrived to it, I discovered that this building was also closed. I was also unable to identify what it was exactly. The part of the structure I had seen jetting out did not seem to be attached to any of the other buildings I came to. However, I did notice something very interesting in the process of trying to identify its purpose.

The street was lined with buildings as described before. Each was separated by color, architecture style, or external material (brick, concrete, wood pannel, etc). Suddenly there was a break in the line of buildings. The break was caused by a tunnel in the form of a red-brick archway. To the left of the tunnel was a carved, square, concrete sign. Inside the square was a golden half-moon with a face. Above the half-moon face was an inscription that read, "Brouwerij." Below the half-moon face was a sign that read, "Brouwerij De Halve Maan." Below that were more words in French. Curious, I walked through the tunnel.

The tunnel then opened up into a courtyard that featured a restaurant, a pub, and (you guessed it) a brewery! The Half Moon Brewery to be exact! Best yet, this place was open and allowing for tours! I signed up for an English-speaking tour without hesitation. Just like the small brewery in Brussels, this tour also came with a complimentary beer (which I would receive after the tour)! There was little wait time before the tour began, but soon a guide appeared to lead the group that had formed in wait.

The brewery was enormous and so was the museum. It was far bigger and more detailed than I could ever have imagined. The museum featured the history of beer brewing in the town and of the Half Moon itself, some history of Brugges in relation to the brewery, fun facts, and an in-depth explanation of how their brews were made. The tour was extremely laid back and it wasn't absolutely required for me to stay with the guide - so I didn't. While the guide was explaining things to the other guests, I went off on my own to explore something interesting that caught my eye. My intention was to have a look before returning to my group. This didn't go according to plan.

I'm not sure how it happened, but somehow I managed to get lost! I ended up finding what I *thought* was my tour group until I realized the guide wasn't speaking English,..and also wasn't my guide! I went through half the museum, then back around before finally finding my tour group again. I somewhat appeared out of nowhere and the guide called me out on it. I made a big joke to make fun of myself for getting lost, and was able to make several people laugh including the guide. From that point on, I stayed with the group to ensure I knew what I was looking at. It was all so interesting, but there was no way to tell what was what without a guide.

A few of the things I learned was that the town had 14 churches and upwards of 100 bars. I was also blown away to learn that for each and every beer made (which was a TON), there was a glass specifically designed for that beer. There was even a large shelf containing one of nearly each of said beer glasses.

At one point we stepped outside to find we were on the roof! The view from here was beautiful. From this vantage point, we could see nearly the entire city. From here I also noticed the unidentifiable structure from earlier. I now saw that it was in fact a part of this very brewery. It finally all made sense.

The tour ended soon after this at which point we were free to collect our complimentary beers. Having no one with me, I asked the tour guide if I could join her. She said she had some friends coming, but I was welcome to join them. I thanked her, and after picking up our beers, I followed her to a table. Her friends soon arrived.

As we all talked, I learned that the tour guide was actually from Alaska while one of her friends was from Pennsylvania I believe. I failed to record where the other was from. We ended up having a few rounds together before they decided to move on.

"You should come with us!" One of them said invitingly. I considered it, but I felt like they were established friends trying to hang out and I didn't want to impose on them.

"Thank you for the invite, but I think I better get going. It was great meeting you all and I appreciate you letting me join you for a few rounds!" I replied gratefully. And with that, we shook hands and parted ways.

I was heading back toward the train station when I saw a beautiful scene. It was part of the canal going through a park. I decided to follow the path along the canal simply because it was so pretty. Taking a seat on a park bench next to a large willow tree overlooking the canal, I sat and took in the site. I really wasn't ready to leave, but felt pretty spent. I remembered the music festival, but decided I didn't feel like waiting around until 8pm. My new plan was to chill on the bench for a minute and reflect on the day before heading back. After nearly a half hour of sitting and journaling, I took my final leave.

It was around 6pm when the train took off from the Brugges station. Suddenly, the train came to a slow stop in the middle of nowhere. The driver came over the intercom and said something about the battery having to be unplugged and plugged in again. He apparently did this, then we were off again. It was a smooth ride for the next hour until we stopped at a small station. The train sat and sat, and sat, and sat, until a woman came over the intercom to inform us that we were waiting on the next driver who hadn't arrived yet. An hour to an hour and a half went by and the driver still had not arrived. We were then instructed to board a different train.

We all got off and did as instructed. This train sat for a while until finally starting to move, though really quite slowly. From here, it took around 2 hours to arrive at a station in Brussels. This station was not the one I needed. It sat for a while again until a man came over the intercom saying that this train would be going no further. He said we could either wait 10 minutes for the next train or go below to the metro. Figuring I could catch the metro more immediately, I chose to head down.

I went down, bought a ticket, went down some stairs, realized they were the wrong stairs, went back up the stairs, found the right ones, went down those stairs, read the sign to figure out where the platform was, and used my map to identify the train I needed. However, I doubted myself for a moment and asked someone nearby to confirm that this was the right train. They confirmed. I then immediately turned to confidently board the subway train, but was too late. The doors to the train closed shut and took off. Classic.

The next subway train wouldn't be leaving for another 20 minutes, and I had already missed the above-ground train! I couldn't help be reminded of my similar experience in Germany coming back from Amsterdam. Needless to say, I was frustrated. It was now nearly 10pm and I was 1 short ride away from my final destination.

I stayed alert to make absolutely sure I caught the next subway train. I did so and made it back to my hostel neighborhood promptly. I then ran over to Regalo's for a late night kebab before returning to my hostel. Once back, I went and set my things down in my room, went and bought a much-needed brew from the bar, then went outside to find a seat and enjoy dinner. It was time to chill.

As I walked out into the courtyard, there was a group playing Truth or Dare from a book. James from Ireland, a few Aussies, and Lillian & Alice of Switzerland. Nothing too exciting was happening. It was mostly truths that you'd tell people you'll never see again but wouldn't tell others, so it was humorous. It was also a fun way to get to know one another. We played this game until around 3am, then I went to bed.

"Tomorrow will 100% be a Chill Day." I thought as I reached my bed. "No doubt."

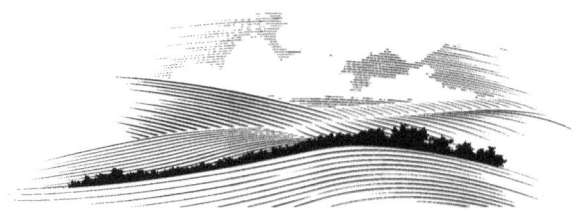

Clarissa And The Dare

Friday, August 1st

I woke up this day at around 11am with a strange craving: American food. I found this particularly odd as I would be heading home the following day. None-the-less, I could not deny my craving. After getting dressed, therefore, I left the hostel and made my way down the road beyond Regalo's. There was a Mc-Donald's on the far corner.

At McDonald's I bought 2 McChickens with a small Coke to drink. In the States, this would have cost maybe $3-$5. The same meal here cost me €10! I couldn't believe the price difference between the States and this country for Mc-Donald's. Yet, I didn't mind paying. As mentioned, I would be leaving the following day and would have money leftover.

I sat inside the restaurant observing the contrasts between this McDonald's and the ones I was used to seeing back home. While very familiar, it was strangely different at the same time. It's hard to explain, but easily observed.

On my way back to the hostel after dinner, I took the opportunity to stop into a few shops. The top priority was of course the chocolate shops. As I walked into one, I was amazed by the aromas produced by the different types of chocolate. Displayed for purchase were anything from bars to syrups, ice cream to fudge, white chocolate, dark chocolate, caramel-peppermint infused, and more. You name it, they probably had it. It was truly mind-boggling,...no to mention expensive. I ended up choosing to buy a few small pieces in a container that were better priced for my budget and conducive to travel. I wanted to bring some back for my family and friends to try - a little taste of Belgium. My only concern was getting it home *uneaten*.

I returned to the hostel after my short venture and decided to spend some time on my tablet. I went swiftly to my hostel, grabbed my tablet, and sat on a comfy chair in the bar/cafe area. Here, considering what my journey home may be like the following day and reflecting on my travels, I couldn't help feeling grateful and inspired. I was immensely thankful for my experiences and not wanting to leave, yet at the same time, feeling quite relieved to be going home. I was both mentally and emotionally exhausted. Why? Because I had been traveling non-stop through foreign countries for the past 2 months, walking around new cities for the better part of 8 hours each day all while having the greatest experiences of my life thus far. I pondered on things I had been so fortunate to see and the people I had been blessed enough to meet (including Conan O'Brian). I also contemplated the misfortunes I experienced and missteps along the way that were sure to make a the greatest stories for those back home.

"The look on Mom's face when I tell of nearly having to sleep outside a few times will be priceless." I thought, chuckling out loud to myself.

As they day drew to a close and evening was upon me, I chose to treat myself this final night abroad. With cash in hand, I strolled down the strip and let my nose guide me. Eventually, it brought me to one of the restaurants leading up to the stock exchange building. It smelled delightful. I went in and was seated quickly. After looking over the menu for a moment without the least worry of price, I chose a salmon pasta with a St. Bernardus (abby style) dark beer to drink. I ate slowly and savored every delicious bite. I smelled the smells, heard the noise, observed the sights, and felt the air as I ate. There was no way to know if I would ever return, so I tried to take as much in as possible.

I arrived back at the hostel a little while later with a nice buzz from the strong drink with dinner. I heard a guy outside playing the guitar and went to join him. He ended up being a Canadian guy named Jeff. I told Jeff about Jay and Nora, and we spent time swapping travel stories. Interestingly enough, he was just beginning his travel adventure as mine was wrapping up. I gave him a few travel tips such as looking for menu prices outside of restaurants and buying drinks for sexy women in red.

He and I then passed his guitar back and fourth. I played him some of my Blues songs while he impressed me with his talent for classical guitar. After a while, he suggested I go grab mine so we could play together. I obliged him, and we had a great time playing together.

As we played, Alice and Lillian from the night before came out. They decided to stop and listen as we played. I supposed we sounded pretty good together, for the next thing I knew, we had a small group gathered around us. In between songs, we would stop to say hello to familiar faces and meet new ones. One of the new faces, which caught my eye, was a Canadian girl named Clarissa. Clarissa was blond with her hair pulled back in a casual bun. Her eyes were green like Irish clover, and her smile was bright as the stars. Jeff and I continued playing as we had been until Lillian left and returned with the Truth or Dare game. Jeff and I then put our guitars down.

During the transition between musical entertainment and getting ready to play the game, Clarissa ran into the bar to grab a drink before we started (as did a few others). People were still grabbing drinks and returning, or joining for the first time. While the circle could always expand, the original spaces were filling up quickly. Call it intuition, but I then received the notion to subtly take up enough space to make up for one other person.

When Clarissa reappeared with her drink, she saw that her seat had been taken. As if without meaning to, I casually shifted myself so that a space "happened" to appear next to me while she was looking around. Meanwhile, I relaxed and became interested in something in the distance so she wouldn't think it happened on purpose. Then, while I was looking ahead, she came over and plopped down next to me. I did my best to play it cool.

"Hi!" She said. "Nice playing earlier!"

"Thank you very much." I replied. "Glad you enjoyed it. I'm Tim, by the way." I reached out my hand for a shake.

"Clarissa," she said, having not yet met me officially.

We shook hands and talked while those taking charge of the game explained to the newcomers how it worked.

Clarissa ended up being really cool and fun to talk to. She proved to be as interesting as she was attractive. One of the things we discussed was our shared anxiety when it came to flying.

"I put my earpods in and crank my music up," I said. "Then hang on tight as if that would do anything." I made a funny face to indicate I realized how silly it was. Yet while I thought my gripping the seat was funny, *her* remedy was hysterical.

"Yeah,...I read porn." She said. If there had been a drink in my mouth, I probably would have spewed it out. I was not expecting such an answer.

"WHAT?" I asked through a laugh.

"Yeah," she replied with a cheeky grin. "It gets me going so my nervousness and the porn counteract each other." I about fell over on myself from laughter. It was too much for me.

I will note, however, that she specifically said, *"read"* porn as opposed to "watch" or "look at," meaning, it was likely one of those romance type novels I'd seen in book stores where there is always a muscular, shirtless guy on the cover, often with a woman worshiping him. There is actually an episode of the tv sitcom FRIENDS about this phenomenon.

Nothing too crazy happened during the Truth or Dare game. It was much like the night before. Some of the dares weren't practical for the setting while others were simply dangerous and could get people into a fight and/or kicked out of the hostel. Other times, people were just too chicken to do anything interesting so they all went with telling an embarrassing truth to strangers. Then, it came to Clarissa. She picked a card and read it.

"Trade clothes with the person sitting on your right or..." I forget what the truth was. I only remember her uncomfortable grin between actually considering it and thinking, 'no, that's funny, but ridiculous. She then looked up at me to gauge my reaction. I looked back at her with an expression of indifference. "Ehh," she finally spoke. "Nah, I don't think so."

"I honestly would have been pretty surprised if you had been up for it." I replied chuckling.

I naturally expected her to go on with a truth before passing the cards to me. Instead, she did something I did not expect. She seemed to start mulling it over. She almost seemed to be concerned about coming off too interested, then getting shut down thereby putting her in an undesirable light in everyone else's eyes. I hope that makes sense. I could completely understand that concern.

"I mean,...ugh, I don't know." She thought out loud. "I'm tired of no one having the guts to do anything but...I don't know. What do you think?" At this point, I felt pretty confident she was up for it, but didn't want to give the audience the wrong idea about her or let me think she was promiscuous. It would be for the sake of a good laugh. I considered it, and thought it would definitely be funny. She wore a spaghetti-string tank-top and skirt with flip-flops.

"I mean.." I paused for a moment as not to seem eager. "I'm down if you're down." My tone was casual with an unenthusiastic confidence. I also shrugged my shoulders a little to reinforce this. "But it's whatever you wanna do." I continued. "If you're not comfortable with it, then let's not. I'll think no less of you either way." I added the last part to calm any concerns she had about me thinking her a wimp if she didn't or promiscuous if she did. Either way, I thought she was great and thought well of her. That wasn't going to change with her decision.

"Let's do it." She said with a certain and confident grin on her face. It seemed my answer accomplished what it needed to. So with that, we got up and left the courtyard as the group excitedly cheered us on. Yet even as we left, I had no idea how we were going to do this. Were we going to grab a second set of clothes to wear while we handed our current clothes to one another to go change into or was there another option?

"So..." I asked. "How do you want to do this?" I figured it was best to let her take the lead lest I suggest something that sounds like I might be trying to take advantage of the situation. I started to ask about going and grabbing separate clothes, but she responded in an unexpected way. Suddenly she took my hand and *pulled* me into the women's bathroom.

"You take that stall, I'll take this one." She said walking into one and shutting the door. I took the next stall to hers as she instructed and cracked a joke as we began stripping down and handing our clothes over the top. We actually had a really nice conversation while we changed into each other's clothes. We then stepped out to see each other and profusely laughed for a solid 3 minutes. She then took my hand again and lead the way, letting go just before entering the courtyard.

To great applause and laughter, we presented ourselves before a captivated audience. I, with her black tank top, her skirt that fell just above my knees, and flip flops while she sported my orange button-up shirt with the sleeves rolled up, my khaki shorts, and boat shoes. The audience couldn't get enough of it, partly because it was funny but partly too because they couldn't believe we actually did it.

We got a couple photos of ourselves to remember the silly experience before returning to the bathroom to change back. This time was about the same as the last time, only our conversation was so enjoyable, time seemed to stand still.

"We better get back out there before they think something's going on." She said, suddenly realizing we had been in there longer than before.

"Oh! Right! I can't have them thinking something happened between me and *YOU*." I replied sarcastically with a wink and a laugh.

"Ha. Ha. Very funny." She retorted jokingly, playfully shoving me towards the bathroom exit.

She and I returned to our spot in the courtyard and were met with curious, questioning looks. We both knew exactly what they were thinking. There was an obvious elephant in the courtyard that a few audible whispers identified. She and I eventually had to set the record straight.

"Na..." I replied lazily with a chuckle. "We didn't." With my answer, I wanted to indicate to Clarissa that it wasn't a bad thought, but I respected her enough to make sure they knew the truth. I was very pleased in the way she responded herself. She answered a few different people in different ways, but the notion each time was "Yeah, something could have,...but no, nothing did."

The game continued and we sat together in the circle. The whole time, we joked back and fourth for as long as the game lasted. I don't think either of us payed close attention to what was going on in the game. It was really great. Eventually, however, I had to force myself to leave. The time was 2am and my flight would be leaving the next day. Clarissa, along with the rest of the group, was sorely disappointed. They were sad to see me go, but understood. I wished them all the best as I reluctantly took my leave.

When I got back to my room, I suddenly realized I had forgotten to get Clarissa's contact information! Part of me wanted to go back. The other part insisted it wouldn't matter because despite feeling like we had a real connection, she lived in Canada and I in Mississippi. Trying to make something work would likely prove more painful than rewarding. Therefore, I chose to let it be. If we were meant to cross paths again; if God willed it, it would happen. Otherwise, leaving it here is probably for the best. However, if I'm being honest, I sometimes wish I had gone back.

As I considered my day, I was amazed by what an incredible experience I had had once again – despite trouble with the train. In this moment, knowing I would be waking up and flying back home in the morning, I felt more satisfied with my life than ever before. Then, as if waiting for the opportune moment, a forgotten voice returned.

"You'll never make it back alive." It whispered from as if returning from a distance in my mind.

Since the start of my adventure, the voices in my mind had slowly been silenced as they were proven to be wrong. I had proven that I had what it took. God proved that he was in fact still with me. Nevertheless, the notion of *never making it back alive* maintained a justifiable foothold. The next day I would be flying back which presented the possibility that something could go wrong and I would not make it back alive. Yet, in spite of this concerning thought, I had peace.

"You know what?" I felt my heart say. "If the plane goes down and I die; if I never in fact make it home, I will die the happiest, most satisfied man alive and my soul will journey up to Heaven full of nothing but joy and thanksgiving."

Sure, I wasn't *excited* about flying,...but **I was no longer afraid**. My fate was in God's hands and I trusted him regardless of what happened because He is good.

As John Newton wrote in 1772, "Through many dangers, toils, and snares, I have already come; 'Tis grace has brought me safe thus far, and grace will lead me home…"

Part X:
The Journey Home

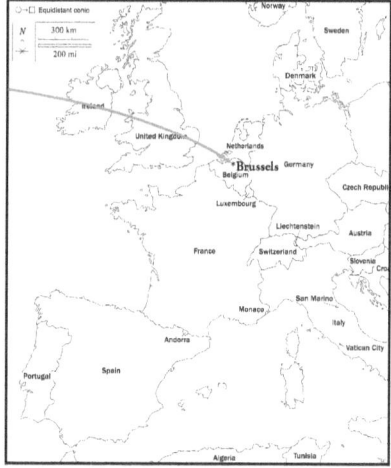

Left Map of Europe: https://d-maps.com/carte.php?num_car=13509&lang=en
- Lines, circles, and words with asterisks are author's annotations and not on original map
Right Map of the USA: https://d-maps.com/carte.php?num_car=24593&lang=en
- Lines, circles, and words with asterisks are author's annotations and not on original map

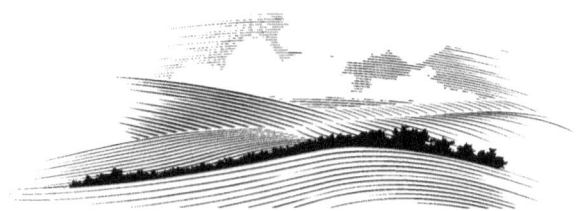

Just A Coke

Saturday, August 2nd

This was the day. While I hated to leave "the old world," I was relieved to be going home. I looked forward to seeing familiar things with new eyes. I further looked forward to seeing if anyone back home noticed anything different about me.

"And if you return,…you will not be the same," said Gandalf to Bilbo in J.R.R. Tolkien's Fellowship Of the Ring. This was certainly true of me. I was not the same Tim I was before I left - even if I still appear to be on the outside.

I woke at 6am and brought my things into the hallway to re-pack lest I wake those still sleeping. The trouble I had was fitting everything in my bag what with the extra items I intended to bring home. These things included the German stein, a coffee mug I picked up in Brugges, a Guinness bottle opener from Dublin, the Belgian chocolate container, and a few other things. Unsurprisingly, I didn't have enough space to bring everything so I was forced to remove a pair of shorts, a couple shirts, and a towel. There was no where I could leave these things except for a trash can. I was certain no one would actually be interested in taking my clothes so I tossed them. I then said a quick and quiet prayer in the dark asking God for a smooth and safe journey home. I then looked up and made my way out.

I easily made it to the metro, caught a ride to Central Station, then hopped a train to the air port. However, just as my luck would have it, I soon realized I was - you guessed it - on the wrong train. The fortunate part was that this train went through the station where the train I needed would be making its first stop. I was therefore able to simply hop of this train and quickly board the one I needed. Soon after making this correction, I was at the air port with time to spare. I was thankful I had factored in time for mishaps.

My first flight was scheduled to take me from Brussels to Charlotte, North Carolina. The flight path, as was shown on a screen, was trans-Atlantic. I much preferred to return the same way as I arrived, flying along the coast. The thought of flying straight across the ocean made me nervous. If an emergency landing were required, it would be to crash into the ocean far from land. At least landing on sold ground provided a chance. Then, to my relief, the plane apparently had some issues with one of the instruments which forced the pilot to alter the flight plan. Instead of flying straight across, we would again trail the coast as before. When my number was called, I boarded with ease.

By the time we landed safely in Charlotte, I was already feeling the jet lag. It was mid-afternoon local time, but it felt like late evening for my accustomed biological clock. The worst of it was the fact that my layover her would be several hours. I considered finding a row of benches and catching a nap like I saw a couple others doing. What stopped me from doing this was a fear of missing my flight and having to buy another plane ticket. I resolved to find somewhere to sit for a while and get some caffeine in me.

I wandered around for a bit until I found a TGI Friday's. I then wandered in and requested a high table with stools so I wouldn't be tempted to lean back and shut my eyes. It wasn't busy, so I was seated quickly. When the waitress came over and asked for my order, I explained my situation.

"…so I'm really not hungry to be honest with you," I said. "I just need really some caffeine. Can I just get a Coke?"

"Of course!" She said chipperly. I meanwhile turned on my phone to send my family a text update. The waitress then returned shortly after with my drink. I thanked her and assured her I would tip her well despite only ordering a drink. She laughed and promised me not to worry.

"Tell me about your adventures!" She demanded intrigued. "Despite working at an air port, I've never flown anywhere exciting." She confessed. I then amused her with a few of my experiences and funny tales such as the hooligans in Dublin, the Harry Potter film studio, the Players in London, the train fiasco in Germany, and meeting Conan O'Brien in Rome. She ate it up, too. Between my Coke and recounting these tales for her in between her taking care of other guests helped keep me awake. Finally, it was time for me to get checked in for my flight so I bid her farewell and headed to my terminal. I also tipped her well as promised.

The jet I boarded was exactly like the one I flew out on from my home town. Just as before, I hated it. Every slight movement was felt the entire time. I attempted to get a little shut-eye, but this proved impossible. I eventually resolved to use the extra time for journaling. I was very much behind. As I was finishing up, the captain came over the intercom.

"Attention passengers," he said. "We are approaching our destination. Please begin preparing to de-board." I looked out of the window into the clear night sky. I could see the city lights of my home town meeting the shores of the gulf below.

I smiled.

I was home.

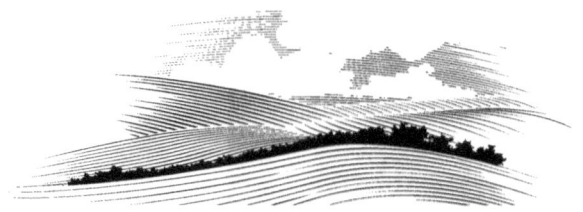

A Final Reflection

Post-Return

If you've made it to the end of this tale, I would like to thank you. I hope you felt as if you were right there with me the whole time, seeing what I saw, hearing what I heard, and experiencing the constant unexpected turn-of-events along the way. My goal in writing this was not to glorify myself, but to share my story as a testament to the goodness of God; to entertain you with humorous and vulnerable failures, encourage you with my sometimes ridiculous successes, but even more so to inspire you to step out of your comfortable life and *live*.

I therefore hope that you too are compelled to take your own travel adventure whether alone, with a trusted friend, or a group. I hope you will resist the temptation to stay in comfortable, fancy, hotels or resorts. I hope you go and experience new places, see new things, and understand just how big this world is and how much bigger the God who created it must be; that you encounter the many amazing people you will inevitably meet along the way and learn how you are really not all that different from one another despite distinct cultural variations and realize how truly insignificant you are as one person in the world yet have the power to impact the lives of strangers. I guarantee you will be humbled by your experiences and grow personally and spiritually.

"The world is not in your books and maps," said J.R.R. Tolkien through Gandalf the wizard in The Fellowship of the Rings, "*It's out there…*"

Out there, however, brings a variable that seems to be a constant reality threaded throughout my deepest reflections of my journey, and one you cannot escape. It must be embraced if you are going to really *live*. I again recall my first journal entry.

"Maybe it is all the unknown variables and risks involved," I wrote that night before I left. "...But isn't that what it's all about? Isn't that what an adventure IS?" After spending some time contemplating, I ultimately concluded that, "I now realize...that my fears are what make an adventure and *adventure*. I must embrace it if I am going to survive and enjoy the experience.

Risk, as I discovered is what made me feel the most alive — more alive than I had ever felt before. Each day was full of uncertainty. Every decision I made could have ended in disaster. I never knew what would happen from one decision or step to the next. The plane I took could have gone down, and I with it. The people I encountered and chose to trust could have had malicious intentions. The mistakes I made with trains could have wound me up in a completely different country than intended with no clue where to go or what to do and no plan whatsoever. More than once, as you'll recall, I could have ended up sleeping outside where I could have potentially been mugged, beaten up, or killed. There are innumerable scenarios I could bring up that would have brought me misery or death. Yet, this was what made it so exciting!

I both surprised and impressed myself a multitude of times in decisions I made and my handling of situations I never would have imagined finding myself in. Not only did I grow into the confident adventurer I had always fancied myself being, but proved to myself that I had what it took all while my faith in God unexpectedly grew exponentially due to His constant faithfulness to come through every time.

If you consider for a moment the stories of people God used throughout scripture, you'll notice one often recurring theme (among others). This theme is RISK, and usually includes real physical danger. In these stories God shows those He calls that they have what it takes (because He is with them), and He always comes through for them. Abraham fears passing through Egypt, Moses fears going before Pharoah, Gideon fears taking his 300 men against the 135,000 Midianite army, and the list goes on. Consider my own story. Was that not the case? I started in fear, afraid and unsure of myself - even questioning if God was with me despite going forward with it anyway. Then, over time, through many toils and snares, God proved to me that I DID have what it took, that I could handle anything that came my way, and that He was faithful to come through for me. Thus I could be absolutely confident in that no matter what happened, I would be alright.

Most people struggle when it comes to living life with a degree of risk. What if you went and told your boss you needed that raise or you'd have to start looking elsewhere? What if you went up to that girl or guy and told them how you really felt about them and asked them out on a date? What if you finally booked that adventure through a foreign country you've dreamed of taking for so long but have always found reasons not to? What if you believed that you had what it takes - because you do. What if you believed that you could handle whatever outcome - because you can. What if you believed that even if the worst possible thing happened that you'd be alright - because you will. What if we lived a life of faith; an adventure outside our safety zones, knowing deeply that God is faithful to come through somehow for those who love Him and are called according to His purpose - because He does and always will.

Imagine you are on your death bed. Are you content? There at the end, do you regret playing it safe when you wish you had taken a chance; never taking a risk?

As I flew home on the long trip back, having spent 2 months living in constant risk, witnessing myself overcome challenges I never imagined facing while becoming the adventurer I had only fancied myself being and all while experiencing God's constant faithfulness by means of always coming through for me, I thought to myself.

"If this plane were to crash right now…I would accept my fate in peace and die the most satisfied with life I've ever been." Imagine feeling that way every day.

Over the years since my return, I've fallen back into the comforts of safety and security. It's easy to do. Yet if we are to live the kind of life God calls us into, we must be willing to take risks. We must be willing to overcome challenges we've never faced before. We must be willing to accept that things may not go according to plan, yet be certain that if they don't, we can handle it; we will be alright, and God is faithful to come through for us.

So with this I leave you: Take a trip, live some risk, have some adventures, and die satisfied. God bless and happy travels.

To learn more about Tim, scan the QR code
to visit his author site.

www.ingramcontent.com/pod-product-compliance
Lightning Source LLC
Chambersburg PA
CBHW030352130626
46549CB00004B/1458